THE DEATH
OF PSYCHOANALYSIS

THE DEATH
OF PSYCHOANALYSIS:

MURDER? SUICIDE?
OR RUMOR
GREATLY EXAGGERATED?

Robert M. Prince, Ph.D., Editor

JASON ARONSON INC.
Northvale, New Jersey
London

140918

The editor gratefully acknowledges permission to reprint material from *Freud's Wishful Dream Book* by A. Welsh, copyright © 1994 by Princeton University Press.

Production Editor: Elaine Lindenblatt

This book was set in 11 pt. Bell by Alpha Graphics of Pittsfield, NH, and printed and bound by Book-mart Press, Inc. of North Bergen, NJ.

Library of Congress Cataloging-in-Publication Data

The Death of psychoanalysis : murder? suicide? or rumor greatly
  exaggerated? / Robert M. Prince, editor.
     p. cm.
  Includes bibliographical references and index.
  ISBN 0-7657-0147-2 (alk. paper)
     1. Psychoanalysis. 2. Psychoanalysis—Methodology. 3. Freud,
  Sigmund, 1856–1939. I. Prince, Robert M., 1948–
  BF175.D39 1998
  150.19'5—dc21   97-37074

Printed in the United States of America on acid-free paper. For information and catalog write to Jason Aronson Inc., 230 Livingston Street, Northvale, NJ 07647-1731. Or visit our website: http://www.aronson.com

To Alex Sandor Prince and Magda Czeisler Prince

and

the memory of their world

Contents

Acknowledgments

First, I would like to thank Section V Psychologist-Psychoanalyst Clinicians, of the Division of Psychoanalysis of the American Psychological Association for giving me the opportunity to arrange the two colloquia that provided the initial exploration of the theme of this book. I also thank the contributors to this volume for their generosity of time and spirit. In addition, I am indebted to Jason Aronson Inc. for making this book a reality; to Michael Moskowitz for his response to the initial proposal, to Norma Pomerantz for her warm helpfulness along the way, to Sigrid Asmus for her thorough copyediting, and to Elaine Lindenblatt for ushering the book into daylight. I would like to thank colleagues too numerous to mention for their ongoing interest and encouragement; these include members of the New York University Postdoctoral Program, the Sandor Ferenczi Institute, and the Suffolk Institute. I need to express my appreciation to my psychoanalytic teachers, amongst whom I include my analysands and students, for providing the *raison d'etre* for this effort. In particular, I am grateful to Dr. Judith Kestenberg who is for me a model of psychoanalytic perception, vision, generosity, and courage. Last but not least, thanks to Andrea, Aaron, and Shawn for understanding why I had to steal precious time from them to do this.

About the Editor

Robert M. Prince, Ph.D., ABPP, is currently on the faculty of the New York University Postdoctoral Program in Psychoanalysis and Psychotherapy, and the Suffolk Institute of Psychoanalysis and Psychotherapy. A member of the Board of the Sandor Ferenczi Institute, he is past president of Psychologist-Psychoanalyst Clinicians, Section V of the Division of Psychoanalysis of the American Psychological Association. He received his Ph.D. in Clinical Psychology from Teachers College, Columbia University and his Postdoctoral Certificate in Psychoanalysis from the New York University Postdoctoral Program. Dr. Prince has written and lectured on the technique of psychotherapy with special attention to the negotiation of therapist activity and the influence of the cultural surround on the psychotherapeutic relationship. He has a further interest in the impact of historical events and epochs on the individual and has been an interviewer of Holocaust survivors for both the Yale Video Archive and Child Development Research. His book *The Legacy of the Holocaust*, along with numerous articles, is a study of what he calls historical trauma. *The Death of Psychoanalysis* is a product of commitment to the idea that psychoanalysis, in order to thrive, must understand itself within its historical, social, and cultural context.

Contributors

Claude Barbre, M.Div., M.Phil., is managing editor of the *Journal of Religion and Health*, and assistant director, child psychotherapist, and training and supervising analyst of the Harlem Family Institute. Recipient of a 1995 and 1997 Gravida Award for poetry and articles, presented by the National Association for the Advancement of Psychoanalysis, he is also the William B. Given Jr. Fellow for 1995–97. He is a psychotherapist in private practice in New York City.

James W. Barron, Ph.D., is a Past President of the Division of Psychoanalysis of the American Psychological Association and Director of the Massachusetts Institute for Psychoanalysis.

Professor **Martin S. Bergmann** is on the faculties of the New York University Postdoctoral Program in Psychoanalysis and Psychotherapy and the New York Freudian Society. His books include *The Evolution of Psychoanalytic Technique* and *The Anatomy of Love*.

Kenneth Eisold, Ph.D., is Director of the Organizational Program at the William Alanson White Institute, where he trains consultants in working psychodynamically with organizations. He is a practicing psychoanalyst as well as an organizational consultant, and he has written extensively on the psychodynamics of large systems. He is a Fellow of the A.K. Rice Institute.

Anne Erreich, Ph.D., is a graduate and faculty member of the New York University Psychoanalytic Institute. She is clinical instructor at the New

York University Medical Center, and Chair of the Research in Progress Subcommittee of the American Psychoanalytic Association.

Caroline C. Grey, Ph.D., ABPP, is on the faculty of the New York University Postdoctoral Program in Psychoanalysis and Psychotherapy and the Fordham University Doctoral Program in Clinical Psychology. She is also a supervisor in psychotherapy at the Ferkauf Graduate School, Yeshiva University. She teaches and writes in the area of culture and psychoanalytic theory and practice. Her interests include the problems of values and gender in psychoanalysis.

Nathan G. Hale, Jr., Ph.D., is Professor Emeritus of History, University of California at Riverside, and an interdisciplinary member of the San Francisco Psychoanalytic Institute. His work includes the two-volume *Freud and the Americans.*

Robert R. Holt, Ph.D., is Professor Emeritus of Psychology, New York University. He has published over 10 books and 100 technical papers including *Freud Reappraised: A Fresh Look at Psychoanalytic Theory.* He received NYU's Great Teacher Award in 1985.

Lawrence Jacobson, Ph.D., is on the faculty of the William Alanson White Institute, a lecturer in psychiatry and religion at Union Theological Seminary, and an associate editor of *Contemporary Psychoanalysis.*

Bertram P. Karon, Ph.D., is Professor of Psychology at Michigan State University, and a Past President of the Division of Psychoanalysis of the American Psychological Association and of the Michigan Psychoanalytic Council. He is best known for his writings on the treatment of schizophrenia, including (with G. R. VandenBos) *Psychotherapy of Schizophrenia: The Treatment of Choice.*

Patrick B. Kavanaugh, Ph.D., is President, International Federation for Psychoanalytic Education; Founding President, Academy for the Study of Psychoanalytic Arts; and Past President, Michigan Society for Psychoanalytic Psychology.

Jonathan Lear, Ph.D., is Professor of Philosophy, Yale University, and a visiting professor at the Committee on Social Thought, University of Chicago. His books include *Love and Its Place in Nature.*

Marylou Lionells, Ph.D., is Director of the William Alanson White Institute. She is senior editor of *The Handbook of Interpersonal Psychoanalysis.*

Esther Menaker, Ph.D., is on the faculty of the New York University Postdoctoral Program in Psychoanalysis and Psychotherapy. Her many books include *Masochism and the Emerging Ego, Appointment in Vienna,* and *The Freedom to Inquire.*

Donald Moss, M.D., is on the faculty of the New York Psychoanalytic Institute and co-editor of *Imago.*

Joseph Newirth, Ph.D., is Director of the Postdoctoral Programs in Psychoanalysis and Psychotherapy, Adelphi University, and a faculty member of the New York University Postdoctoral Program in Psychoanalysis and Psychotherapy.

Nickolas Pappas, Ph.D., is Associate Professor of Philosophy at the City College and Graduate Center of the City University of New York. He has published articles on topics in ancient philosophy and aesthetics, and a book, *Plato and the Republic.*

Arnold William Rachman, Ph.D., is the founder of the Sandor Ferenczi Institute. His latest book is *Sandor Ferenczi: Psychotherapist of Tenderness and Passion.*

Owen Renik, M.D., is a supervising and training analyst at the San Francisco Psychoanalytic Institute; Chair of the Program Committee, American Psychoanalytic Association; and Editor-in-Chief of the *Psychoanalytic Quarterly.*

Paul Roazen, Ph.D., has written or co-edited numerous books, including *Freud and His Followers, Encountering Freud: The Politics and Histories of Psychoanalysis,* and *How Freud Worked: First-Hand Accounts of Patients.*

Jeffrey B. Rubin, Ph.D., is on the faculty of the Postgraduate Center for Mental Health and the Object Relations Institute. He is author of *Psychotherapy and Buddhism: Toward an Integration,* and the forthcoming *Psychoanalysis on the Couch: Exploring the Blindness of the Seeing I.*

Elaine Schwager, Ph.D., is a psychoanalyst and member of the Institute for Psychoanalytic Training and Research. She is also a poet and screenwriter.

Introduction

The report of my death was an exaggeration.
Mark Twain

The idea for this collection grew slowly but from a deeply personal place. My original interest in psychoanalysis occurred in the context of its hegemony in the world of ideas. Psychoanalysis seemed to illuminate every intellectual domain—literature, sociology, philosophy, political science, and even psychology. In the fervor of initial discovery, psychoanalysis offered the key to understanding myself and the world around me. The opposition to it only constituted further evidence of its power and vitality. During my clinical internship, most of my fellow interns had come from graduate programs in the Midwest and West that were dominated by behavioral psychology—which were so limited in comparison to the depth offered by psychoanalytic understanding. Again, to me, their rejection of a psychodynamic point of view only highlighted the limitations of other approaches to the mind and thus further confirmed the primacy of psychoanalysis. As one of my first patients said, disgruntled as he was with my adoption of the stereotypical stance, "This is the only real game in town."

Sometime around the time I received my Certificate in Psychoanalysis, roughly around 1985, I began to notice the sands shifting. Intellectual excitement seemed to spring from outside the psychoanalytic domain, as one psychoanalytic idea after another was superseded, domino like, by contributions from another area. The tone of that great arbiter of culture, the *New Yorker* cartoon, changed from respectful irreverence to pointed cynicism. Opposition, accompanied as it was by loss of support from old friends was no longer confirmatory: it became threatening. At first there seemed to be no notice of all this in the psychoanalytic literature or in discourse among colleagues. We all took pride in seeing ourselves (though subsequent critiques would challenge this self representation) as "against the grain," so we may have been lulled into confusing this sea change with older struggles. Patients too seemed to come to initial consultations with a different mind-set, bringing different expectations and attitudes. My sense of the changing cultural context did not seem to be shared, and I was torn between attributing my perceptions more to my characteristic ways of seeing things than to an objective appreciation of being in the midst of change. Indeed, for psychologist-psychoanalysts, the formation, in 1979, of the Division of Psychoanalysis of the American Psychological Association seemed evidence of growth rather than contraction. However, as managed care came to intrude more and more on the treatment situation, and as the managed care ideology became an explicit, orchestrated assault on psychoanalytic treatment *in principle*, I couldn't help being overwhelmed by the massive denial in psychoanalytic circles that times *were* changing. Sitting in meetings, both scholarly and political, listening to erudite discourse that made no reference to a changing context, I felt like I was the proverbial first person in the movie theater to smell smoke and suspect fire.

Given the incredibly rapid pace of change, denial didn't last long. However avowal took many forms. It was my impression that attitudes had some relationship to, though certainly no exact correlation with, the security the analyst had in a referral base and/or prominence in the profession. Also, explanations of the difficulties varied greatly. Some focused exclusively on the depredations of insurance companies and seemed unwilling to acknowledge that substantive failures *of psychoanalysis* might be contributing to its decline. A particular memory I have is the reaction to a lecture, subsequently published (Holt 1985), given by Robert Holt as the 1984 Division 39, Section V Annual Scientific Lecture. He delivered a Jeremiad disguised as a surgically precise summary of the *previous* ten years' critique of psychoanalytic metapsychology, methodology, and language, along with a vision of and program for psychoanalytic research. Seventeen years later (Holt 1997a), he remembers the smiles of former students but owns that there may have been some "complacency." My own memory is of the coldness of an audience hearing for the first time that the emperor had no clothes. Holt's discussion of the consequences of a failure to fulfill the responsibility of empirical validation would prove all too prophetic. More recently, I was struck by the fact that, in an otherwise splendid issue of the *Psychoanalytic Quarterly* (Renik 1996) devoted to the issue of authority in psychoanalysis, not one article addressed what to me seems to be the single most important contemporary clinical issue, namely the *loss of authority* of psychoanalysis.

There was an interesting range of responses to the current project. When I first began organizing a series of presentations, to be given as invited symposia at the 1996 Spring meetings [here Chapters 1, 3, and 14] and 1996 Summer meetings [here Chapters 6, 7, and 8] of the Division of Psychoanalysis of the American Psychological Association, one of the first people I asked to contribute greeted my stating the title with a sharp, audible intake of breath. Hearing the subtitle M*urder? Suicide? Or Rumor Greatly Exaggerated?* produced a chuckle, the words "Very clever," and a wonderful contribution. Another friend and colleague of many years' standing, now a training and supervising analyst at an Institute of the American Psychoanalytic Association, declined, asserting that psychoanalysis is the only approach to human nature that "has the goods," and would therefore be restored to its rightful status after this period of rejection had passed. In contrast, as word of the project got around, enough people volunteered contributions so that it grew from an initial proposal for twelve to fifteen chapters to the current twenty-three.

By the time the book project was well underway, agreement with the basic premises of the book, that psychoanalysis has fallen from its prominent status and is in danger of becoming marginalized if not extinct, seemed widespread in psychoanalytic circles. The theme of the relationship of psychoanalysis to its surrounding culture and of crisis in psychoanalysis seemed to find its way into psychoanalytic conferences and colloquia as titles or background whispers. Sometimes the theme would emerge when least expected. For example, I remember listening to a clinical symposium of the American Psychoanalytic Association and hearing the moderator, a senior analyst, praise the papers with the offhand comment that although he had been increasingly pessimistic about the future, it was papers like these that renewed some hope that psychoanalysis might survive. Whenever I could, I would try to take a barometric reading. I asked a major figure in the field about his take. Although he was interested in addressing the issue in terms of the impact of finances on psychoanalytic practice, he was very unwilling to discuss any more general disaffection and refused to consider that unhappiness of many patients with their psychoanalytic experience might be a factor to be considered in the current scene. This was all the more striking because this was someone who had made radical contributions to the revision of clinical theory. A great many practicing analysts expressed concern about the lack of opportunity for younger colleagues to find opportunities for clinical psychoanalytic experience and about their own continuing ability to earn a living. People who had sacrificed to become analysts were talking about alternative career possibilities. For some, denial had given way to despair.

The contributors to this volume were asked to consider and explore the relationship of psychoanalysis to its surround and to address the theme *The Death of Psychoanalysis: Murder? Suicide? Or Rumor Greatly Exaggerated?* In our discussions, certain questions would come up:

- What is the writer's view of the current state of psychoanalysis?
- Is psychoanalysis in crisis and what are the dimensions of that crisis?
- What are the causes for the current situation? What historical or social factors contribute to it?
- What are the relevant dynamics of psychoanalytic groups and institutions?
- What is the impact on psychoanalysis of a rapidly changing surrounding culture?
- Why is so much anger and opprobrium directed at psychoanalysis? And who is directing it?
- Can we disentangle the intellectual, scientific critique from the appeal of new paradigms?
- Can we disentangle the assault of insurance companies and a new healthcare model from the dissatisfaction of psychoanalytic patients? If it were all the fault of greedy insurance companies, why weren't we being defended by legions of grateful patients?
- What are appropriate, substantive responses to the charges leveled against psychoanalysis?
- What is encompassed by the term *psychoanalysis*? How large is the psychoanalytic tent?
- Are some psychoanalytic groups more besieged than others?
- What does the future hold? What would be enduring?

Every effort was made to include contributors from diverse backgrounds and traditions. While most contributors are analysts, they also include historians and philosophers, and represent different psychoanalytic perspectives. They bear the legacy of different eras, some having seen psychoanalysis from early on, some entering at its pinnacle, others representing a new generation. They include directors of institutes, past and current presidents or leaders of psychoanalytic organizations, and—just as importantly—positions on the outside looking in.

Initially, I planned to arrange these contributions in groups according to theme, but their breadth and multidimensionality made this task too difficult. I finally decided, as best as I could, to arrange them on a kind of rough narrative basis.

Although one contributor agreed to participate only if she could "have" the suicide option, her chapter, like most of the chapters in this volume, weaves together a tapestry portraying murder, suicide, and exaggerated rumor. The strands of the murder and suicide points of view are sometimes closely joined, as these contributors are uniformly thoughtful about both psychoanalysis and the assaults on psychoanalysis. They reflect Holt's (1997b) comments: "Personally, I don't think the real problem for psychoanalysts is to brush aside the inept ones . . . but to face up to the valid points made by serious critics. . . . Even a sneering and ignorant person . . . has made some original and irrefutable criticisms; it's too easy to dismiss . . . [them] because they so transparently are hostile and unfair at times." Indeed Holt is one of several contributors to this volume who addresses a recent body of criticism, crediting the substantive and distinguishing it from the polemical. In contrast, Paul Roazen, a political scientist I admire for mining historical data about psychoanalysis that can be vital to its self-study, portrays the defensiveness that greeted him.

Part of the problem in addressing criticism of psychoanalysis is defining exactly what is included in the term, and this often depends on who is doing the including or excluding. Esther Menaker regards psychoanalysis as an evolving organism whose very nature it is to be in a state of change. However, many critics insist on seeing psychoanalysis as a monolithic entity, thus putting in place a serious part–whole contamination when psychoanalysis is referred to. At my own institute, the New York University Postdoctoral Program in Psychoanalysis, there are four separate tracks or orientations: the interpersonal, the Freudian, the relational, and the independent. Attributions that are obviously true of one, two, or three may not apply to the fourth. These essays further demonstrate not only the diversity between schools but also within them. They also distinguish between psychoanalysis as a set of ideas, psychoanalysis as social movement, and psychoanalysis as referring to a specific institution which is in fact one of many. There is also a temporal confusion since, as James Barron notes, many "conflate Freud with psychoanalysis as if there have been no new developments since Freud's early discoveries . . ." (p. 82, this volume). Similarly, Marylou Lionells refers to stereotyped ideas and practices that are no longer prominent, while Owen Renik takes the unique tack of referring to psychoanalytic contributions that have so become part of the fabric of the surrounding culture that they now go by another name. It is perhaps part of the fate of psychoanalysis to be subject to criticism no matter what side of a controversy it is perceived as espousing, and the issue of diversity is no exception. Thus when it defends itself against the charge of narrowness with the assertion of its diversity, it is assailed for its incoherence.

The view that psychoanalysis is monolithic does, however, have a basis in history. Martin Bergmann documents the birth of psychoanalytic orthodoxy and also demonstrates the exact moment, in the unfolding of Freud's theory, after which the multiplicity of further development, and, in terms of mathematical Chaos theory, the indeterminacy of psychoanalysis, would become inevitable. A thread elaborating the inherence of conflict in psychoanalytic ideas runs through many of the papers in this book.

This said, the generalization can be made that psychoanalysis is something that has contradiction and paradox as an essential feature. A theory of mind that holds conflict and compromise as essential and posits the fate of resolution to be the creation of a newer conflict will inevitably leave dissatisfaction in its wake. Another paradox is the psychoanalytic ideal of freedom, particularly as contrasted with the historical intolerance that is discussed in many of the essays in this book. While an argument can be made that the attempt to perpetuate an orthodoxy promoted the initial growth of psychoanalysis, its long-term damage to psychoanalysis has been incalculable. It has produced multiple bitter schisms which prevented the integration of conceptually compatible but politically opposite ideas, and intense, bitter hostility from those who were on the receiving end of institutional intolerance. Arnold Rachman, for example, discusses the cost of the exclusion from mainstream psychoanalysis of Sandor Ferenczi's seminal ideas that are only now being appreciated. The anger and hurt of those—including patients, candidates, analysts, and serious critics—who have been victimized by psychoanalytic narrowmindedness is best expressed by paraphrasing Shakespeare: "Hell hath no fury. . . ." It has been my pet theory, one that may even have a kernel of truth, that the psychopharmacological revolution began in the early 1950s as retaliation for the narcissistic injuries endured by a number of psychiatrists in their then professionally mandatory personal analyses. Within the psychoanalytic fold, identification with the aggressor is evidenced as destructive patterns repeated in successive generations of orthodox and dissident groups.

If the centripetal impact of conflict inherent in psychoanalytic ideas is one thread connecting these chapters, another is that it is inherent *in the psychoanalyst*. It should always be remembered that the largest concentration of psychoanalytic patients in any one place at any one time is at a psychoanalytic meeting. Freud's dictum about the impossibility of plumbing the depths of the unconscious and emerging unscathed is now part of psychoanalytic lore. It could be extended to every facet of participation in the psychoanalytic enterprise. Indeed, it is hard to think of any other profession that is so consuming, that so involves every aspect of being at every point in the history of participation. There is more than one reference in this volume to Freud's characterization of "the impossible profession." Lionells addresses the conflicting forces that operate on the developing analyst and the self-destructive patterns that can arise.

It's possible that psychoanalysts were undermined in their ability to appraise the change in their fortunes (in all fairness, there is one chapter in this book that disputes this position) by general misconceptions of their own history. Many of us saw ourselves as outside and above the mainstream of culture, and essentially as having a psychologically constructive but socially destabilizing role. Nathan Hale (1995) makes the opposite case, that American psychoanalysis achieved a position of dominance, its rise enabled by its unique fit with the dynamisms of the developing American culture. However, just as the fortunes of psychoanalysis rose, they would fall as the values of psychoanalysis diverged from the surrounding culture (Prince 1997). In the first place, psychoanalysis has a predominant value for the individual while the surround is increasingly driven by the necessities of a mass society concerned with economies of scale rather than personal fulfillment. Thus the philosophy of care implicit in psychoanalysis is based on a tradition that equates giving with justice. The philosophy of care of the 1990s extends a tradition that assigns the burden of care to those who require it. Where psychoanalysis expects the clinical situation to be designed for the patient, the culture expects all situations to follow the principles of the market. Where psychoanalysis values self-reflection and process, the surround values efficacy and outcome. Where psychoanalysis has a time orientation that blends past, present, and future into a timeless perspective, the surround is preoccupied with the rapidity of change and the tension between progress and reaction. What other intellectual discipline would routinely produce articles with references going back fifty years? Where psychoanalysis values authentic experiences which penetrate appearances, the surround increasingly promotes what the French social critic Jean Baudrillard (1996) calls simulated experiences which are dependent on the creation of appearances. Psychoanalysis remains analogical while the culture is becoming digitalized. The former thrives on associational thinking, the latter demands straightforward, goal-oriented reasoning. Where one common value of all psychoanalytic schools is paradox, the appreciation of which is regarded as evidence of the highest developmental level, paradox causes digital systems to crash. Thus another theme addressed by the contributors to this book is what Donald Moss terms the interface between psychoanalysis and culture.

These essays are more or less explicitly personal. They all implicitly reflect a vision of the future of psychoanalysis. What of psychoanalysis will survive? For some observers, the future requires a look toward the past to rediscover lost treasures. For others, psychoanalysis needs to evolve in step with its surround, to draw strength from an appreciation of its embeddedness in culture, and to move forward in its methods and theories. They also consider the *place* of psychoanalysis: Does it have a future located in medicine, in science, in social science, in philosophy or the arts, or as something sui generis? Should psychoanalysis acknowledge and embrace a spiritual dimension? There is much controversy between these papers, but there are some points of agreement. One is a commitment to the principle that psychoanalysis needs to study itself, to apply its own methods to itself, to attend to what Jeffrey Rubin calls its "self reflexivity." Most of these papers also agree that this is a time of crisis. Dodi Goldman (1996) reflects that, in contrast to times when it is corrupted by unquestioned homogeneity, psychoanalysis may be at its best at such times. However, more than to psychoanalysts, it is my hope that this book will speak to a public whose lives might still be enriched by psychoanalysis. As the bruited expansion of the realm of psychoanalytic ideas proceeds, one searches in vain for mention of psychoanalytic books on the recommended lists of the major book reviews and other voices of contemporary culture. It is hard to escape an impression that analysts are speaking too much to each other and are losing the audience that originally carried psychoanalysis to the center stage of twentieth-century ideas. It is this audience on which the future of psychoanalysis depends. The vital role psychoanalysis has to play in the human future was brought home to me as I heard as allegory the true story someone told me of her analysis (Mohacsy 1997), one that took place in a totalitarian regime in which psychoanalysis was a criminal activity. It was literally an underground analysis, and both she and her analyst risked arrest. Her account challenges the analytic imagination and conveys in shorthand what all of the chapters in this book articulate: an appreciation of why psychoanalysis should survive and why, indeed, it might survive.

Robert M. Prince
January 1999

REFERENCES

Baudrillard, J. (1996). *The Perfect Crime*. New York: Verso.

Goldman, D. (1996). Personal communication.

Hale, N. (1995). *The Rise and Crisis of Psychoanalysis in the United States: Freud and the Americans, 1917–1985*. New York: Oxford University Press.

Holt, R. R. (1985). The current status of psychoanalytic theory. *Psychoanalytic Psychology* 2:289–316.

———— (1997a). Personal communication.

———— (1997b). Letter to Nathan Hale, Jr., March 31.

Mohacsy, I. (1997). Personal communication.

Prince, R. (1997). Psychoanalysis in a cold climate. Colloquium of the Interpersonal Orientation, New York University Post-doctoral Program in Psychoanalysis and Psychotherapy, March.

Renik, O. (1996). Knowledge and authority in the psychoanalytic relationship. *Psychoanalytic Quarterly* 65:1.

1

Thanatos Is Alive and Well and Living in Psychoanalysis

Marylou Lionells

In recent months it has become increasingly clear that psychoanalysts must address a trend that seems to dominate the professional literature as well as the media at large. Hardly a day passes without another headline proclaiming that we are in crisis, that psychoanalysis is on the verge of extinction, or that resuscitation is needed for our careers, our training centers, or ourselves.

Now certainly it is true that psychoanalytic referrals are low, and dealing with managed care presents a daunting challenge. But maintaining a secure income is altogether different from the survival of a professional discipline. Poets worry about their personal fortunes when teaching jobs are scarce, but not about the future of poetry. Anyone with young children knows that fluoridation changed dentistry forever, but no one thinks the dentist is a dinosaur. Despite fewer students, the dental profession remains a major health resource, generally without recourse to insurance coverage, and new subspecialities continue to emerge, refining prophylaxis as well as recovery. This quite parallels the situation of psychoanalysis.

So why do so many assume that our prospects for survival seem so precarious? Why do some of psychoanalysis's staunchest advocates seem the most defensive, and the least confident of its ability to weather political and financial assault? Do we really doubt the value of our work if compared to the quick-fix promises of short-term therapies? Must we we cringe when academics dismiss our results because they defy "scientific" measurement, or when critics cite Freud's errors? Are we so insecure about the conceptual underpinnings of our work that we cannot engage in searching debate? Is it not our responsibility to convince sceptics, challenge competitors, critique fault-finders, and learn from recognition of our past mistakes, oversights, and limitations?

I intend to show that psychoanalysis is indeed in crisis, but that it is one substantially of our own making. I will outline several of the problems leading to our current condition, including how we have curtailed dialogue with the intellectual community and the public, avoided responding to reasonable inquiry and responsible criticism, and systematically shut ourselves off from sources of creativity and stimulation. We have aligned ourselves with economic and political forces that now threaten our very existence. And we have failed to wage a significant battle against the current social climate which is anti-intellectual, materialistic, and newly armed to resist acknowledging the power of the unconscious.

To explicate these self-destructive trends, I will suggest that we have underestimated the Herculean dimensions of the analytic enterprise. Freud discovered the vast continent of the unconscious. But, with nineteenth-century hubris, he also assumed that he had unraveled its mysteries. Working with the most precious and complex objects in the universe, human minds, his followers behaved as if the tools to explain, understand, and cure were already in hand. But, in truth, our field is in its infancy. I will argue that to defend against what has been called the "inevitability of uncertainty" (Witenberg, personal communication), psychoanalysts have erected perfectionistic rules and standards, which in turn, paradoxically, constrict options and increase our unacknowledged awareness of how often our efforts fail. Our organizations and training centers have institutionalized conformity and withdrawn from the mainstream. The unanticipated result, as we near the end of the twentieth century, is social marginality for the entire profession.

Now let me put this in context. In contemporary society, psychoanalytic ideas are virtually a fact of life. No adult, of any class or ethnic group, is unaware of what we do. The analyst/therapist still engenders awe and respect as well as being the target of fear, envy, and ridicule. Incalculable numbers of people seek psychological treatment, and the help they desire is generally informed by psychoanalytic theory, whether acknowledged or not.

Despite this, social commentators and competitive rivals predict the imminent demise of analytic therapy. And they are often joined by our own fellow practitioners. From the beginning of the psychoanalytic enterprise, concern about enemies, social resistances, and the need for vigilant defense has characterized our professional psyche. We traditionally succumb to a mind-set that we deplore (and easily interpret) in contemporary patients. That is, too often we see ourselves as victims, targeted by forces outside of our control that threaten our very survival. And, with this shared siege mentality, we are slow to question whether such assertions might be true.

Let me offer a contrasting view. I see psychoanalysis as a powerful tool, perhaps the most potent yet devised, for revealing the secrets of the human mind. It is a way of thinking and understanding that opens untold and as yet unexplored vistas of psychic functioning, and the infinite varieties of relatedness between and among individuals. Its ideas are expansive, precise, and flexible, and so are its methods. They can be applied, whole or in part, with or without mediation (or medication) to virtually every aspect of the human situation.

HISTORICAL OVERVIEW

In the history of ideas, a hundred years is barely a beginning for a scholarly enterprise. Psychoanalysis is among the youngest independent branches of study, the out-of-wedlock offspring of psychology and neurology, themselves both relative newcomers to the pantheon of medicine. As noted by Kohut (1975), Freud's genius was that he brought scientific understanding to an arena that was previously the province of art and theology. Encompassing the entire range of human experience, psychoanalysis bridges the realms of the humanities and the natural and social sciences. Its profound contribution lies in the assertion that human nature is amenable to rational inquiry and that it is malleable—that is, we can understand people and we can help them change. This simple, radical proposition, and our ability to demonstrate its truth, has wrought major changes in religion, politics, and culture, as well as in psychology, education, and medicine. Far from being outmoded or potentially irrelevant, psychoanalysis struggles with issues that are so vast, with implications so incalculable, that we have barely initiated inquiry down its many paths, either as a hermeneutic or a clinical enterprise.

Psychoanalysis is no longer the brainchild of a single genius. It has become a broad discipline, embracing conflicting conceptualizations, engendering a rich dialogue. Tumultuous changes are presently underway, involving movement from the unidirectional model conceived by Freud, to one that encompasses dyadic relationships. This development, comparable to the emergence of ego psychology in the middle of this century, illustrates the maturing of psychoanalytic theory (and theorists) toward the point where it is possible, and perhaps necessary, to entertain a multitude of competing central concepts. The contemporary recasting of our basic ideas promises a new paradigm for understanding therapeutic action, that is, what really works and why. But the current debate within our field also carries the potential for much, much more. We might anticipate new views of subjective reality, communication, and mutuality of impact, as well as innovative integrations of the dynamics of family, group, and social process. We might also envision a growing ecumenical spirit, including broad affiliation and interaction. This is certainly not a moment to wring our hands at the deathbed of an antiquated view of human nature. Instead, I believe that contemporary analysts are privileged to participate in the vibrant youth of a vigorous, unimaginably fecund way of studying the human mind.

In my view, clinical psychoanalysis is the electron microscope of the human sciences. It is a technology that offers exquisitely detailed images of an unexplored landscape, comparable to fiber optics or the Hubble telescope. It is the basic research of psychological exploration, research that must be nourished (and financed) to provide fundamental data, regardless of immediate utility. The material uncovered by psychoanalysis is inaccessible to any other method. Just as we cannot possibly predict the long-term implications of our work for a particular analysand, we also cannot foresee the eventual understandings that will devolve from current clinical studies. Analysts need never be threatened by advances in related scientific fields. Instead, it is we who should pose questions to be answered by neurophysiology, infant research, genetics, and psychopharmacology, as well as by the cognitive, behaviorist, and experimental psychologists. Oliver Sacks (1996), recanting his involvement in the petition that derailed the Freud exhibit at the Library of Congress, said psychoanalysis is "complimentary and intensely pertinent to neuroscience. The central thrust of psychoanalysis in seeing the mind as creating meanings and creating worlds is also the foundation of the cognitive revolution and of cognitive neuroscience. It's no surprise that one of the most eminent neuroscientists of our time, Nobel Laureate Gerald Edelman, dedicated his last book to Darwin and Freud."

Earlier in this century, our insights provided hypotheses that guided anthropologists' field studies and stimulated social theorists. Our ideas excited students of education, history, and politics, and were appropriated by creative artists in every medium. What changed? A major factor was that our profession did not maintain the dialogue engendered by these studies. We disregarded the findings of Margaret Mead and Talcott Parsons as well as Dewey and Marcuse. Just as we generally dismissed the challenge posed by Piaget, many of us still question the relevance of Daniel Stern and Beatrice Beebe. Rather than learn from Skinner, or Marx, or even from Hitler and Vietnam, analytic theory and practice were insulated from their impact. Psychoanalysts feared the emergence of psychotropic drugs and failed to integrate their effects. We are more prone to preserve our ideas than to enrich them by incorporating new insights. Even though individual analysts read widely, and may be serious students of literature, politics, scientific advances, and the like, our theories and our organizations virtually ignore contributions from outside sources. Similarly, those unusual souls who explored cross-cultural issues, or who tried to integrate psychoanalysis and the arts, or who sought to adapt analytic methods to nontraditional situations, were too often branded mavericks, eccentrics, or heretics.

And, to our great loss, we seldom appreciate those few theorists who do bridge analytic ideas with other disciplines or introduce them to the wider population. For example, Fromm, Jung, and Erikson, second only to Freud, are names the educated public associates with psychoanalysis. Each of them, long dead, still sells more books than any living analyst. Significantly, each, in different ways, forged bridges between psychoanalysis and other areas of sociocultural understanding. Yet within the profession the ideas of these seminal thinkers have had virtually no impact on core theory.

As we increasingly isolated ourselves from other professions and branches of learning, subsequent generations of intellectuals became uninterested in the advances in psychoanalytic understanding and lost the motivation to explore their potential relevance. Starting with Freud, who found a multitude of reasons for his difficulties in obtaining acceptance in the academic establishment, we blame this disinterest on prejudice, or infantile resistance. We even, in the words of Kohut, reject criticism as a "narcissistic rageful defense of the delusional superiority of logic and intellect" (Kohut 1975, pp. 344–345).

Such assertions are defensive and inaccurate. The public does not automatically reject analytic ideas—witness the enormous interest in psychoanalysis in the popular culture. We are the targets of incessant attention, ranging from cartoons, billboards, and media spots to full-length features on film and in print. Accepting that there is no such thing as bad publicity, we realize that in ridicule and harshly critical portrayals, images of analysts receive more than a fair share of media hype. People are deeply curious about who we are and what we do, and they desperately long for the kind of help we have promised. We didn't need *Consumer Reports* to tell us that, when it comes to psychological treatment, people find more is better. The public's appetite for psychological explanations and commentary seems insatiable. But too often the vision of psychoanalytic ideas represented in the press is one that was accurate many decades ago. Few members of the wider community (including the intelligentsia) have any realistic understanding of what we are currently thinking, or about the diversity within the field. I think the wider culture is practically begging us to come out of hiding and add a knowledgeable voice to the current public discussion of human dynamics and motivation. But, until very recently, we steadfastly resisted and maintained our isolation.

This was not always the case. Throughout the past century, compelling sociopolitical issues dominated the awareness of the public and presented challenge and opportunity to psychoanalytic theorists. Starting with Freud, whose interests included cultural systems and ideologies, there have been numerous studies of the impact of social and political turmoil on individual psychological functions. Freud applied his wide-ranging intellect in considering the role of religion and social institutions, as well as in studying the cultural manifestations of individual passions and needs. Following World War I, he was struck by the devastation of physical combat and bombing, and reconsidered the role of trauma in producing war neuroses. After World War II, when governments were desperate to understand the seeds of totalitarianism and aggression, psychoanalysts studied the mentality of war criminals, ideologues, and fascists, and the psychic scarring of Holocaust victims, as well as describing societal personality configurations that fostered authoritarian, militaristic, nationalistic regimes. But quickly, those analysts who retained interest in the psychic impact of sociopolitical forces were deemed "culturalists" and sidelined from the orthodox psychoanalytic movement.

In each succeeding decade, mainstream psychoanalysis moved farther away from such issues, increasingly confining analytic focus to the single individual in the consulting room. The emerging understanding of post-traumatic stress disorder in the aftermath of the Korean conflict and Vietnam never achieved full impact on the psychoanalytic community. While personally gratified by the end of segregation and the promise of racial equality, analysts did little to address the dynamics of bigotry and hatred. We were untouched by the rising competition between the great world powers, maintained immunity from McCarthyism and the rise of ethnic chauvinism, and failed to respond to the questions raised by the antiwar movement of the 1960s and '70s. Just as we ignored the advice of the young Dr. Spock concerning child rearing, we dismissed his later infatuation with youth culture and social change.

The sexual revolution and the explosion in the use of hallucinogens were intriguing to many analysts since they challenged societally enforced repression and brought a new range of symptoms into the consulting room. These too, however, failed to have much impact on theory, just as they eventually proved disappointing in terms of delivering sexual and psychic freedom. The 1980s wave of narcissistic excess in Western culture roughly coincided with an entirely new conceptualization of character pathology, but far too little of the analytic literature concerned the acquisitiveness, greed, and selfishness that gripped American society. Similarly, psychoanalysts have paid scant professional attention to poverty, violent crime, and the development of new street cultures, or to rising divorce rates, new patterns in adoption and fertility, or the rise of single- and same-sex parent families.

The feminist movement forced perhaps the most profound reorganization of social standards of the last century and also launched a major assault on central psychoanalytic tenets. Despite initial resistance, the feminist critique brought profound revisions in analytic theory and practice. This was perhaps the only time that the psychoanalytic establishment engaged in serious revision of key ideas in response to objections raised from outside the profession. Even so, we retain the distinctive—and pejorative—term "feminist-theorists" (or lately, "gender theorists") to segregate those who are deeply concerned with these issues. Think about it. We do not use a special label to distinguish "countertransference-theorists" or "depression-theorists." In a similar vein, on presumably theoretical grounds, psychoanalysts were strong opponents of de-pathologizing homosexuality, despite all our well-known objections to the *DSM* nomenclature. We were among the last of the professions to accept acknowledged homosexuals into our training programs and administrative positions. And, not coincidentally, racial and ethnic minorities and the handicapped are also sadly underrepresented in our ranks. Our record is as dismal as the most hidebound conservative corporation or reactionary social group.

The end of this century has seen a remarkable expansion of psychological awareness within the wider population, spearheaded largely by individuals who have been victimized and/or traumatized in childhood. This movement was initiated some years back with recognition of the effects of substance abuse on family life. At about the same time, significant numbers of military veterans showed psychic scars from experiences in Southeast Asia. It became clear that certain manifestations of posttraumatic stress disorder in adults parallel those resulting from child abuse, especially incest and sexual violation, but including also violence, traumatic bereavement, physical dysfunction, and emotional trauma. Children of alcoholics, identifying themselves as suffering particular forms of neglect and mistreatment, stimulated exploration of the implications of childhood experience on adult personality. Eventually, additional forms of childhood torment were acknowledged and revealed, and the public began to recognize the profound consequences of psychological trauma and its pervasive effects throughout the culture.

One can hardly imagine a situation that could be more significant for psychoanalytic theory and practice! From the first days of psychoanalysis, the traumatized have filled our offices and begged for our expertise. Our theories were forged out of their stories. Yet, analysts seemed to take Freud's famous renunciation of his seduction theory as a signal that trauma itself must be renounced. And, in focusing on the intrapsychic as primary, they also dismissed virtually all meaningful impact of externally generated experience, including parental influence, cultural expectation, and historical and environmental situation (Lear, Chapter 23 this volume). As external events continue to be ignored as central factors in the development of pathology, psychoanalysts as a group have failed to accept the challenge of treating those who suffer from their effects. This entire cluster of patients, which today includes virtually all who would define themselves as needing extensive psychological help, has been relegated to lesstrained professionals who generally offer more superficial treatment.

Some analysts still dismiss reports of incest as confabulations motivated by the inability to accept responsibility for illicit desire. There are still practitioners who believe that to identify the traumatized as a distinct group is at best nonanalytic, if not anti-analytic. There are senior clinicians who still suggest that those who specialize in treating victims of abuse are simply exploiting opportunities for self-aggrandizement. While certain reactionary groups claim to defend analytic principles by pathologizing emergent social movements (notably concerning sexual preferences), there has been little significant interest in expanding analytic understanding by embracing new possibilities. Rather than explore how these data might enrich psychoanalytic understanding, for too long we refused to consider ideas that might radically alter our theories. Instead of welcoming evolving psychological awareness and social concerns, the profession maintains the tradition of turning away from what are dubbed trends or fads. Psychoanalysis ignores AIDS as well as the aged. Psychoanalytic theorists pay little attention to addictions, or bioethical decisions, or delinquency, or organized crime, or societal breakdown. In maintaining immunity from such social issues, we remove ourselves from the array of valued professionals. Karol Marshall (1995) sums up the problem this way: "How . . . can we inspire anyone, let alone our students, if we don't present a strong, clear sense of the role of psychoanalytic knowledge in the real, contemporary world?" (p. 175).

And so, having distanced ourselves from the various branches of academic scholarship, and from the ranks of fellow professionals, and from the problems of the wider population, is it any wonder we are seen as marginal?

Fears for our survival must be taken seriously. They result from a trend that is potentially lethal, and something of a self-fulfilling prophecy. In my title, I semi-seriously used the term "Thanatos" to refer to a self-destructive dynamic, which, if unanalyzed, may render us unable to revive our ailing profession. I plan to consider certain factors that motivated the movement away from the mainstream culture that I have tried to describe, and will then illustrate how these same factors contribute to our current crisis.

CONFRONTING THE IMPOSSIBLE PROFESSION

My thesis is this: the insularity of psychoanalysis reflects an insidious pressure. Within each of us as individuals and within the profession as a whole there is persistent, paradoxical anxiety. We are in awe of the immense powers we possess, while at the same time we recognize that those powers are inadequate to achieve the task we set for ourselves. We assume that psychoanalytic understanding can and should inform every aspect of the human condition. But we are unable to demonstrate how it works, why it works, or even when it works. Therefore, both our assumed strengths and our weaknesses are perpetually in question. Those outside the profession criticize and fear us. We who are inside stifle qualms about our individual inadequacies as well as the limitations of our theory and method, while struggling among ourselves for position and prestige. We are chronically in search of personal and professional affirmation and certainty. This search pervades the privacy of the consulting room, our relationships with superiors and subordinates, and our representation in the community of scholars, of professionals, and of citizens. Our longing for confirmation cannot be satisfied by substantiated knowledge, and is only inadequately met by collegial esteem. Consequently, the search for approval renders us paralyzed. We fear innovation and stifle creativity. We remain perpetually in doubt.

I will argue that the personal qualities of temperament and character that permit an individual to function successfully under these conditions of high expectation (and equally high lack of certainty) lend themselves to a professional image and organizational stance that are, at best, unproductive, and at worst, suicidal. These attributes not only remain unanalyzed in the course of candidacy, but indeed are cultivated within our training centers as affirming central aspects of our shared mind-set.

Contemporary psychoanalysts have accepted a task that is intrinsically impossible, the conquest of the human mind, and therefore struggle with chronic self-doubt and inadequacy. To uphold these unreasonable expectations, we are imprisoned by inevitable insecurity which we can neither openly acknowledge nor escape. Institutional grandiosity, suspicion, and isolation serve to organize and project the fears of failure shared by the individuals within each professional society. That is, if anything is destroying us, it is our self-perpetuated vulnerability to doubt and despair, a tendency that is invasive, corrosive, and potentially lethal.

In offering such a perspective, it is difficult not to appear to be laying all the blame for our current woes at our own doorstep. This of course is inaccurate. We did not create the economic pressures of the '90s. We did not engineer the emergence of managed care. If we were not facing diminished demand and limited insurance coverage for our services, the issues I am raising would still merit discussion, but we would not be concerned about possible extinction. But, as analysts, we know that external events are only traumatic when accommodated by a receptive psyche, and unmitigated by a nurturing environment. The current socioeconomic situation troubles us in part because it resonates with vulnerabilities in our professional mind-set and we lack the internal security to believe we can withstand them.

I believe the problems that threaten us pervade the profession. While certain theoretical positions foster greater involvement with humanitarian concerns or political issues, and certain institutes are more or less heterogeneous and tolerant of diversity, I have not observed that any group differs significantly from the core psychoanalytic stance that I will describe. Here I would include the so-called orthodox as well as the dissidents, the old guard and the young Turks, the newly formed groups and the venerable institutions. And, much as I might wish to assert that the White Institute is free of the problems that beset the rest of the profession, I fear this is not the case.

ANALYTIC TRAINING AND ITS VICISSITUDES

To explicate how we have come to this condition, I will consider certain shared attributes of mind and personality among practitioners. In this discussion I am indebted to Kernberg's (1986) analysis of the difficulties in psychoanalytic training. Kernberg is concerned about the inevitable compromises in neutrality that adulterate the didactic analysis of candidates. He fears that myriad professional concerns and narcissistic investments are beyond the reach of analytic scrutiny because the analyst is inevitably identified with the candidate and has a personal stake in the treatment. We are compromised in exactly those areas that may be most central to our work as analysts. I have chosen a somewhat different aspect of the problem, focusing on how organizational goals and the ideology of analytic institutes contribute further to these limitations. However, I believe my thinking is entirely compatible with Kernberg's criticisms and conclusions.

Whether or not we agree that psychoanalysis is an impossible profession (Malcolm 1980, quoting Freud 1937), most of us are probably flattered by being seen as the kind of brave souls who would attempt it. Indeed, we often employ hyperbolic descriptions of our work, borrowing metaphors from ancient myths and the Bible. We struggle with issues of godlike omniscience and omnipotence. We identify with prophets and saviors. We compare ourselves to surgeons cutting out malignancies, to soldiers at war with dark forces, and to detectives intrepidly pursuing truth. Our training requires more years than virtually any other field, and yet we take pride in the ability to do and say as little as possible. We accept the caricature of stoic silence, although we believe our words have the power to transform lives. And, despite the enormous influence we exert over our patients, we emphasize our neutrality, anonymity, and restraint. Despite all our training and expertise, we deplore the authoritarian position of being more knowledgeable or capable of directing the lives of others. Similarly, we engage in what is perhaps the most intimate of human encounters, yet insist on remaining uninvolved, trained to endure the terrible loneliness of our unresponsiveness. We challenge others to explore uncensored expression of the entire range of psychic experience, yet we require of ourselves terse interpretation formulated along tightly defined theoretical themes (see Bollas 1996). We demand almost inhuman standards of probity, psychic availability, and skill, while denying ourselves even minimal interpersonal satisfactions.

What sort of person chooses and is capable of sustaining such a role? Remarkably little has been written concerning the personal qualities and character traits that correlate to choice of the analytic profession. The data that are available emphasize such issues as the familial experiences that orient individuals toward the helping professions, or the qualities that enhance the capacity to empathize or encourage the patient's ability to identify. Clearly this field does not lure the conventionally ambitious, the openly competitive, or the extroverted. Its rewards are subtle and peculiarly personal. Its demands for forbearance and restraint exclude the more gregarious person who requires active social exchange or mutuality. The deeply introspective interiority that characterizes the analyst involves a willingness to engage one's own mind, and the courage to accept what is found there. The intense responsibility for patients' psychological lives requires a commitment to helping others, while at the same time it precludes obtaining direct gratification from that role. Encouraging the patient to express adoring idealization, often to be followed by venomous rage and deep disillusion, all must be borne with humility and stoicism. Moreover, the analyst must withstand long periods of frustration, confusion, and ambiguity, with little in the way of confirmation or affirmation. One must foreswear certainty, adopting a posture of open-minded inquiry and unfocused attention, and at the very same time be aware of innumerable dimensions of inner and outer reality, theory and concept, ideas and affects, communication and reaction, word and gesture, and, for good measure, every stirring of anatomy and physiology as well.

Even when patients do accomplish some degree of change, it is impossible to determine the exact relationship between cause and effect, or to pin down just what aspects of the analytic relationship are mutative. And, no matter how carefully we adhere to standards and rules, or how impressive are our demonstrations of prescribed technique, patients seldom have any idea of what has been effective, nor can they credit what may have had impact. Indeed, on follow-up they generally cannot even recall much of what transpired. When asked at the end of a treatment what has been the most meaningful or memorable exchange, patients generally recall something inadvertent, spontaneous, and highly personal. Too often, these are incidents that the analyst has forgotten, been ashamed of, or, at best, thought totally insignificant. And finally, despite our fidelity to theory and method, no one knows what we really do in our private offices, including ourselves.

There is no single personality type that represents the ideal analyst. However, certain qualities of self image and presentation seem to transcend temperament or character. In thinking about how to consider the ambiguities and paradoxes described above, I discovered Fiscalini's (1993) description of a particular narcissistic vulnerability that I think is useful. By no means am I suggesting that all practitioners are characterized by narcissistic pathology. Issues of self-esteem are central for every individual at all times. Each person must develop and maintain an accurate self-image, obtain responsiveness and emotional support, and defend against rejection and insignificance. Professional practice expectations create a shared experiential context that resonates with and has an impact upon the individual's mechanisms for maintaining self-esteem.

Here is a summary of Fiscalini's paradigm for the development of the character pattern he calls the "shamed child." He observed that some children who possess particularly outstanding attributes are idealized by their parents. They become objects of inordinate attention and praise, as well as—perhaps—envy. A certain family's social, moral, or other expectations may require stringent rules for behavior. This situation typically results from social position, ethical standards, or religious precepts that demand conformity. Thus a child in such a family is subject to two realms of expectation, one for achievement and the other for behavior. The child becomes acutely aware of the possibility of falling short of parental goals, especially if they are (or at least feel) less talented, skilled, or special than the parents have wished. Such a child is therefore plagued by the possibility of disgrace for having failed. This is the inevitable consequence of unrealistic expectations.

On the other hand, to be able to perform successfully and meet the desired goals may mean that certain of the parents' rules will have to be broken. That is, the price of achievement very often is freedom from external constraint. To use familiar examples, the traveling athlete may miss religious services, the abstinent statesman may offend potential allies if an alcoholic toast is refused. Similarly, the analytic candidate, in danger of losing a patient in crisis, may be trapped between supervisory expectations and the patient's demands for adjusting the analytic frame. In such cases, therefore, a different sort of inadequacy will be exposed, that of infidelity, the failure to behave in accord with familial or professional requirements.

Fiscalini tells us that the family that operates according to such principles in a coercive, inflexible fashion creates the expectation of attaining unrealistic goals while operating under equally impossible constraints. Under such conditions the child is subject to inordinate fears of failure, which, given the circumstances, may be inevitable. One cannot succeed if the rules are rigidly obeyed, but disobedience means betraying relational commitments. Personal freedom or spontaneity is the equivalent of disloyalty. To create and maintain an environment that imposes such expectations, the authority figures are typically harsh disciplinarians. Each generation that subscribes to the agreed upon standards manages its anxiety, competitiveness, and envy by imposing increasingly stringent requirements on those who follow. Thus a system in which expectations are unreasonably high and standards are impossibly rigid perpetuates itself.

Note that the defenses against these impossible demands result in a largely unconscious dynamic. Fiscalini writes,

> Shamed children develop grandiose or unrealistic self-expectations that somehow they *should*, or *could*, or even *must*, be more, or better, or different than the rejected actuality. Such children feel "bad" or "wrong"—in some way that is often hard to verbalize, just not good enough: . . . too needy, not needy enough, too willful, too willing, what have you. . . . [They] become self-centered in direct proportion to their experience with anxiety or shame. . . . [1993, pp. 78–79]

However, and this is most important, such feelings have no outlet for expression within the family structure because "manifest narcissism—such as overt grandiosity, demandingness, self-centeredness—or expansiveness of any kind, is not acceptable . . . and thus it is not manifested, for it, too, would lead to anxiety or hostility" (pp. 78–79).

This, I think, captures a central predicament of psychoanalytic education. The training process and the organization that creates and supports it operate much like the family Fiscalini describes. Analytic candidates are unusual individuals. Drawn to enter training through their dedication, altruism, and sensitivity, they have distinguished records of scholarship, and are willing to submit to years of intense scrutiny of their ideas, their work, and their psyches. After careful screening to accept only the best, we analyze, supervise, and criticize them. We ignore their credentials and previous accomplishments, and consider them analytic neophytes, notoriously infantilizing and humiliating them. We call them "candidates," emphasizing their status as aspiring to acceptance (Kernberg 1996). And we convey the belief, implicit but powerful, that living up to the model of the perfect analyst, employing perfect technique, will eventually result in perfectly analyzed patients. We forget the characterization offered by Freud himself (1937) who wrote, "It almost looks as if analysis were the third of those 'impossible' professions in which one can be sure beforehand of achieving unsatisfying results" (p. 352).

If we have little perspective about our expectations for analytic method and style, we have even less humor. We seldom acknowledge that rules are meant to be broken, or that there is room for spontaneity. We speak of the "art" of clinical technique, yet training makes little allowance for genuine creativity (Kernberg 1986). Even when playfulness is valued, we contextualize and qualify, adding warnings and guidelines, so as to squeeze the life out of it. Now that countertransference has come out of the closet, our own feelings are subjected to the same fate. Not too long ago, before countertransference became respectable, cracks in the analyst's persona were essentially ignored. Out of shame, denial, or perhaps tolerance, analytic life went on around them, a silent accommodation to personal eccentricity. Today however, little of the analyst's personal experience is out of bounds. One is not only expected to attend to every nuance of the patient's presentation, but also to be fully aware of all aspects of one's own experience, wholly cognizant of dynamic history and contemporary association, and to be willing to reveal one's private associations in conversations with colleagues, supervisors, and even patients.

None of us is ever as clear, insightful, attuned, empathic, alert, introspective, or psychologically available as our image requires, and we are surely not unfailingly authentic. Bound by unresolved transferences, does anyone among us sit in the consulting room secretly proud of how much wiser or more effective they are in comparison to their supervisors, or, heaven forfend, their training analyst? We privately measure ourselves against the carefully selected vignettes published in the journals, and generally come up short. Our sessions seem messy and confusing, seldom following the smooth plots laid out by our leading theorists. Our notes do not offer compelling insights, or illustrate systematic working through. An elder statesman at my Institute is reputed to have said that any senior person who willingly presents a verbatim case report is a madman, a masochist, or a fool. The self-perception of every analyst embodies grandiose expectations coupled with the shameful knowledge of inevitable chronic failure. Individually and collectively, we dread that our flaws and shortcomings will be discovered.

One might assume that struggling with common problems and sharing common goals would create strong interpersonal bonds, like comrades huddling in the trenches. But sadly, we find little collegial support for our secret failings. We are restrained in asking peers for reassurance, and from extending unsolicited comfort, lest we add public shame to private misery. I have never read an article extolling the "good enough" analyst! If we cannot ingeniously suggest that our failures somehow paved the way to new insights and eventual success, we simply don't reveal them. We equate failures in results with failures in technique, not with failed assumptions.

SCIENCE ENVY AND ITS EFFECTS

Just as individual practitioners remain hidden, training centers resist the scrutiny of those who might unlock our secrets. We are awed by the so-called "hard sciences," envious of how they expose themselves to replication and possible refutation, and secretly believe we should copy them. Although our work is far more complex, and cannot be subjected to simplistic testing and generalizable proof, for decades we accepted the argument that we should attain similar certainty. I believe that we communally long for some sort of validation for work that is so incredibly demanding yet shows so little in the way of clear results.

This "scientism" fostered the medicalization of psychoanalysis in the United States, and also contributed to the rise of third-party payment. Analysts sought definition as a medical subspeciality, in part because they were seduced by the image of scientific authority and by the lure of financial affirmation. Acceptance by the establishment, ratified by negotiated fees and insurance contracts, seemed to offer a form of validation. We became dependent on third-party payment for psychoanalytic services, a movement that has had far-reaching, perhaps disastrous consequences. We ignored forecasts of potential pitfalls such as loss of control over practice, threats to confidentiality, and the like. Insurance coverage encouraged all mental health professionals to raise fees, keeping pace with medical providers whose charges grew astronomically. Analytic patients who formerly would have been seen at fees that were managed out of pocket became subject to rates that could not be continued if coverage stopped. As practitioners established new living standards and expectations, patients were seen at lower frequency to maintain income levels. While our profession had traditionally accepted compensation at about the level of university educators, we happily joined the financial ranks of "real doctors." Concurrently, insured fees fueled the proliferation of training centers, allowing multitudes of new mental health workers into the field. Analysts failed to question this development, for doing so would challenge the goose that laid the golden eggs, or else mean opening up our own institutes to produce the needed professionals.

To my mind, our participation in the rise of third-party payment was not fueled simply by greed. It was also motivated by a wish for acceptance and affirmation. The insurers' willingness to pay symbolized a ratification of our work. However, in accepting designation as a medical subspecialty, we did not anticipate manualized treatment, evaluation of efficacy, monitoring, and oversight. Nor did we imagine being replaced by lesser-trained practitioners, or finding limitations on prescribed treatment. That is, all the problems that we currently face with the advent of managed care were certainly possibilities we might have anticipated had we not been so eager to enter the world of third-party payers.

RESOLVING UNCERTAINTY

Let me move now to a related matter that contributes to our difficulty. The problems of shame I have outlined are instilled during training as a consequence of failing to meet perfectionistic expectations. Why does psychoanalysis have such unreasonable standards? The disappointment of not living up to professional ideals is inevitable given the virtual impossibility of achieving certainty in the mental health field. Nothing is fixed, invariable, or available to replication, even in one's own practice. Psychoanalytic data are ineffable and ephemeral. We cannot set clear goals, define criteria for success and failure, or even know when the work is completed. We are seldom sure if a patient leaves treatment because they are transformed or simply worn out. And it seems that the more we learn, the more difficult these questions become!

In a particularly insightful essay, Eisold (1994) describes how this inevitable uncertainty leads to an intolerance of diversity within analytic organizations. Plagued by indefiniteness, we create orthodoxies of belief. What we lack in proof, we compensate by faith. The most insidious form of defense against insecurity involves concentrating on means—because we cannot define ends. To gain entry into our arcane world, candidates must be willing to swear allegiance to a system of prescribed techniques. We are sustained in working with ever-shifting realities by adhering to beliefs about methods rather than results. We therefore prefer debating whether or not a treatment is truly psychoanalytic rather than what exactly is being accomplished for the patient. "Right-mindedness" becomes a litmus test of who is accepted. Those who don't share dominant opinions have been treated like heretics. When disagreement arises, we are apt to consider motives rather than reasons. We are as likely to interpret an opponent's character as we are to address their ideas. Argument, too, often, seems a challenge to narcissism rather than to intellect.

So, while shame has isolated us from those in related disciplines, defenses against inevitable uncertainty separate us from one another. Rather than affiliate with the wide range of practitioners who share an analytic orientation, we remain splintered into factions, each claiming to have a more potent truth. Internal battles consume our organizational energy, distracting from wider concerns. This also contributes to what has become an elitist rejection of involvement in social problems and the need to relieve suffering. We have traditionally derogated analysts who bring their work into the popular domain, or act as media consultants. And our mistrust of our associates and our own institutions is corrosive, causing the foundations of our organizations to decay.

In Eisold's view, we have little faith in the very groups that have trained and nurtured us, as well as in those structures that provide links to the wider social world. En masse, we are inordinately suspicious of peers and colleagues. We fear the coercive potential of organizational life, yet we require homogeneity within our groups lest we feel assaulted by diversity. Our professional societies are tight bureaucracies, which in turn define closely held ideologies, many of which eventually fracture under the pressure of internal dissent. Like pressure cookers, institutes are sealed to contain the volatile personalities of candidates and graduates. The profession of psychoanalysis has the dubious distinction of being known for divisiveness, secrecy, competiveness, intolerance, and rigidity. And it is equally identified as besieged by continual splits, factionalism, and disagreement. Each new analytic group, formed out of conflict or schism, goes on to recreate it. To paraphase Hegel, it seems that the major thing to be learned from our century-long history is that we have learned very little from our history.

Among the more profound ironies of our situation is that, as individuals, psychoanalysts are among the more humanitarian, enlightened, dedicated, ethically principled, independent-minded people in our society. In the consulting room we are fearless explorers, willing to assume responsibility for reclaiming the most destroyed lives, passionate in commitment, intensely involved. We are interpersonally accepting, caring, and concerned. Yet as a group we can be conservative to the point of being reactionary, totalitarian, rigid, constricted, and paranoid.

Within professional circles, we seldom manage scholarly examination of our similarities and differences. For example, after reading a panel discussion of alternative theoretical perspectives, Anthony Christiansen (1995) makes the following observation:

> As psychoanalysis undergoes continued assaults upon its integrity . . . we continue to induce a greater ongoing trauma upon ourselves from within. For however fruitful the genuine exchange of psychoanalytic ideas may be when undertaken with the open mind that Freud considered the sine qua non of any psychoanalytic endeavor, we seem as individuals and as a group to be constricted dialogically by the most primitive forms of defensive splitting and infantile rivalry that make true exchange an impossibility. Many of the . . . contributors unfortunately betrayed such tendencies along with an arrogant dismissiveness, a contentiousness that may be seen in equal proportion in some works of the . . . theorists whom they critique. [p. 501]

He was referring to traditional Freudians who discussed the writings of relational analysts, but I inserted the spaces because I believe the name of any school might be inserted into either of the blanks.

A related phenomenon is reflected in the bibliographic citations in our journals (see Hirsch 1996). Rather than encourage systematic expansion of ideas, integration of related findings, or comparison with opposing views, psychoanalytic editors have required adherence to conventional authorities, specified those elders who must necessarily be included, and restricted certain other references. I was publicly chastised for considering the criticisms of known enemies of psychoanalysis in a recent presentation, as if to acknowledge some potential validity in their arguments was to offer them credit and excuse their errors. We have been known to eradicate the writings of heretics as thoroughly as the bureaucrats who expunged Russian history books (e.g., Ferenczi, Jung). Conversely, dissidents who set out to offer a new vision, typically neglect mention of previous theorists or related concepts (e.g., Sullivan, Winnicott, Kohut). And whole schools have emerged that fail to consider the parallels and potential integration between their insights and existing theory (e.g., Fairbairn and Sullivan, or relational theory and interpersonal psychoanalysis).

TOWARD A NEW CONSENSUS

So, where do we go from here? The way I have formulated the predicament in terms of institutionally supported character issues might seem to preclude change—except that, of course, we really believe in the mutative power of analytic understanding. The difficulty in dealing with these issues at an institutional level is compounded by historical tendencies to explain problems by blaming external factors, but the current crisis may facilitate more serious self-examination. Like patients who seek analytic services as a last resort, we may be at the point of acknowledging that we can only understand our situation if we understand ourselves. Jacobson (1995) suggests that to save our profession we must take up the task of psychoanalyzing psychoanalysis, applying a trained analytic eye to introduce a welcome skepticism. When we are prepared to address internal causes, solutions become far less difficult.

The beginning of the second century of psychoanalysis is marked by rapid conceptual advance, heralding upheaval and realignment in every theoretical perspective. No practitioner can ignore it. Whether or not a single overarching psychoanalytic ideology emerges from this ferment, every analyst will become engaged in some degree of rethinking and re-evaluating. This effort, coupled with socioeconomic pressures and the clear societal demand for psychoanalytic insight, would seem to be the ideal condition for the emergence of a new professional ethic. As Emanuel Ghent has noted, "We are all in the same lifeboat, so perhaps we will be able to learn how to row in the same direction" (1996).

As I see it, we are faced with not one but two critical tasks. On the threshold of a new century, we are offered a unique opportunity to transform our professional character at the same time that we revise our ideology. Current revisions in the meanings and uses of countertransference, together with the assault on traditional conceptions of truth, reality, drives, and other pillars of standard theory, encourage, indeed demand, revision of the traditional analytic role. Ironically, conceptual advances in analytic understanding would seem to herald a new synthesis, a rapproachment between the divergent trends in psychoanalytic theory. It is becoming clear that the distinctions between internal and external, intrapsychic and interpersonal, nature and nurture, are essentially false dichotomies. As traditional Freudians have discovered the importance of mutuality, and the impossibility of verifiable truth, even cognitive and behavioral therapists are increasingly recognizing the complex power of unconscious process. Perhaps acknowledging the multiplicity of truths in the consulting room will help us accept the diversity of beliefs among fellow practitioners.

Unlike previous analytic movements, the emerging relational perspective promises a rubric within which a wide spectrum of analytic theorists may comfortably be housed. Object relations, self psychology, interpersonal psychoanalysis, and the new discussions of intersubjectivity are conceptually linked by a common concern with interpersonal process. Meanwhile, what Steve Mitchell (1988) termed the "relational turn" of Freudian theorists has brought the divergent streams of analytic thought into proximity with one another. It remains to be seen, however, whether those factions that have maintained professional enmity for almost a century will be willing and able to submerge differences in pursuit of common understanding. To join as colleagues, recognizing similarities of interest and purpose, need not mean that differences would be eradicated, but rather that they might be mutually respected and openly debated.

I would hope that the evolution of conceptual tolerance might also usher in a movement toward organizational restructuring. We will need a new consensus on technical standards, or the lack of them, if we are to dismantle the pattern of unrealistic expectations within our training institutes that has reinforced narcissistic grandiosity and contributed to the sense of inevitable failure. If there is no unanimity concerning the image of the perfect analyst, there is no inevitable failure in meeting the ideal. If we learn to respect diversity, we are able to tolerate independence. As we struggle to redefine all aspects of the analytic relationship, we become more open to individuality and creativity, can permit exploration of personal styles, and can encourage personal definitions of what to do and how to do it.

I certainly am not arguing that we suspend standards in training or practice. I am deeply committed to stringent educational requirements, extensive experience, and the highest expectations for study, scholarship, and demonstration of talent, skill, and knowledge. But at the same time I feel we must explore the differing validities in our varying approaches rather than insist on a single credo. As an obvious example, we might start by establishing the conditions under which different session frequencies contribute to analytic process and success, rather than this remaining a matter of faith and prejudice. Analytic ideas are always interpreted through the individuality of the practitioner. To my knowledge, we have never openly acknowledged, much less explored, the variability of personal styles. Becoming able to accept and to even cherish the differences among us will permit us to learn more about the nature of the analytic dyad and what aspects are really helpful to patients.

If we cling to our separate life rafts, pushing off those who might join us out of a primitive fear of being swamped, we lose the opportunity to increase our strength and numbers. To thrive, we need to engage the academics, social scientists, pharmacologists, experimentalists, and neuropsychologists, as well as the broad range of mental health workers. This is not a matter of sharing limited resources—that is an inaccurate assessment—this is a time for consolidation. If psychoanalysis can accept differences in goals and techniques while capitalizing on shared core beliefs, we have the possibility of making a profound impact on the wider culture. The alternative is continued marginalization, fragmentation, and relegation to an intellectual backwater.

As we move into the next century, I imagine a psychoanalysis no longer dominated by the internal rivalries that have marked its first hundred years. Warring factions, characterized by the names of individual charismatic leaders, believing that each possessed the single truth, will be replaced by vibrant intellectual competition. Neither an art nor a science, but bearing certain qualities of both, the psychoanalysis of the future will include more heterogeneity along with greater tolerance and respect for divergent views and methods. Our experience in the current debate concerning the nature of fact and truth, and illuminating the nature of interaction and impact, will, I believe, result in a vision of enlarged relevance.

Rather than enshrining our beliefs, secluding them from influence and change, we can learn to expose them to the scrutiny of the intellectual community and the public, encouraging cross-fertilization and mutual enrichment. We must not be so frightened of our own uncertainty that we defend what we do not fully understand and cannot prove. We now know that the patient's defenses arise primarily when we cannot demonstrate our understanding. There is little purpose in accusing the wider society of being unwilling to accept what we ourselves are unable to verify.

Analysts engage in the most absorbing, exciting, demanding, personally and emotionally challenging kind of work. It is not a job, it is a calling—and it is a privilege. I find it unimaginable that once exposed to psychoanalysis, on either side of the couch, anyone could seriously question its eternal value, or its standing among the human arts and sciences. It is our responsibility to present the potency of our ideas, and to illustrate our unique skills. I am fully persuaded that a wide audience eagerly awaits that presentation, if only we are willing to come forward.

REFERENCES

Bollas, C. (1996). Figures and their functions: on the oedipal structure of psychoanalysis. *Psychoanalytic Inquiry* 65(1):1–20.

Christiansen, A. (1995). Commentary: primitive splitting in the field of psychoanalysis. *Psychoanalytic Psychology* 12(4):500–602.

Eisold, K. (1994). The intolerance of diversity in psychoanalytic institutes. *International Journal of Psycho-Analysis* 75(4):785–800.

Fiscalini, J. (1993). Interpersonal relations and the problem of narcissism. In *Narcissism and the Interpersonal Self*, ed. J. Fiscalini and A. Grey. New York: Columbia University Press.

Freud, S. (1937). Analysis terminable and interminable. *Collected Papers, Vol. 5*. New York: Basic Books, 1959.

Ghent, E. (1996). *Discussion of M. Maccoby on Erich Fromm*. William Alanson White Psychoanalytic Society, Scientific Presentation, February 7.

Hirsch, I. (1996). Observing participation, mutual enactment, and the new classical models. *Contemporary Psychoanalysis* 32:359–383.

Jacobson, L. (1995). *The crisis in psychoanalysis*. New York: William Alanson White Institute, Clinical Services presentation.

Kernberg, O. (1986). Institutional problems of psychoanalytic education. *Journal of the American Psychoanalytic Association* 34(4):799–834.

——— (1996). How to stifle creativity in psychoanalytic candidates. *International Journal of Psycho-Analysis* 77:1031–1040.

Kohut, H. (1975). The psychoanalyst in the community of scholars. In *The Annual of Psychoanalysis*, pp. 341–370. New York: International Universities Press.

Malcolm, J. (1980). *The Impossible Profession.* New York: Knopf.

Marshall, K. (1995). Changing times: an impetus to rethink our professional identities. In *Confronting the Challenges to Psychoanalysis*, ed. S. Freidlander. Fifth Annual Conference of the International Federation for Psychoanalytic Education.

Mitchell, S. (1988). *Relational Concepts in Psychoanalysis.* Cambridge, MA: Harvard University Press.

Sacks, O. (1996). Repenting at leisure. *Psychiatric News* 31(1):33.

2

The Future of Psychoanalysis: Getting Real as a Profession

Owen Renik

Psychoanalysts who theorize about clinical process and technique have tended to state without apology—even proudly—that the psychoanalytic treatment method does not concern itself with ordinary reality. This tendency can be noted across epochs and across orientations. Many traditional analysts think of themselves as striving with patients toward a special "analytic" goal which may or may not be associated with therapeutic benefits in everyday life (e.g., Ticho 1972). Avoidance of "reality testing" is understood to be what distinguishes psychoanalysis from other psychotherapies (e.g., Stein 1966). The analytic relationship is considered to be separate from the real relationship between patient and analyst (e.g., Tarachow 1963); analytic collaboration is distinguished as a thing apart from the mundane therapeutic alliance (e.g., Greenson 1968). Analytic treatment frequently has been defined as the study of "psychic reality" rather than "external reality" (e.g., McLaughlin 1981) and patients are expected to explore this psychoanalytically defined reality by entering into "transference regression" (Panel 1958). More recently, the clinical analytic situation has been seen as characterized by "a different level of reality" (e.g., Modell 1991), by a "unique subjectivity" (e.g., Ogden 1994), or located in relation to an "analytic third" that transcends the realities of analyst and patient (e.g., Green 1975). The encounter between analyst and patient is thought to take place in "an area of illusion" (Pizer 1982), within a special "paradoxical" reality (Ghent 1992), or a "potential space" (Viderman 1979).

All in all, I think it is fair to say that *realism* is not widely regarded as being an aspect of the psychoanalytic attitude. Judgments concerning what is real in the world are generally considered not immediately relevant to the clinical analytic enterprise. I have explained in detail elsewhere (Renik 1997) why I think this is a mistake and how I think the mistake can be remedied. For purposes of the present discussion, however, I'll confine my remarks to a description of the current state of affairs in our field and the outlook for the future, as I see it.

My impression is that an unrealistic approach informs not only prevailing conceptions of psychoanalytic process and technique, but the view analysts tend to take of the place of our profession in relation to the rest of the world. Freud called psychoanalysis one of the "impossible professions"—an ironic formulation that has always troubled me because it suggests that we consider our work exceptional. Do we really think that as analysts we're doing, or trying to do, the impossible? And if so, don't we, by adopting that perspective, give ourselves something of a dispensation from full accountability? There is the danger that a self-important sense of special separateness can make us complacent.

All around us—in *New Yorker* cartoons, on television, virtually everywhere but in our own journals—we see cynical portrayals of what analysts are used to conceptualizing as transference regression taking place within the unique reality of the psychoanalytic situation. The popular view of transference regression is that patients in analysis are encouraged to wallow in the past and indulge in self-centered ruminations, providing in the process annuities for their analysts; and the popular view of unique psychoanalytic reality is that clinical analysis facilitates an intellectualized escape from everyday reality, rather than increasing happiness and decreasing distress in dealing with everyday reality. Ordinary people who are suffering emotionally and want to feel better do not usually consult analysts nowadays.

I believe we must take the popular view very seriously and take account of its validity. Hoffman (1983) wrote of the patient's role as interpreter of the analyst's experience, a role which contemporary analysts have increasingly come to acknowledge. We need to listen to and respect the thinking not only of the patients we treat, but of those patients (the overwhelming majority!) whose objections to clinical analysis are such that they do not come to us for treatment. At the moment, what we tend to do all too frequently, I think, is discredit criticism from patients who avoid us.

When the poor state of psychoanalytic practice gets discussed among analysts, the talk is generally about the inevitability of widespread resistance to psychoanalytic truth, the possibility that only a relatively few among the population at large may be suitable to negotiate the difficult path to analytic insight, the need to better educate the public, and so on. The assumption in such discussion is that clinical analysis is effective, and the question then becomes: How can we help more people realize how effective we are? It seems to me that our profession, on the whole, takes a very unrealistic attitude toward criticism from without, and toward events in the marketplace. When a product doesn't sell, the logical first thing to do is to question the quality of the product, but that is the last thing psychoanalysts tend to do, in my experience, when they consider why clinical analysis isn't selling very well.

There is good reason to look closely at whether clinical analysis, as generally practiced, meets patients' needs. We should keep in mind that the term *psychoanalysis*, besides denoting a theory of mental functioning and a treatment modality, is also the name of a social movement. Freud made this abundantly clear when he referred to psychoanalysis as *die Sache*, the cause. At its inception, psychoanalysis was a constructive social movement whose time was ripe: it destigmatized a common kind of emotional distress (*neurosis* became almost fashionable, whereas previously *neurasthenia* had been take to indicate moral weakness and hereditary degeneracy); it modified restrictive Victorian ideals of privacy and decorum by legitimizing self-consciousness and emotional self-expression; it brought sexuality in general, and childhood sexuality in particular, out of the closet. Because psychoanalysis advocated a number of badly needed social reforms, analytic therapy was bound to be successful, even if many of the particulars of clinical analytic procedure were not actually helpful.

However, the fundamentals of psychoanalytic thinking that originally made clinical analysis effective and popular have by now percolated into the culture. One no longer has to consult a psychoanalyst to talk and think freely about sex, or to review one's relationships, past and present. These days, everyone knows and uses those basic principles of psychoanalysis. As a social movement, psychoanalysis is a fait accompli. Psychoanalysis as a therapy must now measure itself against a wide array of other therapies, all psychoanalytically informed because the cultural surround is psychoanalytically informed. Thus, the crucial question becomes: Currently, is the treatment method taught in our institutes actually more effective than the approach any sensible therapist will take toward a patient's emotional difficulties, given virtually universal familiarity with many basic psychoanalytic premises? We have to ask: Has a process of natural selection taken place in which most useful psychoanalytic ideas have become broadly accepted in society at large, while within our relatively small professional subculture, loyalty to tradition perpetuates indiscriminate study of the entire psychoanalytic canon, much of it of questionable value?

Not only are fewer patients currently seeking clinical analysis, but increasingly those who do are members of the mental health community. It has come to the point that the very great majority of patients in analysis are analysts-in-training, would-be analysts, and fellow travelers. This development should warn us that psychoanalysis is continuing as a social movement while failing as a therapy. If analysts are by and large seeing in analysis only people who would like to be analysts themselves, then it is likely that analysts are by and large proselytizing rather than offering a treatment that benefits the individual patient regardless of his or her particular life interests. Clinical analysis appears to be in the process of deteriorating into a kind of secular religious practice.

If the deterioration continues, clinical analysis will suffer the fate of all religious practices: it will become obsolete as the social conditions that originally made it appealing obtain less and less with the passage of time. Certainly, those discoveries made by Freud and clinicians who have come after him that can actually be applied across cultures and epochs to relieve patients' emotional distress will endure, and new understanding will continue to develop. However, psychoanalysis the social movement and psychoanalysis the science are two separate enterprises. The former is time- and culture-bound; the latter is not. Depending upon how long the social movement perseveres, the evolving science and scientifically based treatment method may come to be too burdened by historical associations, in which case the science will have to differentiate from the social movement by abandoning the name *psychoanalysis*. Psychoanalytic organizations, if they retain their generally conservative orientation, are likely to be left behind as the profession evolves. None of this strikes me as discouraging. I believe psychoanalysts do have a bright future, whatever we come to call ourselves. But we need to get real.

REFERENCES

Ghent, E. (1992). Paradoxical process. *Psychoanalytic Dialogues* 3:135–159.

Green, A. (1975). The analyst, symbolization and abstinence in the analytic setting. *International Journal of Psycho-Analysis* 66:1–22.

Greenson, R. (1968). The working alliance and the therapeutic relationship. *Psychoanalytic Quarterly* 34:155–181.

Hoffman, I. Z. (1983). The patient as interpreter of the analyst's experience. *Contemporary Psychoanalysis* 19:389–401.

McLaughlin, J. (1981). Transference, psychic reality, and countertransference. *Psychoanalytic Quarterly* 60:649–664.

Modell, A. (1991). The therapeutic relationship as a paradoxical experience. *Psychoanalytic Dialogues* 1:13–28.

Ogden, T. (1994). The analytic third: working with intersubjective clinical facts. *International Journal of Psycho-Analysis* 75:3–20.

Panel (1958). Technical aspects of regression during psychoanalysis. Reporter: K. Calder. *Journal of the American Psychoanaltyic Association* 6:552–559.

Pizer, S. (1982). The negotiation of paradox and the analytic process. *Psychoanalytic Dialogues* 2:215–240.

Renik, O. (1997). Realism in psychoanalysis. *Psychoanalytic Quarterly*, in press.

Stein, M. (1966). Self-observation, reality and the superego. In *Psychoanalysis: A General Psychology, Essays in Honor of Heinz Hartmann*, ed. R. Lowenstein, L. Newman, M. Schur, and A. Solnit, pp. 275–297. New York: International Universities Press.

Tarachow, S. (1963). *An Introduction to Psychotherapy.* New York: International Universities Press.

Ticho, E. (1972). Termination of psychoanalysis: treatment goals, life goals. *Psychoanalytic Quarterly* 41:315–333.

Viderman, S. (1979). The analytic space: meaning and problems. *Psychoanalytic Quarterly* 48:257–291.

3

Do the Enduring Controversies within Psychoanalysis Endanger Its Future?

Martin S. Bergmann

The original title of this paper* had a question mark behind it; however, the collective unconscious of the Division of Psychoanalysis eliminated the question mark. I hope that those of you who expected me to be a prophet of doom will be able to join me in a more optimistic assessment. What I did mean in my title was that the enduring controversies within psychoanalysis and the different schools that have emerged demand a re-evaluation of the history of psychoanalysis. This is all the more urgent because for the first time we have available the complete exchange of letters between Freud and Fliess, as well as those of his major disciples Abraham, Jung, Ferenczi, and Jones. We also now have available the minutes of the Vienna Psychoanalytical Society. In my plenary address to the American Psychoanalytic Association (Bergmann 1993a), I attempted to find ways to organize the history of psychoanalysis by introducing the concept of extender, modifier, and heretic.

In studying the psychoanalytic past, I found it useful to differentiate three types of contributors: heretics, modifiers, and extenders. The heretics, rare in recent years but prevalent in Freud's lifetime, were typically close to

---

*As presented at the American Psychological Association symposium, Spring 1996, New York.

Freud for some time, made important contributions, and then bolted to start their own schools. They include Adler, Stekel, Jung, Rank, and Wilhelm Reich. During Freud's lifetime there were only heretics and extenders. Modifiers appeared after Freud's death when no one, not even Anna Freud, could lay claim to being the only heir to Freud's legacy.

Modifiers recast psychoanalytic theory or modified psychoanalytical practice, but did not leave the psychoanalytic field. A typical strategy for a modifier is to claim that his or her modification is implicit in Freud's writings or flows directly out of Freud's ideas. While modifiers create controversy in psychoanalysis, they also keep it alive and protect it from stagnation. Early modifiers were Ferenczi and Federn; later ones were Hartmann, Melanie Klein, Winnicott, Lacan, and Kohut. Many modifiers are influenced by movements that take place outside psychoanalysis and attempt a synthesis between psychoanalysis and another discipline. Bowlby (1960) attempted to coordinate psychoanalysis with ethology; Lacan's modifications can be seen as an attempt to recast psychoanalysis in the language of structural linguistics.

Extenders, the third group, usually extend psychoanalysis into areas as yet unexplored, but their findings do not demand modification. Unlike modifiers, they evoke no enmity and their contributions are appreciated. Some of the important extenders are Karl Abraham, Hermann Nunberg, Waelder, and Fenichel. [p. 930]

While controversial issues are continuously debated in psychoanalytic meetings and publications, there is a reluctance to examine the broader question: Why do certain controversies endure with no resolution in sight? The reasons are not difficult to find, for the very topic calls into question what we all would like to believe—that psychoanalysis, like any other science, is making steady progress, solving old problems, and facing new ones. We all would like to believe that we are making progress in conquering the dark continent of the unconscious within ourselves and our patients, harnessing this knowledge into a form of therapy that becomes increasingly more effective.

If we cannot demonstrate that this is so, we become concerned that our detractors will use this argument to demonstrate that psychoanalysis is not a science. But today, when psychoanalysis is celebrating its one hundredth birthday, it is incumbent upon us to face the fact that Freud's bold idea to harness the exploration of the unconscious into a technique of treatment turned out to be a more complex enterprise than had been assumed.

For a number of decades I have been engaged in an educational project in which, with a group of students, we have studied certain clinical entities such as depression, masochism, character analysis, sexual dysfunctioning, or even the history of psychoanalytic technique, each in its own historical sequence, beginning with the earliest papers on the subject and ending with the most contemporary ones. The study of each one of these entities takes about one year to complete in weekly meetings. The results have been instructive. The members of the group feel that the knowledge of the development of this literature has added a great deal to their understanding of these entities and to their skill as therapists. At the same time it becomes clear that one can neither speak of a scientific consensus nor of an ascending curve of knowledge. Rather, it seems that each contributor has captured a part of the truth, or illuminated a certain aspect of the clinical entity. Consequently we do not have the feeling that steady progress is being made in the understanding of any clinical entity. In some instances, as for example in masochism, a deconstruction of the central concept has taken place (Bergmann 1993b).

Anyone who has followed the history of psychoanalysis must have noted that psychoanalytic debates in every decade center on certain issues that seem to excite the participants. After a certain time a kind of fatigue sets in; audiences and editors lose interest in the topic. Other issues emerge that are debated with a similar fervor. This however does not mean that a resolution has taken place. The same problem shelved for a period of time will reappear with other people taking up the same argument, with or without the acknowledgment that this problem has been discussed a decade or two ago. It is not *usual* for psychoanalysts to know a great deal about the history of psychoanalysis, as this history is not taught in psychoanalytic institutions.

THE BIRTH OF PSYCHOANALYTIC ORTHODOXY

Psychoanalytic orthodoxy emerged as the result of two events not anticipated by Freud. The emergence of "wild analysis" (Freud 1910), and, two, the defection of some of Freud's most promising disciples—Adler, Stekel, and Jung.

It may be useful to go back to the main tenets of psychoanalysis before the defections of Adler and Jung. In 1906, Freud's period of "splendid isolation" came to an end when the Wednesday meetings that later turned into the Vienna Psychoanalytic Society began. As this first group of potential analysts assembled, Freud could offer them a sufficiently coherent system that survived as the nucleus of psychoanalysis. It consists of:

1. The unconscious has a logic of its own called by Freud the primary process. In Shakespeare's terms, Freud refound that there is method in madness. Man is not the master of his own house; most of what moves him is unknown to him and motivated by his unconscious.
2. What is unconscious can be made conscious by the technique of "free association." It is of historical interest that two prominent thinkers, both Jews and both living at the same time in the same city, reached opposite conclusions. Wittgenstein, regarded by many as the greatest philosopher of this century, concluded that all that philosophy can do is examine language. What cannot be put into words one should keep silent about. By contrast, Freud found that that which has never been consciously thought and never verbalized could be put into words for the first time during free association.
3. Dreams are particularly useful in exploring the unconscious through free associations but slips of the tongue and pen can also be used.
4. Human sexuality does not begin with puberty, for we go through a period of infantile sexuality. This early sexuality differs from adult sexuality because it is less centered on genital sexuality and finds expression in pregenital forms which correspond to earlier developmental phases of the libido.
   The Oedipus complex is the culminating point of infantile sexuality. It normally undergoes repression during the latency period. If the repression is unsuccessful, it will reemerge during adulthood in the form of neurosis or perversion. It was this item in Freud's structure that was most difficult to accept and that constituted the origins of heresies.
5. In psychoanalysis, investigation and cure coincide. What had been repressed in childhood can be faced by the adult.
6. The journey into the unconscious and the past cannot be undertaken as a purely intellectual endeavor. The psychoanalyst, a modern Virgil who takes his Dante into Purgatory, must evoke powerful emotions of jealousy, hate, envy, anxiety, depression, and love. While the analysand is tossed by these emotions, he learns to understand himself in a new way. Transference is no longer the false connection it was in the "Studies on Hysteria" (Breuer and Freud 1895), but a tool that actual-

izes otherwise latent wishes and fears. No one can expect to be cured without reliving at least some aspects of his past in transference.

7. Psychic life is characterized by dualities and conflicts: conscious versus unconscious, primary process versus secondary process, pleasure principle versus reality principle.

8. Freud had discovered a basic truth unknown to mankind but one of the peculiarities of this truth is that it remains inaccessible, even to people of good will. This is because of the existence of powerful resistances which Freud also discovered. The only way to overcome such resistances is to undergo a personal psychoanalysis.

9. The Oedipus complex shows an enormous variation. It can be positive or negative, strong or weak. The elements of either love or hostility can predominate. It is the task of every analysis to uncover the individual variant of the Oedipus complex and the particular fixation point that it has left behind in every analysand.

Much was still missing in 1906. Narcissism had not yet been discovered, and without its discovery the nature of depression could not be understood. The mechanism of projection had not yet been studied, nor were psychoses understood. The presence of internalized objects was unknown. But enough had been discovered to make the therapeutic journey into the unconscious possible.

The publication of the minutes of the Vienna Psychoanalytic Society meetings (Nunberg and Federn 1974) enables us to date the birth of psychoanalytic orthodoxy. It took place on February 1, 1911. For some time, Adler, a member of the Vienna group, and its chairman, had been reporting his own ideas, which he considered first as additions to Freud's findings, and later as more central than Freud's discoveries. In Adler's view, childhood neuroses were the result of organ inferiority and what he called "the masculine protest," which manifests itself in devaluation of women by men, and in feelings of inadequacy of women toward men. He also gave greater prominence to the aggressive drive over the sexual one: "In the neurotic girl, this defiant attitude produces fantasies and the wish to give herself to a man in order to hurt her mother" (Nunberg and Federn 1974, p. 142). Freud objected to Adler's new vocabulary as unnecessary. For example, what Adler called "psychic hermaphrodism" was not significantly different from Freud's own term, bisexuality. Freud opposed Adler's attempt to deny the existence of infantile sexuality in favor of returning to the belief in the asexual nature of childhood. He also objected to Adler's belief that there is no significant difference between the neuroses. Some attempts were made to reconcile Adler with Freud by suggesting that Adler continues Freud's finding upward, that is, away from the unconscious into the ego and toward sociology. Responding to this suggestion Freud said, "Continuations 'upwards' and 'downwards' are necessary, but he had intentionally limited himself to the psychology of the unconscious. In point of fact, however, Adler's writings are not a continuation upward, nor are they foundation underneath; they are something else entirely. This is not psychoanalysis" (Nunberg and Federn 1975, p. 146). He went on to prophesy that Adler's views will cause damage to psychoanalysis but will be generally accepted because they evoke less resistance than his own (p. 146). From that date onward what is and what is not psychoanalysis will be the subject of continuous controversy.

Within two years Jung's defection followed. This was personally more painful to Freud as he regarded Jung as the Joshua of psychoanalysis, who, unlike the Moses (Freud), would inherit the promised land. Jung was a bright gentile with impeccable academic credentials, in Freud's view a man to whom others were naturally attracted. Freud believed that he himself lacked Jung's charismatic qualities. In 1909 Jung had accompanied Freud on his triumphant visit to Clark University. Freud's relationship to Jung had the earmarks of an idealized son-transference such as Turgenev had described in the novel *Fathers and Sons*. In my book *In the Shadow of Moloch* (1992), I show that the father's hostility toward his son, manifesting itself in the Laius complex, operates as a corollary to the Oedipus complex. As a reaction formation against the Laius complex, some fathers abdicate their place to the son. In Freud's relationship to Jung, such a tendency toward premature abdication is noticeable.

If we look back at Jung's apostasy in the light of subsequent developments, we will become aware of the fact that behind disagreements over the universality of the Oedipus complex powerful sociological forces played a role. Freud's original disciples were, until Jung and Jones joined, predominantly assimilated Jews who no longer believed in the traditional Jewish religious ideas and observances. (After the Napoleonic wars, the Jews of Western Europe lived through a period of emancipation in which they obtained equal rights. But the return of reactionary governments reintroduced a new type of secular anti-Semitism.) Assimilated Jews were eager to undo religious and national prejudices. It was therefore natural for them to create a psychology in which religious differences were excluded. Utopias easily become orthodoxies; it is likely that the Jewish contingent among Freud's followers, recently emancipated from religious orthodoxy, refound in psychoanalysis the orthodoxy they now missed.

Jung was neither willing to nor capable of breaking with his religious past. Unlike Freud's psychoanalysis, Jungian psychology aimed to reconnect estranged men and women to their ancestral and religious roots.

The expulsions of the heretics did not take place after long and dispassionate studies and discussions on what is and what is not psychoanalysis, or even what its limits are. They were the result of emotional disruptions that took place between Freud and his major disciples. Freud was incapable of entrusting the fate of psychoanalysis to history. He thought he could plan its future. The possibility that someday psychoanalysis could once more be forgotten or succumb to repression, and that all his work would have been done in vain haunted Freud throughout his life.

Up to 1920, when Freud made his great reevaluations in theory and practice, psychoanalysis presented a coherent movement, based mainly on the principles I have already enumerated. However, after 1920, when Freud published "Beyond the Pleasure Principle," in which he introduced the dual instinct theory, and when three years later, in "The Ego and the Id" (1923), he introduced the structural point of view, and later the change in the theory of anxiety (1926), he made it inevitable that psychoanalysis would give rise to different schools.

Some analysts, such as Ferenczi and Melanie Klein, would accept the death instinct and make it the center of analytic endeavor, while others, such as Otto Fenichel, would remain sternly opposed to it. Indeed the first controversies on technique took place in 1936 in the Marien Bad Symposium (Glover et al. 1997), where analysts were divided into two groups: those who thought that the analyst should approach the patient essentially from the side of the superego, trying to ameliorate it and lead the patient to accept the psychoanalyst's milder superego; and the other group, led by Fenichel, which insisted that the analytic endeavor should center primarily on the ego. Some analysts will claim that the aim of psychoanalysis is to maximize the power of the transference neurosis and will make the creation and cultivation of the transference neurosis the main difference between psychoanalysis proper and psychoanalytically oriented psychotherapy. Again, some analysts will insist that only transference interpretations are mutative, while others will give equal value to transference and extratransference interpretations. Freud was to a large extent responsible for the establishment of psychoanalytic orthodoxy, but he was equally responsible for its breakup after his reformulations in the 1920s.

Melanie Klein's work was derived from Freud's dual instinct theory. She was one of the few psychoanalysts to endorse the death instinct theory. In her interpretation the death instinct is particularly powerful at birth. The ministrations and love of the mother mitigate the impact of the death instinct. She saw the infant as beginning life in a paranoid position. Gradually, the love of the mother and the fusion of aggression and libido make it possible for the child to reach the next stage in development, the depressive position. Spitz (1945, 1946), who was operating within the Hartmann camp, nevertheless confirmed some of Klein's ideas when he found that infants, whose physical needs are well met but are deprived of contact with a maternal figure, developed marasmus and die.

We are now in a better position to study the controversy between Anna Freud and Melanie Klein since this prolonged and interesting controversy has appeared in print (King and Steiner 1991).

> Anna Freud (1943, p. 631, cited in Steiner 1985) summarized her disagreement with Klein succinctly. For Melanie Klein, the importance of preverbal fantasies is overwhelming compared with happenings after the acquisition of speech, and since these very early fantasies can emerge only in transference, most if not all analytic work takes place though transference interpretation. Transference along Freudian lines assumes that the first contacts between analyst and patient are governed by normal relational attitudes. It is the deepening of the transference that evokes emotions from deeper layers. For Klein the transference is there at the moment of encounter. Experience diminishes rather than enhances the power of transference. Finally, Freudian technique aims to undo repression: Kleinian technique aims to undo projection and introjection. [Bergmann 1993a, pp. 944–946]

As Steiner (1985) noted, the name of Melanie Klein appeared in the Freud–Jones correspondence (Paskauskas 1993) as early as 1925, two years after the publication of "The Ego and the Id." Her reformulations and technique made it possible for psychoanalysts to treat more disturbed patients, those closer to psychosis, than was possible by the standard Freudian technique at that time.

If Anna Freud had her way, Klein would have been destined to become another heretic. However, the mantle of the father did not pass on to the daughter. Melanie Klein was not expelled and thus she became the first modifier in the history of psychoanalysis. Other modifiers would follow.

They include Hartmann, Kohut, Lacan, and Horney, to name only a few. There would also be some future heretics such as Masson and Masud Khan. It is in my opinion pointless to lament the appearance of modifiers or even heretics. They were inevitable given the complex nature of psychoanalysis and the difficulty of assessing its results. When I look at the historical picture I come to the conclusion that every modifier or even heretic discovered a kernel of truth to which psychoanalysis will eventually return. This is particularly striking in the case of Adler, where ego psychology recaptured some of his thinking, and the dual instinct theory returned to some of his emphasis on aggression. Some modifiers, like Freud, conducted their own self-analysis and reached conclusions different from those that were reached in their own analysis. "The Two Analyses of Mr. Z" (Kohut 1979) is a case in point. In a paper (1993a) already alluded to, I pointed out that the emergence of different schools of psychoanalysis was inevitable given its complex structure. We have to face a paradox: ideally psychoanalysis was a rational method to study the irrational. At the same time it did not succeed in preventing an emotional attitude toward and idealization of its own different schools. I suggested that we make use of the different schools of therapy but submit their findings to a more rigorous examination.

I have found it useful to test different theories by asking the following questions:

1. In the view of the theory, how does psychopathology originate?

2. Does the theory lead to the conclusion that some forms of mental illness are not treatable by this method?

3. What does the theory regard as the ideal therapeutic process?

4. What is the theory's model of the mind (Gedo and Goldberg 1973), including its view of human nature and developments during the first years of life?

5. What steps are used by the adherents of the theory to convert the pathology of the patient into the model of mental health held by the theory?

On the whole I find it less productive to search for the common denominator or even compare the theories of the various schools, but useful to study what analysts of various schools say to their patients, particularly in moments of therapeutic crisis. I do not see the existence of different schools of analysis as the curse of the Tower of Babel, but as a unique opportunity to compare the clinical usefulness of different approaches in divergent clinical groups. [Bergmann 1993a, pp. 951–52]

Let me now return to the question I posed at the beginning of this presentation: Do the controversies within psychoanalysis endanger its future?

The problem is a complicated one because we do not know how to define psychoanalysis. Do we mean its core ideas, or its organizational features? As far as I am concerned, both in my clinical and historical thinking, I have been greatly influenced by Freud's dual instinct theory. I see this struggle between the destructive forces threatening civilization and the constructive forces based on humanity's libidinal resources everywhere. Psychoanalysis is not immune to the devastation of the destructive drive, but if the different schools will mean the end of psychoanalysis it will not be, as Freud originally thought, based on differences of opinion, but on the amount of aggression that so often characterizes the emergence of a new school of psychoanalysis. Fortunately in the last decade psychoanalysts have become less certain about their position vis-à-vis their patients and less certain that their school alone contains the only truth. With this more benign attitude, dialogues between different schools are becoming the norm and this decrease in the narcissism attached to preservation of small differences makes the survival of psychoanalysis more likely.

The fact that psychoanalysis is under siege everywhere may have diminished the ferocity of the civil war within its borders. Wars are conducive to coalition governments. In another paper (Bergmann 1985), I have spoken of creativity in the psychoanalytic hour, for in my view the needed creativity is not fostered in our training institutes. Individual differences in our patient populations are so great that no matter how extensive the transmitted knowledge becomes, every analyst will be confronted with the unexpected, and must learn to supplement his knowledge by creativity that is a felicitous coming together of transmitted knowledge accessed through one's own unconscious and the creative ability to make new connections.

When an analysis fails, the presence of other schools offers new help. When the analysand goes to an analyst of a different school he may find the new analyst highly sympathetic, although this sympathy may be based on hostility to other schools rather than focused on the difficulty the analysand presents.

In a recent paper citing many authors, Grossman (1995) showed that the school one chooses is often dependent on unconscious and irrational forces within us. I have found that if the analysis of a candidate was reasonably successful, he will tend to remain in his analyst's school, but that if it fails he is likely to join another competing school.

Freud believed that he discovered psychoanalysis. He was convinced that like Darwin's great discovery, psychoanalysis too could have been discovered by someone else. Only half in jest he asked the Protestant theologian and psychoanalyst Oskar Pfister, why the discovery of psychoanalysis had to wait for him, a "godless Jew." In my view, some of Freud's discoveries, like transference or infantile sexuality, could eventually have been discovered by others. But the totality of psychoanalysis was the creation of Freud alone, and had he not lived it would not have been created at any other time.

Psychoanalysis can grow only within a certain cultural climate, where there is an interest in the inner life of man; where the pursuit of happiness is considered a legitimate goal of life; where life is improving rather than becoming bleaker. It is hardly an accident that in the generation before Freud there were many great artists, such as Dostoevsky, Ibsen, and Nietzsche, who focused their attention on the inner life and even the neuroses prevalent in their time. When these cultural prerequisites are not present, it is likely that psychoanalysis will decline in significance. However, regardless of whether psychoanalysis as an organized entity survives, Freud's major gift to mankind, that traumatic events in our childhood need not wholly determine our life course, and that character need not necessarily mean destiny, will survive. Time may greatly modify the technique of psychoanalysis , but nevertheless it will always remain based on Freud's discovery that so much of our lives is governed by unconscious forces of whose power we remain oblivious unless psychoanalysis intervenes. This too will remain Freud's permanent bequest to mankind.

REFERENCES

Bergmann, M. S. (1985). Reflections on the psychological and social function of remembering the Holocaust. *Psychoanalytic Inquiry* 5(1):9–20.

———(1992). *In the Shadow of Moloch: The Sacrifice of Children and Its Impact on Western Religions.* New York: Columbia University Press.

———(1993a). Reflections on the history of psychoanalysis. *Journal of the American Psychoanalytic Association* 41:929–955.

———(1993b). Psychoanalytic education and the social reality of psychoanalysis. *Psychoanalytic Review* 80(2):199–210.

Bowlby, J. (1960). Grief and mourning in infancy and early childhood. *Psycho-analytic Study of the Child* 15:9–94. New York: International Universities Press. With separate discussions by Anna Freud, Max Schur, and René Spitz.

Breuer, J., and Freud, S. (1895). Studies on hysteria. *Standard Edition* 2.

Freud, S. (1910). "Wild" psycho-analysis. *Standard Edition* 11:219–227.

―――― (1920). Beyond the pleasure principle. *Standard Edition* 18:1–64.

―――― (1923). The ego and the id. *Standard Edition* 19:3–66.

―――― (1926). Inhibition, symptom and anxiety. *Standard Edition* 20:75–175.

Gedo, J. E., and Goldberg, A. (1973). *Models of the Mind.* Chicago: University of Chicago Press.

Glover, E., Fenichel, O., Strachey, J., et al. (1937). Marien Bad symposium on the theory of the therapeutic results of psycho-analysis. *International Journal of Psycho-Analysis* 38:125–188.

Grossman, W. (1995). Psychological vicissitudes of theory in clinical work. *International Journal of Psycho-Analysis* 76(5):885–899.

King, P., and Steiner, R. (1991). *The Freud–Klein Controversies 1941–1945.* New York: Routledge.

Kohut, H. (1979). The two analyses of Mr. Z. *International Journal of Psycho-Analysis* 60:3–27.

Nunberg, H., and Federn, E., eds. (1974). *Minutes of the Vienna Psychoanalytic Society, 1906–1918.* Volume 3. New York: International Universities Press.

Paskauskas, R. A., ed. (1993). *The Complete Correspondence of Sigmund Freud and Ernst Jones, 1908–1939.* Cambridge: Belknap.

Spitz, R. A. (1945). Hospitalism. *Psychoanalytic Study of the Child* 1:53–74. New York: International Universities Press.

―――― (1946). Hospitalism: a follow-up report. *Psychoanalytic Study of the Child* 2:113–117. New York: International Universities Press.

Steiner, R. (1985). Some thoughts about tradition and change arising from the examination of the British Psychoanalytical Society's controversial discussions, 1941–1945. *International Review of Psycho-Analysis* 12:27–71.

4

Separating the Wheat from the Chaff

Esther Menaker

In the course of human history most great ideas, theories, or systems of thought that are destined to interact with society and culture do not remain static, but, like living organisms, change, grow, and evolve. Such has certainly been the destiny of psychoanalysis. This process of change has seldom been welcomed, either by those committed to the orthodoxy of psychoanalytic theory and its accompanying technique, or by those bound by an allegiance to new theories and methods who sometimes look with disdain at the old orthodoxy. This fear of change and difference resides deep in the human creature and expresses itself in a wish to maintain unchanged that which humankind has ventured to create. This fear of challenging the old and creating the new is especially destructive in the case of science, be it based on empirical observation or experimentation. How can we approach the truth if we cannot question theories—systems of thought which are at best approximations? Let us examine how this dilemma plays itself out in the development of psychoanalysis.

Freud, the founder of psychoanalysis, himself feared change despite his many protestations to the contrary. "What will they [referring primarily to psychiatrists in America] do with psychoanalysis?" he is said to have lamented when he learned of the great interest in his theory in the United States. He might have added "*my* psychoanalysis," for he saw it as *his* creation, a closed system of energic forces whose actions and interactions explained the inner life of man. He sometimes spoke and wrote of its incompleteness and the need for further study and research. Yet he allowed only those changes and advances which were compatible with or provided additions to his *closed* system of thought. "Promise me never to abandon the sexual theory," he asked of Jung (1961, p. 150) during their travel to the United States. When Jung's conception of the unconscious differed from his own, or when Adler touched on the issue of the social milieu as an important influence in the development of the feeling of self-worth, Freud saw this as heresy. He wrote a polemical essay on the patient known as the Wolfman (Freud 1918) referring to the "twisted reinterpretations which C. G. Jung and Alfred Adler were endeavoring to give to the findings of psychoanalysis" (p. 7). As a reaction to this heresy he organized the well-known Committee of loyal followers to oversee the publication of psychoanalytic works. Nothing was to be published without the approval of the Committee, which was dedicated to maintaining the basic structure of the psychoanalytic system of thought intact. Freud had created a movement which adhered to a specific ideology. Fortunately its efforts failed. One cannot—and should not—impede the progress of ideas.

Yet for all the strictures imposed on the further development of psychoanalysis, it represented in itself a great advance in human understanding. It is hard to imagine the psychologically two-dimensional world in which people lived a little less than a century ago. Freud's discovery of a dynamic unconscious has changed our world. While philosophers and great writers intuitively sensed the existence of an unconscious aspect of the mind, they did not realize its impact on the emotions and on conscious thinking and behavior as well. It was Freud who discovered the dynamism of the unconscious—its power to intrude on consciousness to express our deep instinctual needs, thus sometimes creating conflict, but also fueling our creativity. In tandem with the unconscious was the discovery of repression—a force which kept unacceptable impulses out of consciousness. What resulted from the ensuing conflict between the repressed impulses and their rejection by the personality was the symptom: initially, the hysterical symptom. This great discovery paved the way to a possible cure for the symptom of hysteria, which in the sexually repressive climate of the Vienna of the late nineteenth and early twentieth century was a common ailment, especially among women.

However, not only was the dynamic process of repression into the unconscious an important discovery, but the *content* of the repressed impulses influenced the entire nature of psychoanalytic theory and ultimately became responsible for some of the most important deviations from classical theory—deviations which we would regard as progress, but by which the psychoanalytic movement felt threatened. Freud observed in the women he treated that at the root of the hysterical symptom there lay either a traumatic *sexual* experience or the fantasy of one. The sexual experience had to be repressed. (For the purposes of this essay, the question of the reality or fantasy of this experience is irrelevant, although it is an important question in other contexts.) Freud fashioned the basic structure of the development of the human psyche on the *primacy* of sexual drives. From Anna O.'s hysterical pregnancy (1895) which Freud interpreted in sexual terms as her wish to have a child with Breuer who was treating her at that time, to the Wolfman's supposed observation of the "primal scene" at the age of five (1918) and to the cause of Little Hans's horse phobia residing in his oedipal wishes toward his mother (1909), an individual's neurotic symptomatology was always and primarily interpreted as having its origin in a disturbance in the normal development of sexuality. In 1905 Freud explicated his conception of normal sexual development in "Three Essays on the Theory of Sexuality." This work contains the essence of libido theory as well as the concept of infantile sexuality. These were revolutionary views in Freud's time and included some measure of truth, and together with the discovery of the dynamic unconscious constitute the "wheat" of psychoanalytic theory. However, there cannot be wheat without chaff. In classic psychoanalytic theory the part has too often been taken for the whole. The knowledge that unconscious factors may play a role—even a large role—in certain human behavior, and also in pathology, should not blind us to the existence of other factors and other realities which profoundly influence human life. We cannot disregard the powerful and profound impact of socioeconomic factors, of the physical environment, or of culture with all its various subcultures on the development of personality and its anomalies. And is sexual development actually as primary for the development of personality as Freud would have us believe? There is a self which represents the total personality, and which from birth defines the unique constitution and character of each individual. Should we not pay attention to the course and nature of its development, and to its deficits and anomalies? And should we not address it therapeutically? The overemphasis on unconscious factors, on sexuality, and on the drives may blur our vision to the importance of understanding the growth and development of the *whole* individual. Heinz Kohut (1977), and Otto Rank (1945) before him, have emphasized the primacy of self-development. I concur with this view. It is the unfolding of growth processes in interaction with the environment that, under favorable circumstances, ultimately leads to the formation of a cohesive self. This is the primary expression of a life force which takes precedence over libidinal development.

The search for the "pure gold" of the unconscious has led to yet another error, especially in the course of the therapeutic process. The temptation to indiscriminately interpret the actions and behavior of the patient in terms of their possible unconscious *symbolic* meaning is a gross error. It can create a loss of contact with reality which threatens the integrity and cohesiveness of the individual's self. This simple fact is captured in verbal caricature in the well-known old joke: "A cigar is sometimes just a cigar"—a response to the implication in the therapist's interpretation that the cigar is inevitably a penis symbol. Not everything has deep unconscious meaning—and even if it does, it is not always productive to interpret it to a patient.

Thus in the overemphasis on the lifting of repression (with the consequent recovery of memories), the over-focus on symbolic meaning, the disregard of the self with its individual uniqueness and its primacy in development, and the dismissal of realities other than familial interactions that exist in an individual's environment and impinge on his or her development, lies a large measure of the chaff of psychoanalysis.

But classical psychoanalysis was impeded in its development by yet another, important piece of chaff. When the patient became the object of study for the analyst, the nature of the relationship between them assumed a specific, limited, and contrived character.

Committed as it was to the view that the neurotic personality was almost solely a product of the conflict between repressed unconscious drives and what it was consciously permissible to do, feel, or think, the therapy of psychoanalysis focused on the uncovering of the unconscious. Not surprisingly it chose the medical model for this undertaking. The patient was the *object* of study. He or she was required merely to express the seemingly random thoughts which came to mind while lying on a couch with the analyst sitting behind, out of the patient's view. The analyst listened carefully and impassively, hoping to find a significant thread in the material presented that would yield a clue to the patient's wishes or impulses.

At a time that the analyst deemed appropriate the meaning of the seemingly random thoughts was revealed to the patient. The cumulative effect of such insights, together with their gradual assimilation (working through) in the mind of the patient, was believed to have the desired therapeutic effect.

True to its origins in the treatment by hypnosis, psychoanalysis was focused on the past—on the patient's recovery of repressed memories. However, these were not always expressed verbally in sensory or emotional imagery, but in enactments in relation to the analyst. Freud discovered that old patterns of behavior, old attitudes, and feelings that began early in the life of the patient within the family were repeated in the analysis vis-à-vis the analyst. The analyst sought specifically for these patterns in the patient's associations. He called this the transference and considered it the surest road to an uncovering of the patient's unconscious conflicts and thus—ultimately—to cure. This was an important discovery and should be considered part of the wheat of analytic development. It came surrounded by much chaff; however, in this case it is not chaff to be discarded but rather to be carefully examined, for it is responsible for many of the advances in psychoanalytic theory and therapy.

While transferences take place in the course of normal life, let us examine the conditions under which the transference flourishes in therapy. It is the analyst's supposed neutrality that is an important factor in precipitating transference reactions. He or she, as analyst, remains solely an observer—not a participant in interaction with the patient—for it is thought that any expression of thought, judgment, or emotion, *any* communication from the analyst, would contaminate the "purity" of the situation in which only the patient's reactions should be examined. This invitation to the patient to project all his or her experience onto a supposedly blank screen proved both impossible and undesirable because, even with a minimum of verbal communication, the analyst reveals his personality, attitudes, and values in every aspect of his being and the patient feels this and resents the contrived effort of the analyst to hide who he or she really is. There is in fact no neutrality. Often the patient's reaction of anger and resentment is interpreted as resistance to an interpretation, thus compounding the negative transference.

Paradoxically Freud, who said "human beings reveal themselves through every pore" (1905, p. 77), advocated the neutral stance of the analyst and the fostering and consistent interpretation of the transference (although he himself did not always adhere to the rule). However, experience showed that, in itself, the analysis of the transference was insufficient for achieving cure or betterment in many if not most cases. While in the early days of psychoanalysis the cure of neurotic symptoms was more likely to be achieved by this analytic procedure, as the nature of the patient population changed to include personality and neurotic character disorders (especially those of a narcissistic nature), and as these individuals came more and more to represent those who sought help from psychoanalysis, the preponderant emphasis on the analysis of the transference and the impersonal stance of the analyst came to be less and less therapeutically fruitful, and was in some cases even destructive.

Certain of Freud's early followers responded to this deficit in the clinical implementation of psychoanalytic theory. Ferenczi was disturbed by the artificial nature of the interaction between patient and analyst. To him, it spoke of inauthenticity and hypocrisy. He abjured the neutral, passive stance of the analyst and opted for interaction between the manifest personalities of the two individuals participating in the therapeutic endeavor. Otto Rank, too, perceived the limitations of classical technique. For him its emphasis was too exclusively on the exposure of unconscious drive needs and wishes, especially those of a libidinal nature, to the neglect of ego phenomena—later to be identified as self issues. He understood that basic human needs could only be met in the context of *relationship with "another"* and that this was equally true for the therapeutic relationship. While transference needs to be perceived and analyzed when it interferes with the progress of the analysis, the basic therapeutic agent is the real relationship of the patient with the analyst, a relationship in which the analyst's affirmation of and respect for the person of the patient, especially of his will, is the most important factor in effecting growth and cure.

This introduction on the part of Ferenczi and Rank, two of Freud's most original and seminally thoughtful followers, of the idea of *relationship* between patient and analyst as crucial to a successful therapeutic outcome was viewed as heretical by the psychoanalytic establishment. They were duly punished by what amounted to excommunication. This however, did not deter them. In Rank's case, he did his most creative work after leaving Freud in the mid-1920s (Menaker 1982). Rank's development as a psychoanalytic thinker is particularly illustrative of the way in which psychoanalytic theory and practice itself evolved under the influence of new empirical observations and experiences, together with changes in the social climate of other times and places. The original doctrine, for all its new discoveries—and while closed to innovative thinking and reformulations—served, nevertheless, as the catalyst for precisely the changes which took place. In Rank's own life, psychoanalysis opened a new world of thought to his already burgeoning mind, and it provided an interested, encouraging, and supportive father figure for him in the person of Freud. But Rank, who had had no supportive background and had essentially created himself, understood the power of life's creative force. When it expressed itself through him in the form of ideas and theories that differed from those of his mentor, he followed them, nourished them, and formulated theories of his own. This is but one example of the innovations—faulty as some of them might be—that sprang up from the roots of Freud's original findings.

The therapeutic importance of the relationship between patient and analyst above and beyond the transference found expression in the works of outstanding English analysts: Fairbairn (1954), Guntrip (1971), and Winnicott (1975). They differed profoundly from Freudian thinking in that they did not consider the drives as the primary instigators of human growth and development, but considered the ego, which was object-seeking from its embryonic beginnings at the onset of life, to be primary. Yet as Rank remarked some decades before, and Martin Buber even earlier, since there is no "I" without a "thou," relationship becomes of paramount importance in the development of personality and in its therapy.

In the United States, too, the acknowledgment that there were *two* individuals in the analytic session and that their interaction needed to be understood and analyzed found expression in Harry Stack Sullivan's (1953) interpersonal theory of psychoanalysis. In this context, the patient's inner psychic life was no longer the sole object of observation and investigation, as was the case in Freudian analysis, but rather his or her interactions with the analyst became the focus of study. The therapeutic endeavor was still strongly influenced by the Freudian emphasis on the uncovering of unconscious impulses—in this case on those that surfaced in the interpersonal interaction. The possible constructive influence of one personality on another within the reality of their beings, as analyst and patient, was not yet accepted as a legitimate aspect of the therapeutic undertaking.

It was Heinz Kohut (1984), with his profound understanding of the way in which the self of an individual is formed in the course of development and the causes of anomalies in this development, who advocated the use of the relationship to rebuild the damaged self of the patient. For him, too, the self was primary; it was the driving force that motivated and defined all action, and thought. If it had been damaged in the course of development, the main function of therapy was to restore it to a fulfilling, joyous functional self.

An individual's self develops through the internalization of aspects of those personalities who have had an important emotional relationship to the developing personality. Initially and generally the parents played this role for the growing child. Kohut referred to those individuals who served this function as "self-objects." In other words, the parents are the child's first self-objects. However, optimally, the growth of the self continues throughout life and new self-objects are incorporated into the structure of the self. It is precisely the human ability to continue psychological growth, that is, growth of self through the choice of new self-objects, of new internalizations, that makes the psychotherapeutic process possible.

Patients who seek out psychoanalytic therapy are suffering not only from the repression of needs and wishes (that is, of drives) of which they are unaware, but from a lack of cohesion and integration of self structure. They are individuals whose early environment failed to provide the nutrients in the form of self-objects for the growing self. A poorly integrated and malfunctioning self is the result. Such patients need help in completing the process of individuation, and to this end the analyst must become a new self-object to be introjected, transmuted, and assimilated as part of the patient's new and more cohesive self structure.

A small vignette will illustrate my point. Not long ago I had been treating a middle-aged woman who came to me because of writer's block. Although a professional writer, she had intermittently had long periods of inhibition in writing. She had had psychoanalytic treatment of a classic nature some years back, but, although she felt that she had been helped in numerous ways involving her general personality functioning, the writing block continued to reappear. During her treatment with me we had talked a good deal about writing, about literature in general, and about her specific interests in this field. She learned in our conversations that I had written several books in my field, and she had in fact acquired my latest books and was reading them. At about this time she was asked to give a talk on a literary theme to an academic audience. The writer's block reasserted itself. Yet she tried to help herself in a very ingenious way—a way which, it seems to me, confirms Kohut's theory about the choice and incorporation of new self-objects throughout life. She reported that she took one of my books from her shelf and began reading my writing. After reading for some time she returned to her desk and found that she could proceed with her writing—with expressing her own ideas. This is a small example of the introjection of some part of a new self-object, transmuting it to harmonize with her own interests, inclinations, and activities to aid in the overcoming of an inhibition. Some readers may object that this does not get at the heart of the matter—to the root cause of my patient's inhibition. While this is true in a sense, it does tell us that the inhibition resulted from a deficit in self-structure, since assistance to the self through an act of identification with the analyst made possible the overcoming of the inhibition.

However, not all patients are open to new identifications—to new self-objects—nor are any of us open to this process at all times. I am aware that there may be conflicts of many kinds, especially those with primary, archaic self-objects that stand in the way of new incorporations. These conflicts must, of course, be resolved first before new implantations can occur. This is the work of psychoanalysis in terms of its original goals: the resolution of conflict. It is to this end that the analysis of the transference is crucial, thus making Freud's discovery of transference phenomena one of the great contributions to the understanding of human psychology. This discovery constitutes some of the "wheat" of psychoanalysis.

It would be a mistake, however, to regard the analysis of the transference as the sole, or even the major therapeutic agent in the resolution of conflict or in the healing of malfunction. Psychoanalysis as a therapeutic method in its over-focus on its most important discoveries—the unconscious, libido theory and childhood sexuality, the transference, and the meaning of dreams and fantasies—has not met its hoped-for goals. To my mind, this is in large measure due to its neglect of the therapeutic situation as a laboratory (in addition to its therapeutic function) for further observations that would ultimately influence, perhaps even change, theory. Instead, despite protestations to the contrary, and thousands of words written in attempts to enlarge some of its concepts, psychoanalysis in its classic form has not changed its deterministic philosophy, nor its energic-economic theory. In its love affair with the unconscious, it has neglected reality. In its focus on the inner life of the individual, it has neglected relationship—not just its importance in all human interactions, but specifically in terms of its therapeutic goals in the analytic situation. In the rigidity with which it set up norms it became value-laden and moralistic. In the narrow limitations of its observations it concluded that all peoples were psychologically alike, and therefore neglected cultural influences. Above all, while it had something to teach us about the ego, especially about its defenses, it failed to contribute to our understanding of the self, the total personality with its indomitable will to live, to grow, and to create. We learn little from classical analysis about the development of the self, although an important seed for our further understanding was planted in Freud's (1917) paper on "Mourning and Melancholia." Here, in a profound way we learn about mechanisms of introjection and identification. It is the understanding of these mechanisms that enabled Kohut, and Rank before him, to gain insights into the structuring of the self, and ultimately to use these insights in the very treatment of the self.

Classical psychoanalysis did not separate the wheat from the chaff. That remains for us to do. But in so doing it is important to gain perspective on the issues. Psychoanalysis is not dead, nor has it in some improbable way destroyed itself. True, its opponents would gladly see its demise. They gloat over its factionalism and internal differences; but this has little to do with its ultimate survival. It has contributed some fundamental truths to our understanding of human psychology; it has organized these into a system of thought, and a method of therapy. But in their original form I do not believe they will survive. For, like a living organism, it will take new influences into itself, it will change, it will evolve—and as it does so it will become clear, to continue the biological analogy, that psychoanalysis is not one species, but rather a genus which in the course of evolution branches out into a number of species.

REFERENCES

Breuer, J., and Freud, S. (1895). Studies on hysteria. *Standard Edition* 2:21–47.

Fairbairn, W. R. D. (1954). *An Object-Relations Theory of the Personality*. New York: Basic Books.

Freud, S. (1905a). Fragment of an analysis of a case of hysteria. *Standard Edition* 7:7–112.

——— (1905b). Three essays on the theory of sexuality. *Standard Edition* 7:123–243.

——— (1909). Analysis of a phobia in a five-year-old boy. *Standard Edition* 10:5–147.

——— (1917). Mourning and melancholia. *Standard Edition* 14:237–258.

——— (1918). From the history of an infantile neurosis. *Standard Edition* 17:7–122.

Guntrip, H. (1971). *Psychoanalytic Theory, Therapy, and the Self.* New York: Basic Books.

Jung, C. G. (1961). *Memories, Dreams, Reflections,* ed. A. Jaffe. New York: Random House.

Kohut, H. (1977). *The Restoration of the Self.* New York: International Universities Press.

———— (1984). *How Does Analysis Cure?* Chicago: University of Chicago Press.

Menaker, E. (1982). *Otto Rank, A Rediscovered Legacy.* New York: Columbia University Press.

Rank, O. (1945). *Truth and Reality.* New York: Knopf.

Sullivan, H. S. (1953). *The International Theory of Psychiatry.* New York: Norton.

Winnicott, D. W. (1975). Birth memories, birth trauma and anxiety (1945). *Through Paediatrics to Psychoanalysis,* pp. 174–193. New York: Basic Books.

5

Does Freud Have a Future in American Psychiatry?

Nathan G. Hale, Jr.

From an historian's perspective, Freud's position in America today reflects much that is perhaps seventy-five to one hundred years old: his role as an agent provocateur of controversy; questions about the scientific status of his theory and therapy; his stature as a hero or a villain. The new factors in Freud's changing reputation are the burgeoning of somatic psychiatry, issues of health care delivery and insurance, the sociology of the psychoanalytic profession, problems of psychotherapy research, and the work of revisionist critics. Let us examine some of these threads from the perspective of an historian, seeking to chart change over time.

Today, Freud is as controversially charged a figure as he was in May of 1896. Then a young, relatively unknown neurologist, he insisted to an audience of Viennese physicians that every case of hysteria resulted from child abuse, sometimes by a stranger, more often by a child's caregiver—nursemaid, governess, tutor—or a close relative (Freud 1896). Since then the battles surrounding Freud have intensified. His present position in America is full of paradox and contradiction. To listen to Freud's critics, his future in America and anywhere else is doomed. A distinguished literary critic has accused Freud of spawning the cult of recovered memories, of distorting his case histories, of browbeating his patients to elicit evidence that would confirm his theories. For some, Freud has become a figure of fun, a dotty Victorian sexist. Purists of the scientific method—often literary critics or philosophers, not practicing scientists themselves—find him unscientific, unworthy to be classed among minds as distinguished as their own. Some conservatives have blamed him for moral decay and the destruction of religious belief and for the cult of victimization.

Freud's defenders argue that he transformed our image of man by his discovery of the unconscious, and created enduring, provocative theories as well as a matchless and fundamental therapeutic technique. But on the whole, Freud's defenders are on the defensive, and Freud bashing has become a major enterprise, almost as extensive as the Freud scholarly industry itself.

FREUD'S UNINTENDED LEGACY TO AMERICA

Both Freud's adherents and his critics demonstrate how deeply the ideas he stands for have become woven into the fabric of American life, both popular and professional. The couch has become a shorthand symbol for psychotherapy of every persuasion. On a professional level, the entrenchment and expansion of the services of the psychological counselor, some of which were once rendered in part by the clergy, is one of Freud's major unintended legacies to American culture. Indeed, there are now experts who will perform psychological autopsies on the deceased to determine whether or not a suicide was induced by depression caused by loss of a job (hence entitling the deceased's widow to workman's compensation), all this without a single pre- and, presumably, no post-mortem interviews with the victim (Felsenthal 1995). The psychobabble involving the "analysis" of politicians, statesmen, athletes, and film stars is notorious.

The range of therapy and counseling for Americans now covers a vast array of human ills, to cite only topics from a recent catalogue of professional books: family therapy, child abuse, teen suicide, incest, recovery from cults, counseling AIDS families, addictions to alcohol or drugs. Without the impetus that psychoanalysis gave historically to psychotherapy, few of these topics would have come within the orbit of the psychiatric or psychological professions, except perhaps for the classical problems of addiction which are surely as old as mankind.

Many current critics hold Freud up to impossibly impeccable standards, drawn as much from a deep strain of American moralism and perfectionism, as from the profound approval and disapproval his ideas still arouse. The American assumption that an investigator must be in every way blameless reflects a deeply rooted need for a flawless healer or for an infallible scientist who never makes a mistake of judgment or claims more for his discoveries than they surely must be worth. Where for instance would the world be without Isaac Newton's confident eccentricities? To blame Freud for ills that affect modern American culture is like blaming Marx, that bibliophile holed up in the British Museum, for Stalin's gulags a hundred years later.

Freud's theories are now almost a hundred years old. It would be astonishing, indeed it would be a major intellectual scandal, if they had not been searchingly criticized—and most of that work has been done by psychoanalysts themselves. Freud himself might have had a reply to both his American admirers and detractors—a deep-seated and ingrained anti-Americanism. America is a mistake, he once observed, gigantic, perhaps, but a mistake all the same. He predicted and feared that his theories would be pigeonholed as merely one method of psychiatric treatment that could become outmoded as medical fashions changed. We shall see later what kind of a prophet he was.

FREUD'S CHANGING REPUTATION

Although never undisputed, Freud's reputation forty years ago was almost magically favorable and heroic. The extraordinary shift in American perceptions of Freud from earlier hero worship to present-day skepticism requires explanation. Some of the twists and turns in Freud's fate can be accounted for by the power of American culture to transform foreign theories. One of those transforming agents can only be described as the powerful need to sell and to popularize an idea, a compulsion that seizes not only journalists, but intellectuals and practitioners as well. We can look at the effects of this American impulse and the dramatic shift in Freud's reputation by examining the American image of Freud at the high point of psychoanalysis in the United States, around 1956.

Then, the American celebrations for the centennial of Freud's birth were orchestrated in part by a typically American institution, a public relations firm. Perhaps prompted by PR, President Eisenhower sent congratulations to American psychoanalysts, and Freud was lauded as one of the major scientists of the twentieth century. Taking an expansive historical view, some of his followers proclaimed him the equal of Copernicus, Galileo, Einstein, and, just possibly, Moses, as the fountainhead of a new dispensation. For those who read Ernest Jones's biography, hailed then by some critics as one of the world's greatest, Freud was a supernaturally virtuous man, austere, uxorious, and a driven, compulsive scientist, if at the same time neurotic and given to odd superstitions.

THE EXPANDED SCOPE
OF AMERICAN PSYCHOANALYSIS

In the 1940s and '50s, psychoanalysis and its derivatives were touted by some popularizers, and even by a few psychoanalysts themselves, as a remedy or an explanation for physical ailments from migraines to asthma, for some accidents, and for psychological disorders as various as compulsions, character defects, and severe mental illness—including schizophrenia. This was an extraordinary expansion of the rather limited ills Freud thought his method could treat.

This therapeutic expansion of psychoanalysis reflected the hopeful environmentalism of American popular culture. One reason for this therapeutic expansion had been the success of psychoanalysts in treating and theorizing about the war neuroses during World War II. After the war, it was deemed essential to bring mental health services to as wide a public as possible, to train an army of psychiatrists, clinical psychologists, and psychiatric social workers, many of them, if not most, under psychoanalytic auspices. Early treatment, it was hoped, would prevent the development of serious mental illness. And in those early postwar years psychoanalysis faced as yet no developed rivals in the field of psychotherapy.

The superhuman virtues Americans ascribed to Freud and the magical powers ascribed to psychoanalysis in magazines and films set both up for serious falls. Perhaps the apogee of extravagance was this astonishing paean of praise printed in the *Chicago Sun Times* in 1956:

> Do we have a new concept of individual dignity? Do more employers recognize the psychological as well as the economic needs of their employees?

Are we more self expressive in our clothes, in the blither colors of our homes and cars?

Do we merely lock up criminals and juvenile delinquents as hopeless defectives beyond redemption? Or do we try to cure them by seeking out causes in their homes and childhood? . . . Where the answer is yes, there are many authorities who trace this indirectly to Freud and those who followed him. [Hale 1995, p. 286]

THE CAUSES OF CHANGE

What happened between the exuberant 1950s and today? How can the reputation of both Freud and psychoanalysis have changed so drastically, and what does the future hold for both? A number of factors came into play: somatic psychiatry and its breakthroughs; the proliferation of therapists and therapeutic schools; the sociology of the psychoanalytic profession and its training; issues of high treatment costs and insurance costcutting; the closely related problem of psychoanalytic outcome research; and finally, revisionist scholarship about Freud and psychoanalysis.

Neo-Somatic Psychiatry

With the advent of tranquilizers in the 1950s, treatment of the mentally ill was revolutionized, marking a dramatic resurgence of somatic psychiatry—that is, a psychiatry seeking the cause and the cure of nervous and mental illness in physiological factors—in, for instance, drugs and genetics rather than in environmental and psychological forces. These somatic ambitions had had a long history stretching back into the nineteenth century. Despite strenuous efforts up through the 1940s, and with the possible exceptions of electroshock, insulin shock, or lobotomy, the results of treatment had been relatively meager in serious mental illness.

The new somatic psychiatry that began in the 1950s created not only promising new drug treatments, but also extraordinary discoveries about the nature of brain and neurological functioning, an explosion of knowledge that has become even more spectacular today. Drug treatments have recently been developed that have shown remarkable success for a percentage of patients with anxiety and other conditions that used to be considered neuroses of psychological origin.

Genetic Research and Mental Illness

With this new knowledge has come more stringent genetic research, focusing on controlled studies of twins raised apart. These findings suggest, at least for some mental illness, a constitutional factor ranging from perhaps 37 percent to 60 percent or more. The *Harvard Mental Health Letter* (1995), a compendium of the up-to-date, recently suggested that the heritability of depression ran at about 37 percent. The *New York Times* has reported that a genetic basis for persistent bed wetting, a condition often thought to have partly psychological origins, is on the verge of discovery. But it is important to recall, in this new enthusiasm for a genetic factor, that an estimate of 37 percent would still attribute some 63 percent of mental illness to nongenetic elements in depression. These would include birth trauma as well as interactions with the environment, such as the early response to caretakers, given the inborn temperament of the very young child. Some recent psychoanalytic research has focused precisely on these early interactions (Emde and Harmon 1982, Holmes 1993). The search for a genetic basis for an increasing number of mind states and behaviors has grown rapidly, from temperament to sexual orientation. This movement in psychiatry was part of a neo-somaticism that also held sway in the social sciences, and there has been a good deal of theorizing about the evolutionary function of say, aggression in the male. Some of the neo-Darwinism in social science has been more speculative than anything the psychoanalysts theorized on the basis of what their patients told them.

New Psychological Therapies and Therapists

In addition to neo-somaticism, alternative psychological treatments have proliferated, beginning with behavior therapy; none of them had been developed much before 1950. The example of psychoanalysis inspired the dramatic growth of psychotherapists of all kinds, from orthodox analysts to school counselors, although mind cures in America had had a long history, particularly in the middle and late nineteenth century. Mind-cure enthusiasts had in fact helped to introduce Freud to Americans in the first decade of the twentieth century. Indeed, psychological treatment has reflected the ingrained American concern for reshaping and improving the self. The number of psychotherapies is now legion—by some estimates more than 400—and they are plied by therapists with the most disparate training and skills and with no universal standards of competence.

THE SOCIOLOGY OF THE PSYCHOANALYSTS

Against the proliferation of such psychotherapists, the psychoanalysts have upheld the concept of an elite profession, with a systematic set of evolving theories. And this laudable aim sometimes has had unintended consequences for the sociology of the profession. Psychoanalytic candidates in institutes of the American Psychoanalytic Association are allowed to graduate only after protracted scrutiny; they must complete not only a personal analysis, but also present several cases, with one of them virtually completed, each treated under the supervision of a senior analyst. A profession at first limited in America to physicians by the American Psychoanalytic Association, the Association has most recently been forced to allow the training of selected lay candidates under threat of a lawsuit filed by members of the American Psychological Association. The latter's psychoanalytic Division 39 has become the single largest psychoanalytic organization in America, with more than 3,400 members by 1992. (The American Psychoanalytic Association claimed more than 3,000, the American Academy of Psychoanalysis about 800.) The Division's recommendations for training are close to the traditional ones and include a substantial personal analysis, intensive supervision of patients, and substantial didactic work. These recommendations were reached after conflicts reminiscent of earlier debates within the American Psychoanalytic Association over how lengthy and intense training should be, including required hours of personal therapy and supervision. Some of Division 39's programs are affiliated with university settings, notably in New York. There are a number of local chapters, four of which have been recognized by the International Psychoanalytic Association, thus breaking the mold of training and certification of the American Psychoanalytic Association (Lane 1994).

Despite frequent conflicts over training requirements, the psychoanalysts, both medical and nonmedical, probably remain the most meticulously trained of all the psychotherapists. However, the current psychoanalytic training programs of both the American Psychoanalytic and American Psychological Associations, as well as earlier independent training centers, have meant an increase in the number of nonmedical psychoanalysts, with unforeseen effects on the psychoanalytic profession and its relation to psychiatry.

For historical reasons, psychoanalysts have remained largely a profession of practitioners. For the most part they create and support their own training centers, and these—with a few exceptions such as Tulane, Columbia, and New York University—are outside the traditional system of medical schools and universities. This very sociology of a group of private practitioners has militated against research, even among the psychologist-psychoanalysts.

To do psychoanalytic research, unless funded by the government or a university, a private foundation, or an endowment, a practitioner would have to give up earning time spent with patients. The lengthy and expensive demands of psychoanalytic education have ensured that analysts are no longer young when they complete their training, sometimes with large debts—not the best age or status for innovation and discovery. However, most of them practice psychiatry and/or psychotherapy during their apprenticeship, so age at completion of training may be less significant as a factor in their development than the bare graduation statistics would suggest. And the growth of nonmedical practitioners could result in a younger cohort of psychoanalysts. Thus, superannuation is not the whole story. Analysts currently do not represent a collection of aging introspectives, uncritical in their Freudian allegiance. There has been a remarkable ferment of ideas within the profession, a new openness to a variety of theoretical positions, and a willingness to rethink fundamentals. Exposure to diverging viewpoints is one of the goals of the institutes founded by members of the American Psychological Association. But the concept of a carefully trained profession remains, and its members perforce must compete with many who have had far less lengthy a scrutiny. The very notion of a profession, rigorous by reason of training (and presumably competence), has come up against the fad of anti-elitism, a holdover from the counterculture of the 1960s when psychoanalysis was decried as part and parcel of the psychiatric establishment.

THE ISSUE OF COST

Recently problems of professionalism have been overshadowed by the ubiquitous current issue of cost constraints, which suggests a frivolous question: Does the film actor–director Woody Allen's lifelong addiction to psychoanalysis suggest that psychoanalysis has a future for anyone else? One of the most pressing issues psychoanalysts face today is one that Allen presumably has not had to deal with, that is, the high cost of analytic treatment, treatment in many cases lasting five years or more at $100 or more an hour. Historians, myself obviously included, are by no means gifted prophets, and I am undoubtedly being highly presumptuous, but I think the future may be reasonable for a flexible psychoanalytic psychotherapy, perhaps dismal for four- or five-day-a-week classical analysis. One reason is obvious. Given current rates, a classical analysis of four hours a week could run to a minimum of $1,760 per month, about the rental of a modest apartment in some large American cities, while a five-year analysis might total $114,000. However the increase in the number of psychoanalysts may mean reduced fees, and this already has happened in some areas.

PROBLEMS OF OUTCOME RESEARCH

The problem of high cost is directly related to the problems of psychotherapy outcome research. Insurance companies and government agencies in the United States have been unwilling to fund a therapy whose results have not been demonstrated. But that judgment often has been based on standards, sometimes inappropriately derived from medicine, such as the current emphasis on randomly selected patients and double-blind procedures.

Here I am not suggesting that the National Institute of Mental Health's massive research in therapy for depression, for example—with matched groups of patients, and therapists trained to follow standardized therapeutic interventions—is useless. Quite the contrary. And the results have been favorable for psychotherapy. A writer in the *Harvard Mental Health Letter* recently insisted that behavioral, interpersonal, and cognitive behavioral therapies were as effective as antidepressant drugs in the treatment of major depression without psychotic features. He argued that psychodynamic therapies were less useful, and that the results of long-term therapy remained untested. He also noted that controlled studies of psychotherapy have concerned short-term treatment almost exclusively (Kingsbury 1995). Recently in the same publication, a psychologist noted that a survey of long-term therapy by *Consumer Reports* demonstrated that it was highly effective. But here again, no particular therapy "was better than any other for any problem or disorder" (Seligman 1996).

Because of the current reluctance to fund long-term therapy, and the decline in insurance benefits (often limited to twenty hours or less), the patient's financing of analysis has become increasingly onerous. Unless these limitations can be changed, the pool of patients for long-term psychotherapy, not to speak of psychoanalysis, becomes more and more narrowed to those who are able to pay, reinforcing the stereotype of the wealthy psychotherapeutic or psychoanalytic patient. What seems to be replacing classical analysis is a briefer psychotherapy based on psychoanalytic principles. But psychodynamic therapy also can be considered lengthy by current insurance standards. Today, the press is full of reports of therapists of many persuasions who complain that HMOs or insurance companies have cut off psychotherapeutic treatment far too soon, leaving patients to flounder. There seems to be an unholy alliance between cost-cutting insurers and those who assume that a pill will suffice for every emotional or mental disorder.

THE PROBLEM OF EVIDENCE

But cost is not the only challenge to the psychoanalytic profession, a challenge only partly met by psychoanalytic clinics or practitioners who charge reduced fees. The second challenge, closely related, is to make the claims for psychoanalysis convincing to non-analysts. There are two subordinate issues here. One is to make psychoanalytic clinical data objective, and the second is to compare the results of psychoanalysis or dynamic psychotherapy with those obtained by other methods. Clinical evidence based on case histories has provided psychoanalysis with some of its most striking data. It is difficult to read the careful case history of a successful psychoanalysis without believing that a serious therapeutic intervention has taken place. For example, the psychosomatic psychoanalyst Morton Reiser's account of analyst and patient's discovery of the basis of a particularly severe phobic episode supplies convincing evidence that the discovery was clinically crucial. Indeed, the phobia was resolved (Reiser 1985). Leaving aside the comparative issue for the moment, are we to assume that all the analysts' case histories of lengthy successful treatment are fairy stories, made up by self-deluded practitioners? Is it impossible for a therapist to create an honest clinical report of extended psychological treatment of a patient? Of course not. The problem is to make this clinical evidence objective and therefore convincing.

PSYCHOANALYTIC RESEARCH
IN PROCESS AND OUTCOME

There has been some progress in this direction. For example, both clinical evidence and controlled psychoanalytic research suggest that the careful working through of transference patterns is one of the hallmarks of successful psychoanalytic treatment. This has been the conclusion of several psychoanalytic research projects, including Lester Luborsky's research at the University of Pennsylvania into the Core Conflictual Relationship Theme, a pattern that seems to distinguish a patient's relationships to not only his or her therapist, but to truly significant others in his or her life, especially parents (Luborsky 1985). Increasingly, the psychoanalytic focus has been on the relationship between therapist and patient, particularly on the analyst's special emotional and intellectual relationship to his or her patient, the patient's relation to the analyst, and how these intricate interactions can affect therapeutic outcomes. John Gunderson's careful study (1990) of the psychotherapy of schizophrenia suggests that successful outcomes depend on the establishment of a strong therapeutic alliance. Luborsky (1996a) has advanced some evidence that accuracy of interpretation is related to outcome. Other psychoanalytic research by Joseph Weiss and Harold Sampson (1986) suggests that when the therapist's interventions accord with the patient's own unconscious plan of recovery, anxiety is relieved and progress takes place. Patients formulate such plans in order to overcome their "pathogenic beliefs," faulty cognitive and evaluative structures rooted in early experience. The Boston, Columbia, and New York psychoanalytic institutes have used standardized tests and blind raters since the 1950s to demonstrate that both psychoanalytic psychotherapy and psychoanalysis achieve substantial results. And several of these studies included follow-ups from a year to six years after treatment. Attempts to predict outcome were unsuccessful. However, one important finding was that the treating therapist's final assessment of outcome correlated closely with the findings of blind judging therapists and standardized outcome measures, and this strongly suggests the accuracy of clinical judgment. Certainly, far more such research needs to be done. Because these studies have not compared treatment outcomes to patients on a waiting list or similar control, some psychotherapy researchers are skeptical about the results.

However, research in long-term therapy presents two serious problems. First, patients drop out of studies—the longer the study, the greater the attrition. Second, would it be fair to patients to make them wait for four or five years without treatment in order to organize a comparative study with patients who in fact are being treated?

Still another issue, part of the problem of evidence, is the lack of comparison of the results of analytic treatment with those of other methods. The first meta-analyses of psychotherapy research, notably by Smith, Glass, and Miller in 1980, concluded that there was little difference in the outcome of most therapeutic methods. But then, psychoanalysis was not represented in this research, and much of the therapy was extremely brief. Psychotherapy research sometimes has been limited and of poor quality, using college student subjects and untrained graduate student therapists, hardly a cross-section of the usual patient population with serious problems treated by skilled and experienced therapists. And there certainly is growing evidence that some therapists are far more skilled than others and achieve substantially better results.

The major comparisons so far have been between psychoanalysis proper and supportive psychoanalytic psychotherapy, as in the massive study carried out by the Menninger Foundation under the leadership of Robert Wallerstein and Otto Kernberg (Wallerstein 1986). These results, like those of the Institutes, suggest that psychotherapy achieves outcomes as satisfactory as does analysis proper. The best results were obtained in patients with perhaps florid symptoms, but with the most ego strength. But the question remains: Why were both supportive psychotherapy and psychoanalysis successful? Does it mean that psychoanalysis really is the underlying model of therapy or that in addition to the therapist–client relationship, there are factors that we don't yet know that may provide a still more basic model for therapeutic change?

There have been a few comparisons between psychoanalytic psychotherapy and behavior therapy, notably Bruce Sloan's study (1975), in which both methods achieved relatively comparable results, with a slightly more favorable edge to behavior therapy. Today, group therapy for the families of psychotic patients seems to be almost entirely behavioral or cognitive behavioral in nature.

EXPERIENCE IN OTHER COUNTRIES

Treatment results and costs have dominated debate over the insurance issue, affecting not only psychoanalysis but other psychotherapies as well, and these problems are especially acute in the United States. But America is not the only country where psychoanalysis is established. Experience elsewhere has been more encouraging to psychoanalysts. For example, psychoanalysis has survived hardily in Britain where it never has been part of the national health insurance system. And in Germany, where 300 hours of psychoanalytic therapy per patient have been funded by government health insurance programs, there is evidence that the cost of this treatment is offset by analyzed patients' lessened use of other health services, including hospitalization. However, at the moment, the German government has restricted psychoanalysis to not more than three hours a week (Willock 1996). (Studies in the United States also have demonstrated that outpatient mental health treatment has distinct offset benefits, reducing medical costs for patients with chronic diseases in which psychological factors are assumed to be one element [Sands 1996].) Psychoanalysis flourishes in much of Europe and Latin America. In Ontario, Canada, where psychoanalysis is fully funded, a recent survey recorded the following facts about patients in analysis lasting an average of five years: first, they suffered from severe disorders including serious childhood traumas, and second, a large number of them had turned to analysis after first trying other, briefer therapies that proved to be ineffective (Doidge 1994).

ISSUES AND IFS

Despite these encouraging signs abroad, large doubts remain to plague the issue of psychoanalytic survival in America. Let me leave the historical role and take on once again the very doubtful role of prophet. Can Freud's psychoanalysis survive? I think it can, with a series of caveats:

1. IF psychoanalysts can demonstrate with more convincing evidence, either by single-case research but preferably by controlled comparisons with other methods, that psychoanalytic treatment works and indeed may work where other modalities fail. Some quite sophisticated research is already underway, particularly for evaluating and measuring change in individual patients.

2. IF analysts can define clearly what their methods treat more effectively than other therapies. Today, long-standing character disorders and those that involve ongoing internal conflict seem to be the targets of choice for analytic therapy, but they need to be more clearly circumscribed and defined. New techniques for dealing with character disorders and border-

line patients also need to become a standard part of institute training. It is only recently that training in psychotherapy has become part of the curriculum in some psychoanalytic institutes, despite the fact that psychotherapy has become a growing part, and in many instances the major part, of the psychoanalyst's practice.

3. IF psychoanalytic training broadens to make analysts and candidates at least aware of the wide range of alternative therapies, their techniques and results; that is, behavioral, group, cognitive, and so on. There is one clear reason for this messy eclecticism: we cannot yet match patients' symptoms or problems with appropriately optimal therapies. It is possible that given the wide gamut of patients and problems, a wide spectrum of techniques needs to be available; some may work better with some patients than with others.

However, it is reassuring that new psychoanalytic institutes are being started in some areas and some institutes are faced with a growing number of candidates, many of whom already are experienced psychotherapists who seek psychoanalytic training to enhance their therapeutic skills. Thus the future for psychoanalysis within psychotherapy seems reasonably assured.

4. IF candidates and analysts can keep abreast of both the merits and limitations of available somatic therapies by maintaining close contact with the most recent advances in psychiatric medicine. Because advances in somatic psychiatry are developing fast and furiously, knowledge about this area is especially critical for nonmedical therapists. Indeed, a recent book answers this very need: *Understanding Biological Psychiatry* (Hedaya 1996). One study of the San Francisco Institute by a sociologist (Nunes 1984) suggested that as analysts, including medical analysts, advanced in their training, their knowledge of somatic therapies declined and their exclusive commitment to talk therapy increased. For this reason alone, some knowledge of somatic interventions needs to be part of psychoanalytic education.

All of the above suggests a radical restructuring of psychoanalytic training away from the notion that the sole paradigm of effective treatment and the only topic to instruct candidates about is classical psychoanalysis.

But by the same token a knowledge of psychotherapy needs to be an essential part of the medical and psychiatric curriculum. One survey of psychiatric education indicated that exposure to intensive psychotherapy is much less than it was twenty or thirty years ago, and indeed is almost nonexistent (Altshuler 1990).

It is ironic that nearly all the objections that have been raised in the past about psychoanalysis—impressionistic clinical evaluations, unclear definitions, lack of control groups, small sample size, incautious evangelism, and so on could be raised against many of the initial discussions of somatic therapies or genetic factors. Take Prozac, for instance. Peter Kramer, the author of *Listening to Prozac* (1993), seemed to commit every one of the errors just mentioned for which psychoanalysts had sometimes been damned. Prozac seemed precisely to promise the deep characterological changes that psychoanalysts have sought for their patients. But the basis for this judgment was highly impressionistic. As the psychoanalyst Franz Alexander once observed, no matter what the advances in somatic psychiatry, there will remain an irreducible core of psychological and interpersonal problems for which psychological methods are uniquely appropriate—and indeed, Kramer used psychotherapy as well as Prozac.

Finally, probably there always will be patients who seek greater understanding of their own conscious and unconscious processes and who are willing to make the sacrifices in time and money that that requires. And for patients who have not found relief in other treatments, psychoanalysis may be, as Freud once argued, the best method for substituting ordinary unhappiness for dreary and unwanted neurotic symptoms.

All these highly complex problems of research, cost, and training have eroded the once prestigious position of psychoanalysis. But there is another factor, the revisionist scholarship of the Freud industry.

REVISIONIST SCHOLARSHIP

An unseemly brouhaha has recently been resolved about the Freud Exhibit the Library of Congress has been planning. Had it been captured by devotees of the Freudian flame? Would there be enough room for revisionist critics? Indeed, the Library postponed the exhibit, probably bowing to the winds of controversy, then rescheduled it for 1998. It is the repository of the Freud Archives and has an unparalleled collection of the papers of psychoanalysts. One can only add that the Freud Archives' policies of restriction have contributed to endless speculation about Freud's life and integrity, matters which open access could have clarified.

Finally, the superhuman virtues Americans ascribed to Freud in the 1950s neatly set him up for a serious fall. The sweeping and almost inane praise typified by the *Chicago Sun Times* (Hale 1995, p. 286) was too exaggerated to remain unchallenged. In the last two or three decades there have been a number of revisionist views of Freud, some of them dotty, some more reasonable. Jeffrey Masson (1984), for instance, has argued that Freud gave up his theory that neuroses were due to sexual abuse by parents because he feared condemnation by his Viennese colleagues. Yet, as Peter Gay (1988) has noted, Freud then propounded an even more outrageously offensive theory, that is, that these presumed memories often represented fantasies that expressed the inchoate desires and jealousies of the very young child. So much for the pusillanimous Freud afraid of colleagues. In revising his theory, Freud also decided that there probably was far more neurosis than there was abuse, although in many cases abuse and its effects were real and traumatic, a position he maintained to the end of his life. One of the most moving descriptions of the discrepancy between the powerful adult and the powerless, awkward child victim occurs in one of Freud's early works on hysteria:

> People who have no hesitation in satisfying their sexual desires upon children cannot be expected to [have scruples about] the methods of obtaining that satisfaction; and the sexual impotence which is inherent in children inevitably forces them into the same substitutive actions as those to which adults descend if they become impotent. All the singular conditions under which the ill-matched pair conduct their love making—on the one hand the adult who cannot escape his share in the mutual dependence necessarily entailed by a sexual relationship, and who is yet armed with complete authority and the right to punish, and can exchange the one role for the other to the uninhibited satisfaction of his moods, and on the other hand the child, who in his helplessness is at the mercy of this arbitrary will, who is prematurely aroused to every kind of sensibility and exposed to every sort of disappointment, and whose performance of the sexual activities assigned to him is often interrupted by his imperfect control of his natural needs—all these grotesque and yet tragic incongruities reveal themselves as stamped upon the later development of the individual and of his neurosis, in countless permanent effects which deserve to be traced in the greatest detail. . . . [Freud 1896, pp. 214–215]

And this is the Freud who has been accused by some critics of being indifferent to the child victim.

An English writer, E. M. Thornton (1983) regards psychoanalysis as the product of Freud's cocaine-driven imagination. One need only read the "Interpretation of Dreams" (1900), "Jokes and their Relation to the

Unconscious" (1905), and "Three Essays on the Theory of Sexuality" (1905), all written before 1912 (after which, Thornton argues, the influence of cocaine was no longer observable), to conclude that a drug-besotted imagination could hardly have produced these eloquent if sometimes tortured arguments.

The contention that Freud exaggerated the therapeutic action of his own psychoanalyses seems exaggerated but more plausible, as several critics have argued. Fisher and Greenberg (1977, 1996), in their surveys of Freud's scientific status, suggested that many of his cases were incomplete or failures. And a devastating account of Freud's analysis of his daughter, Anna, has come from the Canadian psychoanalyst Patrick J. Mahony (1992). Frank Sulloway (1992), without offering additional evidence, has sharply criticized two of Freud's most famous cases, the Rat Man and the Wolfman, arguing that these were therapeutic failures, glossed over by Freud. However, a critical look at the revisionists suggests that their judgments are sometimes faulty, their evidence slender and often purely speculative, and their conclusions sometimes malicious.

Most recently Freud has been accused of being a closet devotee of the Judeo-Christian tradition in matters of sexuality (Webster 1995). Then again, he has been accused of possessing a personal paranoid pathology and style that has definitively contributed to what another critic regards as the paranoid suspiciousness of modern culture, a culture that besmirches tradition and high achievement with vulgar reductionism (Farrell 1996).

Finally, Freud's uxorious reputation, so devoutly established by Ernest Jones to counteract rumors already circulating, has been questioned by one or two writers who think he had an affair with his sister in law, Minna Bernays, a rumor spread by Carl Jung. It's possible, but certainly not proven, and the one systematic attempt to demonstrate it is riddled with conjecture and implausible conclusions. Until the Freud Archives makes available the full correspondence between Freud and Bernays, and possibly the Jung records yield additional material, the issue remains undecided—and no matter what the outcome, will remain irrelevant to any judgment of Freud's intellectual achievement. This is one more instance where the Freud Archives' policies have done Freud a serious disservice.

One hopeful sign for the future of Freud's ideas has been their capacity to generate hypotheses in a number of humanistic fields outside psychiatry. After the first feminist onslaughts of the 1970s and 1980s, a number of Freudian feminists have begun writing. Schools of literary and aesthetic criticism have been heavily influenced by Freud, and he has been a minor presence in the social sciences—less strong than, say, twenty years ago, but an ongoing presence nevertheless, particularly in anthropology.

PSYCHOANALYTIC RESEARCH PROJECTS AND FREUD AS PROPHET

In recent years, some analysts have been attempting to verify their hypotheses by replicable methods. Such research utilizes transcripts or videos of therapy sessions, blind raters, and a number of converging strategies made possible in part through computer techniques. These strategies attempt to simplify the therapeutic process into a few structural patterns that can be universally applied, compared, and perhaps ultimately quantified. The aim is to seek similar conceptualization and measurement of the patient's problem, the treatment, and the outcome (Strupp 1992, p. 316). It is assumed that patients present dysfunctional, repetitive modes of behavior that can be isolated and conceptualized and that these modes repeat themselves in the patient's relation to the therapist. Luborsky's group categorizes these transactions in terms of the subject's wishes, the anticipated response of others, the actual response of others, and the subject's view of him or herself (Luborsky 1996b, p. 18). Hartwig Dahl of the SUNY Health Sciences Center in Brooklyn, has attempted the content analysis of recorded psychoanalytic sessions in terms of "frames" or stereotyped structures of behavior. For example, a "support" frame might include the patient's sense of conflict, an appeal for support from a spouse, the spouse's denial of support, and the patient's subsequent fury at the spouse (Dahl 1988). At Vanderbilt University Strupp and his colleagues have combined process and outcome studies, focusing on the patient–therapist dyad in short-term dynamic psychotherapy. This therapy, too, seeks recurrent problematic patterns in the patient's behavior, also described as vicious circles or positive feedback cycles. The aim of therapy is to discover these patterns, and for the patient to explore alternative behaviors that disrupt the self-sustaining vicious circles (Strupp and Binder 1984, p. 73). Other examples of psychoanalytically informed research include Mardi Horowitz's important studies of "states of mind" that organize and structure emotions and perceptions of the self interacting with others, in process at the University of California, San Francisco (Horowitz 1991). At the University of California, Berkeley, the psychoanalytic psychologist Enrico Jones is using a computerized analysis of changes in patient language as a possible reflection of underlying structural change during the course of therapy (Jones 1995). Most of these projects bypass traditional psychoanalytic theory in favor of simpler, more accessible—and ultimately measurable—categories.

Surprisingly, then, despite the burgeoning criticism, the psychoanalytic profession and Freud as a major thinker are both alive and well. While as a prophet he had his successes and failures, Freud is still provocative, and his theories still generate applicable hypotheses in a wide variety of fields. He remains a marvelous writer, if just now a rather beleaguered genius, and he has been a major influence in the history of western thought. For all these reasons, Freud has a future, even as the most slavish applications of his theory and therapy may disappear.

Undoubtedly he would have welcomed the recent advances in biological and genetic research. As one of the best neurologists of his time, who wrote a definitive text on the cerebral palsies of children, he would no doubt have welcomed the recent explosion of knowledge about functioning of the brain and nervous system and the somatic interventions that alter both. After all, he predicted and hoped that one day somatic research would solve the problems of the psychoses and the relative strength or weakness of biologically based drives within the individual patient (Freud 1933). Toward the end of his life, Freud wrote: "The future may teach us to exercise a direct influence, by means of particular chemical substances, on the amount of energy and their distribution in the mental apparatus. It may be that there are other still undreamt-of possibilities of therapy" (Freud 1938, p. 182).

Fortunately for his own reputation, Freud was a bad prophet about America. His ideas have not yet been reduced to the category of one more tiresome and outmoded psychiatric technique.

REFERENCES

Altshuler, K. Z. (1990). Whatever happened to intensive psychotherapy? *American Journal of Psychiatry* 147:428–430.

Dahl, H. (1988). Frames of mind. In *Psychoanalytic Process and Research Strategies*, ed. H. Dahl and H. Kachele, pp. 51–68. New York: Springer-Verlag.

Doidge, N., et al. (1994). Characteristics of psychoanalytic patients under a nationalized health plan. *American Journal of Psychiatry* 151:586.

Emde, R. N., and Harmon, R. J., eds. (1982). *The Development of Attachment and Affiliative Systems*. New York: Plenum.

Farrell, J. (1996). *Freud's Paranoid Quest.* New York: New York University Press.

Felsenthal, E. (1995). Courts hear mental-health experts in more civil cases. *Wall Street Journal,* August 23, pp. B–1, B–6.

Fisher, S., and Greenberg, R. (1977). *The Scientific Credibility of Freud's Theory and Therapy.* New York: Basic Books.

────── (1996). *Freud Scientifically Reappraised.* New York: Wiley.

Freud, S. (1896). The aetiology of hysteria. *Standard Edition* 3:191–221.

────── (1900). The interpretation of dreams. *Standard Edition* 4–5.

────── (1905). Jokes and their relation to the unconscious. *Standard Edition* 8.

────── (1933). New introductory lectures on psycho-analysis. *Standard Edition* 20:154.

────── (1938). An outline of psycho-analysis. *Standard Edition* 23:182.

Gay, P. (1988). *Freud: A Life for Our Time.* New York: Norton.

Gelfand, T., and Kerr, J. (1992). *Freud and the History of Psychoanalysis.* Hillsdale, NJ: Analytic Press.

Gunderson, J., et al. (1990). The role of the therapeutic alliance in the treatment of schizophrenia. *Archives of General Psychiatry* 45:228–236.

Hale, N. G. (1995). *The Rise and Crisis of Psychoanalysis, 1917–1985.* New York: Oxford University Press.

Harvard Mental Health Letter (1995). Heredity vs. environment in depression. July.

Hedaya, R. (1996). *Understanding Biological Psychiatry.* New York: Norton.

Holmes, J. (1993). *John Bowlby and Attachment Theory.* New York: Routledge.

Horowitz, M., ed. (1991). *Personal Schemas and Maladaptive Interpersonal Patterns.* Chicago: University of Chicago Press.

Jones, E. (1995). How will psychoanalysis study itself? In *Research in Psychoanalysis,* ed. T. Shapiro and R. Emde, pp. 91–108. Madison, CT: International Universities Press.

Kingsbury S. J. (1995). Where does research on the effectiveness of psychotherapy stand today? *Harvard Mental Health Letter* 12:3.

Kramer, P. (1993). *Listening to Prozac.* New York: Viking.

Lane, R. C., and Meisels, M. (1994). *A History of the Division of Psychoanalysis of the American Psychological Association.* Hillsdale, NJ: Erlbaum.

Luborsky, L. (1985). A verification of Freud's grandest hypothesis. *Clinical Psychology Review* 56:501–512.

────── (1996a). Theories of cure in psychoanalytic psychotherapies and the evidence for them. *Psychoanalytic Inquiry* 16(2):257–264.

──────, ed. (1996b). *The Symptom-Context Method.* Washington, DC: American Psychological Association.

Mahony, P. (1992). Freud as family therapist reflections. In *Freud and the History of Psychoanalysis,* ed. T. Gelfand and J. Kerr, pp. 307–317. Hillsdale, NJ: Analytic Press.

Masson, J. M. (1984). *The Assault on Truth: Freud's Suppression of the Seduction Theory.* New York: Farrar, Straus and Giroux.

Nunes, M. B. (1984). *Professional culture and professional practice: a case study of psychoanalysis in the United States.* Ph.D. dissertation, Northwestern University.

Reiser, M. (1985). Converging sectors of psychoanalysis and neurobiology. *Journal of the American Psychoanalytic Association* 33:11–34.

Sands, H. (1996). Psychoanalysis and dynamic psychotherapy, the mental health provider and managed care. In *Impact of Managed Care on Psychodynamic Treatment*, ed. J. W. Barron and H. Sands, pp. 3–14. Madison, CT: International Universities Press.

Seligman, M. E. P. (1996). Long term psychotherapy is highly effective: the *Consumer Reports* study. *Harvard Mental Health Letter* 13(1):6.

Sloan, H. B., et al. (1975). *Psychotherapy vs. Behavior Therapy.* Cambridge, MA: Harvard University Press.

Smith, M. L., Glass, G. V., and Miller, T. I. (1980). *The Benefits of Psychotherapy.* Baltimore: Johns Hopkins University.

Strupp, H. H. (1992). A brief history of psychotherapy research. In *History of Psychotherapy*, ed. D. K. Freedheim, pp. 309–334. Washington, DC: American Psychological Association.

Strupp, H. H., and Binder, J. L. (1984). *Psychotherapy in a New Key.* New York: Basic Books.

Sulloway, F. (1992). Reassessing Freud's case histories. In *Freud and the History of Psychoanalysis*, ed. T. Gelfand and J. Kerr, pp. 153–192. Hillsdale, NJ: Analytic Press.

Thornton, E. M. (1983). *Freud and Cocaine.* London: Blond and Briggs.

Wallerstein, R. (1986). *Forty-Two Lives in Treatment: A Study of Psychoanalysis and Psychotherapy.* New York: Guilford.

Webster, R. (1995). *Why Freud Was Wrong.* New York: Basic Books.

Weiss, J., and Sampson, H. (1986). *The Psychoanalytic Process.* New York: Guilford.

Willock, B. (1996). Psychoanalysis and psychotherapy under national health insurance plans around the world. In *Impact of Managed Care on Psychodynamic Treatment*, ed. J. W. Barron and H. Sands, pp. 281–295. Madison, CT: International Universities Press.

6

Contemporary Psychoanalysis: Crisis and Creativity

James W. Barron

At a recent meeting of the American Psychological Association in Toronto, Canada, I was one of the participants at an early morning symposium examining the current status of psychoanalysis. As I was walking to the convention hotel and mulling over my presentation, I saw a large building with a huge sign proclaiming "Doctors Hospital—Managed Health Care." A little bit farther down the road, I noticed a much smaller sign in front of the Art Gallery of Ontario, annoucing an exhibit of modern art, "presenting works from different periods which are grouped together to demonstrate various themes, for example the place of the dream and the unconscious in 20th century thought."

The hospital sign forcefully reminded me of the powerful economic forces rearranging the healthcare landscape and creating a climate so inhospitable to psychoanalytic practice. The museum sign suggested that, while psychochoanalytic ideas have successfully permeated popular culture, they are increasingly relegated to its margins.

From the perspective of the sociology of knowledge, it is a cruel irony that the survival of psychoanalysis is threatened by external forces precisely at a time when psychoanalysis is internally experiencing creative growth. Psychoanalysis is not unified theoretically, clinically, or organizationally. Nevertheless, as psychoanalysts of different persuasions, we are inexorably drawn to the questions of human motivation and meaning which psychoanalysis, in its various guises, explores, and we find psychoanalytic modes of inquiry to be compelling.

Psychoanalytic views of human nature and of the functioning of the psyche are in flux. We feel anxious because of the challenging of traditional psychoanalytic wisdom, the breaking up of old verities and orthodoxies, the fragmentation of theory and practice, and the resulting "crisis of representation," as described by Dr. Kavanaugh (see Chapter 7, this volume), both to ourselves and to those outside our psychoanalytic communities.

That psychoanalytic views of human nature are complex, sometimes complementary, and frequently contradictory comes as no surprise. William James's description of infancy as a state of blooming, buzzing confusion, it turns out, does not fit the surprisingly organized unfolding of the infant's potentialities and the orchestrated patterns of mother–infant interaction. James's description more aptly describes our own internal states as we confront multiple frames of reference and controversies within psychoanalysis. But we also are excited by the intellectual ferment within our field.

At the same time we are alarmed by the intense hostility toward psychoanalysis in our culture. The environment in which we practice, research, write, supervise, and teach constantly impinges upon and constrains us, our patients, our supervisees, and our students. To a certain extent, the tension between psychoanalysis and its sociocultural surround is inevitable.

In his historical review, leavened with well-chosen anecdotes from his personal odyssey, Dr. Karon (Chapter 8) offers us the salutary reminder that psychoanalysis has always been and will always be in crisis; that is, that psychoanalysis is fundamentally in opposition to individual and group tendencies to hug the shores of rationality and deny the existence, potency, and complexities of unconscious motivations. When viewed through that historical lens, the contemporary hostility, while virulent, is not new, but merely an exaggerated expression of the negative side of this chronic ambivalence toward psychoanalysis.

At its best, psychoanalysis is a radical, even a revolutionary theory of mind which shatters our illusions about the unity and transparency of our psyches. People today recoil from the narcissistic assault the way earlier generations, as Freud suggested, recoiled from the theories of Copernicus and Darwin. Psychoanalysis inevitably stirs up covert resistance and overt opposition. But we know that is only part of the story.

We are cognizant of other factors contributing to the hostility surrounding psychoanalysis, some of which are directly attributable to ourselves and our psychoanalytic progenitors. Not as a masochistic exercise, but in the spirit of self-analysis, we need to confront our historic, and to a lesser extent, our current contributions to the crisis. These factors include: the rejection of Freud's emphatic advice that psychoanalysis not become the handmaiden of psychiatry; the resulting medicalization of psychoanalysis; the widespread rigidity, arrogance, and self-righteousness of many psychoanalytic practitioners; the stultifying dogmatism, fortress mentality and intellectual isolationism of many psychoanalytic institutes, under the guise of protecting the "pure gold" of psychoanalysis; the overselling of the applicability and efficacy of psychoanalytically based treatments; and the excessive reliance on case histories, clinical vignettes, and anecdotal reports to buttress the scientific claims of psychoanalysis. Other factors include: the erosion, and in some cases the elimination, of psychoanalytic input and influence in graduate programs in psychology and clinical internships, and in departments of psychiatry in hospitals and medical schools; the proliferation of psychotherapies in the healthcare marketplace; the ubiquity and intensity of the pleasure principle, and many patients' and practitioners' attraction to quick fixes; and the genuine advances in neuroscience and psychopharmacology combined with the marketing power of the pharmaceutical companies that are, in their turn, overselling the efficacy and applicability of psychotropic medications, although we are beginning to witness an early stage of public skepticism regarding the "magic" of drug treatments.

All these factors are significant, but they pale in comparison to the emergence of the healthcare-industrial complex, or managed care for short. In his commentary, "The Greening of the HMO: Implications for Prepaid Psychiatry," Bennett (1988) observed:

There has . . . been a change in the organizational mission and its derivative, system values: yesterday's HMO was designed to organize and deliver health care; today's is likely to be a product line, one activity of an organization seeking to prosper in the marketplace. Ginzburg (1984) has termed this "the monetarization of medical care," i.e. increasing domination of health care by those whose primary business is the preservation and increase of capital. These changes create a crosscurrent that threatens to confuse and inundate those who work in such settings. [p. 1546]

More than a decade has passed since Bennett made his prescient remarks, and the trends he noted have only accelerated. In the *Impact of Managed Care on Psychodynamic Treatment* (Barron and Sands 1996), I trace the evolution and implications of these massive changes, and contend that:

Managed care, at least as it is currently conceived and executed, is inimical to psychoanalysis and psychodynamic treatment. Indeed it remains questionable whether managed care (even when its more flagrant abuses are curtailed) and psychodynamic approaches can coexist within the same framework. One conclusion is that, at a minimum, psychodynamic therapists should strive to protect the right of patient and therapist to contract privately with one another outside of systems of managed mental healthcare. With the collapse of large-scale national healthcare reform efforts (at least for the foreseeable future), psychotherapists will have to continue to monitor healthcare law carefully on a state by state basis. While protecting the right of patient and therapist to contract privately is essential, it is not enough. Many patients are dependent upon their health insurance to afford treatment of any kind. Therapists should not abandon those patients, but should fight to make appropriately meaningful treatment, including intensive dynamically oriented psychotherapy, available to them as their needs require. [pp. 301–302]

Although I am attracted to the idea, espoused by Dr. Kavanaugh (Chapter 7) and other experienced, thoughtful psychoanalysts, of altogether withdrawing psychoanalysis and its derivative psychodynamic psychotherapies from the healthcare arena, I remain skeptical about whether such a course of action would achieve the desired result of liberating psychoanalysis from the thrall of managed care and enabling it to flourish. I worry that we may be seduced by our wish to enact the romantic myth, promulgated by Freud in his official history of the psychoanalytic movement and accepted uncritically by some of his followers, of psychoanalysis's early splendid isolation from its scientific and professional surround. In any event, we need to be mindful of the substantial differences between the origin of psychoanalysis in fin de siècle Vienna and psychoanalysis in the United States a hundred years later.

The danger posed by managed care entities is not simply that they maximize profits by discouraging patients from seeking psychotherapeutic help, by placing gatekeepers, case-managers, and other obstacles in the paths of patients, by routinely violating confidentiality, by exclusively advocating pharmacologic, group, crisis-intervention and brief-treatment modalities, by attempting to suppress dissenting patients and therapists, and by resisting regulatory-legislative reforms which may subtract from the bottom line. We have already started to witness public pressure and outrage forcing legislators to curb the more flagrant abuses of managed care. The more serious threat is that the healthcare–industrial complex has enormous resources at its disposal, and a willingness to use them to create a climate of opinion in which psychoanalysis, to the extent to which it is referred to at all, is portrayed as a dangerous unscientific aberration, an enemy of progress, or as a quaint, harmless anachronism destined to wither away. These views deny the existence or relevance of unconscious factors in personality development and organization, as well in the process of therapeutic change (Barron, in press b). They rely upon a utilitarian positivism which recognizes only conscious phenomena and observable behaviors organized according to the prevailing diagnostic system. *Making Diagnosis Meaningful: Enhancing Evaluation and Treatment of Psychological Disorders* (Barron, in press a) attempts to critique aspects of that diagnostic system, to suggest necessary modifications, and to explore possible alternatives which make room for motivation and meaning and are more closely aligned with clinical process.

The obvious proximal cause of fewer patients entering into intensive psychodynamic psychotherapy is that more individuals have health insurance administered by managed-care entities which rarely authorize payment for such treatment. The distal cause is the negative climate of opinion which deters many individuals from seriously considering more intensive treatment, either inside an HMO with a therapist who is a member of the panel of providers, or outside an HMO with an independent therapist. Of course, even when indemnity insurance prevailed, psychoanalysis or its derivative therapies were rarely covered beyond a relatively small initial amount, so that those who entered such treatments ended up contracting directly with their therapists. Nevertheless, many chose to do so. Now the situation has changed drastically. Of those individuals who can afford direct payment, far fewer believe psychodynamic treatments are necessary, or even valuable.

By and large, clinging to our habit of insularity, we have done a poor job of conveying the creativity and excitement of contemporary psychoanalysis to those outside our professional communities. To be sure, the media prefer dramatic stories about the death of psychoanalysis to those about its vitality. In addition the media conflate Freud with psychoanalysis as if there have been no new developments since Freud's early discoveries and formulations.

Paradoxically Freud's death has enlivened psychoanalysis. To be more precise, his transformation in the psyches of succeeding generations of analysts from haunting ghost to revered ancestor, to use Loewald's evocative phrase, has decreased slavish adherence to real and imagined Freudian doctrine. Paralleling this change has been an organizational transformation. Psychoanalysis in this country is no longer primarily the franchise of the American Psychoanalytic Association. Psychoanalysis has evolved into a multipolar world, more chaotic, more competitive and challenging, and more conducive to creativity in the potential space of organizational interstices.

New psychoanalytic institutes have sprung up across the country, responding to strong local interests, and experiments with alternative models of training and education. The set of assumptions loosely characterized as classical or ego psychological no longer enjoys theoretical hegemony. Hermeneutic, constructivist, self psychological, interpersonal, intersubjective, relational, Lacanian, Kleinian, and other object-relational models compete in the psychoanalytic marketplace.

Feminist critiques, gender theory, infant research, cognitive science, and neuroscience are interacting with and transforming psychoanalytic theory and practice. These trends suggest that psychoanalyis is enjoying a renaissance, a vitalizing rebirth. Furthermore these trends are in many ways independent of the metastasizing growth of managed care, although not entirely so.

There remains the necessary link to clinical practice, which is indeed adversely affected by managed care—so much so as to become an endangered species. To give but one concrete example, for the past fifteen years I have supervised the clinical work of psychology interns at an American Psychological Association-approved traineeship in the department of psychiatry at a large teaching hospital in Boston. The traineeship was well known for being psychodynamically oriented, for attracting extremely bright, capable interns, and for providing them with the opportunity of working intensively with a wide variety of patients. In order to survive, the hospital recently merged with another major hospital. To compete effectively for capitated contracts, this merged healthcare complex is increasingly adopting prevailing managed-care policies and procedures.

These large-scale changes have rapidly affected all clinical services. The immediate impact on the psychology interns is that they can no longer see patients more frequently than once every two weeks. (At the time of my writing this chapter, the leaders of the department of psychology are attempting to create an alternative model of service delivery which would permit a few trainees to work with patients once a week.) The implications of these changes, which are occurring at a rapid rate throughout the country, are ominous for the next generation of psychodynamically oriented therapists. Will they constitute a lost generation? Certainly far fewer psychologists are able to enter or sustain themselves in private practice, which traditionally has been the most congenial work setting for psychoanalysis and psychodynamic psychotherapy. Over the past five years, I have seen decreasing numbers of my supervisees find work in clinical settings in which they can make direct, and in some cases, even indirect use of their psychodynamic interests, and fewer still will eventually pursue psychoanalytic training. Extrapolating from these data, we can predict that, at least for the foreseeable future, the clinical base will be eroded, and the vital links between theory and practice attenuated.

Despite these assaults, psychoanalysis, including its clinical applications, will survive because the questions and problems it grapples with will endure. Despite powerful wishes to the contrary, there is no royal road to the unconscious. The paths are narrow and tortuous. There are no easy answers to questions posed by our multilayered, contradictorious psyches and to the complex intrapsychic—interpersonal problems which arise.

At the beginning of his essay on the history of the psychoanalytic movement, Freud (1914) referred to the motto *fluctuat nec mergitur*, which Strachey translated as: "It is tossed by the waves, but does not sink." Although the motto described the odyssey of psychoanalysis early in the twentieth century, it appears even more apt as the century draws to a close.

Crisis and creativity each characterize contemporary psychoanalysis. We are well aware that psychoanalysis encompasses much more than therapeutic technique. Yet, like the mythical giant Antaeus who renewed his strength by touching Mother Earth, psychoanalysis, to remain strong and vital, must remain in close contact with its clinical base.[1] Intensive analytic work with patients helps to generate and test hypotheses of personality development and functioning, intersubjective experience, and

---

1. Hercules succeeded in killing Antaeus first by lifting him up and separating him from Mother Earth and then by strangling him.

therapeutic action. While we may readily agree that maintaining and strengthening the clinical foundations of our work are essential, we are also aware that pursuit of those goals requires considerable courage and creativity on our parts during these challenging times.

REFERENCES

Barron, J. (in press a). *Making Diagnosis Meaningful: Enhancing Evaluation and Treatment of Psychological Disorders.* Washington, DC: American Psychological Association.

———— (in press b). Managed care and the denial of the unconscious. In *Psychoanalytic Therapy as Health Care,* ed. H. Kaley, M. Eagle, and D. Wolitzky. Hillsdale, NJ: Analytic Press.

Barron, J., and Sands, H., eds. (1996). *Impact of Managed Care on Psychodynamic Treatment.* Madison, CT: International Universities Press.

Bennett, M. J. (1988). The greening of the HMO: implications for prepaid psychiatry. *American Journal of Psychiatry* 145:1544–1549.

Freud, S. (1914). On the history of the psychoanalytic movement. *Standard Edition* 14:7–66.

Ginzburg, E. (1984). The monetarization of medical care. *New England Journal of Medicine* 310:1162–1165.

7

Is Psychoanalysis in Crisis? It All Depends on the Premise of Your Analysis

Patrick B. Kavanaugh

INTRODUCTION

Is psychoanalysis in crisis? Recent years have witnessed the juggernaut-like onset of healthcare reformation. Massive changes in healthcare policies and revolutionary transformations in the design of healthcare delivery systems have impacted most dramatically upon the psychoanalytic community. These have been desperate times. And desperate times have called for desperate measures. Organized psychoanalysis and psychology have responded by directing vast allocations of their meager organizational resources into political-legislative efforts to soften, if not blunt, the impact of the industrialization and commercialization of the healthcare professions. The question remains, however: "Is *psychoanalysis* in crisis?" And the question invites the reply, "It all depends. . . ." Crisis and that which might constitute *psychoanalysis* being in crisis resides in the eye of the beholder and is inextricably linked to one's particular understanding and version of psychoanalysis. Put in a slightly different way, the determination of crisis in psychoanalysis depends upon one's understanding of psychoanalysis itself, and the premise upon which this understanding proceeds.

As my contribution to this volume, I would like to consider the question before us—"Is psychoanalysis in crisis?"—from three different perspectives. First, to consider "Is psychoanalysis in crisis?" from the rather narrowed perspective that proceeds from the premise that psychoanalysis is a healthcare profession, or a specialty thereof. And, as such, to consider some of the implications for psychoanalysis as *the standards of the healthcare model* and *the principles of industrialization and commercialization* are applied to psychoanalysis as theory, as practice, and as education. Second, to consider the question "Is psychoanalysis in crisis?" from a somewhat broader perspective that proceeds from the premise that the creative ferment of recent years in psychoanalysis has led to the development of what could be thought of as a "crisis in representation" within organized psychoanalysis and the psychoanalytic community at large. This crisis in representation refers to a *series* of interrelated, interconnected, and intersecting crises having to do with psychoanalytic conceptualization and education, and the politics of representation in organized psychoanalysis. More specifically, there has been a growing crisis in conceptualization as to which theory best represents psychoanalysis in terms of purpose and objectives. There has been a developing crisis in education as to which set of objectivized standards of training best represents the legitimate psychoanalytic institute and authorizes the authentic psychoanalyst. And there has been a divisive political crisis developing among various organizational representatives as to which psychoanalytic organization or consortium best represents psychoanalysis to the professional, lay, and political communities. And, third, to consider the question "Is psychoanalysis in crisis?" from an even broader perspective, a cultural–historical perspective. From this broader perspective, the current conceptual, educational, and political crisis in representation taking place within organized psychoanalysis *reflects* and *contributes to* an even more profound and farther-reaching "crisis"—a different kind of crisis in representation. This crisis (Gergen 1994, Smith 1994) has been taking place within the very epistemological fabric and design of the westernized cultures during the past quarter of a century, with the emergence of the postmodern era. As a cultural epoch, the postmodern era provides a historical perspective and a cultural context in which to consider the question: "Is psychoanalysis in crisis?" It is this emerging and revolutionary epistemological field of the postmodern era that provides the opportunity to reexamine, reconsider, and rethink psychoanalysis as theory, practice, and education. And it is within this discourse of the postmodern that is to be found a basis for directional guidance for the future of psychoanalysis.

THE INDUSTRIAL AGE OF THE MODERN ERA

In the history of people and of ideas, it is possible to discern at least three cultural epochs in which civilization was organized in a characteristic and distinctive manner. In the first era, the *agricultural era*, civilization was organized around the requirements and tempos of agriculture, with the rhythms of the earth and other quasi-mystical explanations inherent in religion, magic, superstition, and folk wisdom coming to constitute the body of knowledge for that particular time. In the second era, the *modern era*, civilization was organized around the Enlightenment, with its emphasis on rationality and science during the accompanying emergence of civilization from the darkened intellect of the agricultural era. Within this schema of historification, the industrial age of the modern era is believed to have had its beginnings sometime in the early 1700s, with civilization organized around the characteristic and inexorable trend toward the industrialization of the westernized cultures.

In the history of people and of ideas, psychoanalysis had its earliest of beginnings within the sociocultural context of the industrial age of the modern era. As a child of the westernized cultures, psychoanalysis was born out of the then emergent and revolutionary epistemological matrix and cultural ideology of the industrial age. The episteme of the industrial age was to proceed from within a philosophic tradition of objectivism in which objective reality was believed to be self-evident and its essence was to be found in solid matter, with each object occupying its own sharply demarcated place in space and time. This "world" was understood to be a predictable and mind-independent entity that had an essential state. In its essence, it was both objective and knowable, through the discovery of universal and unifying laws that existed "out there." A linearized one-to-one correspondence between the world, these natural laws, and the concepts that represented them was assumed by this classical epistemology. Language, it was believed, was object-based and simply reflected reality as it really was. The world of the industrial age, however, was more than just "objective and knowable." This world was a Cartesian-Newtonian world, a world based upon a particular way of thinking about institutions, people, and life.

A Cartesian certainty of knowledge about the world was possible only through the application of Newtonian-based science, method, and explanation. A central preoccupation of the modern era was to be the discovery of nomothetic laws that would explain the world and people, make it possible to predict, influence, and control natural events and human behavior, and to eventually construct a better world through the discovery of such empirically derived knowledge. The applications of this discovered knowledge were to provide for better adaptations by people to the objective realities of everyday life, to contribute to more informed social policies for government, and, in general, to further the development of a better and more civilized world. The scientific method was to occupy a privileged relationship with this discovered truth. The industrial age of the modern era was to become the age of science and technology, the age of quantification and objectivization. This was to become the age in which the assembly line of the factory and the component parts of complex machinery were to serve as the mental model for the ordering of and thinking about people and events.

It was this rational-objectivist view of reality, of the world, and of people as being like complex machines, that was to be developed during the seventeenth, eighteenth, and nineteenth centuries. The industrial age of the modern era was, also, to be the age in which certain principles were to be developed for the mass production, mass distribution, and mass consumption of goods and services. It was to be the age in which "the producer" and "the consumer" were to become the hyphenated basic unit of society. The industrial age of the modern era provided the cultural context and ideology, the objectivist epistemological premise and world view, and the historical tradition of industrialization which were to contextualize the development of psychoanalysis. It was to be this Cartesian-Newtonian way of thinking that was to provide the epistemological assumptions, premises, core values, and context for the development of classical psychoanalysis. Psychoanalysis has been a child of the westernized cultures. Psychoanalysis as theory, practice, and education has been a product of these times. It is this industrial age that has provided the cultural context in which health care has become the most recently identified and regulated of the major industries in this country—the behavioral care industry. And in which industry the principles of industrialization and commercialization are being systematically applied to psychoanalysis as a healthcare profession.

PSYCHOANALYSIS AS A HEALTHCARE PROFESSION

In the United States, the history of the conceptual development, education, training, and practice of psychoanalysis has been closely interwoven with medicalized concepts and practices, and has been tightly intertwined with the history of the development of the healthcare professions. Largely unquestioned medicalized conceptual models and unexamined ways of thinking have had a profound impact on the development of psychoanalysis as theory, and, in the minds of many, upon its identity as being a healthcare profession. As a profession situated within the matrix of health care, psychoanalysis has come to be understood within the contextual metaphor of disease, diagnosis, and treatment. And people have come to be understood within the conceptual framework of symptomatology, etiology, and pathology. In this country, particularly, this favored conceptual framework of symptomatology, etiology, and pathology has come to understand psychodynamics as evidence signifying psychopathology. In many respects, it has been this medicalized contextual metaphor and its organizing conceptual framework that has become *the strongest weakness* of contemporary psychoanalysis.

Redefinition of Professional Standards

As a professional situated within health care, psychoanalysis has become subject to the ongoing industrialization of the healthcare professions and the systematic redefinition of professional standards. The psychoanalytic practitioner and the psychoanalytic educator have been captured and imprisoned in the image of themselves as healthcare professionals. They have become confined in the prison of their contextualizing and defining metaphors as healthcare providers. They remain captive in this conceptual prison through the ongoing *redefinition of the standards*—of practice, standards of care, and standards of education and training. And this redefinition of professional standards has extended to include the *rewriting of the ethical standards* of the profession. This newer version of ethical standards derives from medicalized conceptualizations of people and psychopathology, core values and attitudes more appropriate for issues of sickness and treatment, and with the presumptive responsibility for people and their lives more consistent with people afflicted with physical disease and illness. The reification of traditional contextualizing metaphors for psychoanalysis, such as "psychopathology," "mental illness," "cure," and "curative factors" has contributed significantly to the redefinition of that which has come to constitute "quality," "integrity," "reliability," and "value" as the healthcare professions become more industrialized (Hall 1995). This rewriting of ethical standards proceeds from the medicalized conceptualizations underlying the current revision of other professional standards by various bureaucratic entities, national committees, and other healthcare interest groups. And, it will be these industrialized and industrializing standards that will determine the psychologist-psychoanalyst's legal exposure and liability in future malpractice actions.

These institutional(ized) bureaucracies, national committees, and various special interest groups have been developing policies and proscribing procedures that have dramatically restructured the professional standards of psychoanalysis and psychology as more clearly in alignment with the standards of a healthcare profession. These professional standards are being articulated, established, and encoded in the maze of new healthcare rules, regulations, policies, and procedures. The altering of these professional standards has redefined the professional functioning and everyday life of each psychologist-psychoanalyst as that of a healthcare professional. Succinctly stated: the current identification of psychoanalysis as a specialty of the mental health disciplines has come to define psychoanalysis as a regulated craft to be further subjected to the regulatory constraints imposed by the industrialization and commercialization of the healthcare professions. In recent years, the psychoanalytic community has been witness to a massive, systematic, and literal dismantling of an educational and practice milieu by various governmental entities, legislative bodies, professional organizations, and regulatory agencies. Currently, the psychoanalytic community is witnessing the semiotic construction of a new professional identity for the psychologist-psychoanalyst as that of a craftsperson.

Psychoanalytic Practice

The industrialization of the health care professions has resulted in the "Narrowing Scope of Psychoanalysis" (Kavanaugh 1995b). As a healthcare profession, psychoanalysis has been subsumed by this current industrialization and commercialization, with far-reaching consequences. As the standards of the healthcare model and the principles of industrialization have been applied to psychoanalysis, the scope of psychoanalysis narrows— through the increased centralizations of information, authority, and decision-making power in various bureaucracies; through the uniformity of policies and procedures that are coming to define and assure so-called quality in psychoanalytic practice and education; and through the templates that indicate the appropriate treatments for specified diagnostic categories and determine the expected outcomes for education. As a medical procedure, psychoanalysis is considered to be appropriate for only certain diagnostic conditions. And, as a method of treatment, psychoanalysis is considered to be among the least cost-effective of those medical procedures to be included in the prepackaged healthcare product lines marketed by the insurance industry. It is significant to note that neither organized psychology nor organized psychoanalysis has questioned or challenged the framework of health care that presumes an integral relationship between health care and psychoanalysis as these healthcare policies are being formulated, standards of practice are being redefined, and revisions to state mental health codes are taking place. To the contrary, the stated strategic objective of the American Psychological Association Practice Directorate has been to maintain psychology's stake in American health care and, more recently, the Practice Directorate's organizational focus has been to address the need for a better balance between cost containment and efforts to ensure quality services in the healthcare delivery system (Newman 1996). The centralization of information, authority, and power in various bureaucracies includes the overlapping bureaucratic structures of organized psychology and organized psychoanalysis. The rather narrowed focus and effort of organized psychoanalysis has been to deal with "the managed care threat" through the education and lobbying of legislators, the providing of information to consumers, and the organization of various coalitions in the service of influencing and shaping these healthcare policies, plans, and delivery systems (Eagle 1966).

Psychoanalytic Education

The same industrializing principles for the mass production, mass distribution, and mass consumption of psychoanalysis as a treatment procedure are now being applied to psychoanalytic education. The industrialization of the healthcare professions, with its emphasis upon outcome-based treatment, has led to the industrialization of education, with its emphasis upon outcome-based education. Among the other consequences of healthcare reformation for the psychoanalytic educator has been the increased emphasis upon the development of more *standardized programs* of study, the *predetermination of educational objectives and outcomes* to be attained, and a predefined and *standardized set of core competencies* to be mastered by new practitioners. These educational objectives have been adopted by the American Psychological Association as "priority objectives" for graduate school education in psychology (Resnick 1995a,b).

Competency in education has come to be defined as the mastery of certain pre-thought thoughts and ways of thinking. And this standardizing, qualitizing, and homogenizing educational philosophy has been organized around the rapidly developing trend of *increased specializations* within the healthcare professions. Provider-specific credentials are becoming the standard by which competency in specific areas of ability is measured: "Since 'quality' in health care has proven so difficult to advertise based on *outcomes of care*, those who assemble networks of providers usually resort to asserting quality based on the *inputs, i.e. the providers' credentials*" (Stromberg and Ratcliff 1995, p. 3 [italics added]). This emerging trend of proficiency credentialing in designated areas of competence is taking place throughout the healthcare professions.

This increased emphasis on specialization, standards, and proficiency credentialing is actively embraced and advanced in organized psychology *and* organized psychoanalysis. The increased specialization and credentialing in designated proficiency areas within the profession of psychology-psychoanalysis has kept pace with this larger industrializing trend. As reported in the *Psychologist's Legal Update* (Stromberg and Ratcliff 1995), the expectation is that these credentialing requirements will increase in the years ahead. This increased emphasis on specialization and credentialing for the psychologist-psychoanalyst follows in the footsteps of the medicalized model of specialization, contributes to the further conceptual fragmentation of people, and serves as both the "effect" and the further "cause" of industrialization. Such industrializing efforts tacitly advance and endorse the principle and practice of "economic credentialing," in which efforts are made to include only those who meet certain levels of "efficiency" in managing the costs of treatment.

As a profession situated within the matrix of health care, psychoanalysis in the United States is quickly becoming a psychoanalysis of conformity and compliance: conforming to the healthcare standards that contextualize psychoanalytic ethics, practice, and education. And, through such conformity and compliance, people who seek psychoanalytic consultation or education are encouraged to conform and comply to the standardized, qualitized, homogenized, and idealized normative outcomes, from the rather narrowed perspective that proceeds from the axiomatic premise that psychoanalysis is a healthcare profession or a specialty thereof. Yes! It would appear that psychoanalysis is in crisis! The industrialization and commercialization of the healthcare professions have enveloped the psychoanalytic community and have come to define for the psychoanalytic community how to conceptualize, how to practice, and how to educate. . . .

The defining issue confronting the profession has been rather narrowly identified by organized psychoanalysis as "the managed care threat." These are desperate times. And desperate measures have come from desperate times. Efforts to redress this so-called crisis in psychoanalysis have centered, for the most part, upon attempts to humanize the harshness of the industrializing principles that have come to contextualize psychoanalytic practice and education, and to enlighten various legislative, regulatory, and policy-making bodies as to the worth of having psychoanalysis included in the healthcare product lines marketed by the insurance industry.

There is, however, a noteworthy alternative position developing among a significant minority of colleagues. They have reidentified the defining issue as psychoanalysis having located itself in the healthcare professions in the first instance. Their more radicalized solution, which appears to be gathering support in some sectors of the psychoanalytic community, is to extricate psychoanalysis from the healthcare professions and to declare psychoanalysis to be an independent and separate profession. Cloaked within the developmental notions of "progress," the establishment of psychoanalysis as a separate and autonomous profession is presented as the next logical and evolutionary step. Psychologist-psychoanalysts could then practice independently and educate their own, it is advanced, and in so doing "the natural destiny" of the psychologist-psychoanalyst could be then fulfilled.

To move in either of these directions in the pursuit of a (re)solution to the so-called "crisis in psychoanalysis as a healthcare profession," however, is to risk underappreciating something that has been happening in recent years within psychoanalysis and within the westernized cultures at large. Indeed, as we look inward and outward for direction in psychoanalysis, we might do well to collectively consider a broader perspective, an historical-cultural perspective, contained within which are to be found several crises in representation that bear quite directly on the future of psychoanalysis.

CRISES IN REPRESENTATION

Within the past quarter of a century, a new sociocultural epoch has been making its largely unexpected, if not unwelcomed, appearance. A third era in the history of people and of ideas has been emerging: *the informa-tion age of the postmodern era.* Its discourse speaks loudly to an unrelenting questioning of the largely unquestioned and presumed realities of the so-called truth that had come to constitute science and the body of knowl-edge of the industrial age of the modern era. A deconstructive question-ing of the modern-era notions of history, literature, art, education, physics, science, conceptualizations of the self, the referents of language, logic and reasoning, the nature of reality, and other questions philosophic in nature, has profoundly shaken if not eroded confidence in the logical-objectivist epistemological premise of the modern era. A profound and far-reaching "crisis in representation" (Gergen 1994, Smith 1994) has been appearing in the westernized cultures as certain fixed, foundational, and enduring "rules" that had prescribed "the reality" and "the natural order of things" are being requestioned, reconsidered, and reconceptualized, rules that had provided for what constituted the discursive rationality and social coher-ence of the modern era (Foucault 1973). And for what had constituted its goodness, beauty, and truth. The discursive power of the monologic rules of discourse has been shaken. The fundamental and foundational codes that have constituted, authorized, and sanctioned "appropriateness" in perceiving, thinking, and knowing during the modern era have been changing dramatically and radically. There have been rather abrupt and ruptured breaks with traditional ways of thinking about, understanding, and conceptualizing people, ideas, life, and the world. The westernized cultures are currently immersed in a turbulent transition from the indus-trial age of the modern era to the information age of the postmodern era. The episteme of the modern era is becoming as obsolete and nonfunctional for the merging postmodern era as the episteme of the agricultural era was for the modern era. As Barratt succinctly states: "We are now wit-nessing the death throes of this episteme" (1993, p. 3). A profound and far-reaching conceptual revolution has been taking place. Uncertainty has been spreading as the unquestioned fundamental assumptions, traditional epistemological premises, and presumed realities of the industrial age elusively evaporate and transform into the unexpected, the unfamiliar, and the unknown.

This "crisis in representation" has had a disturbing, disorganizing, and disorienting impact on institutional structures and individuals alike. A related series of crises has been developing in organized psychoanalysis as this irreverential discourse of deconstructive questioning gathers synergistic momentum and pragmatic consequence in its reexamination and reconsideration of the once seemingly natural and unquestioned ideology of a monolithic psychoanalysis. Within organized psychoanalysis, these have become times of profound uncertainty. A conceptual *crisis in representation* has appeared in psychoanalytic theory as the monolithic view of psychoanalysis era has been disappearing, if not disintegrating, and as a plurality of heterogeneous theories have emerged in contemporary psychoanalytic thinking. There has been a proliferation of conceptualizations of what psychoanalysis "is," each version having little in common with the others. Theoretical pluralism, at least for the time being, has been accommodated, if not appropriated, through innovations within traditional organizational structures and educational curricula. The epistemological-philosophical premise of the industrial age, which had provided a seemingly eternal and unquestioned justification for psychoanalysis in the Newtonian-Cartesian tradition, and psychoanalytic education fashioned in the image of the Berlin Model, have been disappearing beneath our feet (Kavanaugh 1995a). The once axiomatic epistemological premises, assumptions, and core values of a monolithic psychoanalytic theory have been drawn into deconstructive question. There had been a natural and commonsensical organic bond between psychoanalysis and its largely unquestioned and unexamined medicalized concepts, attitudes, values, and ways of thinking, along with a similarly natural and commonsensical one between psychoanalytic education and its institutional(ized) structure, educational philosophy, and the educational model, methods and objectives of the modern era. It is this natural and commonsensical organic bond that is decaying.

This crisis in representation gathers considerable significance as it raises questions of *pragmatic, economic, and political consequence* as this plurality of heterogeneous theories makes its appearance. For example: Who is to be represented as being the authorized psychoanalyst? As defined by which set of objectivized standards? Or levels of certifications? Or tiers of credentialing? And a competitive crisis in representation is developing between groups within organized psychoanalysis, centering upon such questions as: Which psychoanalytic organization or consortium is to be the recognized standard bearer for psychoanalysis? or to represent the standards of psychoanalytic education? or, Which psychoanalytic institute is to be the legitimate guardian and authorized transmitter of psychoanalytic truth? (particularly as there are increasingly different and contradictory truths of psychoanalysis). This crisis in representation extends to such political of questions as: Which psychoanalytic organization is to represent and speak with the authentic voice of psychoanalysis? in the professional community? in congress? to insurance companies? to the public? Such a series of crises may be understood and dismissively responded to as simply a part and consequence of the creative ferment and tensions that have defined the tradition of restless and searching inquiry within psychoanalysis. As a profession whose basic theoretical constructs, principles, and philosophy are conceptually situated and located within the epistemological premises and roots of the modern era, however, it would appear that Yes! Mainstream psychoanalysis is in a profound state of crisis!

Paradoxically, these "crises of psychoanalysis," as the consequences of the principles of industrialization and commercialization being applied to the healthcare professions, or of being buffeted about in the throes of a political crisis in representation within organized psychoanalysis, or of being caught up in the fractured turbulence of an epistemological crisis in representation within westernized culture, are not to be construed to mean that *psychoanalysis* is in crisis. Organized psychoanalysis might be in crisis. And organized psychology might be in crisis. However, that does not translate to mean that *psychoanalysis* is. The position advanced is that psychoanalysis is neither a healthcare profession nor is it an entity defined by or housed within organized psychoanalysis. Further, it is advanced that direction for the future of psychoanalytic theory, practice, and education is to be found by *looking inward* to these crises in representation in organized psychoanalysis brought about by the recent creative ferment, and by *looking outward* to the epistemological crisis in representation in westernized culture. Indeed, contained within these so-called crises themselves is to be found a reexamination, a reconsideration, and radicalized rethinking of psychoanalysis that has been going on from within and from without for quite some time.

INWARD AND OUTWARD DIRECTIONS: PHILOSOPHY, THE HUMANITIES, AND THE ARTS

As confidence in the various mythologies that had come to envelop and define psychoanalysis of the modern era has shattered, there has emerged, phoenixlike, a new psychoanalysis of extraordinary power, passion, and poetics. This psychoanalysis proceeds from an epistemological premise of radicalized relativism, and phenomenalism, and is situated within philosophy, the humanities, and the arts. Its conceptual premise and understandings are to be found within the realm of human experience. This psychoanalysis speaks from different and unfamiliar ways of thinking about the world, people, and life, and presumes neither the reparative purposes nor the normalizing objectives of the psychologies of psychoanalysis of the modern era. As has been noted by the philosopher Vattimo (1988), the world is a *world of differences* in that there is an infinite interpretability of reality amongst people. The only world that can ever exist and be known is this "world of difference," that is, this world of interpretations of the world.

This philosophic premise of an infinite interpretability of reality leads to an understanding of a psychoanalysis of a much different purpose, objective, and set of core values than have the various psychologies of psychoanalysis of the modern era. From his philosophic premise, the center of the universe in psychoanalysis becomes the human experience, and the quest(ion) of discovery in psychoanalysis becomes the quest of the enunciating subject (Kavanaugh 1992). The focus and purpose of psychoanalysis becomes the understanding of that person's way of thinking, knowing, perceiving, and the subject's way of constructing "reality," the world, and the nature of that world. In this phenomenalistic world of the individual, foundational essence is whatever the senses of the individual reveal it to be; that which exists is whatever it is that the senses experience (Eacker 1975). This world is one in which reason and "truth" are situated in the realm of the human experiences of the subject and are to be found within the ideographic and provisional laws of the perceiver. Truth as to the question of essence is reduced to the values of the subject. It is the subject who has the privileged relationship to truth; it is the privilege of the discourse of the analysis to attempt to understand that truth.

Situated within philosophy, the humanities, and the arts, the essence of psychoanalysis derives from such sources of knowledge and understanding as literature, poetry, and the theater. As recently noted by Jonathan Lear (Chapter 23, this volume), "Creativity is no longer the exclusive preserve of the divinely inspired or the few great poets. From a psychoanalytic point of view, everyone is poetic; everyone dreams in metaphor and generates symbolic meanings in the process of living. Even in their prose, people have unwittingly been speaking poetry all along" (p. 25). As a unique psychological discourse, psychoanalysis ventures into this poetic communication of everyday life via the associative method within a contextual metaphor from the arts such as, for example, the psychic theatre of the mind (Kavanaugh 1995b, McDougall 1985).

As a venture into this vitally metaphoric communication, psychoanalytic discourse is understood to be semiotic discourse, to be understood as one would understand a poetic text. From this perspective, psychoanalytic discourse is considered to be, much like poetry, one of the most complex and intricate forms of human discourse, one in which all thinking is considered to be radically and vitally metaphoric. Here, there are no "facts" except as are construed within the mind of each person. Indeed, the subject is both the maker and the interpreter of meaning. The discourse of psychoanalysis is concerned with the understanding of these idiosyncratic meanings, ideas, desires, passions, beliefs, motivational causalities, and psychic laws of the subject—the ideographic meanings of which derive from the associative context of the analytic moment (Kavanaugh 1995c). As a work of art, the psychoanalysis of the postmodern era is concerned with attempting to understand the psyche, that is, the soul, the spirit, the mind of the person. As a poetic work of art, psychoanalysis speaks to such enduring and fixed traditions of the subject's phenomenal past as are coexistent and codeterminant with the subject's present wishes, desires, and longings, and with their future purposes and goals. In so doing, psychoanalysis speaks with the voices of the dead in the present moment of the past. Psychoanalysis, as derived from philosophy and the arts, is considered to be a poetic work of art in that it registers, monumentalizes, and attempts to speak to the subject's passage of time.

Such versions of psychoanalysis as are derived from philosophy and the arts carry with them radically different visions for psychoanalytic education in terms of institutional structure, educational philosophy, and educational model. As we enter the postmodern era, it would seem that a rethinking of what is meant by psychoanalytic education in itself constitutes a major and ongoing postmodern project (Kavanaugh 1991, 1995a, 1996).

To return, however, to the question most immediately before us: Is psychoanalysis in crisis? Of course it is! Unless, of course, it isn't! It all depends on the premise of your analysis. And it all depends on the premise of your psychoanalysis.

REFERENCES

Barratt, B. (1993). *The Postmodern Impulse: Knowing and Being Since Freud's Psychology*. Baltimore, MD: Johns Hopkins University Press.

Eacker, J. N. (1975). *Problems of Philosophy and Psychology*. Chicago: Nelson-Hall.

Eagle, M. (1966). From the president's desk. *Psychologist-Psychoanalyst* 16(1):1–2.

Foucault, M. (1973). *The Order of Things: An Archaeology of the Human Sciences.* New York: Vintage.

Gergen, K. J. (1994). Exploring the postmodern: perils or potentials? *American Psychologist* 49(5):417–427.

Hall, J. E. (1995). The editor's desk: a perspective on the evolving healthcare environment: quality, integrity, reliability, and value. *Register Report, The Newsletter for Health Service Providers in Psychology* 20:3, 21:1.

Kavanaugh, P. B. (1991). Moving forward into the '90s with an alternative to "progress." *Psychologist-Psychoanalyst* 11(4):26–30.

———— (1992). The quest in psychoanalysis: philosophical underpinnings of theory and technique. *MSPP Newsletter* 2(3):21–26.

———— (1995a). *Postmodernism, psychoanalysis and philosophy: a world of difference for the future of psychoanalytic education.* Paper presented at the International Federation for Psychoanalytic Education, Toronto, Canada.

———— (1995b). The narrowing scope of psychoanalysis. *Psychologist-Psychoanalyst* 15(4):29–30.

———— (1995c). Influences from philosophy, the theatre, and the poets on psychoanalytic theory and technique. *MSPP* (Michigan Society for Psychoanalytic Psychology) *Newsletter* 5(2):4–13.

———— (1996). *The impossible patient meets the impossible profession under impossible conditions: implications for psychoanalytic education.* Paper presented at the International Federation for Psychoanalytic Education. Boca Raton, FL, September.

McDougall, J. (1985). *Theaters of the Mind: Illusion and Truth on the Psychoanalytic Stage.* New York: Basic Books.

Newman, R. (1996). APA practice directorate: 1995 year in review. *Practitioner Focus. APA Practice Directorate* 9(1):1–12.

Resnick, R. J. (1995a). APA president's column. *APA Monitor*, March.

———— (1995b). Dr. Resnick focuses on core of competence during presidential year. *APA Education Directorate News*, Summer.

Smith, M. B. (1994). Selfhood at risk: postmodern perils and the perils of post-modernism. *American Psychologist* 49(5):412–416.

Stromberg, C., and Dellinger, A. (1993). Malpractice and other professional liability. *The Psychologist's Legal Update*, pp. 3–10, December.

Stromberg, C., and Ratcliff, R. (1995). A legal update on provider credentialing. *The Psychologist's Legal Update*, pp. 3–10, June.

Vattimo, G. (1988). *The End of Modernity*, trans. J. P. Snyder. Baltimore, MD: Johns Hopkins University Press.

8

"The Struggle Is Not Yet Over"

Bertram P. Karon

Psychoanalysis has no future. It has no future as a treatment or as a theory. There are few psychoanalysts, but they are too many. There are very few psychoanalytic patients. Psychoanalysis has little impact on intellectual work outside of psychology and psychiatry, almost none within psychology. What impact it does have will disappear. You cannot make a living as a psychoanalyst and certainly not as a psychologist-psychoanalyst.

These statements are commonly heard today. When did they begin to be made?

With the advent of managed care? With the rise of cognitive therapy? Within the last five years when university departments of psychology became antipsychoanalytic? In the last ten years when departments of psychiatry became biological?

One of the most effective passages in literature is on the first two pages of Dickens's *A Tale of Two Cities* (1859). The author makes these contrasts: "It was the best of times; it was the worst of times. Never had the world sunk so low, never had the world risen so high," and so on for two pages, ending with: "In short, it was no different from any other time."

Psychoanalysis is now in crisis. It is endangered and scorned. But it has always been in crisis, it has always been endangered and scorned, and it will always be in crisis, always endangered, always scorned. It will survive because it is fascinating intellectually, its most important ideas are scientifically valid, it is generative of new ideas, and it is therapeutically effective.

I began college at Harvard in 1948. In those days, as now, most psychologists were opposed to psychoanalysis. The few undergraduates I knew who were undergoing psychoanalysis did so because the psychiatrists at the Harvard Health Center told them that psychoanalysis was nonsense. Gordon Allport was smart enough to make his students learn about psychoanalysis, but he defined it ambivalently as that psychology which goes down deepest, stays down longest, and comes up dirtiest. B. F. Skinner redefined psychoanalytic variables in behavioral terms in his introductory course in psychology. The reading for his course was a book by Skinner, a book by two students of Skinner, and Freud's *General Introduction to Psychoanalysis* (1935). Skinner then had the view that if you were going to be a psychologist you should know two people: Skinner and Freud. Skinner was right that if something were scientifically tenable it could be defined in terms of relations among observables, and he was remarkably ingenious at redefining Freudian concepts in terms of relations among observables. But the relationships were so complex and subtle that they would never have been discovered working only at the level of observables. One of my ex-students told Skinner in the '60s that I had said that after reading Freud, Skinner was done. He replied, "Those were the early days—I don't assign Freud any more."

That was not my first exposure to psychoanalysis. In the late 1940s, a patient was advised by a nationally prominent psychiatrist connected with the Harvard Medical School, "If you were a rich man, I would suggest psychoanalysis. But you are not rich, and therefore I recommend electric shock, and if that doesn't work, lobotomy." The patient was a bright but uneducated man who went to the public library, read about electric shock and lobotomy, and was appropriately scared by what he read.

Luckily he found a psychoanalytic M.A. psychologist, Edward Karon, who saw him in psychoanalytic psychotherapy twice a week for six months. When he started treatment, the patient had been unable to work and hardly able to leave the house. His nearly daily functional heart attacks ceased, were replaced by asthma, which was replaced by stomach ulcers, which were replaced by migraine headaches. After six months, his therapist left town. But the patient was back at work at a job that was so physically difficult that, at age 17, I would not have attempted it. As he moved a heavy load, he said to me, "This psychoanalytic stuff is all bullshit. I feel just as bad as I ever did." He then moved another heavy load. Once a month he had to leave work early because of a migraine attack. His life satisfaction, marital problems, and feeling of choice in his life were all greatly improved. I was impressed. It was then that I first read Freud's *General Introduction.*

At Harvard in the 1930s and '40s, there had been a remarkable group of psychologists, including Erik Erikson, Samuel Beck, David Levy, Rudy Ekstein, Silvan Tomkins, and Robert White, among others, who were assembled by Henry Murray at the Harvard Psychological Clinic. It is now fashionable to remember that group with awe. But at the time it was controversial. There were years when the psychology department refused to provide any money to continue their research, and Henry Murray, who was independently wealthy, funded it out of his own pocket.

When Henry Murray came up for tenure, Karl Lashley threatened to resign if Murray were given tenure. At that point, Allport threatened to resign if Murray were not given tenure. James Conant, then president of Harvard, intervened, gave Lashley a research professorship without teaching duties (Lashley did not like to teach), and Murray got tenure.

When was the heyday of psychoanalysis, when it was popular and accepted? Certainly not in the beginning when Freud wrote despairingly to Fliess (Bonaparte et al. 1957) that he was going to give up, because no one could do all the reading that was necessary to learn all the things he needed to know to get anywhere with these problems. Certainly not in 1900 when "The Interpretation of Dreams" was first published and sold a few hundred copies. Or around 1910 when a discussant of Freud's paper at the Vienna Medical Society said that he had tried Professor Freud's methods. "But if they begin to talk about sexual matters, I shut their mouths" (Freud 1926, p. 207).

Or was it the 1920s? In 1924 the Vienna Psychoanalytic Institute was formally organized, because psychoanalysis had clearly established itself and Freud's work was well known. The first four candidates were Richard and Editha Sterba and Edward and Grete Bibring. At the University of Vienna Medical School, Richard Sterba had studied with Wagner-Jauregg, who won the Nobel Prize for his development of the malaria treatment for general paresis. Jauregg told him, "You are a bright young man with a good future in psychiatry. Why do you want to waste it by studying with Freud?" (Sterba, personal communication). In the 1920s when permission was requested to start a low-cost psychoanalytic center in Vienna, the authorities refused and ordered it shut down when it started. It was started and continued without permission (Fine 1990, p. 107).

In the late 1930s, when the Bibrings were considering coming to United States, even Helene Deutsch said to them, "There are already too many psychoanalysts in the United States. You will not be able to make a living" (Sterba, personal communication).

In the 1940s Otto Will entered a residency in psychiatry and was so appalled that he switched back to internal medicine. Only after he entered psychoanalysis with Frieda Fromm-Reichmann, and realized that there was a way of being a psychiatrist that actually helped people, did he return to psychiatry as a psychoanalyst.

In 1945 when Silvan Tomkins came to Princeton University, there was not a copy of Freud's *Collected Papers* (1924–1950) in that very large university library.

Some people think of the 1950s as the heyday of psychoanalysis because it was talked about more. The chairs of prestigious departments of psychiatry were psychoanalysts. Nonetheless, according to Vamık Volkan, at no time in the United States has more than one psychiatrist in 400 been a fully trained psychoanalyst. Very, very few psychologists were trained as psychoanalysts. Indeed, few psychologists were trained to do psychotherapy. Most state psychological associations were opposed to psychotherapy. The American Psychological Association (APA) was opposed to psychologists doing psychotherapy. There were a few institutes in New York that would train psychologists as analysts, and none anywhere else in the United States.

In the late 1950s, Hollingshead and Redlich (1958) pointed out that most good private psychiatric hospitals emphasized psychoanalysis and psychoanalytic therapy in their brochures, but earned the bulk of their income on the basis of electric shock treatments, which were then and still are the most profitable treatments in psychiatry. Hollingshead and Redlich made the distinction between "directive-organic" psychiatrists and "psychoanalytic-psychotherapeutic psychiatrists," and described them as two separate professions in the United States in the 1950s, who read different journals and went to different professional meetings. The psychoanalytic-psychotherapeutic psychiatrists, in addition to their residency, had to get their own psychotherapy or analysis, and supervision, which made their training longer and more expensive. The most prestigious of these psychiatrists were the fully trained psychoanalysts. Despite the fact that their training was longer and more expensive, they earned less money than their directive-organic colleagues, who gave advice, medication, shock treatment, and, in some cases, lobotomy. Directive-organic psychiatrists in the 1950s and '60s spent much less time with each patient and therefore could earn more. Since there were two ways to be a psychiatrist, one of which required longer and more expensive training and earned less money and one of which required less training and earned more money, there was no contest as to which kind of psychiatrist was more numerous.

The psychoanalytic-psychotherapeutic psychiatrists in the 1950s were mainly to be found in large cities and around universities, and even there were outnumbered by directive-organic psychiatrists.

It was in the 1950s that I met V. K. Alexander. He was an experimental psychologist from Union Christian College in Alwaye, South India. He read Freud and he read Brenner's *Elementary Textbook* (1955). He treated a classic conversion hysteric on a couch five days a week, as best he could. He took careful notes. The patient said just what Freud said she would, he interpreted as well as he could, and the process continued just as Freud described. The patient got better. He took other patients and did psychoanalysis and psychoanalytic therapy as well as he could. He treated a multiple personality, read Morton Prince (1913), and adapted the psychoanalytic thinking to successfully cure his patient in six months. He has since published some of his early brilliant cases (e.g., Alexander 1956). He decided he needed systematic training and came to the United States. As a graduate student he had trouble accepting the fact that most professors of clinical psychology in the United States of the 1950s knew less about psychoanalysis and about treating patients than he had found for himself.

He once told me sadly that there were faculty who do not like him. "They think I'm a Freudian. You know me, Bert, I'm no Freudian." (He was a deeply religious man who found Freud's emphasis on sex and aggression troubling.) "I don't like Freud's ideas. But all my patients are Freudians."

When he finished his Ph.D., he was startled by a clinical psychologist on the faculty who told him, "Now that you are finished, you can forget all that Freud nonsense, and do what works in India!"

"What was he talking about, Bert? I know what works in India. Freud works in India."

There was one important positive development in the late 1940s and the '50s. William Menninger, Chief of Army Psychiatry, said that there would be a need for therapy for veterans of World War II and that there were not enough psychiatrists in the United States. Even with a large training program in psychiatry, there would not be enough, and so there had better be large training programs in clinical psychology and social work as well. He had enough prestige—and Americans cared enough about the veterans of World War II—so that large training programs in the three mental health professions were started, and they frequently, but not always, were psychoanalytic. But the resistance to psychoanalysis was also there.

Unfortunately, government subsidies for training programs in the mental health professions, begun in the late '40s, have now largely ended. Universities and medical schools follow the money and emphasize anything for which they can get grants, and today that is rarely psychoanalysis or psychodynamic treatment. The Veterans Administration continues but with reduced programs.

From 1958 to 1960, I had a postdoctoral fellowship at supposedly the most psychoanalytic hospital in Philadelphia, a hospital which was unusual in that all the psychiatric residents were in training to be psychoanalysts, and most of the medical staff were psychoanalysts. Nonetheless, fifty outpatients and almost all the inpatients were given electric shock treatments every Monday, Wednesday, and Friday. When I asked the chief psychologist about it, he said, "It depends what you mean by psychoanalysis. We mean the treatment of the classical syndromes four or five days a week on a couch if they can afford it. What do you do if they can't afford it, or if something else is wrong with them? Either you don't treat them or you shock them. We shock them, we think it's kinder."

It was at this same hospital in 1960 that a psychological intern told me that I was the first psychologist he had met who told him that his being psychoanalyzed was a good thing. He had previously worked at a Veterans Administration hospital where even the psychologists told him it was a mistake that would be held against him.

Similarly, a graduate student in history at Princeton in the 1950s was told that his being psychoanalyzed was a problem that the department chairman would have to state in any recommendation letter, and that probably would prevent him from being accepted for an academic position. The student, who had been influenced by Crane Brinton and other psychoanalytically sophisticated historians, was startled to discover that many prestigious departments, like Princeton, considered psychoanalysis totally unacceptable.

Philadelphia was unusual for the number of psychiatrists who combined being a psychoanalyst, for the prestige, with a shock practice for the income. But Robert Knight (1953) described the typical analytic candidate of the 1950s as interested in learning as little about psychoanalysis as was necessary, and opening an office and making money, unlike earlier analysts whom he described as less well-adjusted but better psychoanalysts. Knight justified rigidifying the requirements for psychoanalytic training on that basis, not realizing that rigidifying and proliferating requirements appealed to the obsessive and commercially minded candidates he deplored, and discouraged the creative ones.

In Philadelphia at that time there was a prestigious medical psychoanalyst doing so-called "important" research on depression. Let me say here that when I hear a clinical paper, I translate the technical language into what did the patient say, what did the patient experience either in therapy or in life, what did the therapist hear and say, and what did the therapist experience. When I can make such translations I know what we are talking about, no matter what technical language is being used; if I cannot make such translations, I do not know what we are talking about. But nothing this psychoanalyst said lent itself to any such translation. I concluded that I was defective in my ability to think abstractly and that consequently I could never become a psychoanalyst. But that seemed like a good thing, because he reported research that found there was little anger in the TATs of depressed patients, and concluded, consequently, that anger was their central problem. If it had come out just the opposite, it seemed to me, he would have drawn the same conclusion. That did not seem like science.

Ten years later, in the late '60s, a psychiatrist gave a paper about cognitive behavior therapy for depression at the Society for Psychotherapy Research. A colleague said, "That's unbelievable. That man sounds as if he's never even heard of Sigmund Freud." I shrugged my shoulders. We have many colleagues who haven't heard of Sigmund Freud. But then I did a double-take. It was the same medical psychoanalyst referred to above, whose version of psychoanalysis was so sterile and therapeutically ineffective that it had even turned him off psychoanalysis!

It was in Philadelphia that I came to the intellectual conclusion that in most settings which were not entirely psychoanalytic, the most psychoanalytic member of the staff was also likely to be the most competent therapist. But there was a point beyond which psychoanalysts became rigid and being more psychoanalytic was not synonymous with being more helpful.

There were some analysts even in Philadelphia who earned my respect as therapists and intellectuals. Most notable was Robert Waelder, whose book *The Basic Theory of Psychoanalysis* (1960) I still recommend. At no time was he bothered by genuine questions and genuine disagreement as long as you were willing to think about the issues honestly and consider the evidence, especially the clinical evidence from analytic hours.

Most memorable was a colloquium at the hospital on "Totem and Taboo" (Freud 1913) and related ideas. The colloquium began jointly with Dr. Waelder and a medical psychoanalyst who was director of resident training. If the ideas had been challenged when presented by the medical psychoanalyst alone, the questioner would have been squelched. Luckily the medical psychoanalyst left early. During the question period, I asked Dr. Waelder, "It seems to me that you have postulated an inheritance of acquired characteristics. While that was good biology in Freud's day, there are few good geneticists who would accept such an idea today."

His immediate response was, "Are you an anthropologist?"

"No, I'm a psychologist."

"The anthropologists always ask that question. You listen very carefully, young man. I did not postulate an inheritance of acquired characteristics, but I came very close to postulating an inheritance of acquired characteristics. But you are quite wrong, young man. It is not true that very few good geneticists would accept such an idea today. No good geneticist would accept such an idea today." It became clear, as he went on to discuss the issue and how Darwin himself had veered to such a view, that this was an explanatory idea that he had liked, but was now convinced was scientifically untenable. He was doing further reading on it. The only thing that was important was what was true.

On the other hand, it was an analysand of Waelder, now a distinguished psychoanalyst, who provided my favorite stupidity. He denies this conversation, but it really did occur.

"What," I asked, "is the difference between the two psychoanalytic institutes?"

"Everyone knows," he said.

"I don't know. I'm not from Philadelphia." (Indeed, neither institute would take a psychologist for training, so from my standpoint they were the same.)

"But everyone knows."

"I'm not from Philadelphia. I don't know."

"Either you practice psychoanalysis or you don't practice psychoanalysis. We practice psychoanalysis. They don't practice psychoanalysis. We practice psychoanalysis just exactly the way Freud did it. As a matter of fact, I don't know what Freud was doing. Freud wasn't practicing psychoanalysis."

That Freud would be too creative and questioning to be acceptable at a psychoanalytic institute of the American Psychoanalytic Association in the late 1950s was probably true—but to know it and be proud of it was a measure of sickness.

In the late '50s and early 1960s, the eastern universities were no longer interested in faculty who were psychoanalytic. Harvard did away with its clinical program and with the Harvard Psychological Clinic of Morton Prince and Henry Murray. Princeton fired all of its faculty in clinical, social, and personality psychology who did not have tenure, and harassed Silvan Tomkins and Hadley Cantril until they resigned. A graduate student at the University of Pennsylvania told me that reading Freud was something that he did not dare to let his faculty know about. A graduate student in clinical psychology at Temple University, who sought statistical advice on his dissertation, was tempted to fudge his data because the findings were in keeping with Freud's ideas—he thought that would be too upsetting to his committee. I reassured him that he was not responsible for the real world, even if it was Freudian.

In his dissertation orals, when asked if he were a Freudian, he said, "No, it's much too primitive a theory." As he explained later, "I wanted to get through."

I was surprised in the 1960s when the psychologists at Michigan State University were not turned off by my interest in psychoanalytic ideas. But the fact that I was a competent psychometrician had at least as much to do with my being hired as my clinical competence. That made me acceptable to the experimentalists. From that time until now, the experimental psychologists, with a few exceptions, were opposed to psychoanalysis. But in the 1960s, and every decade since, the most adamantly anti-psychoanalytic faculty have been clinical psychologists, who were clinically incompetent.

In the '60s, the American Psychological Association (APA) was still opposed to psychotherapy. Division 12, the only clinical division, did not include psychotherapy in its definition of clinical psychology. I refused to join on that basis. I later learned that there had been a political fight as to whether to include psychotherapy in Division 12's definition.

Division 29 (psychotherapy) was originally an organization outside the APA formed by Reuben Fine, Carl Rogers, and other serious therapists. Eventually, the APA asked those of us who were APA members to join

Division 12, and it became a subdivision. Eventually, its members became restive and, despite Division 12's opposition, became Division 29. It was not until the 1980s that Division 39 (psychoanalysis) was formed.

The bulk of academic psychologists, pseudoclinical as well as experimental, are anti-psychoanalytic today. But the bulk of academic psychologists have always been antipsychoanalytic. Wundt said Freud's work was immoral. G. Stanley Hall invited Freud, Ferenczi, and Jung to the United States and they met with distinguished academic experimental psychologists, including William James. This was Freud's first acceptance by scientists, according to Boring (1950). But American psychology and psychoanalysis split again and stayed apart.

From the beginning, many philosophers condemned psychoanalysis as irrational; since mental means conscious, unconscious mental processes are a logical contradiction and can have no meaning, it was said. Adolf Grünbaum's (1988) is just the latest bad philosophy aimed at dismissing the discoveries of psychoanalysis. But Americans hear less of European philosophers who are positive about psychoanalysis. The Belgian philosopher and psychoanalyst Antoine Vergote (Huber et al. 1964) is especially worth reading, particularly on the subject of depression.

Literary critics, economists, sociologists, political scientists, and anthropologists have all found psychoanalysis useful and generative. Within each field there are also ardent critics, as there always have been.

But psychoanalysts themselves have contributed to the resistance to psychoanalysis. Thus, in the 1970s when Heinz Kohut's ideas were new, the American Psychoanalytic Association's institute in Detroit had a meeting on Kohut's ideas. The discussant, a medical analyst, proclaimed pompously that the self was an unscientific concept that no social scientist would take seriously, and that Kohut did not use such clearly scientifically accepted ideas as the "instincts." There are interesting questions to raise about what is or is not useful and valid in Kohutian theory and technique, but none of the real issues were included in that discussion.

In the 1980s, at that same institute, the two discussants of a paper by Henry Krystal were both ego-analysts. One smiled throughout his discussion, noted that the paper was different from the draft, but the draft was eight weeks old, and said, "I know Henry; he, of course, would change something in eight weeks." He went on to thank Krystal for bringing knowledge with which most psychoanalysts are unfamiliar to bear on psychoanalytic theory and technique. He agreed with most of the conclusions, but drew one implication that he felt was wrong, and described why he disagreed with that implication. Obviously, he appreciated and enjoyed considering the ideas of a bright and creative colleague. The other discussant had a fixed frown on his face, and informed the audience that "We have a theory and we don't need any other." He went on to state, "Nothing outside the analytic hour is relevant."

One of my students asked me what I thought.

"You have just heard a discussion by two orthodox ego psychoanalysts, one of whom is very bright and one of whom is very stupid."

There are problems now. Managed care refuses to pay for ethical, intensive, and confidential treatment. But managed care is a war, not a state of the world that needs to be accepted. In the long run, we will win if we do not assume we have lost.

But even if we lose, all we are losing is insurance company funding. Psychoanalysis and psychotherapy did not die when *no* insurance would pay a psychologist. As Nat Stockhamer (personal communication) has said, "We were spoiled." In East Lansing, Michigan, most of my patients in the 1960s, '70s, '80s, and '90s have had to pay out of their own pocket.

I have a colleague, an M.A. psychologist practicing in a town of 12,000 people. There are eight other psychologists in practice in that town and a highly publicized psychiatric clinic. Blue Cross and most other insurance companies will not pay her. Recently I asked how she is doing.

"I have a problem. I really do not want to carry more than forty clinical hours a week and they are filled."

Of course, she is an extremely competent psychoanalyst, and her colleagues and patients know it.

The government has stopped funding training in the mental health professions. Academic psychologists did not like psychoanalysis or clinical psychology but they went along with it for the money. Now they have become more aggressive, trying to reduce or eliminate clinical programs and co-opt resources. Within the APA governance and in Division 42 (private practice), surprisingly enough, there are strong voices saying there are too many clinical psychologists and we should only train what managed care can use. At the same time there is a push for prescription privileges from psychologists, including supposed psychoanalysts, who do not believe they can help people with psychotherapy.

In psychiatry, grants have been most available to study biological treatments (the ratio is ten to one from government sources, and probably a hundred to one from private sources). Biological psychiatrists are hired because they have grants and they teach what they know. Psychiatry, since it has been "medicalized," is not maintaining its numbers. While biological psychiatrists make more money, there are even more lucrative specialties. The intellectual challenge is almost nonexistent; there are far more interesting drug treatments in other specialties. Unfortunately, the stream of bright psychiatrists who, despite being told to become surgeons or internists, became psychiatrists because they were fascinated by psychoanalysis, has been turned off in recent years by the so-called medicalizing of psychiatry.

A study by the American Psychiatric Association concluded that no matter what fee one charged, one could not reasonably expect to earn more than $100,000 per year doing psychotherapy, but one would could easily earn $300,000 doing evaluations and medication. For the last ten years, young psychiatrists have asked, "But can you make a decent living as a psychoanalyst?" Recently, data suggest that medicating psychiatrists are now making only $100,000 a year while doing work they despise. This is similar to the finding in California that the psychologists who are going out of business are those who trusted the managed care companies.

In psychology departments, clinical programs frequently are being cut back, or moved in antipsychoanalytic directions. On the other hand, there are psychoanalytic programs that are growing. It is a struggle.

Yet there are more psychoanalysts now than there have ever been. Psychoanalysts are treating more varied and disturbed patients than ever. There are more psychoanalytic journals than ever, with forty-nine cited in the latest *Psychoanalytic Abstracts* (1997). Psychoanalysis is incorporated in constructive interventions that are not thought of as psychoanalysis, and in intellectual ideas whose origins are ignored.

A social psychologist told me that psychoanalysis was a poor personality theory.

"What is a good one?"

"Erikson," he said.

In the end, Freud's (1938) statement is still apt:

I started my professional activity as a neurologist trying to bring relief to my neurotic patients. Under the influence of an older friend and by my own efforts, I discovered some important new facts about the unconscious and the psychic life, the role of instinctual urges, and so on. Out of these findings grew a new science, Psychoanalysis, a part of psychology, as the new method of treatment of the neuroses. I had to pay heavily for this bit of good luck. People did not believe in my facts and thought my theories unsavory. In the end, I succeeded in acquiring pupils and bringing up an international psychoanalytic association. But the struggle is not yet over.

Nor will it ever be.

REFERENCES

Alexander, V. K. (1956). A case study of a multiple personality. *Journal of Abnormal and Social Psychology* 52:272–276.

Bonaparte, M., Freud, A., and Kris, E. (1957). *The Origins of Psychoanalysis: Letters to Fliess.* Garden City, NY: Doubleday.

Boring, E. G. (1950). *A History of Experimental Psychology, 2nd ed.* New York: Appleton-Century-Crofts.

Brenner, C. (1955). *An Elementary Textbook of Psychoanalysis.* Garden City, NY: Doubleday.

Dickens, C. (1859). *A Tale of Two Cities.* New York: Hurd & Houghton, 1868.

Fine, R. (1990). *The History of Psychoanalysis.* Northvale, NJ: Jason Aronson.

Freud, S. (1900). The interpretation of dreams. *Standard Edition* 4–5.

——— (1913). Totem and taboo. *Standard Edition* 13:1–162.

——— (1924–1950). *Collected Papers* (5 Vols). London: Hogarth.

——— (1926). The question of lay analysis. *Standard Edition* 20:183–250.

——— (1935). A general introduction to psychoanalysis. New York: Liveright.

——— (1938). The Psychoanalytic Review *Presents the Voice of Sigmund Freud.* Audio cassette, prod. D. M. Kaplan, National Psychological Association for Psychoanalysis.

Grünbaum, A. (1988). *The Foundations of Psychoanalysis: A Philosophical Critique.* Berkeley, CA: University of California Press.

Hollingshead, A. B., and Redlich, F. C. (1958). *Social Class and Mental Illness.* New York: Wiley.

Huber, W., Piron, H., and Vergote, A. (1964). *La Psychanalyse: Science de l'homme.* Brussels: C. Dessart.

Knight, R. (1953). The present status of organized psychoanalysis in the U.S. *Journal of the American Psychoanalytic Association* 1:197–221.

Prince, M. (1913). *The Dissociation of a Personality.* New York: Longmans, Green.

Psychoanalytic Abstracts (1997). Vol. 11, no. 3, pp. 1–72.

Waelder, R. (1960). *The Basic Theory of Psychoanalysis.* New York: International Universities Press.

9
Freud as Leader: The Early Years of the Viennese Society*

Kenneth Eisold

"Freud never lost control of the group as a whole; he proved a masterful leader," Nunberg wrote in his introduction to the *Minutes of the Vienna Psychoanalytic Society* (Nunberg and Federn 1962, p. xxiv). But Freud's own assessment of his leadership was very different. In his "History of the Psychoanalytic Movement," he disparaged his ability to lead the group of Viennese supporters he had gathered around himself starting in 1902: "I could not succeed in establishing among its members the friendly relations that ought to obtain between men who are all engaged upon the same difficult work" (Freud 1914, p. 25).

As a generalization, Freud's statement has a good deal of superficial plausibility, given the fact that the period he describes included the notorious splits with Adler and Jung. Indeed, he wrote his *History* (Freud 1914) in order to explain and justify what appeared to the larger world as sectarian schisms, damaging to the reputation of psychoanalysis as a serious

*This chapter is reprinted from *The International Journal of Psycho-Analysis*, Vol. 78, Part 1, pp. 87–104, copyright © 1997 by *The International Journal of Psycho-Analysis* and used by permission.

scientific endeavor. In that context, it adds to his account of those conflicts a modest confession of his inadequacy as a leader. And, I think, moreover, he truly believed he lacked such skills.

On several occasions Freud expressed his distaste for the burdens of leadership and doubts about his ability. In 1907 he wrote to Jung: "I have always felt that there is something about my personality, my ideas and manner of speaking, that people find strange and repellent," which he attributed to being an "'obsessional' type, each specimen of which vegetates in a sealed-off world of his own" (McGuire 1988, p. 82). And again, in 1908: "I am certainly unfit to be a chief, the 'splendid isolation' of my decisive years has set its stamp upon my character" (p. 141). Many times during these years, moreover, he spoke of being too old for the burdens of leadership.

But Freud's "failure to establish friendly relations" in Vienna also casts a shadow on the Viennese and alludes to what had by then become a common attitude within the psychoanalytic community. Binswanger reported Freud's discouraged remark following an early meeting: "Well, now you have seen the gang" (Binswanger 1957). And Jones reported Jung's description of the Viennese group "as a medley of artists, decadents and mediocrities" (Jones 1955, p. 33).

Much of this is attributable to competition between the locals and the visitors from abroad. Abraham wrote Eitingon, following his 1907 visit to the Society, "I am not too thrilled by the Viennese adherents. . . . *He* is all too far ahead of the others" (Gay 1988, p. 178). Jones, in his autobiography (1959), wrote that the Viennese "seemed an unworthy accompaniment to Freud's genius" (pp. 159–160). Nor, I think, was Freud above stimulating rivalry as a means of encouraging his followers.

Moreover, as we shall see, relations between Freud and the Viennese group became strained and, at times, acrimonious: as the Society grew in size, transformed itself into a professional organization, encountered competition from outside, and redefined its relationship with its founder and most precious member, it went through stormy times. But it has never fully escaped this early reputation as a collection of rivalrous, petty, and contentious men. Gay (1988), with seeming definitiveness, characterized their meetings as "testy, even acrimonious, as members sparred for position, vaunted their originality, or voiced dislike of their fellows with a brutal hostility masquerading as analytic frankness" (p. 176).

The other side to this story, of course, is Freud's reputation as the tyrannical father who could not let his sons grow up to become independent (Puner 1947, Roustang 1982). Jung, in several bitter letters during his break with Freud, accused him of "playing the father" (McGuire 1988, p. 535). Wittels (1924) links Freud to the tyrannical father of "Totem and Taboo," and he offered the tart comment about the stifling of dissent: "Suppression makes people snappish" (p. 142). Roazen (1969), not untypically, voices the conclusion that, "the best of Freud's male pupils left because the atmosphere was too narrow and ultimately degrading" (p. 48).

The most poignant evidence of this comes from Freud himself. In April 1910, he wrote Ferenczi he felt threatened by "falling into the role of the dissatisfied and superfluous old man" (Brabant et al. 1993, p. 155). In November of 1910, he complained to Jung of his growing difficulties with Adler: "He is . . . forcing me into the unwelcome role of the aging despot who prevents young men from getting ahead" (McGuire 1988, p. 373).

But, if we examine the evidence of what went on in the Viennese group more closely, these characterizations become more and more puzzling. Freud's own description of this group in his *History* is unquestionably if somewhat grudgingly positive: "On the whole I could tell myself that it was hardly inferior, in wealth and variety of talent, to the staff of any clinical teacher one could think of" (Freud 1914, p. 25). Indeed, individually, many of the members of the group are viewed today as important and distinguished contributors to the development of psychoanalysis. Moreover, an examination of the minutes of the Society from 1906 through 1915, carefully edited by Nunberg and Federn (1962, 1967, 1974, 1975), reveals that, in fact, those meetings were lively, obviously stimulating to the members, and productive. They may not have been in Freud's term "friendly"; indeed, they were often contentious and competitive. But by any measure they were successful and precisely in the way that Freud had hoped, in developing the ideas and practice of psychoanalysis.

The objective success of these meetings hardly needs to be dwelt upon, and Freud unquestionably played a major role in this success. There is a substantial psychoanalytic literature on the qualities of the successful leader that can help us grasp how Freud contributed to this success. Zaleznik (1989) for example, notes that the successful leader is often "twice born," distinct in his identity from others as a result, and exceptionally purposive in pursuing his vision (see Newton 1995). Similarly, Lapierre (1991) notes the importance of the personal authority of the leader, stemming from the clarity of his "inner truth," enabling him to project his desires and fantasies into his followers. Zoner and Offer (1985), working from a self-psychological perspective, identify the type of the "wise leader" who has transformed his primary narcissistic needs, on the one hand actively pursuing his ego ideal, but, on the other, able to appraise himself realistically. All of these perspectives capture something of Freud's personal achievement that, at this stage in his life, enabled him to lead the psychoanalytic movement. He became a compelling—at times, mesmerizing—leader.

And yet the story of Freud's leadership is also profoundly disappointing. In his own terms, he failed to turn over the leadership to others, as he repeatedly sought to do, and he lost the intellectual companionship of the men he loved the most. Moreover, starting with these early years, psychoanalysis became encumbered with a reputation for sectarian intolerance—a reputation subsequently reiterated and reinforced—damaging to its efforts to establish its scientific standing and inhibiting to its internal development.

Clearly, the responsibility for all this cannot be attributed to Freud. He played a vital role in bringing this about, but so did his followers. Freud was a leader insofar as and in the manner that was allowed by his followers.

There is a strand of psychoanalytic thinking on this subject that begins with the pioneering observations of Bion (1969), stressing the control that groups exert over leaders. Noting that all groups are simultaneously engaged in pursuing a task as well as defending against anxiety—they are what he called "work groups" and "basic assumption groups"—he called attention to the unconscious ways in which groups manipulate leaders in the service of their defensive needs. Menzies-Lyth (1967) has elucidated the largely hidden impact of "social defenses" in social systems, affecting task performance and controlling the scope of leadership. Shapiro (1979), also working in this tradition, has suggested the impact of group regression on leadership, as has Kernberg (1980a,b). Other theorists stressing the power of unconscious dynamics in groups have looked at it somewhat differently. Anzieu (1984) has studied the powerful role of unconscious fantasy in groups in subverting rational planning. Strozier (1985), working from a self-psychology perspective, has explored the constraints on the leader stemming from his role as self-object; the increasingly fragmentation of selves in groups, accompanied by narcissistic rage, produces an increasing need for an idealized leader.

I will use here Bion's framework for understanding the process of the group, although other frameworks accounting for the dynamic interplay between leaders and followers could also serve. The Viennese Society was a relatively small group, close to the size of the groups with which Bion made his initial clinical observations, but I also follow Bion because his terms are descriptive and parsimonious—and they closely fit the phenomena for which we have evidence. At the same time, I follow Rice (1963) and Kernberg (1980c) in looking at such dynamics in the framework of a task system: regression leading to "basic assumption" behavior tends to occur in groups when there is a conflict between tasks or a discontinuity between the task and the requisite structures for carrying it out.

A close look at the records of the Society, as we shall see, strongly supports the presence of basic assumptions. Freud and his followers, feeling continually besieged by the medical and cultural establishment, could hardly avoid the basic assumption of fight/flight, that is, the belief that their primary need was to defend themselves against external dangers. On the other hand, given the power and importance of Freud to the group, neither could they avoid the basic assumption of dependency, the belief that they needed Freud's support and protection to survive. At the same time, they all were engaged in trying to develop the organizational structures they needed to address the various tasks they faced; and, as we shall see, there was an essential conflict in their understanding of those tasks.

Clearly, Freud was not entirely the "masterful leader" Nunberg described. Neither was he the domineering despot he has sometimes been made out to be—nor the ineffective leader he sometimes felt he was. The Viennese, on the other hand, were not a petty and squabbling band of mediocre followers; neither were they heroes or victims. They were, at various times, to be sure, all of these as they attempted to rise to the challenges they faced and react to pressures they did not understand. Above all, they were passionately engaged in an enterprise that brought out the best and the worst in them. Together, they brought psychoanalysis into the world and, stimulated by profound anxiety, engaged in destructive unconscious defensive acts as well.

BEFORE SALZBURG

Begun in 1902, at the suggestion of Stekel, the Vienna group first came into being when Freud sent postcards to four physicians—Stekel, Adler, Kahane, and Reitler—to meet informally with him in his waiting room. The "first evenings were inspiring. . . . We were so enthralled by these meetings that we decided new members could be added to our circle only by unanimous consent" (Stekel 1950, p. 116). By the time minutes were

first recorded in October 1906 by Rank, the group had become more struc-
tured. The decision to hire Rank and keep formal records must, in itself,
have marked a decisive moment in the development of the group; after
four years of meeting, it had developed a sense of its own permanence and
importance. According to Rank's minutes, it now consisted of seventeen
members: "Prof. Dr. Freud chairs the meetings, Otto Rank acts as sala-
ried secretary. The meetings take place, as a rule, every Wednesday
evening at eight thirty o'clock at Prof. Freud's home . . ." (Nunberg and
Federn 1962, p. 6).

At this stage in its development, the group had something of a hybrid
character: in the words of a subcommittee formed to consider new rules
in 1908, it was "something in between a group invited by Professor Freud
and a society" (Nunberg and Federn 1962, p. 315). That is, it continued
to be a group of members who had ties to Freud and to whom Freud looked
to carry on the enterprise of psychoanalysis he had founded. At the same
time, members had ties to each other and to the enterprise on their own,
ties that were increasingly formalized as rights and obligations to the
Society: presenting papers, participating in the discussions, paying dues,
voting on new members, and so on. Clearly, these overlapping structures—
"a group invited by Professor Freud and a society"—were profoundly
bound together: without Freud, the society would lack the guidance and
support of the primary authority for the understanding and practice of its
discipline; on the other hand, without the society, Freud would lack a vital
means to extend the influence of his ideas. Yet, indissoluble as the two
were at this point, their interests were not identical. The "group invited
by Professor Freud" had as its primary purpose the development of Freud's
ideas and influence; the "society" was there to further the professional
development of its members (Levinson 1994).

There are early signs of this tension, as Freud struggled to distinguish
his authority from that of the group. At the start of the first meeting in
the fall of 1906, for example, he retracted an earlier agreement to share
decisions on publications with the group (Nunberg and Federn 1962,
pp. 6–7). Again, over the summer of 1907, he announced that he had dissolved the Society, giving each member the opportunity to renew his membership. His ostensible reason was to reestablish "the personal freedom of
each individual" (Nunberg and Federn 1962, p. 203). But his deferential
tactfulness also had the effect of reminding members that only Freud himself had the power to take such a step; it was his group. Moreover, fram-
ing his concern in terms of the members' "personal freedom" obscured the

extent to which they possessed a formal organization of their own. Sachs (1944) recalled that Freud opened annual business meetings with the remark "Now we must play highschool fraternity" (p. 62).

This "fraternity" was becoming increasingly assertive. Binswanger (1957) had been impressed by the fact that "conflicting opinions were voiced freely, and that no one pulled his punches—Freud himself, for all the respect shown him, was often contradicted." Indeed, there were a number of occasions on which they criticized each other's dependence upon Freud. In October 1906, for example, Stekel noted that "everything in [Rank's] book is seen through spectacles colored by Freudian teachings, without going beyond Freud" (Nunberg and Federn 1962, p. 25). In February 1907, Sadger complains that the group as a whole is "inclined to overestimate the significance of the Freudian teachings for psychology; that is to say, the importance of the sexual factor for psychology, for the unconscious" (p. 132). Two months later, Federn "sees the error of those who, totally imbued with the Freudian way of thinking, ignore all other points of view" (p. 165).

At the meeting of February 5, 1908, "Adler and Federn make motions and proposals concerning the reorganization of the meetings" (Nunberg and Federn 1962, p. 298). Federn added a motion of his own to abolish the Society's "'intellectual communism.' No idea may be used without the authorization of its author" (p. 299). Subsequently, Sadger proposed: "Personal invectives and attacks should immediately be suppressed by the Chairman who shall be given authority to do so" (p. 300). Graf commented, shortly afterwards, on the proposals and the discussion: they "stem from a feeling of uneasiness. We no longer are the type of gathering we once were. Although we are still guests of the Professor, we are about to become an organization. Therefore, he suggests the following motion. . . . To move the meetings from the Professor's apartment to another place" (p. 301).

Freud's response to this upsurge of organizational activity on the part of the group was tactful and tactical. He opposed Sadger's proposal on the grounds that he found it painful to reprimand anyone, but he also warned the group that if they could not collaborate better, "then he cannot help but close down [shop]" (p. 301). He proposed setting up a committee to make recommendations; the discussions concluded with a unanimous reaffirmation of their "intellectual communism."

At the next meeting of the Society, on February 12, the committee proposed by Freud made recommendations that were primarily procedural.

They rejected Graf's suggestion of a change of locale. Adler proposed, however, "monthly meetings in some other locality (perhaps a small auditorium at the University), to which all those who apply should be admitted if they have been approved by a two-third majority. From this group some could be selected for membership in the more intimate Wednesday circle by the voting procedure practiced until now" (pp. 315–316). According to the minutes: "Adler's minority motion evokes a lively discussion" (p. 317). But Adler withdrew his motion as Freud suggested the formation of a larger group entirely separate from the Wednesday Society.

The net result of these proposals and discussions was, on the surface at least, very little. Nothing was done about the formation of a larger group. What, then, was at stake?

As Graf's comments at the February 5th meeting suggest, the group was no longer the same group; it had evolved to the point where it felt more keenly its own authority and the need to assert more control over its own functioning. In this respect, these struggles of February 1908 are extensions of the struggle over Freud's authority that we could see signs of earlier. The proposals were counterparts to Freud's subtle declaration of ownership the previous summer in "dissolving" the Society. And, I think, Freud recognized this in reminding the group that he could "close down [shop]."

There is another aspect of this struggle, however, that links to the group's anxiety about its relationship with Freud. Sadger's proposal to give the chairman power to suppress personal attacks speaks to the growing dismay in the group about its own contentiousness and conflict, a situation that was referred to in the minutes of the following meeting, February 12th, as, "the 'ill humor in the empire' which has lately arisen" (p. 316).

It is not difficult to trace this "ill humor" back to the meeting two months before, on December 4, 1907, at the start of which Freud "reports Jung's suggestion that in the Spring a congress of all 'followers' be held (perhaps in Salzburg)" (p. 254). That meeting, formally devoted to the presentation and discussion of a paper by Sadger, erupted in unprecedented vitriol. "Stekel is horrified and fears that [Sadger's] work will harm our cause" (p. 255). "Federn is indignant. Sadger has not said a single word about . . . sexual development" (p. 256). "Wittels first takes exception to the personal outburst of rage and indignation on the part of Stekel and Federn. He considers these entirely out of place" (p. 257). In response, Freud advised moderation, obviously attempting to calm the frayed tempers, but at the end Sadger declared: "He expected to receive information and instruction, but takes home nothing but some invectives" (p. 258).

Clearly, the precipitant for these unprecedented conflicts was Freud's announcement of Jung's plan for the congress: the group was confronted for the first time by the fact that Freud had other followers who might in fact accomplish more for him than they. Sadger became the scapegoat of the meeting on one level because, I suspect, his work aroused the immediate feeling in the group that it was not good enough to represent psychoanalysis and satisfy Freud. On another level, I suspect, he was a stand-in for Freud himself, receiving the helpless rage they dared not direct at the Professor.

But, of course, the anxiety in the group could not be contained by blaming Sadger. At the January 8, 1908 meeting, when it was Stekel's turn to present, Sadger counterattacked. Stekel rejoined: "he is horrified at the lack of understanding which he has encountered tonight" (p. 280). On March 4, Stekel attacked Adler in turn. The normal give-and-take of the meetings had become bitter and personal.

The Society was caught in a dilemma. On the one hand, how could its members preserve it as an instrument for their own professional development, a need that was all the more apparent now as Freud was finding disciples elsewhere? This question lay behind the proposals to move the meetings from Freud's waiting room, to form a separate society, and to abolish "intellectual communism." On the other hand, how could they eliminate the self-destructive conflicts that only served to further alienate Freud? The proposals to streamline the meetings and to give Freud greater authority to quell dissent were designed to accomplish this end.

The deepest fear expressed in these meetings, though, was the loss of Freud's allegiance, and that fear appears to have been most completely addressed in their submitting entirely to his recommendations for reform. The outcome reassured them and confirmed their dependence.

For Freud, the outcome was a group of adherents who more fully recognized their reliance upon him. They had worked through their panic of being abandoned, and were now prepared to present an orderly presence at the Salzburg Congress. Thus he could more fully depend upon them to take their place among the other adherents of psychoanalysis elsewhere in the world—not only Jung but also Jones, Abraham, and Ferenczi, as well as A. A. Brill and Morton Prince from America—who were preparing to join up at Salzburg.

Adler's proposal for two groups in Vienna was a last-ditch effort at the meeting to affirm the notion of an independent society as well as preserve the intimate connection with Freud. The "larger group" could continue the freewheeling discussions and foster the competition over developing original ideas and formulations that the group's renewed dedication to "intellectual communism" would only inhibit. On the other hand, Adler's proposal raised the specter of competition for access to Freud. The "lively discussion" provoked by Adler's proposal suggests that the idea must have had significant support, but Freud's counterproposal to preserve the Wednesday group intact while creating an entirely separate larger organization, in effect, reassured the group that he was not prepared—at this point, certainly—to kick anyone out. They could all continue to meet with him—if they behaved, which is to say, if they contained their anxiety about competition with Freud's followers outside of Vienna.

But the idea of the "larger group" was inevitable. Two years later at the Nuremberg Congress, when the International Psychoanalytic Association was formed under Jung's leadership, it provoked another crisis for the Viennese.

TO NUREMBERG AND THE INTERNATIONAL PSYCHOANALYTIC ASSOCIATION

The minutes of the meetings before the Nuremberg Congress, at the end of March 1910, show no anticipatory anxiety, as Freud apparently played his cards close to his vest; no one knew in advance what he had planned with Ferenczi and Jung. And for good reason. Ferenczi's proposal, first announced in his address, "On the Organization of the Psychoanalytic Movement" (Ferenczi 1911), but obviously approved by Freud, called for the creation of the International Psychoanalytic Association, with Jung the designated president for life, possessing the power to censor all psychoanalytic publications. Adding insult to injury, Ferenczi, in his introductory remarks on the history of psychoanalysis, completely omitted any reference to the contributions of the Viennese; indeed, he characterized the first "heroic" age of psychoanalysis—before "the appearance of Jung and the 'Zurichers'"—as a time when Freud was "entirely alone" (Ferenczi 1955, p. 300).

The Viennese, predictably, were outraged. According to Wittels, they met in Stekel's room, secretly, to plan their opposition, when suddenly Freud appeared: "Never before had I seen him so greatly excited. He said: 'Most of you are Jews, and therefore incompetent to win friends for the new teaching. . . . We are all in danger.' Seizing his coat by the lapels, he said: 'They won't even leave me a coat to my back. The Swiss will save us—will save me, and all of you as well'" (Wittels 1924, p. 140). They reached a compromise in which some of the more onerous features of Ferenczi's proposal were modified. There was to be no censorship, and Jung's term was limited to two years.

When meetings of the Society resumed in Vienna on April 6, 1910, Freud pointed out that "the implementing of these resolutions will signify a new period for the activities of our Society." Until now, the members of the Society have been his guests: "now this is no longer feasible. The society must constitute itself and elect a president." Declining to be president of the new society, Freud proposed Adler (Nunberg and Federn 1967, pp. 463–464).

Adler responded, as if on behalf of the Viennese group; he explained their actions in Nuremberg, calling Freud to account for his part in the conflict and blaming the "harshness" of Ferenczi's "Memorandum." He then went on to speak in a proudly affirmative if not defiant manner: "We can therefore say today that from now on we belong to an association that chooses its president in a free election by members with equal rights, like every other association" (p. 464).

The mood of the meeting was sad and defensive. Stekel commented that he "cannot imagine how we would exist . . . without Freud—who seems to harbor deep hatred towards Vienna" (p. 466). Federn disavowed "any hostile intentions towards Zurich," blaming instead "the aloof behavior of the members from Zurich. . . . Even though it is difficult to imagine the old patriarchal relationship ceasing to exist, surely Freud has good reasons for his decision, and to fight against them will, he supposes, be in vain" (p. 466). Sadger "thinks that he has observed that Freud has been fed up with the Viennese for the last two years now" (p. 465). "However, the fact is that we need him" (p. 467).

Gradually the mood of the meeting shifted. Freud reminded them of the "many compelling reasons" for Zurich becoming the center, but more importantly reassured them of his continued presence and involvement. The group searched for a way to define Freud's continuing special role, and at his suggestion made him "scientific chairman." It then elected Adler president.

It is clear from the subsequent meetings that an effective transition was made with relative smoothness. The group got down to the business of electing an executive committee, setting up a committee to oversee the *Zentralblatt*, finding a new location for its meetings, setting new dues, establishing a library, and, by the following fall, establishing its statutes. Freud himself commented in a letter to Jung that the founding of the IPA in Vienna, while perhaps premature for the development of the group in Zurich, "has definitely helped. The style has improved and enthusiasm is great" (McGuire 1988, p. 321).

The relative ease with which the Viennese surmounted this crisis, I believe, can be attributed to the fact that they had been preparing for it for two years—in effect, since their recognition in February 1908 of their hybrid status. They were ready now to take the step of becoming, in Adler's proud words, "an association that chooses its president in a free election by members with equal rights" (Nunberg and Federn 1967, p. 464). But also in the intervening two years, the group had developed in Adler a leader who was felt to be capable of taking over from Freud. Freud, of course, clearly recognized that development in proposing Adler, and the group recognized it as well in tacitly assigning him the role of its spokesman.

As Stepansky (1983) has carefully shown, Adler was far from the rebellious and difficult member of the Viennese Society he has been retrospectively identified as being throughout these years. Indeed, he was frequently approvingly cited by Freud for his thoughtful and original contributions. Moreover, unlike Stekel, Sadger, and even Federn, he refrained from comments that could incite opposition to Freud's ideas, while at the same time developing his own thoughts and, as we have seen, his own proposals for the development of the society.

At the last Scientific Meeting of the Society before the summer break of 1909, for example, Adler gave a paper, "The Oneness of the Neuroses," developing ideas that clearly departed from Freud's. The minutes report Freud's judicious and extensive comments: "Prof. Freud sees little to find fault with, in the details of Adler's unusually lucid and consistent train of thought, but he must confess that in general, he has a different standpoint" (Nunberg and Federn 1967, p. 265).

A few days later, Jung wrote Freud that he had heard through a patient that Adler "is moving away from you and is going off on his own, in the opposite direction to you, even. Is there any truth in it?" (McGuire 1988, p. 232). To which Freud replied: "Yes, I believe there is truth in the story. He is a theorist, astute and original, but not attuned to psychology. . . . A decent sort, though; he won't desert in the immediate future, but neither will he participate as we should like him to. We must hold him as long as possible" (p. 235). Throughout this period, it seems clear, neither

Freud nor Adler wished to stress their differences; both chose to see their ideas as essentially compatible.

A year later, anticipating Adler's election as president of the Vienna Society, Freud wrote Ferenczi about his reasons for selecting Adler: "I will transfer the leadership to Adler, not out of inclination or satisfaction but because he is the only [prominent] personality and because in this position it will perhaps be necessary for him to share the defense of the common ground" (Brabant et al. 1993, p. 155). Several months later, Freud wrote Jung: "Adler is hypersensitive and deeply embittered because I consistently reject his theories" (McGuire 1988, p. 331). But this is in the context of Freud's criticism of Jung's dilatoriness in setting up the IPA and underscores his appeal to Jung to act more promptly and collaboratively with the Viennese group. Clearly he wanted Jung to know how awkward his position had become with the Viennese as a result of his delays. "You know how jealous they all are—here and elsewhere—over your privileged position with me, . . . and I think I am justified in feeling that what people say against you as a result is being said against me" (McGuire 1988, p. 330; see also Kerr 1993).

In a similar vein, Freud exhorted Jung on October 31, 1910: "I also believe that you have not overcome your dislike of our Viennese colleagues. . . . You are unquestionably right in your characterization of Stekel and Adler. . . . But it does not befit a superior man like you to bear a grudge against them. Take it with humour as I do except on days when weakness gets the better of me" (McGuire 1988, p. 366).

A month later, it appears that his "weakness" is more frequently getting the better of him; he writes Jung: "My spirits are dampened by the irritations with Adler and Stekel, with whom it is very hard to get along. . . . Adler is a very decent and highly intelligent man, but he is paranoid. . . . He is always claiming priority, putting new names on everything, complaining that he is disappearing under my shadow, and forcing me into the unwelcome role of the aging despot who prevents young men from getting ahead. They are also rude to me personally, and I'd gladly get rid of them both. But it won't be possible. . . . And on top of it all, this absurd Viennese local pride and jealousy of you and Zurich!" (p. 373). December 3rd, Freud writes again: "It is getting really bad with Adler. You see a resemblance to Bleuler; in me he awakens the memory of Fliess, but an octave lower. . . . The crux of the matter—and that is what really alarms me—is that he minimized the sexual drive and our opponents will soon be able to speak of an experienced psychoanalyst whose conclusions are radically different from ours" (p. 376).

The minutes for this period, the fall of 1910, following the euphoria of the spring response to the Nuremberg Congress, show that in fact the Wednesday night discussions in Vienna were increasingly crystallized around the theoretical differences between Adler and Freud. At the meeting of November 16th, Hitschmann offered the proposal that "Adler's theories be for once thoroughly discussed in their interconnections, with particular attention to their divergence from Freud's doctrine" (Nunberg and Federn 1974, p. 59). Hitschmann's proposal, ostensibly aimed at introducing clarity into the debates, set the stage for a confrontation that led three and a half months later to Adler's resignation.

Far more was at stake, obviously, than the clarification of theoretical differences. As Freud reportedly confided to Wortis (1940) years later: "personal differences—jealously or revenge or some other kind of animosity always came first. . . . scientific differences came later" (p. 848). In retrospect, I believe it is possible to see that the increasing tension between Freud and Adler derived from conflicts between their roles, exacerbated by the Society's new status. The developments since Nuremberg had placed the underlying conflict about the purpose of the Society and the Society's relationship with Freud into greater and greater prominence.

Adler had always stood for the independence of the Society, which he now formally led, as well as for the development of independent theoretical thinking within it. He had successfully rallied the members in the wake of the Nuremberg crisis and managed the transition into this new phase. But the dependence that all the members had felt as "guests of Professor Freud"—the dependence that had caused them to feel anxious and depressed in the aftermath of the Nuremberg Congress when they lost "the old patriarchal relationship" (Nunberg and Federn 1967, p. 466)—continued to be felt in the group. Freud had reassured them that he would not withdraw, that all relationships would remain as they had been, but it must have been increasingly apparent that, in fact, this was not so.

For one thing, it must have been clear to members of the Society that Freud was in fact siding with Jung in the disputes that arose between them. Neither his heart nor his loyalty remained with the Viennese. Freud's letters to Jung show that he was anything but complacent about Jung's shortcomings as leader of the IPA; he not only exhorted Jung to behave better toward the Viennese and take up his role as president more aggressively, but also he offered to intervene as "go-between" with Adler and Stekel, the editors of the *Zentralblatt*: "I can put through all your demands and block anything that doesn't suit you" (McGuire 1988, p. 367). But the minutes of the Society suggest that to the Viennese he was apologetic if not merely silent; he either defended Jung casually or ignored their complaints about him. Moreover, as he himself attests in his letters to Jung, he became increasingly irritable and impatient. The Viennese could not help but wonder on whose side he was.

But things could not remain the same for another reason as well. An independent Society would have to tolerate competition and differences, theoretical and otherwise. Adler's selection as its president, indeed, followed from the stature he had gained as a thinker. In this sense, the more outspoken debates of the fall of 1910 were inevitable outgrowths of the new status of the Society as, in Kanzer's (1971) words, "a congregation of scientists with varying views and degrees of competence . . . no longer an assemblage of students who sat at the feet of a master" (p. 39). Indeed, the debates were undoubtedly meant to test the limits of this tolerance—and, of course, the limits of Freud's tolerance.

Throughout the final months of 1910, Freud's impatience mounted. Ostensibly he was irritated with Adler's behavior, as well as Stekel's, but they were only the most obvious targets for his growing irritation with the Society and the increasingly difficult position he felt himself in between the Society and Jung. When Hitschmann, then, made his seemingly innocuous proposal, the group unconsciously set the stage for a showdown by pitting against each other the two men who represented the poles of their ambivalence. Adler was prodded into a more exposed position, while Freud was prodded into deciding how far he would allow such theoretical independence to be tolerated.

By the time the debate actually occurred, Freud had clearly decided that Adler had to go. The minutes for February 1, 1911, describe Adler's presentation of his paper and Freud's lengthy and detailed response in relatively straightforward terms, but there is no mistaking Freud's tone. The bulk of his criticism focused on his view that because it minimizes the power of libido and the "ego's fear of the libido" (Nunberg and Federn 1974, p. 149), Adler's is a surface psychology, merely "ego psychology, deepened by the knowledge of the psychology of the unconscious" (p. 147). As such, Freud seemed willing to concede, it can be a useful supplement to psychoanalysis, but, he states: "This is not psychoanalysis" (p. 146). Worse, he affirms, it will "do great harm to psychoanalysis. . . . It will . . .

make use of the latent resistances that are still alive in every psychoanalyst, in order to make its influence felt" (p. 147).

Wittels's account, largely based on Stekel's recollections, concentrates on the drama of the occasion: the "Freudian adepts made a mass attack on Adler, an attack almost unexampled for its ferocity even in the fiercely contested field of psychoanalytic controversy. . . . Freud had a sheaf of notes before him, and with gloomy mien seemed prepared to annihilate his adversary" (Wittels 1924, pp. 150–151). Graf noted that Adler "quietly and firmly" defended his point of view, but was nonetheless "banished" (Graf 1942, pp. 472–473).

Those who spoke on behalf of Adler confined themselves, primarily, to defending his right to develop his ideas; they seem taken off guard by the coordinated detail and intensity of the attack. "Furtmuller considers it premature to assume a *pro* or *con* attitude . . . [and tries] to refute some of Prof. Freud's objections" (Nunberg and Federn 1974, p. 156). In the third meeting both Freud and Adler make efforts to temporize: "Prof. Freud considers Adler's doctrines to be wrong and, as far as the development of psychoanalysis is concerned, dangerous. But these are scientific errors . . . that do great credit to their creator" (p. 172). Adler commented that his writings "would not have been possible if Freud had not been his teacher." If he is at fault for endangering psychoanalysis, "he will not hesitate to draw the necessary conclusions" (p. 174). Following the meeting, the minutes announce, Adler resigned as president "because of the incompatibility of his scientific attitude with his position in the society" (p. 177).

Adler, I think, struggled to account for the ferocity of Freud's affect, by seeing it as motivated by his fear for the future of psychoanalysis, much as he and the other members of the Society had seen Freud's ferocity mobilized in Nuremberg. If psychoanalysis is endangered—or, more to the point, if Freud saw it as endangered—the appropriate response would be to reassure him and soberly take stock of the danger his actions may inadvertently evoke.

"I have decided, after this unsuccessful attempt, to take the reins back into my own hands and I mean to keep a tight hold on them" (McGuire 1988, p. 400) Freud announced to Jung in his letter of March 1, 1911. Two weeks later, he added, "Naturally, I am only waiting for an occasion to throw them both out, but they both know it and are being very cautious and conciliatory, so there is nothing I can do for the present" (McGuire 1988, p. 403).

At the March 1st meeting, when Freud took over the presidency, we can see the members of the society pulling back from the consequences of the "discussion" of Adler's theories. After voting unanimously to thank both Adler and Stekel for their services, the society passed an addendum in which it refused "to acknowledge any incompatibility" (p. 179). The editors of the minutes comment in a footnote: "It is actually rather puzzling that the majority of the members, despite the clear state of affairs, and against Freud's expressed wish, nevertheless voted in favor of the amendment" (p. 179). But it is not so puzzling if one is willing to see in this defiant gesture the remnant of the Society's independence. They would bow to Freud's wish and reinstate themselves in his good graces by deposing Adler, but they would also remind him again of their capacity to defy him.

With the "palace revolution in Vienna" (McGuire 1988, p. 403) Freud seemed to turn more fully against the group he now formally led. On March 30th, he writes Jung: "You have been very kind to the Viennese in your handling of the Congress question. Unfortunately they are a lot of rabble and I shall feel neither horror nor regret if the whole show here collapses one of these days" (p. 411).

The Viennese had succeeded in preventing Freud's withdrawal from active leadership in the Society; he was forced into shouldering the unwanted burden of leadership. That, in itself, may account for his irritation, especially at the point when he longed for stronger ties with Jung, not with them. But, I suspect, his contempt came from his sense that he had been manipulated into becoming the object of the group's dependency, while at the same time, ambivalently, they continued to remind him of their power to thwart him. They had played upon his fears of the internal enemy, provided a scapegoat, and placed themselves once again under his care.

By October 1911, Freud decided on the expulsion of Adler's associates from the Society and forced a vote. The Society that defiantly refused to see incompatibility between Adler's role and beliefs in March was forced into taking the stand that no one could belong to the Society as well as Adler's new group. But it seems that, by then, both sides were prepared for the break.

Stekel's resignation the following year, in October 1912, was over his refusal to cede editorial control of the *Zentralblatt.* For Freud it was unpardonable that Stekel should resign from the Society and yet insist that he retain the editorship of its journal. But in fact Stekel had the power to do just that—and did, forcing the Society to found a new journal in its stead. Ironically, in this ultimately self-defeating gesture, Stekel affirmed the independence of his editorial role and the power of Society members to thwart Freud's control. Like Adler, the year before, however, his gesture of independence only seemed to confirm the dependence of the Society upon Freud.

But curiously there is no mention of this in the minutes of the Society. Indeed, virtually all references to organizational matters disappear after October 1911, elections to posts, appointments, new members. All that is noted are the names of those in attendance, and increasingly perfunctory accounts of the discussion.

Nunberg, one of the editors of Volume Four, notes "something that is quite puzzling—namely, that Freud's most devoted followers are beginning to minimize his achievements, and on certain occasions it almost looks as if there were a mutual understanding among them to do so, one in which even Tausk, Federn, Hitschmann, Sadger—those most devoted pupils of Freud—are taking part. At times, these men seem to have forgotten Freud's teachings" (Nunberg and Federn 1975, p. xv). It is not clear to me precisely what occasions Nunberg has in mind; I cannot find any overt minimizations of Freud's achievements, certainly none comparable to those notable in the years 1906–1908. But one does find, I think, a loss of vigor and excitement in the discussions, as well as occasions in which Freud does appear to be patiently providing elementary lessons.

One sees, in effect, the presence of the "basic assumption" (Bion 1969) of dependency. Members on occasion argue or dispute, but it does seem as if they have lost the capacity to clarify things for themselves. Grinker (1940), observing somewhat later, suggested their meetings were "like a religious ritual the meaning of which has long been forgotten and the necessity for it long passed" (p. 854). Sterba (1982) noted the atmosphere of reverence and strict hierarchy (Rustin 1985). Weiss (1970) confessed: "The truth is, no one felt completely free to express ideas very divergent from Freud's basic concepts" (p. 12).

FREUD'S LEADERSHIP

There is something of a tragedy in this outcome for Freud. As many who knew him agreed, he did not enjoy veneration and he was impatient with the dependency of his followers. Deutsch (1940), for example, commenting on the "atmosphere of absolute and infallible authority" created by his Viennese followers throughout the '20s and '30s, notes: "It was never any fault of Freud's that they cast him in this role and that they—so rumor has it—became mere 'yes men.' Quite the contrary; Freud had no love for 'yes men'. . . . He loved those who were critical, who were independent, who were of interest for their brilliance, who were original" (pp. 189–190). Similarly, Sachs (1944) has written movingly of knowing that he was not among those who had the capacity to stimulate this interest and intimacy with Freud.

Deutsch points to Freud's disappointment in losing his original and brilliant followers. Much has been made of a kind of paradox in Freud that accounted for this: his need to work things out on his own, in his own way and at his own pace (see Jones 1955, p. 428). Thus Freud could find himself at cross-purposes with the men he was attracted to and sought out, stubbornly unable to appreciate the very source of stimulation he required.

On one level, of course, are the "oedipal" explanations that Freud and his followers themselves favored. Each disciple was a son, bound to be in competition with the father as well as the other sons for the approval and favors of the father. The correspondence of Freud and his followers is, in fact, peppered with confessions of rivalry and protestations that more analysis has cured the problem. No less significant was the jealousy and rivalry among the Viennese.

Freud's own version of this explanation for group conflict was worked out in "Totem and Taboo" (1913). And it is possible to see in that an acknowledgment of the father's reciprocal role with respect to his rebellious sons, certainly the fear evoked in him by the extent and depth of the murderous oedipal feelings in the group of sons. He was once reported to have said he could not stand the "parricidal look" in the eyes of one of the younger members of the Society (Alexander 1940, p. 200). No doubt we see here Freud's underlying justification for his seizing the reins of control and acting in so decisive if not brutal a manner.

But on a deeper level, the drama was between Freud and the group as a whole. The very fact that Freud felt forced into seizing control through a "palace revolution" represented a victory for the group and a defeat of Freud's wish for greater independence. The group that feared abandonment by him, that experienced directly the transfer of his enthusiasm elsewhere, that was betrayed by him, in fact, as he planned with Jung to minimize their interests—this group finally succeeded in getting him to bind himself indissolubly to them. Moreover, they succeeded in getting him to weed out of their ranks any possible threat that they themselves might pose to his future control. Passively, indirectly, they manipulated him into the role of president for life he had sought to avoid.

How did Freud let this happen? We have seen all along how he struggled to maintain control over the independent-minded and even unruly group he had called into being. Clearly, he wanted to control the development of psychoanalysis.

Moreover, he had difficulty grasping the need of his followers to establish their independence from him. He was fiercely independent—counterdependent, more likely—intolerant of the dependency of others and of their struggles for independence. Indeed, it is what blinded him in his relations with others and made him, in Jones's (1957) phrase, so poor a judge of men (not a "Menschenkenner"); see also Grosskurth (1991), and Rosensweig (1992). Thus, even in promoting the independent status of the Viennese Society following the establishment of the IPA, I doubt he understood how complex and stormy the process was likely to be.

Roustang (1982) has argued, "Although he denied it, Freud was possessed by an uncontrollable need to have disciples and to surround himself with completely devoted followers" (p. 15). But this is too simple a view. Freud did want to control the development of psychoanalysis, and he was fiercely punitive and unforgiving. But I believe he was right to disparage his leadership ability. Despite his profound intellectual leadership, he failed to understand what was required to manage the development of a professional society (Levinson 1994). And he was able to be manipulated by the group into the role of "aging despot."

In Bion's (1969) term, Freud's "valency"—his predisposition for a role in the group—was for the role of fight leader. The efforts of the Viennese to cast Freud in the role of the dependency leader, the one who could cause them to feel nurtured and protected, encountered his hostility. In midlife, he characterized himself to Fliess as "a conquistador by temperament, an adventurer" (Masson 1985, p. 398). His boyhood idol was Hannibal, the conqueror of Rome (Freud 1900, p. 197). Sachs (1944) called Freud a fighter: "untiring and unbending, hard and sharp like steel, a 'good hater'" (p. 117). He saw psychoanalysis as constantly besieged by enemies; Stefan Zweig noted "above all when he is at war, fighting alone against a multitude, that there develops [in him] the unqualified pugnacity of a nature ready to face overwhelming odds" (Zweig 1932, p. 94). Sulloway (1979) has emphasized this aspect of Freud's heroic identity, and Ellenberger (1970) has pointed out the exaggerated degree to which Freud viewed himself as under attack. As we saw, he successfully mobilized the Viennese behind his plan to place Jung at the head of the psychoanalytic movement, despite their intense opposition, with his desperate portrayal of the threat they all faced from a hostile world.

Given the intense rivalry that characterized Freud's earliest followers and, moreover, given his characteristic dislike of dependency in his followers, we can easily see how his valency for the role of fight leader allowed him to incite high levels of aggression and competition in the group and to channel those into attacks on the group's external enemies. He never tired—nor did the group—of referring to their "enemies," their "opponents," their "adversaries," and the group gained coherence and confidence from this sense of being engaged in an embattled struggle under his leadership. They were, as Freud wrote Abraham, "partisans" (Abraham and Freud 1966, p. 19). But the appearance of external rivals—most particularly, of course, Jung and the Zurichers—altered this dynamic pattern. As we saw in the meeting at which Freud first announced the Salzburg Congress, the Viennese immediately began to seek out a scapegoat to blame for the threatened loss of their leader.

Two years later, Freud himself had become convinced that a danger at least as great as that posed by external enemies lurked within. I believe that this is precisely true: much as Freud disapproved of these divergent ideas, and much as he disliked the covert attempts to get him to endorse them, what truly alarmed him and galvanized him into action was his fear of the enemy within.

But this fear did not originate solely with Freud. It was an intrinsic belief within the embattled Society that any internal weakness or failure could aid the external enemy. So that, throughout the fall of 1910, as the Society faced a real external danger in the form of Jung, newly installed as president of the IPA, and a growing internal danger in the form of Freud's support of Jung against them, an unconscious plan emerged in the Society to put forward Adler as a target. Paradoxically, Adler—who represented the Society's intellectual and organizational independence—became seen as the major threat to its existence.

Freud's valency for fight, then, which was so helpful in galvanizing his initial band of followers into action—providing a "sophisticated work group" in Bion's term, a work group in which the underlying basic assumption is supportive of the task—proved also to be an Achilles' heel.

His aversion to dependency meant that his followers could only bond to him and securely experience his leadership when he was engaged in a fight, when he had an enemy. To hold on to him, they had to continue to provide an enemy.

"An intimate friend and a hated enemy have always been requirements of my emotional life," he wrote in "The Interpretation of Dreams" (Freud 1900, p. 483). But only the enemies proved enduringly reliable.

REFLECTIONS

From an institutional perspective, there are two points about Freud's leadership that emerge from this account: one is about his legacy to psychoanalysis, the other is about leadership in general.

Adler's was but the first of the notorious "defections" in the history of psychoanalysis, and his founding of a rival school the first of the "schisms." Psychoanalysis has been bedeviled ever since by this tendency toward institutional splitting. I do not think that the responsibility for this can be placed on Freud's shoulders, just as I think it is clear from this narrative that he did not bring about Adler's expulsion alone. But Freud set his stamp upon the movement so that the dynamic processes that were at work in the case of Adler were encouraged to develop elsewhere. That is, in placing emphasis upon leadership based on fight and, more importantly, fearing leadership based upon dependency, Freud left little room for psychoanalysts to acknowledge their dependencies. Indeed, the implicit lesson of these early years in Vienna is that the only way Freud's followers could be able to feel dependent upon him was to convince him that they would be faithful soldiers under his flag.

This is Freud's legacy. I have argued elsewhere (Eisold 1994) that psychoanalytic organizations are weak and vulnerable to schisms in part because the real allegiances of their members are to their analysts and the lineages of analysts that define particular schools of thought. Thus, as dependency upon one's analyst has traditionally been thought a sign of unresolved transference, the way to ensure one's place in the lineage, one's secure relationship with one's analyst and his school, has been to be willing to fight on his behalf. Moreover, in doing so, one is able to project into the rival school one's own displaced fear and hatred of the leader. This is precisely the story of Freud and the early Viennese. From this perspective, the threat to psychoanalysis, far from being the internal enemy that has to be identified and rooted out, is the unacknowledged dependencies of analysts themselves.

The larger point I wish to make is about leadership in general. Turquet (1978), in an important article on leadership building on Bion's work on "basic assumptions," pointed out that the leader will inevitably have projected into him all the group's anxiety and doubt: group members simultaneously attempt to rid themselves of their fears while inciting the leader to act on their behalf. Thus the leader must not only be able to tolerate anxiety and doubt himself, he must be able to not act in response to these incitements and pressures. The point I wish to make is that, in holding onto his capacity to not act, the leader has to reflect on the meaning of his action for the group he leads.

We analysts are accustomed to probing our own unconscious motivations, exploring our countertransferences in order to shed light on the transferences of our patients. We know what it is like to not act in our consulting rooms, subject to the pressure of an individual. But we tend to be far less aware of pressures emanating from the group. We are less likely to think of unconscious collusive forces permeating our relationship with colleagues. We have not been trained, by and large, to detect the unconscious at work in our institutional relationships. More particularly, we are not used to looking at how our leaders are creatures of those they lead. We avert our eyes from the unconscious collusive pact we establish with our leaders, who are allowed to feel venerated and strong precisely because they act as they are required to act. Or, as is now increasingly the case, we disparage the leaders who carry out the agendas we require but who fail to protect us from the problems we face.

If there is a lesson to be drawn from this story it is that we need to learn about the unconscious at work in our group and institutional relations. Our leaders ignore this at their peril—and ours.

REFERENCES

Abraham, H. C., and Freud, E. L., eds. (1966). *A Psycho-Analytic Dialogue: The Letters of Sigmund Freud and Karl Abraham, 1907–1926*. New York: Basic Books.

Alexander, F. (1940). Recollections of Bergasse 19. *Psychoanalytic Quarterly* 9(2):195–204.

Anzieu, D. (1984). *The Group and the Unconscious*, trans. B. Kilborne. London: Routledge & Kegan Paul.

Binswanger, L. (1957). *Sigmund Freud: Reminiscences of a Friendship.* New York: Grune & Stratton.

Bion, W. (1969). *Experiences in Groups.* New York: Basic Books.

Brabant, E., Falzeder, E., and Giampieri-Deutsch, P. (1993). *The Correspondence of Sigmund Freud and Sándor Ferenczi. Vol. 1, 1908–1914.* Cambridge, MA: Harvard University Press.

Deutsch, H. (1940). Freud and his pupils. *Psychoanalytic Quarterly* 9(1):184–194.

Eisold, K. (1994). The intolerance of diversity in psychoanalytic institutes. *International Journal of Psycho-Analysis* 75:785–800.

Ellenberger, H. (1970). *The Discovery of the Unconscious.* New York: Basic Books.

Ferenczi, S. (1911). On the organization of the psycho-analytic movement. In *Final Contributions to the Problems and Methods of Psychoanalysis,* ed. M. Balint, pp. 299–307. New York: Basic Books, 1955.

Freud, S. (1900). The interpretation of dreams. *Standard Edition* 4–5.

———— (1913). Totem and taboo. *Standard Edition* 13:1–161.

———— (1914). On the history of the psychoanalytic movement. *Standard Edition* 14:1–66.

———— (1921). Group psychology and the analysis of the ego. *Standard Edition* 18:65–143.

Gay, P. (1988). *Freud: A Life for Our Time.* New York: Norton.

Graf, M. (1942). Reminiscences of Freud. *Psychoanalytic Quarterly* 11:465–476.

Grinker, R. R. (1940). Reminiscences of a personal contact with Freud. *American Journal of Orthopsychiatry* 10:850–854.

Grosskurth, P. (1991). *The Secret Ring.* Reading, MA: Addison-Wesley.

Jones, E. (1955). *The Life and Work of Sigmund Freud,* vol 2. New York: Basic Books.

———— (1957). *The Life and Work of Sigmund Freud,* vol. 3. New York: Basic Books.

———— (1959). *Free Associations: Memories of a Psycho-Analyst.* New York: Basic Books.

Kanzer, M. (1971). Freud: the first psychoanalytic group leader. In *Comprehensive Group Psychotherapy,* ed. H. I. Kaplan and B. J. Sadock, pp. 27–40. Baltimore, MD: Williams & Wilkins.

Kernberg, O. F. (1980a). Regression in groups. In *Internal World and External Reality,* pp. 211–234. New York: Jason Aronson.

———— (1980b). Organizational regression. In *Internal World and External Reality,* pp. 235–252. New York: Jason Aronson.

———— (1980c). Regression in leaders. In *Internal World and External Reality,* pp. 253–273. New York: Jason Aronson.

Kerr, J. (1993). *A Most Dangerous Method.* New York: Knopf.

Lapierre, L. (1991). Exploring the dynamics of leadership. In *Organizations on the Couch,* ed. M. F. R. Kets de Vries, pp. 69–93. San Francisco: Jossey-Bass.

Levinson, H. (1994). The changing psychoanalytic organization and its influence on the ego ideal of psychoanalysis. *Psychoanalytic Psychology* 11(2):233–249.

Masson, J. M. (1985). *The Complete Letters of Sigmund Freud to Wilhelm Fliess, 1887–1904.* Cambridge, MA: Harvard University Press.

McGuire, W. (1988). *The Freud/Jung Letters: The Correspondence between Sigmund Freud and C. G. Jung.* Cambridge, MA: Harvard University Press.

Menzies-Lyth, I. E. P. (1967). A Case Study in the Functioning of Social Systems as a Defense against Anxiety. *Tavistock Pamphlet No. 3.* London: Tavistock.

Newton, P. (1995). *Freud: From Youthful Dream to Mid-Life Crisis.* New York: Guilford.

Nunberg, H., and Federn, E. (1962). *Minutes of the Vienna Psychoanalytic Society, vol. 1, 1906–1908.* New York: International Universities Press.

——— (1967). *Minutes of the Vienna Psychoanalytic Society, vol. 2, 1908–1910.* New York: International Universities Press.

——— (1974). *Minutes of the Vienna Psychoanalytic Society, vol. 3, 1910–1911.* New York: International Universities Press.

——— (1975). *Minutes of the Vienna Psychoanalytic Society, vol. 4, 1912–1915.* New York: International Universities Press.

Puner, H. W. (1947). *Sigmund Freud: His Life and Mind.* New York: Howell, Soskin.

Rice, A. K. (1963). *The Enterprise and Its Environment.* London: Tavistock.

Roazen, P. (1969). *Brother Animal.* New York: Knopf.

Rosensweig, S. (1992). *Freud, Jung, and Hall the Kingmaker: The Historic Expedition to America (1909).* St. Louis, MO: Rana House/Hogrefe & Huber.

Roustang, F. (1982). *Dire Mastery: Discipleship from Freud to Lacan.* Baltimore, MD: Johns Hopkins University Press.

Rustin, M. (1985). The social organization of secrets: towards a sociology of psychoanalysis. *International Review of Psycho-Analysis* 12(2):143–160.

Sachs, H. (1944). *Freud: Master and Friend.* Cambridge, MA: Harvard University Press.

Shapiro, R. L. (1979). In panel: Psychoanalytic knowledge of group process. Reporter K. T. Calder. *Journal of the American Psychoanalytic Association* 27:145–156.

Stekel, W. (1950). *The Autobiography of Wilhelm Stekel.* New York: Liveright.

Stepansky, P. E. (1983). *In Freud's Shadow: Adler in Context.* Hillsdale, NJ: Analytic Press.

Sterba, R. (1982). *Reminiscences of a Viennese Psychoanalyst.* Detroit, MI: Wayne State University Press.

Strozier, C. D. (1985). Lincoln and the crisis of the 1850's: thoughts on the group itself. In *The Leader: Psychohistorical Essays,* ed. C. D. Strozier and D. Offer, pp. 211–233. New York: Plenum.

Sulloway, F. J. (1979). *Freud, Biologist of the Mind.* New York: Basic Books.

Turquet, P. M. (1978). Leadership: the individual and the group. In *Analysis of Groups,* ed. G. S. Gibbard and J. J. Mann, pp. 349–371. San Francisco: Jossey-Bass.

Weiss, E. (1970). *Sigmund Freud as a Consultant.* London: Intercontinental Medical Books.

Wittels, F. (1924). *Sigmund Freud: His Personality, His Teaching, and His School.* New York: Dodd, Mead.

Wortis, J. (1940). Fragments of a Freudian analysis. *American Journal of Orthopsychiatry* 10(4):843–849.

Zaleznik, A. (1989). *The Managerial Mystique.* New York: Harper & Row.

Zoner, M., and Offer, D. (1985). Leaders and the Arab-Israeli conflict: a psychoanalytic interpretation. In *The Leader: Psychohistorical Essays,* ed. C. D. Strozier and D. Offer, pp. 156–179. New York: Plenum.

Zweig, S. (1932). Portrait of Freud. In *Freud as We Knew Him,* ed. H. M. Ruitenbeck, pp. 85–96. Detroit, MI: Wayne State University Press, 1973.

10

Freud's Analysis of Anna

Paul Roazen

The kinds of normal scholarly debate which characterize intellectual history as a whole have never succeeded in being welcomed within the tale of the origins of psychoanalysis. This is not just a simple-seeming matter associated with either sectarianism or trade-unionism, although both factors have for instance played their part in ensuring that as momentous a conflict in the history of ideas as that between Freud and Jung has still not been adequately surveyed. It has been as if the ideal of science led analytic practitioners to believe that entertaining a variety of perspectives on the past of the discipline would constitute a breech in the ranks of those who should be, supposedly, supporting the field by maintaining a monolithic conception of history. Pluralism is more fashionable in theory than practice, and literary critics can be doctrinaire in a way that clinicians, aware of the complexities of their work, are not.

It should come as no surprise if historians of French psychoanalysis have been unaware of the many years in which a "dissident" like Otto Rank practiced in Paris (Roazen 1991b). And an influential biography of Freud completely ignored the name of Wilhelm Reich, and therefore his role in Viennese analysis, presumably because a discussion of such a controversial figure would be disagreeably painful to have to entertain (Roazen 1990b). Although in academic life in general careers can be made by concentrating on neglected thinkers, the history of psychoanalysis is littered with instances of unconsciously suppressed conflicts.

Given the nature of the work that has failed to be done in this area, it follows that as I look back over all the possible changes that have taken place in the study of the history of analysis during the more than thirty years this subject has interested me, the polarized nature of the controversies that have succeeded in coming up continues to stand out. Even during Freud's lifetime, as a matter of fact predating the outbreak of World War I, people tended to be either passionately favorable to his work or else adamantly antagonistic. Unfortunately, people have been too easily made angry in this field, at the same time that it has continued to be simple to be original, since a little bit of tolerance goes a long way in making one open to the legitimacy of the various rival points of view which have been contesting for public allegiance.

These preliminary considerations may help explain how Freud's analysis of his youngest child went publicly unmentioned for over four decades; yet that analysis constituted such a striking ethical transgression that I am even today left bewildered about its implications. This violation of his own stated rules for the practice of technique has to leave one questioning what he intended to accomplish with his written recommendations for future analysts. I am inclined to think that Freud's behavior here, and that of Anna too, stemmed from a kind of Nietzschean conviction that the chosen few were entitled to go beyond the normal bounds of conventional distinctions between good and evil (Roazen 1991a). Freud did think of analysis as a source of new moral teachings, and out of this treatment setting he hoped to be able to evolve fresh ethical standards. If the superior few had special entitlements, then lesser beings were to be controlled by a different set of restraints. In this context, though, I am forced to recall Lord Acton's famous maxim: power corrupts, and absolute power tends to corrupt absolutely.

It is now over a quarter of a century since 1969, when I first published a paragraph about Freud's having analyzed Anna (Roazen 1969, p. 100). I had some idea ahead of time how potentially explosive this analysis was capable of being. I was revealing this information in the larger context of the story of Freud's relationship with Victor Tausk, and that reconstruction itself, including Freud's complex reaction to Tausk's suicide, was inevitably going to be controversial. I have no idea how high a professional price I paid for my stubbornness in going ahead and revealing Freud's analysis of Anna.

For a group of old loyalist analysts, this revelation about Freud and Anna was bound to seem debunking. Yet I thought I was proceeding in the spirit of Freud's own idealistic argument in his "Future of an Illusion" (1927). In that assault on traditional religious faith, Freud held out the norm of scientific knowledge and the precious enlightenment that the truth was capable of bringing. Although I never thought only one set of interpretations could be put on Freud's having analyzed Anna, it did seem to me that the reality of what had happened was worth making public.

While Anna Freud was alive, and capable of contesting anything that I wrote, there was a fallback position for her advocates and defenders. It might be the case that Freud had analyzed her, but then it was commonly said that later she had had a second analysis with Lou Andreas-Salomé. Presumably that extra therapeutic experience acted as a sort of check on what Anna had experienced with her father. Oddly enough, Anna seems to have preferred to think of herself as solely analyzed by her father, as she downplayed the significance of Andreas-Salomé in her life.

The note at the back of the book, where I first supplied the oral evidence about this then startling bit of information about Freud and Anna, was contrived, in that I was deliberately writing while she was capable of reacting to my assertion (Roazen 1969, pp. xiv–xvi). Now that I have examined the lengthy letter she wrote to Kurt R. Eissler, who was put in charge of polemically answering me about Tausk, it has to be noticeable that she did not even discuss the point about her having been analyzed by her father. Presumably Eissler already knew about it himself, since he somehow claimed in print that it was already a "well-known" fact (Roazen 1990, p. 105).

I had purposefully left some key names out of my roster of sources, on the grounds that a few of them could not withstand Anna's possible anger at their willingness to discuss such a sensitive matter with me. One of my informants, an old friend and analysand of Anna's, waited a period of many months before writing to Anna denying that she had ever talked about the subject with me; Anna's official biographer never bothered to check the truth of the matter, and instead chose in 1988 to broaden the possible allegations against me by saying that I had invented interviews with people who "insisted that they had refused to be interviewed" (Young-Bruehl 1988, p. 433).

A few years later I spent several pages (Roazen 1975) discussing the whole subject of Freud's analysis of Anna, which had still failed to make its way into the professional psychoanalytic literature. Although I had naively expected that clinicians would have a good deal to contribute in understanding this highly unusual situation, the silence continued pretty much as before. Since some misguided die-hard loyalists have mistakenly sought to give another the credit for having first put into print the news of Anna's analysis, I returned to the whole issue in another text (Roazen 1993).

Finally some public dialogue is getting going on this still sensitive matter. I hope that it proves possible to explore the implications of what went on between Freud and Anna without calling forth outraged wrath. Partisan fervor seems to lurk just below the surface of almost every aspect of the historiography of psychoanalysis. I suppose this sort of passion can be attributed to Freud's success in making analysis a powerful secular religion. But moralistic fervor will not accomplish much, other than to discredit the whole tradition of depth psychology at a time when biological psychiatry is as much in factor as before Freud wrote a psychological line. It is unfortunately the case that in the public mind as well as in the historical literature an all or nothing approach continues to prevail; and it has been hard to get people to pick and choose what deserves to survive from Freud's teachings, without either completely endorsing everything he wrote or else rejecting analysis root and branch.

Unfortunately the critics who challenged Freud in his lifetime have still by and large not been credited adequately for the blind spots in Freud's system that they accurately observed. It was always possible to be respectful of Freud without absorbing his whole outlook, and a substantial literature exists of skeptics who were willing to learn from what Freud had proposed.

Up to now, however, after all these years, I can think of only one article in the literature that concentrates on Freud's analysis of Anna; although it was written by an analyst it appeared in a book intended for a general audience concerned with the history of psychoanalysis (Mahony 1992). My own tentative explorations of the implications of what Freud and Anna cooperated in doing were conceived pretty much in a vacuum, although I did have the benefit of discussing the matter with many who had personally known both the creator of psychoanalysis and his daughter. If, as I think may have been partly the case, Freud was trying to protect Anna, aware of the damage that any other analyst could do to her, I am not proposing this hypothesis in order to gloss over the negative sides to what he did. Freud's kindliness could sometimes lead him to extend the scope of analysis too broadly; it should be our job, I think, to under-stand the mixture of motives that went into what Freud did, even if in the end we assess the analysis to have been one which had consequences which we might not want to see repeated.

I was gently warned by at least one famous analyst in New York that I ought not to publish such news, since it was bound to be "misused." Al-though fortunately I did not understand the full force of the fury which would be aroused by my making public a secret which was broadly shared among the oldest analysts, it was never my intention to stack the deck one way or another. Freud was, I believed, a great enough figure in the history of ideas to be able to take the full scrutiny of historical research.

Another Viennese analyst told me that Anna, when directly asked whether her father had indeed analyzed her, lied about it in the 1920s. There were many ways of Anna then rationalizing an evasion of the truth—either that it had not been a genuine analysis, or else that it was nobody else's business. Still a third source told me that when Anna had, within the confines of old friends, been straightforwardly asked about who her own analyst had been, her response had been silence.

It is hard to know what sorts of meanings to attribute to such reticence, and I want to refrain from undue psychologizing. But it does seem to me, as someone who has had to withstand considerable attack for bringing up a variety of what once seemed unwelcome news, that secrecy can be a powerful political weapon. For example, with certain of the early analysts, when I raised the issue of Anna's own analysis by her father, it was as if I had never said anything at all.

The truth of what had happened was a bit of commonly shared knowl-edge, even if almost all chose not to want to elaborate on it. As an out-sider, with a special interest in the history of ideas, I was immediately struck with how various figures in the history of analysis had been un-fairly stigmatized as "deviants" if not heretics for daring to propose vari-ous technical alternatives to Freud's own written recommended rules of therapeutic procedure. I want to suggest now that it seems to me that the very impropriety of such an analysis, given the standards of orthodox analysis of a generation ago, meant that all those who shared in such secret information were thereby members of a tightly knit band of true believers who felt themselves able to bear such knowledge, even if the out-side world was deemed too weak to absorb the burden of insight. I cannot offer any firsthand knowledge of what it may have seemed like to those in the 1920s who learned of the analysis then, although many I met were neither shocked nor upset about what had happened. (I have never been entirely sure, when Ernest Jones brazenly wrote Freud that Anna had been inadequately analyzed, whether Jones knew for certain who her analyst had been.) At least by the 1960s, when I was most actively pursuing the fieldwork for my research, it was such an impolitic matter to be investigating that I am tempted to think of there then existing some sort of group complicity to blot out an unwelcome aspect of the past.

It would not be surprising if the negative transferences these pioneers had toward Freud were rarely explored or interpreted. To the extent to which critical feelings were kept under wraps then, it was all the more reasonable to anticipate the worst possible consequences flowing from historical honesty. In the imaginations of the oldest analysts, Freud's stature had still to be achieved, while for those of us who took Freud's standing within intellectual history for granted, it seemed unnecessarily insecure for his followers to be worried about being sure that Freud's contribution was safely established.

To the extent that the inner circle shared in such knowledge, while the outside world remained in the dark, then such hidden complicity was a powerful weapon in explaining how they were all so intimately tied with one another. Of course what I have called trade-unionism, or a desire to protect safe therapeutic turf, ought not to be underestimated. Analysis in the 1960s was successful in worldly terms beyond the wildest expectations of Freud's early followers, even if by now the tide has turned in a different direction.

It would not have been unusual, though, for Freud's own disciples to have thought he had erred, even if some of them went on to analyze their own children. (Another explosive chapter in the history of analysis would be an examination of the tale of the relation between the early analysts and their own children.) If it was ever thought that Freud had been capable of being mistaken in having treated Anna himself, then such a belief would have inspired guilt and a desire to cover up the truth.

Defensiveness, however, can only lead historiographically to bad consequences. The best way, I believe, to honor Freud's memory is by accepting him as the daring innovator he was; of course he was capable of making mistakes, even if that has to include his analyzing Anna. (He did succeed in creating a leader who watched over the movement he had founded.) Freud was always his own person, although succeeding generations of analysts have not taken seriously enough Freud's admission that his own way of proceeding as a therapist was simply the procedure that suited him personally best.

Fraudulence arises when analysts are unwilling to accept Freud's limitations as well as their own. Consciously or not, too much idolization has been found necessary. Freud does not need to have been perfect for him to be worthy of immense admiration. Nor need everything he said, wrote, or did become sacred writ. It does appear established that he was the greatest writer among twentieth-century psychologists, and a great deal of his influence has flowed from his literary prowess. But a lot of his power also came from the impact of unanalyzed transferences, such as must have been the case with his daughter Anna.

It should not be necessary to lose hold of the possibility of identifying with Freud as a genuine original. The historical cover-ups, including the prettifications of what Freud was like, made it necessary later on to unveil the sides of Freud that an earlier generation of analysts might have thought it wise to disguise. I believe he will endure as a thinker and writer long after any particular recommendations that he might have had in mind have evaporated.

Freud was an immensely hard-working clinician, and he sought to generalize from what he encountered. With the advantages of hindsight it is possible to see all sorts of ways in which Freud might have been misguided. Perhaps the analysis of Anna was one of his larger errors, and many will argue that he should have been more cautious in how he tried to implement his insights.

It should go almost without saying that this analysis was something that Anna herself must have wanted very much. I do not think that this was a procedure that was somehow imposed on Freud's youngest child. We do not know at whose initiative the analysis started, but my best hunch would be that it was a collaborative enterprise. For both Anna as well as Freud analysis was the central ethical standard, and in that case who should she have been expected to turn to for instruction except her father?

Even if one bends over backwards in order to appreciate how this situation could have come about, there still seems something appalling about what took place. Freud had made privacy and autonomy absolutely central analytic goals, and yet with Anna he was willy-nilly compromising everything he held morally dear. He was, whether he knew it or not, intensifying her attachment to him at the same time that he said he wanted to wean her a bit from her dependence on him. Later he would be proud of her original work as a child analyst, at the same time that he worried about how she would manage after his death.

For myself it is gratifying now to have had a panel presentation about Anna's analysis at a 1995 New York University conference, and I hope that different interpretive points of view will continue to be explored as time passes. There have been occasions, especially over the last Freud-bashing decade, when I have felt a bit like the legendary sorcerer who helped unleash forces that he did not anticipate. It should be obvious that it cannot have been my intention to spend so much time on a figure that I did not regard as heroic in terms of intellectual history.

The pendulum has swing against Freud lately, in North America although by no means only there, and oddly enough he might be gratified by some of the grounds for analysis getting discarded. All along he had anticipated that it would be possible in the future to found psychology on a biochemical basis, and the striking developments that have taken place over the last years have largely been in the area of psychopharmacology. Science inevitably means that one era's point of view will be replaced by a superior subsequent orientation. The biochemistry of dreams has made so many advances that even if Freud's particular theories cannot be confirmed, I think his emphasis on the significance of dreaming has been established as legitimate. Great playwriters, novelists, and poets have long understood this, although there are some scientists now who do insist that we have succumbed to a set of illusions about dreams.

The problem continues to be the extent to which, as I said at the outset, polarities in this area have been allowed to get out of hand. And so there is a danger that the baby will go out along with the bathwater, and all the important interpersonal aspects to analytic therapy will be replaced by a strictly organic outlook.

I would argue that despite the success of the Freudian revolution in the history of ideas that has marked this past century, in some sense we are now more or less back to where Freud was at the outset of his career. There is a clinical interest in classification almost for its own sake, and reluctance to spend an adequate amount of time in getting to know patients. There must be some common-sense middle ground, so that therapeutic ambitiousness does not dominate the latest innovations. Powerful medication can alas be recommended on the basis of premature diagnoses.

My job is, however, not that of a therapist, but as a historical witness. I consciously intended that others more knowledgeable than myself would pursue the implications of the therapeutic interaction between Freud and

Anna. It has taken a remarkably long time to get this debate under way, and it may in the end not add to the luster of the myth about Freud which orthodox analysts have liked to entertain.

Thirty years ago it was not even a real temptation for me to think of concealing the truth about this analysis of Anna by her father. I do not think I calculated the full consequences of revealing what I did; although I had been warned of the dangers of doctrinal excommunication, and seen how earlier people in the history of analysis had been abused for their daring to be true to themselves, somehow I thought I could get around the worst consequences of being straightforward.

Analysis, Freud once said, requires three things—courage, courage, and courage. I wish it were not the case that honesty and integrity stir up so much discontent. The benefits of conventional success often come to those who are bent on promoting conformist values. But one of the reasons that the history of analysis has attracted so many controversies is that as a field it has drawn to itself those who are dissatisfied with knowledge as it has been bureaucratically defined.

It is still true today, for example in my own field of political science, and in particular political philosophy, that Freud has so far failed to become a secure part of the established canon. A career would be better advanced by studying Augustine, Rousseau, Marx, or Locke, than by paying attention to the works of Freud. The concept of the unconscious, no matter how it be construed, is no more widely accepted by political scientists now than it was over sixty years ago when Harold Lasswell first wrote his *Psychopathology and Politics* (Roazen 1990a, pp. 241–244).

So the old French adage still holds: the more things change, the more they stay the same. That maxim applies to much in the life of the mind. For anyone publicly to talk about Freud's analysis of Anna should not, I hope, bring down the anathemas hurled by those who think of themselves as defenders of the faith. There has been enough in the way of ideological warfare in the history of analytic doctrine.

Analysis, despite what Freud sometimes liked to argue, does entail certain moral values and ethical beliefs. Think of what it has been like to try to practice analysis under dictatorial political and social conditions. It is only possible to exclude the philosophic dimensions of analysis by virtue of cutting off the basic lifelines to all genuine clinical endeavors, and analysis is doing better elsewhere in the world wherever philosophy is studied alongside Freud's teachings. How we assess Freud's analysis of Anna is going to depend on our prior moral convictions. Even if we should conclude that Freud's treating Anna himself was wrong, and at odds with some of his own most central principles, historically and morally it is impossible to sweep this whole episode under the rug.

There are aspects to Freud which take one's breath away. I recall how that was the immediate nonverbal response I got from one of Anna Freud's own patients when I first informally let the news out about who her own analyst had been. Freud felt proud about his ability to think and utter certain shocking thoughts, something that takes us back to his identification with Nietzsche. There is no way of successfully shrinking Freud down to fit the practical needs of what we might now like the creator of psychoanalysis to have been like. He was a struggling innovator who defied preexisting categories, and it is only if we appreciate him in the round that we can begin to come to terms with some of the central aspects of the legacy he left us.

Perhaps it is possible to look on Freud's analysis of Anna from a strictly political point of view, in terms of the wielding of power. How different was this one analysis from the way other analysts have been trained? Here I am broadening the implications of Freud's treating Anna to question the possibilities of authoritarianism implicit in training analyses in general.

Sectarianism has meant that too little debate about the institution of training analysis has been allowed to take place in public. Privately, many analysts have reported being unable to tell anything like what they felt as the truth while in training, and that in hindsight it would have enriched their analyses to have been emancipated from the constraints of their formal education. The suppressions of feelings that take place in such a setting are of course all the more powerful for being unconscious at the time.

Although orthodox analysts have rarely understood the point, both Edward Glover in England and Jacques Lacan in France have long ago protested against the effects of training analyses. Outsiders warned all along that training analysis might be an act of spiritual violence. My belief is that Jung, when he first proposed before World War I that all analysts in the future be analyzed, was implicitly saying that Freud necessarily had not been able to overcome his own personal neurosis.

When in 1918 it was initially proposed as a rule that analysts undergo analyses, both Rank and Tausk opposed it, and I doubt that they would have done so without the secure inkling that Freud himself was no enthusiast for the idea. In fact it only went into effect after Freud had fallen ill of cancer of the jaw in the 1920s, after which he could no longer hope to take personal charge of the future of analysis.

It has to remain an open question whether Freud ever thought that Anna could take over as head of the psychoanalytic movement as we know she later did, or whether his analysis of her was part of any such planning on their side. And it is unclear to what extent one can suppose that she was trying to protect her father's creation by undergoing the analysis in the first place.

Now I have broadened the issue of Freud's analysis of Anna beyond anything I have ever put in print before, and I hope it will be apparent how tentative and uncertain I remain. It can only serve the "cause" Freud first started if we continue to ask all possible questions, considering nothing as too great a taboo to challenge.

REFERENCES

Freud, S. (1927). The future of an illusion. *Standard Edition* 21:3–56.

Mahony, P. (1992). Freud as a family therapist. In *Freud and the History of Psychoanalysis*, ed. T. Gelfand and J. Kerr, pp. 307–317. New York: Analytic Press.

Roazen, P. (1969). *Brother Animal: The Story of Freud and Tausk*, 2nd ed. New York: Knopf; New Brunswick, NJ: Transaction, 1990.

——— (1975). *Freud and His Followers*, pp. 436–440. New York: Knopf; New York: Da Capo, 1992.

——— (1990a). *Encountering Freud: The Politics and Histories of Psychoanalysis*. New Brunswick, NJ: Transaction.

——— (1990b). Review of Gay's *Freud: A Life for Our Time*. *Psychoanalytic Books*, January, pp. 10–17.

——— (1991a). Nietzsche and Freud: two voices from the underground. *Psychohistory Review*, Spring, pp. 327–349.

——— (1991b). Review of Roudinesco's *Jacques Lacan & Co. Virginia Quarterly Review*, pp. 780–784, Autumn.

——— (1993). *Meeting Freud's Family*, pp. 105–118. Amherst, MA: University of Massachusetts Press.

Young-Bruehl, E. (1988). *Anna Freud: A Biography*. New York: Summit.

11

Death by Silence (*Todschweigen*): The Traditional Method of Silencing the Dissident in Psychoanalysis

Arnold William Rachman

TODSCHWEIGEN: DEATH BY SILENCE

There is a phenomenon prevalent in traditional psychoanalysis that can be called *Todschweigen*, death by silence [from the German: *Sie haben ihn todgeschweigen*. They silenced him into death] (Rachman et al. 1997). The process involves the analytic establishment deciding to remove a dissident's work from study and not referring to him or her in discussions. Esther Menaker reported the result of Ferenczi's *todschweigen* while she was a candidate at the Vienna Psychoanalytic Institute in the 1930s. During a seminar in 1933, with Helena Deutsch, Ferenczi's death was announced. Menaker reported a silence which hung so thick in the air that it seemed to say, "Ferenczi is someone of whom we do not speak" (Rachman 1997a).

The most relevant consideration regarding the mental health of psychoanalysis is the climate for dissidence, within what is considered the mainstream of analytic thought and practice. Dissidence within the pioneering circle of psychoanalysis was considered undesirable. In fact, the secret circle was founded not only to surround Freud with support, but to act as a form of suppression and censorship of any deviant ideas by the members of the circle as well as the greater analytic community (Grosskurth 1991). This negative attitude toward dissidence had been established from the earliest days of psychoanalysis, when Freud, and those who would sacrifice their independence (including Ferenczi) to maintain their loyalty to him, excommunicated dissidents such as Adler, Jung, and Rank. (The irony is that Ferenczi participated in Jung's and Rank's excommunications before he suffered the same fate [Rachman 1997a,b].) Ferenczi was an example of someone, for all his creative insight, who needed Freud's approval so intensely that he could not show his dissidence openly (Thompson 1964) or became a "company man" (Fromm 1959), and finally found his own voice during his last clinical period (Rachman 1997a, 1998) expressed in a secret diary (Ferenczi 1932). In reviewing the literature on this event I found a decided absence of resentment or outrage both when the suppression and censorship occurred and in subsequent reviews.

If one examines the relational dimension of *todschweigen*, we can see how detrimental silence can be in any significant interpersonal interaction, especially in experience of the family, education, or religious institutions. Clinical experience indicates the deleterious effects parental silence can have on child development. In one such instance, a controlling and dominating mother who demanded obedience regularly practiced *todschweigen*. The mother would not speak to her child for periods of a week or more, in retaliation for the child's exertion of her own will or "dissident" voice (nonapproved parental behavior). The mother would not relent. As an adult this individual, whose "dissidence" (exhibiting a different view that the mother) was treated by deadly silence, felt profoundly rejected and alienated from her family. She felt her mother hated her and wanted to abandon her. In a sense she never recovered from her *todschweigen* experience. This example offers a parallel to the impact of *todschweigen* on organized psychoanalysis.

Todschweigen in Institute Training

My own experiences as a candidate in an analytic training institute, during the late 1960s–1970s, reflect what, I believe, was wrong with analytic training, and psychoanalysis. In another paper I have outlined fifteen incidents that have remained vivid in my thinking and feeling over twenty-five years later, which reflect the problems that psychoanalysis faced then and now (Rachman 1997c). I have recently chronicled my difficulties in being an analytic candidate (Rachman 1998), emphasizing my struggle to retain a humanistic perspective in a conservative analytic setting. I believe silence is so integrated into the theory and method of traditional psychoanalysis that *todschweigen* is actually a natural outgrowth. The deprivation paradigm of classical analysis, where visual, verbal, and emotional responsiveness is reduced to a minimum by design, supports silence and withholding as appropriate and valued ways of being.

One such experience was my attempt to gain supervision for a very difficult case. I had complained to a senior faculty member, training analyst and department head, whom I respected, about an analysand with whom I was very frustrated because her diagnosed passive-aggressive personality was thwarting my effort to analyze her. She recommended that I deliberately remain silent as a response to my analysand's "attempts to manipulate me." I thought I should bow to the expertise of a senior analyst I respected even though I felt that deliberately withholding a response was manipulative and antitherapeutic. I did try the silent technique but it only exacerbated the analysand's difficulty in responding and so I changed my tack. Rather than be silent, I intuitively practiced what I would now call "active empathy" (Rachman 1996). In reality, I became more engaged in the analytic encounter, while explaining that my more assertive attempts to reach her were not because I was angry. She was very responsive to my assertive, yet empathic approach. From then on the analysis proceeded in a very successful way although I was left feeling this was a success achieved through opposition to received wisdom.

Two other events left a lasting impression on me indicating the institute's view of dissidence or any non-approved frame of reference:

"Carl Rogers never discovered anything, did not contribute to the field of psychotherapy. In fact, he stole from others and never gave them credit."

I will never forget these words from a senior faculty member, department head, training and supervising analyst, and someone intimately connected to the founder of the institute. I cite this individual's formal and informal status because it would suggest a well-informed, thoughtful, and intelligent assessment of contributors to the field of psychotherapy. Her bias was so deeply seated that it blinded her to a valid assessment. This is not the kind of intellectual atmosphere that should be part of a training institute. This analyst clearly set a tone, one reenforced by another negative experience: the institute would only endorse certain ideas by individuals who were designated "mainstream" by the analytic establishment.

When I graduated from the institute and investigated other perspectives to psychoanalysis, first the interpersonal/humanistic, then the object relations, and recently the self psychology perspectives, I saw that these orientations were significantly more receptive to a diversity of psychodynamic approaches as well as integrating nonanalytic ideas and methods.

"If you believe in Erich Fromm's work you are in the wrong church and wrong pew." During an orientation meeting, on the first day of my training at the institute, the dean of training made a point of emphasizing the phrase cited above to drive home the point that we were being trained in the Freudian view of psychoanalysis. What is more, if any of us candidates felt that a dissident viewpoint like Fromm's was meaningful, then we should terminate our training right then and there. Coming from the liberal and democratic atmosphere of the University of Chicago, I was shocked to hear an institution of higher learning openly challenge academic freedom. I had read Fromm's work in graduate school and found it stimulating and was looking forward to studying its clinical application.

When I rediscovered Fromm's work, during the investigation of Ferenczi's unacknowledged contributions, I realized that Fromm was a courageous champion of dissidence—and of Ferenczi (Fromm 1959), especially, during a period when almost no one in the analytic community cited his work (Rachman 1997a). During these investigations into the history of psychoanalysis, it became clear that Fromm became a persona non grata because he dared to criticize Freud's ideas, clinical functioning and, worst of all, his personal functioning.

A third experience of deadly silence occurred when a distinguished and revered faculty member decided to experiment in an experimental course on group psychotherapy. Rather than respond to overwhelming requests for a demonstration of his unique approach to clinical interaction, he decided to remain silent during the sessions of the training course. A dramatic event occurred midway through this "silent treatment." The class became increasingly frustrated, angry, and confused. Finally, they plotted a revenge, and locked the faculty member out of the class (Rachman and Wolf 1986). In this educational experience, *todschweigen* was not consciously intended to be a negative response to a dissident viewpoint, but the faculty member's continued silence, after the class lockout, suggested that he was involved in a countertransference reaction, punishing the class by not acknowledging its protest.

I believe *todschweigen* is woven into the fabric of this psychoanalytic institute because its founder and the "keeper of the keys" who succeeded

him did not value democracy and dissidence as much as they did perpetuating "a movement" and encouraging conformity (Fromm 1959). In the
training program of this particular analytic training institute, silence was
actually a part of the philosophy. Witness the rationale of such training:

> The . . . instructor took the attitude that he would be himself at all times,
> that is, would give or refuse as he determined. His position was based on
> the observation of Freud, further developed by Hartmann, Kris and
> Loewenstein, that the ego comes into being and matures as a sense of self
> as a result of the experience of frustration by the object which comes to be
> perceived as having separate existence outside the self. [Markowitz et al.
> 1965, p. 221]

The rationale was used to initiate an "ongoing experimental approach"
to training where silence was deliberately used (Markowitz et al. 1965,
Schwartz and Rabin 1968). I remember one of these faculty members registering his surprise that the analytic candidates tolerated such "experiments." In fact, he was shocked that only one candidate left such a training session when he decided to respond to what was said only with incest
interpretations (Schwartz and Rabin 1968). What was more shocking to
me was that at least two senior psychoanalysts found it acceptable to
manipulate and control analytic candidates by silence and incest interpretations and did not understand they were being emotionally abusive.
Clearly, they did not comprehend the "Confusion of Tongues" paradigm
(Ferenczi 1933) where an authority figure can emotionally seduce a
subordinate into tolerating an abusive situation by virtue of the power,
control, and status they possess over a candidate's training, professional
life, and career. Of course, Ferenczi's genius for explicating the inherent
opportunity for retraumatization in the psychoanalytic situation was unknown to these senior analysts, since they continued the *todschweigen*
practice, insuring that no dissident viewpoint, whether from Ferenczi,
Fromm, or Rogers, was taught at the institute (Rachman 1997a).

PSYCHOANALYSIS'S DARKEST HOUR:
THE SUPPRESSION OF SÁNDOR FERENCZI

Psychoanalysis shot itself in its heart and soul when it suppressed and
censored Ferenczi's ideas and techniques. In my opinion, the decline of
psychoanalysis can be traced to the campaign Freud and the conservative

members of his inner circle (Abraham, Eitingon, Jones, Sachs) launched to suppress Ferenczi's ideas and techniques.

Clearly, the removal of Ferenczi's ideas and methods from mainstream psychoanalysis, particularly his relaxation therapy (Ferenczi 1930) and the theory of childhood trauma caused by sexual seduction (Ferenczi 1933), left a theoretical and clinical void. His ideas were not viewed as having sufficient merit for serious psychoanalytic thinkers. The process of censorship was so complete that, up until the 1970s, Ferenczi's work was not formally studied at any International Psychoanalytic Association approved psychoanalytic training institute in North America. He was only briefly mentioned, if at all, at dissident institutes, such as William Alanson White (Ortmeyer 1992). The founder of the institute I attended was an analysand of Clara Thompson, a Ferenczi analysand. He was considered a modern pioneer in the active method of psychoanalysis and was considered to be flexible, innovative, and daring. Yet, in all my training, which took place from 1964 to 1968, whether it was course work, supervision, special lectures, or seminars by invited scholars and personal analysis, Ferenczi's name was never spoken, nor did it ever appear on a reading list. I was able to rectify this oversight when I taught the first course on Ferenczi's work at this same institute in 1989 (Rachman 1997a, 1998).

The practice of *todschweigen* was best exemplified by Freud and the orthodox analytic community which surrounded him in the suppression and censorship of Ferenczi's last formal presentation, the "Confusion of Tongues" paper (Ferenczi 1933). I have attempted to chronicle the actual acts of suppression in order to understand the practice of *todschweigen* as a traditional method for dealing with dissidence (Rachman 1989, 1993, 1994, 1997a,b, Rachman and Mattick 1997). The suppression of the Confusion of Tongues paper was actually the most dramatic act of *todschweigen*, but there were a series of acts both before and after the Confusion of Tongues trauma as well (Balint 1968, Rachman 1997a,b).

There were many events in the Freud/Ferenczi relationship that caused great emotional difficulty for Ferenczi (Rachman 1997a,b). But the most emotionally damaging experience was the practice of *Todschweigen* by Freud in reaction to Ferenczi's Confusion of Tongues paper. As a member of Freud's secret circle, it was Ferenczi's mandate to gain approval for his papers from the Master. Ferenczi, however, also needed Freud's approval for his self-esteem, an unfortunate personal difficulty.

First, Freud attempted to extract a promise from Ferenczi that he would not present the Confusion of Tongues paper (Rachman 1997a). On August 29, 1932, Freud sent a letter to a conservative member of the secret circle, Eitingon. Before Ferenczi read the contents of the Confusion of Tongues paper, Freud was prepared to censor it.

He must be prevented from reading his essay [on the Confusion of Tongues]. *Either he will present another one, or not at all.* . . . Our behavior will depend first on his acceptance of the cancellation [of the reading of his paper] and then the impression you all have of him in Wiesbaden. [Sylwan 1984, p. 108, translated from the French by S. Teicher and A. W. Rachman, italics added]

On a fateful day in September of 1932, three days before the 12th International Psychoanalytic Congress in Wiesbaden, Ferenczi gathered his courage and went to Freud in Vienna to read his paper. It was a meeting filled with anxiety, disturbance, and interpersonal conflict for both Freud and Ferenczi. Ferenczi was devastated by Freud's very negative and abusive reaction to him. The details of this experience were told to his student and analysand, Izette De Forest, who in turn conveyed it, in detail, to Eric Fromm over twenty years after it occurred:

I [Ferenczi] told him of my latest technical ideas . . . I have tried to discover . . . my patients' . . . desires and longings, the manner in which they suffered rejection at the hands of their mothers or their parents or surrogates. And I have also endeavored through empathy to imagine what kind of loving care . . . the patient really needed at that early age—a loving care and nurture which would have allowed his self-confidence, his self-enjoyment to develop wholesomely. . . . It is possible to sense when I am on the right track, for the patient immediately unconsciously gives the signal by a number of slight changes in mood and behavior. Even his dreams show a response to the new and beneficial treatment. All this should be confided to the patient—the analyst's new understanding of his needs, his ensuing change of relationship to the patient and his expression of this, and the patient's own evident response. Whenever mistakes are made by the analyst, the patient again gives the signal by becoming angry or despondent. And this can be elicited from the patient and explained to him. It must be absolutely honest and genuine. [Fromm 1959, pp. 63–64]

Ferenczi presented in this conversation a remarkably clear and compelling overview of the empirical evidence he gathered in his clinical work with "difficult cases" and the relaxation therapy he developed to work analytically with individuals traumatized by sexual, physical, and emotional abuse. He was, of course, talking to Freud about his Confusion of Tongues paper, trying to convince the Professor to approve his ideas and humanistic method and rescind his prohibition against Ferenczi delivering the material at the upcoming 12th International Psychoanalytic Congress. This conversation was in August, prior to that tragic meeting when Ferenczi would be ridiculed by the analytic community for his prophetic views on the relationship between childhood sexual abuse and the development of psychological disorder.

Ferenczi finished his exposition of that last fateful meeting with Freud by telling De Forest the Professor's reaction to the Confusion of Tongues material:

> The Professor listened to my exposition with increasing impatience and finally warned me that I was treading on dangerous ground and was departing fundamentally from the traditional customs and techniques of psychoanalysis. Such yielding to the patient's longings and desires—no matter how genuine—would increase his dependence on the analyst. Such dependence can only be destroyed by the emotional withdrawal of the analyst. In the hands of unskilled analysts, my method, the Professor said, might easily lead to sexual indulgence rather than an expression of parental devotion. *This warning ended the interview. I held out my hand in affectionate adieu. The Professor turned his back on me and walked out of the room.* [Fromm 1959, pp. 64–65, n3, italics added]

Ferenczi, I believe, never recovered from this silent treatment. He died about a year later—physically of pernicious anemia, emotionally of a broken heart.

THE FERENCZI RENAISSANCE

Part of my mission in the Ferenczi renaissance has been to set the record straight regarding Ferenczi (Rachman 1989, 1993, 1994, 1995, 1997b). Ferenczi's suppression and censorship was the darkest hour in the history of psychoanalysis, because the most clinically creative, daring, and innovative individual was politically assassinated, his work deliberately removed from the mainstream, with no significant protest launched by anyone, including his own students. No outrage was forthcoming, either then or now, regarding the practice of *todschweigen*. Ferenczi's fall from analytic grace (Rachman 1997a,b, 1998) became the standard punishment of dissidence for generations to come. Balint (1968) felt the suppression and censorship of Ferenczi's work produced a trauma for the analytic community that did not allow, over twenty-five years after Ferenczi's death, the British middle group (the object relations orientation) to feel part of mainstream psychoanalysis because they focused their work on the more difficult cases and therapeutic regression. Balint was discussing not only his work, but that of other members of the British middle group, such as Guntrip, Khan, Little, Winnicott, and others, who can be seen as continuing to work clinically in the tradition of Ferenczi. And as if alienation from the mainstream were not enough of a punishment for clinicians who dared to believe in the concept of a therapeutic regression, rumors apparently circulated that Ferenczi and Winnicott were homosexuals because they emphasized the tender aspects of the maternal transference (Roazen 1990).

"MAINSTREAM PSYCHOANALYSIS": THE MODERN FORM OF *TODSCHWEIGEN*

There are some indications that traditional psychoanalysis is making changes that could make a positive difference in our field. Otto Kernberg, president-elect of the International Psycho-Analytic Association, recently wrote an article aimed at acknowledging the way the traditional analytic community destroys creativity in analytic candidates (Kernberg 1996). Kernberg (1996) referred to thirty features characteristic of traditional psychoanalytic institutes which need attention by the analytic community. Among these inhibitors of creativity are "repetitive and unquestioning teaching of key papers by Freud: monolithic tendencies regarding theoretical approaches: . . . neglect of studies of controversies regarding psychoanalytic technique. . . ." (p. 1031).

As welcome as I find Kernberg's reflections that traditional psychoanalysis needs to admit and change its functioning to encourage enhanced functioning of candidates, he still reflects tradition. In a recent paper, advertised as an attempt to integrate contemporary approaches with tradition, he re-evoked the designation of "mainstream psychoanalysis" as being synonymous with what is acceptable and appropriate from the traditional perspective. By implication, the other contemporary developments he discussed, for example, post-Kohutian self psychology or the relational perspective, were not given the seal of approval, and were considered out of the so-called mainstream (Kernberg 1997).

Alternative viewpoints are emerging. To this end I have begun a Sándor Ferenczi Institute to celebrate the life and work of one of psychoanalysis's greatest dissidents and creative spirits. By gathering together analysts who respect dissent, diversity, and innovation, we will attempt to keep alive Ferenczi's significant contributions to psychoanalysis, contributions that have influenced all the contemporary non-Freudian perspectives, and rekindle interest in other pioneers, like Adler, Groddeck, and Rank, whose work has been forgotten and assigned to the designation "not psychoanalysis."

THE NEW PSYCHOANALYSIS

There are several areas that would indicate there are signs of health in psychoanalysis, such as the Ferenczi renaissance (Rachman 1996, 1997a) which attempts to return Ferenczi's neglected ideas and work to mainstream psychoanalysis; the growing popularity of other dissident frameworks, such as object relations and self psychology; the reevaluation of the significant contribution made by dissidents who were removed from psychoanalysis, such as Adler (Stepansky 1983), Jung (Roazen 1975), Rank (Kramer 1996, Lieberman 1985, Menaker 1982); the appearance of revisionist histories of psychoanalysis (Grosskurth 1991, Masson 1984, Roazen 1975); the recognition of the analysand's contribution to the understanding of the analytic relationship and process (Aron 1992, Harris and Ragen 1992, Rachman 1997a); the growing acceptance of the reality of actual sexual molestation as a contribution to psychological disorders (Herman 1981, 1992, Masson 1984, Miller 1984, 1991); and, very importantly, self-criticism from within the psychoanalytic establishment (Kernberg 1996).

REFERENCES

Aron, L. (1992). From Ferenczi to Searles and contemporary relational approaches. *Psychoanalytic Dialogues* 2:181–190.
Balint, M. (1968). *The Basic Fault: Therapeutic Aspects of Regression*. London: Tavistock.
Ferenczi, S. (1930). The principle of relaxation and neo-catharsis. In *Final Contributions to the Problems and Methods of Psycho-Analysis, Vol. 3*, ed. M. Balint, pp. 108–125. New York: Brunner/Mazel, 1980.

———— (1932). *The Clinical Diary of Sándor Ferenczi: January–October 1932*, ed. J. Dupont, trans., M. Balint and N. Z. Jackson. Cambridge, MA: Harvard University Press, 1988.

———— (1933). The confusion of tongues between adults and children: the language of tenderness and passion. In *Final Contributions to the Problems and Methods of Psycho-Analysis, Vol. 3*, ed. M. Balint, pp. 156–167. New York: Brunner/Mazel, 1980.

Fromm, E. (1959). *Sigmund Freud's Mission.* New York: Harper & Row.

Grosskurth, P. (1991). *The Secret Ring: Freud's Inner Circle and the Politics of Psychoanalysis.* New York: Addison-Wesley.

Harris, A., and Ragen, T. (1992). Mutual analysis in supervision. Presentation at the Division of Psychoanalysis. *American Psychological Association Conference* Philadelphia, April.

Herman, J. L. (1981). *Father–Daughter Incest.* Cambridge, MA: Harvard University Press.

———— (1992). *Trauma and Recovery.* New York: Basic Books.

Kernberg, O. (1996). Thirty methods to destroy the creativity of psychoanalytic candidates. *International Journal of Psycho-Analysis* 77:1031–1040.

———— (1997). *Karen Horney memorial lecture.* Karen Horney Institute and Clinic, New York, February.

Kramer, R., ed. (1996). *Otto Rank—A Psychology of Difference: The American Lectures.* Princeton, NJ: Princeton University Press.

Lieberman, E. J. (1985). *Acts of Will: The Life and Work of Otto Rank.* New York: Free Press.

Markowitz, M., Schwartz, E. K., and Liff, Z. (1965). Nondidactic methods of group psychotherapy training based on frustration experience. *International Journal of Group Psychotherapy* 15:220–227.

Masson, J. M. (1984). *The Assault on Truth: Freud's Suppression of the Seduction Theory.* New York: Farrar, Straus & Giroux.

Menaker, E. (1982). *Otto Rank: A Rediscovered Legacy.* New York: Columbia University Press.

Miller, A. (1984). *For Your Own Good: Hidden Cruelty in Child-Bearing and the Roots of Violence.* New York: Farrar, Straus & Giroux.

———— (1991). *Breaking Down the Wall of Silence.* New York: Dutton.

Ortmeyer, D. (1992). Discussion. Sándor Ferenczi Symposium, American Psychological Association Conference, Philadelphia, April.

Rachman, A. W. (1989). The confusion of tongues: the Ferenczian metaphor for childhood seduction and emotional trauma. *Journal of the American Academy of Psychoanalysis* 17(2):182–205.

———— (1993). Ferenczi and sexuality. In *The Theoretical and Clinical Contributions of Sándor Ferenczi*, ed. L. Aron and A. Harris, pp. 81–100. Hillsdale, NJ: Analytic Press.

———— (1994). The confusion of tongues theory: Ferenczi's legacy of psycho-analysis. In *100 Years of Psychoanalysis*, eds. A. Haynal and E. Falzeder, pp. 235–255. London: Karmac.

———— (1995). Theoretical issues in the treatment of childhood sexual trauma in spinal cord injured patients: the confusion of tongues theory of childhood seduction. *SCI Psychosocial Process* 8(1):20–25.

———— (1996). *A contemporary clinical model for the Budapest School of Psychoanalysis and Psychotherapy*. Grand Rapids Seminar. Grand Rapids, MI, November 16.

———— (1997a). *Sándor Ferenczi: The Psychotherapist of Tenderness and Passion*. Northvale, NJ: Jason Aronson.

———— (1997b). The suppression and censorship of Ferenczi's confusion of tongues paper. *Psychoanalytic Inquiry* 17(4):459–485.

———— (1997c). *The view from the couch: the contributions of patients, the theory and method of psychotherapy and psychoanalysis*. Unpublished.

———— (1998). *Psychotherapy of "difficult cases."* Unpublished.

Rachman, A. W., and Mattick, P. (1997). *The confusion of tongues: dynamics of power, control and status in human relations*. Unpublished.

Rachman, A. W., and Wolf, A. (1986). *An experimental group experience with a silent group leader*. American Group Psychotherapy Association Conference, New York, February.

Rachman, A. W., Menaker, E., and Roazen, P. (1997). *Freud's Analysis of His Daughter Anna*. In preparation.

Roazen, P. (1975). *Freud and His Followers*. New York: Knopf.

———— (1990). *The history of the psychoanalytic movement*. Symposium on Jung, Freud, Ferenczi, Sullivan: their relationship and their contributions. Jungian Institute, New York City, January 28.

Schwartz, E. K., and Rabin, H. M. (1968). A training group with one non-verbal co-leader. *Journal of Psychoanalysis In Groups* 2(2):35–40.

Stepansky, P. E. (1983). *In Freud's Shadow: Adler in Context*. Hillsdale, NJ: Analytic Press.

Sylwan, B. (1984). An untoward event: où la guerre du trauma de Breuer à Freud de Jones à Ferenczi. *Cahiers Confrontation* 12:101–122.

Thompson, C. (1964). Sándor Ferenczi, 1873–1933. *Contemporary Psychoanalysis* 24(2):182–195, 1988.

12
Beyond Prometheus: A Reevaluation of Psychoanalytic Pedagogy and Morality

Claude Barbre

> Progress is never simple and unidirectional—the previously
> established order, the old morality, the prior sytem of values
> being overcome are not only waning, but simultaneously
> waxing, channeling their influence into covert but silently
> effective activities, and feeling threatened, pursuing their aims
> with intensified exertions.
>
> —Heinz Kohut

In Greek mythology, it was the destiny of Prometheus, the resistance hero, to rescue humanity from ignorance by deceiving the heavenly gods and proclaiming the spirit of human progress. To speak of a Promethean spirit, then, is to acknowledge the creative power, the fire in human striving which revolts against static tyrannies of any kind, exulting in the fullness of life. Resonant with a Promethean defiance, Sigmund Freud's epitaph to the *Interpretation of Dreams* (1900), taken from the seventh book of Virgil's *Aeneid,* proclaimed his creative intent: *Flectere si nequeo Superos, Acheronta movebo* ("If I cannot bend the higher powers, I will move the infernal regions"). His volition would prove prescient (indeed, Prometheus means "forethought"), for his book on dreams, as Peter Gay (1988) writes, "was going to leave the higher powers of Vienna unmoved, the unimaginative professors who had called his ideas a fairy tale, the bigoted bureaucrats who would not give him his professorship, were not likely to be converted to his views. No matter: he would raise the powers of hell against them" (p. 105). The Promethean Freud would aspire to teach humanity ways to contain and use the fires of self-knowledge, thereby saving civilization from its own destruction and darkness.

As Freud developed his revolutionary ideas into more conservative notions of "the psychoanalytic cause," however, he would gradually stray from the Promethean character. A good example of Freud's resistance to changing ideas is clear in a 1930 meeting where he objects to Otto Rank's writing on creative will (Sterba 1982) calling him a "con man" and "a low type of fraudulence":

> He uses the theory of relativity, the quantum theory, and the principle of indeterminism to express doubts about psychic causality, so that there is nothing left except soul and free will. But psychoanalysis cannot possibly be an illusion [here Freud was obviously referring to the principle of determinism in our science]. *The new discoveries might be bewildering to physicists, but psychology has always suffered when the standpoints of other sciences are applied to it.... Leave psychology finally in peace; leave psychology to the psychologists.* [p. 116, italics added]

By attacking Rank for introducing "new discoveries" in science which question the principles of psychic causality, debunking quantum theory and further understandings of the nature of life, Freud betrays a refusal to reexamine his own pedagogy and suffer the inevitable realities of change. Rank, whose name appeared on the title page of the *Interpretation of Dreams* (a book he had helped Freud to revise, word by word, for every edition since 1911), now became the Promethean "trickster" defying the higher powers of psychoanalysis. In fact, with Freud's remarkable statement that psychology should be "left alone, left in peace" from the impingements of other forms of knowledge, he unwittingly sounds a death-dealing inference, almost as if he is saying that for psychologists a separate peace is preferable to the influx of discoveries and new world views. Rank would criticize Freud's gradually more recalcitrant stances with respect to cultural and individual initiatives, indeed playing Prometheus to his mentor turned Zeus, most notably in his observations that psychoanalysis needed to reclaim the spirit of the early Freud by challenging the intractability of existing pedagogies. Rank believed that to leave psychoanalysis "in peace" was to leave it to die, and that such a death would be brought about not only by new discoveries and novel interventions, but also by its practitioners' identification with the founder of psychoanalysis who would not move beyond his own teachings. Rank believed that psychoanalytic ideas must change, and that Freud's later refusal to reappraise aspects of his "science" imperiled the spirit of inquiry that had informed their past collaborations. We would do well to reexamine Rank's explorations and criticism of psychoanalytic pedagogy, for they continue to address present-day concerns that refuse to leave psychoanalysis in peace, that argue for an evolving spirit and the fire of creative striving. Indeed, any discussion about the life and death of psychoanalysis must recall that while the search for knowledge can lead us to important values that may contain abiding validities, their positions may also change in response to the developing psychological and sociocultural milieus in which we live (Kohut 1984, pp. 49–64).

Speaking to one of her trainees in the 1930s, Anna Freud told the story of her first child-patient, a 7-year-old boy. As she met the child at the door, she directed him to take his place on the couch and say whatever came to his mind. The child reclined dutifully, but said nothing. Following the therapeutic procedure of her father's method, Anna sat and waited. The child squirmed and fidgeted, but remained quiet, looking around the room. After a while, there came a sound outside, a rustling of packages and paper. The boy looked at the door. "What does that sound make you think of?" Anna asked. The boy replied, "They are wrapping something to take to the pawn shop." Another long pause. Anna asked him to associate to the pawn shop image, but the boy fell silent again, and the session soon came to a close (Menaker, personal communication).[1]

Anna Freud's recounting of the story was not so much to highlight the terrible depression in Austria at the time, nor was it offered as an example of how therapeutic methods had greatly shifted to accommodate more nuanced interactions with children by less formal techniques of analysis. Rather, for the most part, Anna Freud told the story simply as an example of the early history of child analysis and how it started. Even so, such a

---

1. This story, conveyed to me by Esther Menaker, was recounted by Anna Freud to the trainees of the Child Therapy Seminar, Vienna, 1932. For further accounts of Dr. Menaker's training in Vienna, see Menaker 1995.

story underscores the important fact that experience can teach us a great deal about the need for change, be it in the context of therapeutic viability or the powerful dynamic of cultural influences. We must remember that Anna Freud would later say, "You can't do child analysis unless you sit on the floor!"—quite a shift from her initial therapeutic stance where the clinical relationship, following what is now termed the "classical technique," was more experience-distant and often overly interpretive.

Anna Freud's interaction with her first child-patient illustrates well the struggles inherent in the pioneering work of the psychoanalytic founding practitioners as they searched for ways to relieve the mental suffering of their clients. It also illustrates the extent to which the history of psychoanalysis conveys an ever-changing frame of reference, as evidenced by today's increasing reevaluation of how cultural and historical influences can determine theoretical formations in regard to what constitutes the "self" in particular, and therapy overall. For example, the application of hermeneutics and social constructionism to the practice of psychotherapy has accentuated a greater awareness of the sociohistorical contexts that affect both psychological theories and the therapeutic relationship by heightening our awareness of how we construct the world the way we do. However, by historically situating the therapeutic setting, the result does not necessarily preclude, as Philip Cushman (1997) suggests, "our making use of roles, power relations, or authority hierarchies, such as the asymmetry of the therapist–patient relation. It simply helps the therapist to be more conscious of them, and more mindful of their potential influences" (p. 291). The necessity of such "mindfulness" in regard to shifting power dynamics remains today as important as the moment Anna Freud moved from behind the couch to the play space of the open floor.

In a recent study, Theo L. Dorpat (1997) notes that from Freud to our present time—despite the variety of psychotherapy theories and changing interventions and methods—psychoanalytic treatment "has often been compromised by a set of controlling attitudes and indoctrination methods contrary to its avowed values and technical precepts" (p. xiii). These attitudes and methods, when institutionalized and sanctioned, continue to pose significant dangers to the viability of psychoanalytic inquiry. Since changes in psychoanalytic theory and therapy clearly constitute an experience of separation from the protection and safety of established beliefs—a death, if you will—then the possibilities of transformation and growth into new forms of thinking may be curtailed when groups unite against the threat of loss by positing their ideologies deeper in accustomed systems of procedure and preferred conceptualizations. Such entrenchments reveal how cultural and historical changes can be experienced by psychoanalytic groups as potentially "murderous" or annihilating. Hence, the survival of psychoanalysis as a profession may appear to become contingent on resisting change as a way of alleviating a tandem death-anxiety. At the same time, when psychoanalytic groups disparage the inevitability of theoretical and practical evolution, they risk estrangement from the cultures that might benefit from their more successful legacies of care. William Blake's warning remains relevant as ever: "Still water breeds poison."

In the event of changing times, as psychoanalytic practitioners ponder the future of their profession, many look to contemporary wisdom for guidance and revelation. In the history of psychoanalysis, however, Otto Rank's writing speaks vividly to our age in its farsighted focus on how the powerful influences of separation and change on individual and group ideologies, most notably reflected in pedagogical attitudes, affect the growth and development of new world views. In fact, Dorpat's current (1997) insights concerning his belief that psychoanalytic theories and therapies continue to reveal intransigent methods of indoctrination in the face of changing value systems, have a dramatic antecedent in Rank's evaluation of Freud's moral and pedagogical perspectives. We would do well to recall such assessments, for they remain germane to any discussion of psychoanalytic traditions in transition. As Rank (1928) observed, as if conveying Dorpat's recent thesis, psychology adopts a particular attitude toward the development of humanity, for "it is purely individualistic, aims at knowledge of I, of the internal, but also uses in its material data concerning the external—reality, Thou. Thus it is in essence a science of relations (*Beziehungswissenschaft*) which easily runs into the danger of overestimating either one or the other factor, instead of dealing with the relationship between the two" (Kramer 1996, p. 235). Indeed, Rank's thinking on the social self anticipated the moving horizons of psychoanalytic history. In short, Rank's objection to Freud's tendency to instruct the analysand—a method Anna Freud (1932) would later call "practicing psychology" (*Psychologie treiben*), where the analyst must explain analysis to his or her clients and teach them about what the mind is *before* the treatment can be addressed in a personal sense—anticipates by seventy years current expositions concerning the status of psychoanalytic pedagogy and its positive and negative effects on the therapeutic relationship.

Dorpat (1997) might have been quoting Rank when he surmises that in Freud, *as with many other analysts following him,* "there developed a vertical split in the ego in which one complex of conscious attitudes upholding values of freedom, autonomy, and self-determination was separated by the defense of disavowal from a largely unconscious complex of controlling and authoritarian attitudes contradictory to his consciously avowed values" (p. xix). Such a split, he thinks, often remains unbridged today in psychoanalytic work, and continues to polarize the value of interpretative interventions from an overarching and underlying tendency toward "stereotyped approaches" where the analyst manipulates a client into compliance with his or her clinical theories, usually in the form of the analyst's initial formulation about the patient (Peterfreund 1989). Approaches such as these become covert methods of interpersonal control where the client's self-determination is co-opted and undermined. Dorpat warns of the widening of this split as contemporary practitioners "increasingly become *engineers of the soul,* what with the impressive and powerful array of biological, social, and psychological modalities they have available for manipulating the minds as well as the brains of their patients" (Dorpat 1997, p. xv, italics added). With such power comes a greater possibility of the abuse of power, and the viability of psychoanalytic evolution depends not only on the recognition and elimination as much as possible of the more egregious manipulations of human beings, but on discerning hidden dynamics of ideological indoctrinations. As well.

Nancy Schnog's words (Pfister and Schnog 1997) act an as introduction to Rank's *precursory* observations. We must:

> *Develop the concerns of these earlier critics* by focusing on the power of the psychological profession to naturalize oppressive standards of social adjustment, to perpetuate social inequities, to legitimate dangerously personalized visions of pain, and to speak, for better or worse, to widespread needs for self-disclosure and solace. [p. xiii, italics added]

Indeed, Rank's earlier criticizing of scientific determinism, and his challenge to the psychoanalytic moral and ethical worldview of his time remain apposite as ever, especially when we are reminded, as the work of Dorpat and Schnog conveys, that although the emphasis has shifted in the current panoply of therapeutic practice, and present-day theories may no longer be ostensibly Freudian, nevertheless they have descended from the founder of psychoanalysis. Lawrence Josephs (1994) underscores this point by noting that many analysts and training analysts today are indoctrinated into what Karen Horney called "the tyranny of the shoulds," pedagogical rules that prescribe the ideal practice of psychoanalysis:

The preconceptions are often along the lines of such ideas as: One should never answer a patient's questions; one should answer a question with a question. One should never reveal any personal information about oneself; one should never tell the patient what to do. One should never give one's opinion; one should not talk too much. One should not share feelings. One should never take things at face value and always look for deeper meanings. One should not direct or focus a patient's associations. One should always be empathic, but should never shy away from difficult issues. One should call attention to all of a patient's hidden resistances to treatment and to all of the patient's hidden feelings toward the analyst—and so on. [pp. 149–150]

Josephs (1994) observes that such preconceptions continue to "afflict" current analysts, and arise from what he calls a "Freudian superego," an internalized image of Freud, that, although often caricatured, nevertheless acts as a persecuting and austere ideal. Such pedagogical remnants, he concludes, must be alleviated to give practitioners "the inner freedom to learn from experience" (p. 151). As we shall see, Rank's discomfort with the notions of "practicing psychoanalysis" pertains to Josephs's timely views. Even so, Rank's careful scrutiny of psychoanalytic pedagogy moved beyond mere methodological criticism and eisegetical positioning (Rank 1930); rather, most importantly, he understood that the struggle of therapists and healing practitioners to separate from their affirming group ideologies in order to embrace new creative initiatives was largely due to a dramatic predicament inherent in the psychological makeup of humanity: the will–guilt conflict. As psychoanalytic ideas evolve, meaning that certain theoretical essentialisms must die in order to allow learning to grow out of experience, Rank's exploration of the will–guilt dynamic continues to offer meaning and understanding in place of pedagogy.

To fully grasp the relevance of Rank's criticism of early practitioners' tendency to reduce psychoanalytic thinking to fixed criteria for evaluating life, and how such foundationalisms continue to imperil the evolving life of psychoanalysis, we must return briefly to Rank's pivotal views, and in doing so recognize their present-day resonance to the importance of psychoanalytic revaluations of pedagogical influences in theory and practice. Rank (1926) rejected the prominent psychology of his time in which the "principle of causality is applied to the psychic," pointing out that such an application "is in fact an attempt to equalize or equate men; this principle was to reduce the infinite variety of men to an ordered, indiscriminate set of causes-and-effects in which differences were effectively ignored or were condemned" (p. 82). Instead, Rank stressed that truth is as variable as the infinite variety of individuals who strive to express and perpetuate themselves creatively through the psychological birth of innumerable and unique selves, and that this striving dynamic emanates from the force of life itself, the will. Unlike Freud in his structural model, Rank did not think that human development depended upon ego responses torn between instinctual forces and repressive environmental influences. Rather, he stressed that through the responses and choices a person makes, he or she begins to make use of both inner and outer forces for his or her own growth and development. To these organizing, volitional, and choosing processes Rank (1941) ascribed the term "will," which he defined as "an autonomous organizing force in the individual which does not represent any particular biological impulse or social drive, but constitutes the creative expression of the total personality and distinguishes one individual from another" (p. 50).

Rank's notion of the will (1941) is central to the meaning behind his words: "Our psychological age was inaugurated by Nietzsche and brought to a close by Freud" (p. 271). Did Rank believe that the death of psychoanalysis had already come even as "the new science" was burgeoning in America? How could this be? One answer may lie in the way Rank resonated strongly with Nietzsche in his attempt to free human psychology from its tendency to become confined to moral absolutes by questioning the a priori acceptance by Western society of the moral judgment of the will as evil. At the same time, he differed strongly with Freud's "making evil" of the will, suggesting that psychoanalysis often resembled "a covert moralistic 'philosophy' or ideology (terms which he used interchangeably) disguised as an objective, logical science" (Seif 1980, p. 114). Indeed, Rank was well aware of the way a strong adherence to natural science had influenced Freud's attempt to translate psychoanalytic standards into epistemological norms, conveying the spirit of scientific classifications as in the case of biology. Noting this, Rank concluded, "since what is being classified concerns the nature of man . . . these norms automatically acquire *moral import*" (p. 146). Hence, Rank warned that the attempt by analysts to fix norms of behavior forced the patient to fit into a particular pattern of behavior (e.g., *Psychologie treiben*). Neurosis, then, represents a failure on the part of the individual to reach a certain norm or average. Establishing the analyst as the one who decides the range of normality led Rank to contend that such a position reflected a reductionistic ideology "that worships knowledge for the purpose of controlling and predicting human behavior," rather than addressing the emotional experience of the person's life (Taft 1958, p. 150).

Rank's affirmation of the will as the creative force in human beings repudiates the *moral scope of Freud's thinking*, rejecting the notions that human beings lack entirely an internal ethical system "and would be ruthlessly savage if not externally controlled by fearsome authority" (Seif 1980, p. 144). This is to say that the id can be understood as having ethical ideals and inhibitions (Kurtz 1989, p. 220). Further, Rank's view of the will phenomenon presents a paradox inherent in the life-force: we require, indeed must have, closeness, connection, and acceptance from others in order to survive. Yet, self-actualization requires separation and differentiation. Hence, too much closeness can impede separateness and the birth of individuality, leading persons to fear the loss of their own distinctiveness, their unique, creative idiom. This can create what Rank calls a "death fear" in regard to the stifling of individuation. However, the fear of death from too much separation is clear from the start of life. The movement toward independence gives rise then to a fear of abandonment, isolation, and destruction. Rank calls this fear of individuation "the life fear." We are caught between the desire for and fear of self-affirmation, which becomes heightened as we develop greater cognitive capacities and notice the consequences of our actions as well as the reactions of others. Thus, Rank asserts that the affirmation of one's difference is a manifestation of the will toward individuation that is expressed in a person's creative activities and life experience. The will originates in the drive for self-actualization which, in turn, introduces the human dilemmas of separation and relatedness. Indeed, this inevitable predicament at the level of life and death fears confronts the world of psychoanalysis as individuals and groups strive for distinctive identities necessary for self-development. The presence of such a paradoxical reality is indicative of life itself.

Rank (1926) understood that relatedness is jeopardized by self-assertion, and guilt arises when separation creates a presumption of injury to the other's need for togetherness. Therein lies a dramatic human struggle: how to live out one's unique expression when it opposes the wishes and needs of another. He calls this dynamic "ethical guilt," an inner reaction from the fear of hurting the other through separation. By "ethical," Rank means the capacity for relatedness originally experienced when the child and mother were one. In fact, Rank sees guilt as an ethical problem, and in doing so contrasts "ethical" to "moral" connotations, instead referring to the inherent and inevitable relations of self to other. Thus, when we express our will (as, for example, in creative innovations in psychoanalysis) the empathic response may be charged with the assumption that the "other" (or group) does not wish us to separate. Guilt, then, is a natural consequence of the creative urge toward individuality, a by-product of the experience of separateness. Indeed, as we have seen, psychoanalytic practitioners may experience an ethical guilt as they separate from the pedagogy of therapeutic rules in order to learn by experience. Changing attitudes about psychoanalysis among analysts may be experienced, then, as oppositional stances toward group ideologies, creating the impression that analysts' innovations will hurt or even lead to the death of psychoanalysis. Rank's views offer an important understanding of the impact of separation guilt on individuals and groups as they grow and develop.

Dorpat's (1997) contemporary examinations of covert control in psychotherapy recall Rank's earlier discomfort with the extent to which value judgments implicit in psychoanalytic theory condemn individual difference or deviation from a so-called "social norm." In fact, Rank's trenchant remark (1941) gives pause: "almost every manifestation of human thought and behavior has been labeled "pathological" or "abnormal," except the psychology itself which is claimed as an unfailing standard" (p. 288). In short, Rank underscores the fact that Freud did not for the most part acknowledge the necessary relativeness and general limitation of his idea of normality. Freud's scientific-psychological system of typology, as Nancy Seif contends, "was a model of his own, or society's, a moral code of classification in which, in Rank's opinion, the term 'neurotic' denotes 'everything with which we do not agree, or of which we disapprove' (Rank 1941, p. 289). As such, individual difference becomes immoral" (Seif 1980, p. 151).

As we have seen, Rank was critical of the way Freud "taught" his patients, suggesting that analysis at the time measured the patient by the minimum scale of his assumed Oedipus complex with its related sadistic and narcissistic features, and taught the client about himself through these terms. The psychoanalytic striving to educate the individual exclusively according to Freudian assumptions betrayed, Rank thought, a moral-pedagogical attitude, the very opposite of the attitude necessary for constructive therapy. Such a view relegated the patient's own productions of thoughts and feelings to a coercive orientation to theories rather than emotional experience. As Esther Menaker (1995) recalls of her analysis at the time of Rank's writing, "On the one hand, I was supposedly permitted to express whatever came to mind; on the other, I was made to feel that I was saying the wrong thing or revealing some very pathological part of myself" (p. 41). Indeed, as Robert Kramer (1996) suggests, "Rank implies that patients may feel emotionally exploited by an analytic method that sees itself as a form of reparenting or reeducation—what Freud called *Nacherziehung*" (p. 210, n1). Further, analysts do not always have to infuse their patients with a morality which at bottom they themselves purportedly lack. In short, Rank (1926) described the treatment process, when it resembles such an overly pedagogical situation, as a "ritual of atonement" (p. 224) which discourages and moreover condemns the individual's inhibited desire to assert his or her individual idiom—that is, will—as an expression of primitive or Oedipal evil. The outcome of this atonement, Rank laments, is socialized conformity as prescribed by the analyst. As Dorpat has shown, such indoctrination exists today even as the history of psychoanalytic writing has shown its damaging effects. We would be well advised to review Rank's warnings about the history of such indoctrinations in order to discern where psychoanalysis can avoid their deadening as well as self-defeating effects.

How can psychoanalysis today avoid the pitfalls of indoctrination and covert manipulation that have threatened its lasting power as a healing source of potential benefit? Again, we find Rank anticipating our modern interrogative. In his 1927 essay, "The Prometheus Complex," Rank observes that the analytic situation "represents chiefly an educational problem" (p. 201). As we have seen, this insight still pertains. By suggesting that the parental relationship can provide a prototype of the pedagogic situation in analysis, Rank warns of the potential for the educator (analyst) to "enforce his personality and his views on the child's ego (analysand)" (p. 201). The child's revolt against subjection of his or her ego by the primary caretakers, which in psychoanalytic understanding culminates in Oedipal conflicts, is contrasted in Rank's view with a *parental complex*, which he designates as the *Prometheus complex*. As Rank writes, "Whereas the Oedipus complex is founded on identification. ... [and] symbolizes identification, the Prometheus complex is not only the symbol of the need or desire to create but also arises in the individual creatively, that is, spontaneously, at a crucial point, and *not* in identification with parents" (p. 201). Expressed positively, this Promethean urge to create furthers a person's development and the unfolding of his or her own personality. However, it may also take a negative form in the therapy relationship as the *analyst's* need, often unconscious, to recreate the patient in his or her image, leading to the pathogenic misuse of the analyst's creative will.

Following Greek mythology and his previous work on hero motifs, Rank underscores that Prometheus symbolizes a threefold role. First, Prometheus assumes that he is a creator of humanity, and hence views himself as a Man–God, the hero prototype. In doing so, Prometheus cancels "the earlier projection by means of which the gods themselves had been created," thus symbolizing the "dethroning of the gods created by men, and in the place of the gods, man now installs himself with his fully developed personality and his need to create" (Rank 1927, p. 202). Second, Prometheus creates human beings after his own image, people who "live their own lives—to which he himself has to adjust by means of identification" (p. 202). Finally, Prometheus creates a love object, Pandora, which Rank likens to the creation of a love object by projection—a wish fulfillment on whom the creator wants *to imprint his own characteristics*, not unlike the pedagogic situation in which the same imprinting occurs. Rank is clearly suggesting that psychoanalysis often reflects these Promethean roles when it dethrones earlier ideologies and creates practitioners who, in turn, identify with the new pedagogy.

In the Promethean saga, the hero's acts of creation lead to his punishment, but not because he steals fire from the gods. Rather, since fire originally belonged to humanity, "he is punished because he wants to practice with it the same misuse that apparently was allowed the gods and in which creators of men—*parents, educators, or therapists*—can so easily fall. This misuse is to impose one's own personality on the creature and so to make it first of all a willing object, and, in the future, the successor of one's own ego" (Rank 1927, p. 202, italics added). Rank concludes that the Oedipus complex (the infantile situation), suggesting our developing adjustments by means of identification, and the Prometheus complex (the pedagogic situation), pointing to our individual and group potentialities to create by means of projection, contrast with the analytical situation which, ideally, becomes a union of both and, at the same time, something "beyond" (Rank 1927, p. 203). In suggesting that the analytical situation not only includes a union of the Oedipus and Promethean complexes (infantile and pedagogic), but eventually must lead to something "beyond," Rank is suggesting that the *overcoming* of both complexes is vital for the patient's formation of his or her own personality, which is designated as "self-guidance" (p. 203). The "beyond," then, includes the therapeutic situation where the analyst must resist the temptation *to compel the other to his or her own thought, exploiting the patient's natural position of power in an emotional sense.* Overcoming the Promethean complex, in Rank's developmental stages, conveys that the pedagogic situation "must be transformed and developed into a mutual emotional relationship (*Gefühlsbeziehung*) in which parents and children (i.e., analyst and analysand) grow up with—and develop—one another" (p. 210). This mutual development becomes the hallmark of the therapeutic relationship.

Rank (1938) underscored that "all living psychology is relationship psychology" (Kramer 1996, p. 271), meaning that a psychology that propounds an asymmetry between analyst and patient by neglecting the mutuality between persons is a "dead psychology." He understood that in the uniqueness of each individual's will there exists the potential for the creation of the new, a potential that includes the irrational forces of lived experiences where human creativity and self-expression transcend the universalized interpretations of human behavior. Out of this will to create, new values and possibilities are discovered. So must the moving horizons of psychoanalysis as a field of exploration and inquiry extend beyond the Promethean domains, beyond the Pandoran fulfillments that create worlds according to their own perspective; instead, psychoanalysis must measure what Rank called "the volitional affirmation of the obligatory"— that is, as Menaker (1996) describes it, "To the extent that therapy is geared to the cultivation of the creative will, it is volitional; in helping the individual to accept rather than condemn his will, it is affirmative; and *in fostering an awareness of the duality of life and death it places the obligatory in perspective, thus creating the opportunity for the individual to say "yes" to the tragic nature of life"* (p. 129, italics added). Refusing what is obligatory— that is, the inevitable changes in psychoanalytic ideas—has become the modern dilemma of the psychoanalytic world where defensive retreats to training indoctrinations and methods of covert control provide intermittent respites from the rumors of life and death fears, avoiding the inevitable expressions of individual will and collective affirmations of difference.

Rank was prophetic in his understanding that, as humanity develops and changes, the emotional experience of nonsurvival and death mirrors its transformation. Likewise, it is not surprising that the very field of psychoanalysis, as it separates from its accustomed identities to address cultural needs and protean worldviews, must affirm what is obligatory: the experience of its own death in the formation of the new, and this experience may indeed lead the psychoanalytic communities to feel threatened by eradication, immolation, and the rumors of isolation and degeneration. Indeed, self-actualization requires separation and differentiation, and this phenomenon applies to group formation and change as well. As Joseph

Vining (1995) writes, "the what of an idea escapes, always escapes. It leads on, unfolds, is not captured, and cannot be made into a unit, a bit, a package, not even represented by a word or symbol by itself . . . it leads on and takes the self with it" (p. 10). Not surprisingly then, psychoanalytic ideas escape their own historical and ideological contexts and unfold where the worlds of social transformation and the personal life meet; and as they do, meaning the more we individualize ourselves, as Rank (1928) reminds us, "the stronger is the formation of guilt-feeling that originates from this individualization and that again in turn unites us emotionally with others. This is the psychological basis of our ethical socialization" (p. 236). It also makes possible the uniting presence of love, which Rank considered in the end the real task of psychotherapy.

In the Prometheus myth, the culture-hero must acknowledge the limits of conquering the incomprehensible. Subsequently, he learns that in the end he must also concede something, namely the impetus to rule others through the powers of personal sanction through conquest. This theme of transformation becomes most apparent by the story's conclusion. As Prometheus suffers Zeus's punishment, chained to a rock at the edge of the world, Chiron, the beloved teacher of gods, enters the drama. Chiron, doomed to eternal suffering because he had been accidentally wounded by one of Heracles's poisoned arrows, gladly offers to give up his own immortality to end his own and Prometheus's suffering. Zeus consents to the exchange and Prometheus is freed. The theme of pedagogical change with respect to life and death is clear: the teacher of gods (Chiron) and the instructor of humanity (Prometheus) find a mutual release from their sufferings through giving up their respective presumptions, their "higher powers." Chiron experiences death and a loss of immortality; Prometheus finds renewal through a willingness to share the world of human vulnerability. Even Zeus must compromise, transforming his own unalterable decree into choice and deed. As the gods become more human, they teach each other the limitations of their own power, and this experience, paradoxically, empowers them with a wisdom beyond their expectations.

Keeping the Promethean myth in mind, Rank understood that the analytic situation must move beyond its own pedagogy. By drawing from the legacy of Promethean identities that make up the history of psychoanalysis, it becomes clear that the necessity of mutual development through an acknowledgment of limitation and the experience of change transforms this myth into a story for our times. As Rank understood so well, the Promethean fire must inevitably yield to the hearths of human love, where the higher or infernal powers, be they analogous to psychoanalytic ideologies or the un-compromising pedagogy of one individual, must dare to learn the strength of dying into the unknown possibilities of growth and change.

REFERENCES

Cushman, P. (1997). *Constructing the Self, Constructing America: A Cultural History of Psychoanalysis.* New York: Addison-Wesley.

Dorpat, T. L. (1997). *Gaslighting, the Double Whammy, Interrogation, and Other Methods of Covert Control in Psychotherapy and Analysis.* Northvale, NJ: Jason Aronson.

Freud, S. (1900). The interpretation of dreams. *Standard Edition 4, 5.*

Gay, P. (1988). *Freud: A Life For Our Times.* New York: Norton.

Josephs, L. (1994). The Freudian superego. *Journal of Religion and Health* 2:149–153.

Kramer, R., ed. (1996). *A Psychology of Difference.* Princeton, NJ: Princeton University Press.

Kohut, H. (1984). *How Does Analysis Cure?* Chicago: University of Chicago Press.

Kurtz, S. (1989). *The Art of Unknowing.* Northvale, NJ: Jason Aronson.

Menaker, E. (1995). *Misplaced Loyalties.* New Brunswick, NJ: Transaction Press.

——— (1996). *Separation, Will, and Creativity.* Northvale, NJ: Jason Aronson.

Peterfreund, E. (1989). *The Process of Psychotherapy.* Northvale, NJ: Jason Aronson.

Pfister, J., and Schnog, N., eds. (1997). *Inventing the Psychological.* New Haven, CT: Yale University Press.

Rank, O. (1926). *Will Therapy.* New York: Knopf, 1972.

——— (1927). The Prometheus complex. In *A Psychology of Difference,* ed. R. Kramer, pp. 201–210. Princeton: Princeton University Press, 1996.

——— (1928). Beyond psychoanalysis. In *A Psychology of Difference,* ed. R. Kramer, pp. 229–239. Princeton: Princeton University Press, 1996.

——— (1930). Speech at mental hygiene congress. In *A Psychology of Difference,* ed. R. Kramer, pp. 221–227. Princeton: Princeton University Press, 1996.

——— (1938). Modern psychology, social change. In *A Psychology of Difference,* ed. R. Kramer, pp. 265–275. Princeton: Princeton University Press, 1996.

——— (1941). *Beyond Psychology.* New York: Dover, 1958.

Seif, N. (1980). *Otto Rank: On Human Evil.* Unpublished dissertation, Yeshiva University, New York.

Sterba, R. (1982). *Reminiscences of a Viennese Psychoanalyst.* Detroit, MI: Wayne State University Press.

Taft, J. (1958) . *Otto Rank: A Biographical Study on Notebooks, Letters, Collected Writings, Therapeutic Achievements and Personal Associations.* New York: Julian Press.

Vining, J. (1995) *From Newton's Sleep.* Princeton, NJ: Princeton University Press.

13

Psychoanalysis and the Unconscious: The Phoenix Rising from the Ashes

Joseph Newirth

The development of a two-person, relational paradigm in psychoanalysis has resulted in a shift in the central focus of psychoanalytic treatment from the analysis of unconscious wishes and impulses to the analysis of current relational patterns. Contemporary technique (Kernberg 1993, Schafer 1994) that has developed out of this evolving two-person constructivist perspective has focused on the analysis of the transference–countertransference interaction as a way of addressing and changing the patient's maladaptive repetitive childhood relational schemas. In this important theoretical shift to a two-person psychology, the unconscious has been redefined as a reflection of either inaccurate childhood patterns of relationship which distort current relationships or as current relational patterns that remain outside of awareness. As psychoanalysis has developed into a two-person theory, it has lost its primary identification with the unconscious defined as the frightening, irrational, bestial, mysterious, but also creative and powerful care of the earlier one-person concept of the unconscious. In the present chapter I will argue that the rejection of the classical notions of the unconscious has led to an overly rational view of the unconscious; I will suggest an integration of recent theoretical trends into an alternative conceptualization of the unconscious as a developing structure of mind which contains the powerful forces traditionally associated with the unconscious.

THE UNCONSCIOUS IN CONTEMPORARY PSYCHOANALYSIS

Many authors have commented on the loss in psychoanalysis of a central focus on the unconscious. Fromm (1970, p. 16) criticized the failure of contemporary psychoanalysis to pursue "The most creative and radical achievement of Freud's theory (which) was the founding of a 'science of the irrational'—i.e., the theory of the unconscious." He believed this failure was a result of conservative political forces in the development of the psychoanalytic movement which focused on increasing the control of the profession and its conforming to the bourgeois constraints of society. Fromm's argument suggests that the importance of Freud's revolutionary concept of the unconscious became lost in the conservative development of the profession of psychoanalysis, and the parallel development of theory in which the emphasis moved from an id psychology to ego psychology and the patient's adaptation to reality.

Fromm's radical critique of the development of psychoanalysis is echoed in current debates on how to define psychoanalysis. These debates focus on the importance of the "extrinsic criteria" (Gill 1994) of psychoanalysis; the frequency of sessions, the duration of sessions, and the use of the couch. Gill (p. 63) argues that more important then these extrinsic factors in the psychoanalytic situation are the "intrinsic factors" of the psychoanalytic situation which involve "the intent to analyze the interaction as much as possible" (p. 63). Gill (1994) poignantly states his position: "What I am struggling against is the rote acceptance of the idea that an analysis can be conducted only with at least four or five sessions a week and on the couch . . . I want the frequency to be the *least* that is compatible with an analytic process for a particular patient so that analysis can be made available to more people" (p. 76, italics added).

Gill, who has been one of the central theorists in the development of the contemporary two-person, constructivist perspective in psychoanalysis, suggested a radical approach to the psychoanalytic situation which emphasizes the analyst's active engagement with the patient and the importance of the interpretation and explication of the analyst–patient interaction as the critical dimension of psychoanalytic treatment. However, at the same time that he presents a radical approach to analytic technique he seems to present a conservative approach to the unconscious as a structure, and defines it as distortion, as the source of pathology, and as the core difficulty in adapting to reality. Gill argues that the analysis of the interaction is the effective means of addressing the patient's pathological transferences which are rooted in childhood experience; that is, the analysis of the interaction becomes the means of transforming the irrational past into the rational present. The following statement illustrates both the radical and conservative elements in Gill's (1994) argument:

> The analyst will remember that he is always interacting with the patient and that the interaction is so complex and multifaceted that it is fatuous to think he can always be aware of what is going on. The analyst will work toward the establishment of a psychoanalytic situation . . . in which, however they temporarily stray from it, analyst and patient both remain committed to the idea that the proximal goal is to understand the relationship, not only to engage in it, while the distal goal is to understand the patient's psychopathology in the light of the patient's development. [p. 116]

This view of the unconscious as the repository of the historical, pathological, and irrational interpersonal or relational schemas has encouraged the development in contemporary psychoanalysis of a view of the unconscious, like Freud's topographic model, in which the unconscious is thought of as meanings outside of awareness rather than as a structure of the mind which is a source of energy and which encompasses the irrational as an important counterforce to the rational. This contemporary view of the unconscious, as relational schemas outside of awareness, has resulted in the emphasis in contemporary technique on the rational analysis of the transference–countertransference relationship in a process that increasingly resembles discriminant learning theory, in which interpretations are focused on differentiating the analyst (a contemporary object) from the patient's historical objects.

Hirsch and Roth (1995), in reviewing contemporary views of the unconscious, present the interpersonal and relational views of the unconscious as essentially unarticulated schemas of past interpersonal relationships. They point out that for many contemporary authors the central dimension of the unconscious and of the treatment is the patient's "rigid patterns of relating that truncate a more dimensional experience in living. Specifically people's difficulties result from their adhesion to loved ones of the past with whom they are embedded and from whom they cannot separate" (p. 271). These authors, in harmony with Gill and many other contemporary theorists, state that the goal of treatment is "to demystify the analyst in the transference and thereby to also demystify the family in the patient's internal world" (p. 273). It is as if psychoanalytic cure is simply thought of as the demystification of the past and the conscious recognition of the inappropriateness of the old patterns to current situations, thus allowing the freedom to develop appropriate healthy relationships.

The view of the unconscious as unarticulated relational patterns and the treatment corollary of the patient learning a more realistic or functionally accurate view of self in relation to others—that is, of differentiating the repetitive, self-destructive, relationship patterns through a current relationship with the analyst—is the central theme in many contemporary psychoanalytic approaches. For example, the *control-mastery* approach developed by Weiss and Sampson (Sampson 1992) describes two aspects of effective treatment; the first involves insight into the pathological beliefs and the problems to which they give rise, and the second involves the patient's unconsciously (that is, outside of awareness) testing his/her beliefs in relation to the analyst. The critical treatment events are whether the patient perceives the analyst's behavior and attitudes as disconfirming the belief he is testing. Sampson breaks with the tradition of emphasizing the singular importance of verbal interpretation and points out that "direct experience with the analyst sometimes may lead to significant analytic progress even without interpretation" (p. 519). Again, the unconscious is defined as the individual's repetitive relational patterns which are outside of awareness; issues of energy, specific content such as sexuality and aggression, or different modes of organizing experience such as primary and secondary process thought are not considered in this and similar positions.

THE UNCONSCIOUS IN KLEIN, WINNICOTT, AND BION

André Green (1995), in a critique of contemporary psychoanalytic theory and technique, raises the ironic question "Has sexuality anything to do with psychoanalysis?" He argues against the current emphasis on the analysis of repetitive relational patterns to the exclusion of references to sexuality and the unconscious. His discussion of sexuality in psychoanalysis points to our inability to develop a contemporary view of the unconscious because of literal interpretations of Freud's concept of sexuality and drive. He presents the argument that the essence of Freud's concerns with sexuality involved the capacity for "pleasurable enjoyment" and the ability "to feel alive and to cathect the many possibilities offered by the diversity of life, in spite of its inevitable disappointments, sources of unhappiness and loads of pain" (p. 874). Green's (1995) emphasis on pleasure and aliveness are attempts to address the concepts of drive and energy which were thought from a one-person perspective as reflecting biological drives, and in a two-person perspective can be thought of as reflecting the individual's capacity for pleasure and joy. Green seems to be calling for a revision of the concept of the unconscious so as to maintain this concept as the powerful center of psychological structure which is the source of energy, passion, and aliveness.

Winnicott, Bion, and Kleinian analysts have been ambiguous in their presentation of the concept of the unconscious. They continue to use the one-person, metapsychological language of Freud's structural model, implying that the unconscious is an organization of instinct, drives, and energy displacements, while through their dramatic and poetic descriptions of clinical process they suggest a two-person perspective in which the analyst is involved in an interactive process of growth and development with the unconscious defined as a critical life force. It would seem that they have implicitly modified the one-person, biological concept of drive into a two-person, psychological concept of passion, pleasure, and joy in their view of the unconscious as a source of energy, which they define as creativity. Hana Segal (1994) describes a children's story, *Haroun and the Sea of Stories*, the novel by Salman Rushdie, as a parable for the psychoanalytic endeavor and the experience of the unconscious, which Segal describes as having the characteristics of either deadness and domination by external reality, or aliveness, creativity, and joy. She describes the universal struggle to resolve the "inner conflict between creativity and the anti-creative forces" (p. 612) in the development of the unconscious through the integration of love and hate, and the evolving capacity to use symbols.

The concept of the unconscious suggested by Segal, Winnicott, Bion, and other Kleinians involves a view that the unconscious as a developing set of capacities which organizes experience in progressively integrated and symbolic forms. This developmental view of the unconscious is radically different from the static view of the unconscious as a container for either drive derivatives or childhood relational schemas. This view of the unconscious which emphasizes the capacity for creativity and a sense of aliveness is discussed by Eigen (1981) as a critical outcome of the analytic process. Eigen describes this quality of the unconscious as a capacity for a passionate commitment to life, *faith*, which he defines as a "way of experiencing which is undertaken with one's whole being, all out, with all one's heart, with all one's soul, and with all one's might" (p. 413). He contrasts this dimension of the unconscious with operations which emphasize ego mastery, introjection, and processes of internalization, or of successful adaptations, and is critical of contemporary psychoanalytic approaches in which the analyst attempts to become a new, more realistic internal object replacing the patient's historical, pathological objects. Eigen points out that Winnicott, Bion, and Lacan: "maintain the critical importance of not confusing creative experiencing with introjection (or internalization) of mother and father images or functions" (p. 431). For Eigen,

> The sources of creative experiencing run deeper than internalization and go beyond it . . . If one reads these authors carefully, one discovers that the *primary object of creative experiencing is not mother or father but the unknowable ground of creativeness as such.* Winnicott, for example, emphasizes that what is at stake in transitional experiencing is not a self or object (mother) substitute, but the creation of a symbol, of symbolizing experience itself. [1981, p. 431]

The implicit Kleinian and Winnicottian view of the unconscious argues that more important than the patient's internalized childhood relational patterns is the development of the capacity to integrate experience in an intense, committed, alive, creative, and symbolic form. This dimension of the unconscious, the individual's creative capacity, was initially thought of as an aspect of the development of the depressive position, in which concrete experiences of love and hate, self and other, are transformed into symbolic experiences. However, Ogden (1992) has recently suggested that it is more accurate to think of this development as involving a dialectic relationship between the paranoid-schizoid position and the depressive positions. Winnicott's (1971, Newirth 1996) concept of transitional experiences can be thought of as a means of understanding the transformation of external, concrete experience to subjective, symbolic experience in terms of both internal representations and interpersonal enactments. The theory of transitional experience describes a developmental process, between parent and child or patient and analyst, through which the individual's concrete experiences are enacted and, through this experience, become internalized as powerful symbolic and unconscious fantasies. This developmental dimension of the unconscious which is implicit in Klein's and Winnicott's two-person perspective, is reflected in the individual's evolving capacity for pleasure, joy, a passionate commitment to life, and the capacity to create symbolic and transitional experiences which are expanding sources of power and energy.

THE UNCONSCIOUS IN MATTE-BLANCO'S THEORY

Because of the poetic and literary language that has been the preferred style of many contemporary Kleinian and Winnicottian analysts, it has been difficult to develop a new conceptualization of the unconscious as a two-person relational structure. This preference for literary language reflects both these analysts' critique of the biomechanical language of traditional psychoanalysis as well as an important personal quality of those analysts (C. Bollas, M. Eigen, M. Khan, M. Little, and A. Philips) who found the constraints and language of traditional one-person theory not in keeping with their experiences as psychoanalysts. The work of Matte-Blanco provides an interesting and original structural approach to the two-person, Kleinian and Winnicottian view of the unconscious. He sees the unconscious as a source of energy, creativity, and power which can be conceptualized as sets of mathematical equations, that are able to integrate and organize vast amounts of simple experience into more complex and powerful systems and organizations of experience.

Matte-Blanco (1988, Rayner 1995) conceptualized the mind as a system of mathematical or logical functions rather than as a container for physical energy transformations, a hierarchy of control apparatuses, or sets of biological systems. He conceptualized consciousness and unconsciousness as different systems of classification involving two different forms of logic or mathematical functions which exist in a parallel and dialectical relationship with each other. This view of the conscious and unconscious systems as different forms of logic or thought process is similar to Freud's concept of primary and secondary process thinking; however, it is also different in that for Matte-Blanco the conscious process is not considered to supersede or control the unconscious thought process. Implicit in Matte-Blanco's concept, as in Winnicott's, Klein's, and Bion's, is the idea that the unconscious continues to and *needs to* develop throughout life; it is not a static system of physical drives or childhood relational schema but systems of organization which potentially grow in their capacity to generate powerful, creative experiences of self in the world.

Matte-Blanco (Rayner 1981) defined the operation of the two sets of functions or ways of organizing experience in the following way: "consciousness is defined by asymmetrical logic and is concerned with, and operates to form discrimination of differences; the unconscious is defined by symmetry and is concerned with registering and creating sameness, identity or homogeneity" (p. 405). Asymmetrical logic (Fink 1995)

> allows the conceptualization of time and space and the differentiation of the whole and its parts. It is ruled by the laws of contradiction or antinomy, negation, causality, numerical, spatial and temporal sequence, and the ability to distinguish between subject and object. Thus it is possible to conceive of time, the idea of past, present and future; in terms of space, the here and there, inside and outside, left and right, below and above, external and internal world, self and non-self, etc.; and in terms of whole and parts, the idea of part objects versus complete objects formed by many parts, leading to concepts of individuality, identity. [p. 137]

This is the logic of consciousness and of the usual form of interpretation which is directed at increasing the patient's awareness of difference in the areas of time, space, and the experience of people as whole objects. In symmetrical logic the distinctions of time, space, part and whole, and subject and object are effaced; all relationships are equal to their converse and therefore there cannot be concepts of sequence, time, or space. Matte-Blanco thought the equation of a part with the whole and the tendency to experience emotion at all-or-nothing levels is related to a specific quality of symmetrical logic and of the unconscious; that the unconscious operates as if it is a series of mathematical infinite sets. The psychological experience of an infinite set is (Rayner 1995) "limitlessness, of there being no end, no boundary, no constriction, no control, a lack of negative feedback and so on" (p. 56). Although Matte-Blanco's mathematically based theory can sound quite abstract, these infinite, limitless, or absolute experiences are commonplace and easily recognized. For example, dreams, poetry, art, ideals, love, friendship, and feelings of purpose and identity all reflect the experience of infinite sets and symmetrical experience. Matte-Blanco's concept of the unconscious as symmetrical experience can be thought of as providing a structure which supports the Kleinian and

Winnicottian view of the unconscious as the capacity to create symbolic and transitional experiences which function as expanding sources of power and energy. Experiences of joy, terror, creativity, and a passionate commitment to life are both symmetrical and experienced as belonging to an infinite set, which is why dreams and love poems compare one's lover to absolute experiences such as the depth of the ocean rather than to asymmetrical experiences such as comparisons of qualities or between several specific real people.

Matte-Blanco's theory presents a means to understand the pathological and constructive aspects of symmetrical and asymmetrical thought process. For example, Rayner (1995) illustrates the dialectical relationship between symmetrical and asymmetrical logic with the following illustration, which seems to echo Winnicott's theory of transitional experience:

> A child may lie on the beach lapped by the waves and declaim "I am a stone."
> If he is playing he will know very well that he is not a stone but the point
> of the game is that he is a stone. This is a paradox inherent in any make-
> believe play. Without symmetry there is no metaphor and with no meta-
> phor there is no make-believe play. But without the self having a contain-
> ing framework of awareness of asymmetrical relations play breaks down
> into delusion. The child becomes a stone. This occurs in psychosis of course
> and also normally in dreams. It is muted in affective states and in neurotic
> anxiety when a person may feel he has turned to stone but knows very well
> consciously that he has not. [p. 37]

Matte-Blanco's theory provides a system with which we can begin to understand the interplay of conscious and unconscious processes without losing the power and richness of the earlier one-person view of the unconscious.

The following fragment of a psychoanalytic dialogue (Rayner 1995) presents an interesting illustration of the complexity of the relationship between symmetrical and asymmetrical experience in the transference–countertransference relationship. A woman patient says to her male analyst, while talking about her husband "with dismissive abandon: 'He's the same as all you men, of course, an exploiting capitalist'" (p. 34). In equating her husband and the analyst with all men and with capitalist exploitation there is a lack of discrimination or, in Matte-Blanco's terms, a symmetrization of the historical, current, and transference objects. However, we might also think of the patient as projecting or evacuating her greed, aggressiveness, hostility, and power into her husband, analyst, and all men, and in that way applying the rules of asymmetrical logic in her attempt to differentiate those aggressive affects, in effect saying that they are not me. It would not be surprising for a contemporary analyst to inquire or comment on the apparent symmetrical equation with the expectation that the patient become able to differentiate, that is, to bring an asymmetrical and conscious focus to her historical and current relationships. That approach, which is characteristic of many contemporary approaches, would suggest a view of the unconscious as relational distortions, with the analyst's function that of differentiating the historical from the current experiences—that is, to have the patient use an asymmetrical framework to organize her experience or, in classical language, to make the unconscious conscious. However, an alternative approach, based on the developmental view of the unconscious which I have suggested is implicit in the work of Klein, Winnicott, Bion, and others as it is joined with Matte-Blanco's theory, would instead focus on increasing the degree of symmetry and on the dissociated, concrete unconscious experience which is presented (projected) as if it were objective reality and not-me. In this alternative view of the unconscious, the focus would not be on facilitating the patient's ability to differentiate, or to become conscious of the differences between the various men in her world, but on dedifferentiating (Newirth 1989) her experience as an exploited person and the exploiting other; that is, the analyst would introduce the principles of symmetrical logic through an enactment in order to facilitate the integration of her disowned aggression, greed, and power which she projects into her husband, the analyst, and all men. In order to facilitate a beginning enactment of a symmetrical experience in the transference the analyst might have said: "yes, we men are a greedy and exploitive lot." With this symmetrical intervention, the analyst would explicitly identify himself with the patient's dissociated aggression as well as acknowledge her view that all men and perhaps all women are greedy and exploitative. The goal is not the differentiation of past and present but the dedifferentiation of the transference and countertransference so that they are experienced as part of the same infinite set.

This example suggests the complex interweaving of symmetrical and asymmetrical logic as the unconscious and conscious organizations of experience interpenetrate and control each other in the same way that gravitational fields of adjacent planets control and influence each other's movements. The analyst's concept of the unconscious and his ability to facilitate the development of the unconscious as a source of energy is particularly important in our contemporary age, when many patients seem to be imprisoned in the asymmetrical world of external reality and have not developed the capacity for make-believe, for play, joy, creativity, and for a passionate commitment to life. Psychoanalytic technique that focuses on discriminating the historical distortions in the current transference–countertransference relationship ignores the positive and powerful importance of the unconscious as having the capacity for symbolic and symmetrical experience. Focusing on the development of the symmetrical and symbolic aspects of the unconscious takes the opposite therapeutic tack from those contemporary approaches which encourage a differentiation of the historical from the current analytic objects. The approach that I have described involves a symmetrization or a dedifferentiation of the historical and current analytic objects. This approach involves a volitional shift in the therapist's strategy from asymmetrical interventions that, through objective or rational discourse, attempt to make the unconscious conscious, to interventions which are directed at the development, elaboration, and internalization of unconscious experience which we might think of as making the conscious unconscious. This shift in therapeutic strategy reflects a view of the unconscious as a center of creativity, power, and pleasure, and of the symmetrical fantasies which organize the individual's action in the world. From my perspective, what is necessary for the rebirth of psychoanalysis is to focus our understanding of pathology and of the psychoanalytic process on the development of the patient's unconscious. Then like the phoenix rising from the ashes, the unconscious may again become the central focus of psychoanalytic theory and technique.

REFERENCES

Eigen, M. (1981). The area of faith in Winnicott, Lacan and Bion. *International Journal of Psycho-Analysis* 62:413–433.

Fink, K. (1995). Projection, identification and bi-logic. *Psychoanalytic Quarterly* 14(1):136–154.

Fromm, E. (1970). *The Crisis of Psychoanalysis.* New York: Holt, Rinehart & Winston.

Gill, M. M. (1994). *Psychoanalysis in Transition.* Hillsdale, NJ: Analytic Press.

Green, A. (1995). Has sexuality anything to do with psychoanalysis? *International Journal of Psycho-Analysis* 76:871–883.

Hirsch, I., and Roth, J. (1995). Changing conceptions of the unconscious. *Contemporary Psychoanalysis* 31(2):263–276.

Kernberg, O. F. (1993). Convergences and divergences in contemporary psycho-analytic technique. *International Journal of Psycho-Analysis* 74:659–673.

Matte-Blanco, I. (1988). *Thinking, Feeling and Being.* London: Routledge.

Newirth, J. (1989). *Psychological structure, regression and clinical psychoanalysis.* Paper presented at the annual meeting of the division of Psychoanalysis, American Psychological Association, Boston, April 6.

———— (1996). On not interpreting: the metaphor of the baby, enactment and transitional experience. *American Journal of Psychoanalysis* 56:415–430.

Ogden, T. H. (1992). The dialectically constituted/decentered subject of psycho-analysis: II: The contributions of Klein and Winnicott. *International Journal of Psycho-Analysis* 73:613–626.

Rayner, E. (1995). *Unconscious Logic: An Introduction to Matte-Blanco's Bi-Logic and Its Uses.* London: Routledge.

Sampson, H. (1992). The role of "real" experience in psychopathology and treatment. *Psychoanalytic Dialogues* 3:509–528.

Schafer, R. (1994). Traditional Freudian and Kleinian Freudian analysis. *Psychoanalytic Inquiry* 14:462–475.

Segal, H. (1994). Salman Rushdie and *The Sea of Stories. International Journal of Psycho-Analysis* 75:611–618.

Winnicott, D. W. (1971). *Playing and Reality.* London: Tavistock.

14
The Poem and Reason
Elaine Schwager

OVERVIEW AND HISTORICAL BACKGROUND

In the origins of psychoanalysis, Freud and his followers, feeling the fragility of its revolutionary premises and dangers of attack from the outside, tried to secure its method of exploring the irrational in a rational, scientific system of thought. At this time the religious ideals of the church and moral ideals of the culture viewed sexuality and the sensual aspect of the self as enemies. Triumph over this weaker aspect of the self resulted in superior moral feelings. Through psychoanalysis a new character ideal was born, a person liberated of these restraining moralistic (superego) feelings, a person who could satisfy his or her sexual and sensual self in a love relationship. In shifting the balance in this mind/body duality, Freud was revolutionary and courageous.

While there have always been disagreements among Freudians on aspects of theory and technique, the institutionalization of this position became in some ways another church. While the ways in which psychoanalysis secured itself in its beginnings seemed to be politically and culturally necessary, they were also related to unexamined issues of power, narcissism, and defensive rationalizing both by Freud and by its leaders. For this reason, its ways of institutionalizing were at odds with what it was trying to accomplish as a clinical method. In the long run, its convictions and exclusions became a source of its fragility; they created unexamined "principles" for its constituents, creating blind spots in its practitioners that led to unexamined countertransference problems with patients. This initial orthodoxy set a course in which future differing points of view would vie for rightness or power, rather than be subsumed under a roof of differences, all of which might contribute to a greater whole.

Not only did Freud feel that it was necessary to make the sexual theory the bedrock of psychoanalysis, he found it difficult to integrate ideas of thinkers who might have threatened some of its premises. Early on, Jung, Rank, and Ferenczi seriously questioned many of the accepted concepts of psychoanalytic theory. They warned against the limitations of a rationalistic, moralistic, and scientific approach—against viewing sexual instincts as primary, excluding "soul," spirituality, and creativity as central instincts or aspects of the self, and against the potential of psychoanalysis to repeat the traumas of childhood through its rigidity. Ferenczi was concerned about psychoanalysis serving its own interests, at times at the expense of patients, and of not educating patients, particularly those traumatized into compliance, in how to contradict and fight back.

Otto Rank (1930) said, "All human problems are in the last resort, problems of the soul," and warned that it is "essential . . . to resist the temptation to accept any definite psychological theory as the principle of exegesis" (p. xv). He also emphasized that the "artist cannot be explained on purely individual-psychological grounds" (p. xvii).

Soul is thought of here as an immaterial aspect of the self connected with a greater consciousness or unconsciousness for which it is the conduit. Its driving instinct is the discovery of truth both universal and personal, as opposed to the sexual, aggressive instincts that are considered basic to our biological nature or the relational instincts basic to our emotional nature. This search—and the expression of this search—is highly unique and often puts one at odds with the conventions and established truths of the existing culture and institutions. Art is the attempt to give aesthetic, concrete expression to the abstract and ineffable ideas of the soul. The poetic aspect of the self, as Coleridge (1817) states, emerges from the soul, and the poet is one "who brings the whole soul of man into activity . . . by that synthetic and magical power to which we have designated the name imagination" (p. 235). It is an aspect of the self that exists in the world a-causally, in the dialects of non-reason, paradox, image, and passion. To keep his theory coherent and based in a scientific and rational framework, Freud eliminated or marginalized this aspect of self from the domain of psychoanalysis. He did so as often by elevating it—claiming psychoanalysis had not developed the capacity to understand this realm thereby debunking it, seeing institutionalized religion as a way the common man used to blind himself rather than bear reality. Neither healing nor development of the soul's profound and aesthetic capacities can be part of treatment if theory holds in doubt their existences.

Jung (1910) reported Freud saying to him: "My dear Jung, promise me never to abandon the sexual theory. That is the most essential thing of all. You see, we must make a dogma of it, an unshakable bulwark 'against occultism.'" To which Jung thought in response: A dogma . . . is set up only when the aim is to suppress doubts once and for all. But that no longer has anything to do with personal judgment, only a personal power drive . . . (pp. 150–152).

Ferenczi felt that Freud's reluctance to deal with certain of his negative feelings led him to focus on the patient's resistance, analyzability, or negative transference. He felt that this was itself traumatizing, echoing early denials and blame by parents. He saw the importance early on of understanding countertransference, and also criticized the paradigm of the sick patient and the healthy clinician. He believed acknowledging limitations in theory had great importance in the patient's well-being.

Threatened, psychoanalysts pathologized their opponents, suffering them to be ostracized for forging their own path.

Despite early—and later—attempts to "freeze" psychoanalytic theory, the discipline has evolved in numerous positive directions. Many of its gains, ironically, have been retrievals of what Freud excluded in such areas as creativity and spirituality; these gains were made only after hard battles against accepted theory.

When Freud excluded spirituality and the artist's experience from the theoretical domain of psychoanalysis, he also excluded or diminished aims, instincts, and wisdom of the soul that could balance reason, scientific inquiry, and instinctual life and could prevent psychoanalysis from getting too comfortable with its own discoveries. Spirituality was more or less flatly considered self-deception, a pacification of the human condition and false consolation for the inevitability of untamed aggression, war, tragedies, corruption, envy, and death. It was seen as that which falsifies and blinds, rather than as what illuminates and helps people to create context for and find meaning in the most horrific aspects of life.

The unknown is always a threat to dogma. It unsettles, creates exceptions, defies, or questions. What science establishes is thought to be known, even proved. But both are necessary for the whole process. It would be unbearable to endure the continual anxiety and uncertainty of living in the unknown. One needs way stations of security and structure. However, security and structure should not then be used to tyrannize by becoming unquestioned conviction.

In Freud's view, creative energy and drives, as well as spiritual drives for wholeness, were considered secondary to or sublimations of sexual drives and energy. The unconscious was viewed primarily as the reservoir of the repressed and forbidden, with far less emphasis on the equally frightening capacity for the aesthetic and sublime, and an alternate order of thought that might be at odds with conscious reality. It made the mode of paradox, the bedrock of spiritual and artistic thinking, apologetic to reason and dualistic thinking. Psychoanalysis established fixed images and myths through which to understand human nature that overpowered the soul's hunger for images that partake of the new and unexpected, and plumbed the depths of being for the eternal and primitive. It put greater value on success and fear of success as these were connected to oedipal issues than on the value of failure, as it allowed for the collapse of limiting conscious structures. It tended to pathologize the darker side of the self and certain by-products or phases of the spirit's struggle—periods of depression, despair, terror, aloneness, elation, even suicidal feelings or hallucinations, all of which may be responses to leaps of courage, heightened aesthetic awareness, or encounters of deeper relatedness to oneself or others. Such experiences were more often to be cured than valued for what they taught and how they contributed to becoming a whole person; or they were used to justify a diagnosis that might disqualify people from psychoanalytic treatment.

The intensity of one side lends strength to the other and vice versa. To get identified with too narrow an idea of health or normality, one that excludes the darker sides of the self, creates fragility, not strength. This was why, when patients came in to report the loss of a job or relationship, a so-called failure, Jung might take out a bottle of wine and offer to celebrate. He saw that such "failure" offered the possibility of the collapse of some conscious system, thus allowing a person to encounter new aspects of the self and so achieve a reorganization based on deeper or more encompassing needs.

A conception of maturity or "happiness" that emphasizes mutual genital satisfaction in a love relationship, or success in love and work, while giving less attention to a capacity for paradox, involving owning one's dark side and transforming it to a place of dignity, seems to value the "pleasure principle" more than developing strength of character and compassion. Development of instincts of soul, as opposed to development of instincts of sexuality and aggression—what Schopenhauer called the nonegotistical instincts of compassion, self-denial, and sacrifice—were also not given equal place in early psychoanalytic theory as central to maturity.

DUALITY VS. PARADOX (OR, REASON VS. THE POETIC)

Freud did describe the ability to tolerate and endure ambivalence, ambiguity, and contradictory experience as a turning point in the attainment of maturity and in the establishment of a therapeutic persona. This ability in the analyst to be equally disposed toward contradictory thoughts or feelings is what allows a patient maximum freedom, generally more than was permitted in his family of origin and culture, where a particular point of view, moral code, or emotional demand directs him toward one outcome or another. But the ideal analytic stance of neutrality, lack of bias toward any position, being without "memory and desire" (Bion 1963) is not one of decision, not a rule one memorizes in graduate school and then hides one's personal life and ideas behind. It involves the lifetime work of analysts confronting their biases, morality, countertransferential issues, and the way their securities and convictions may be impeding as well as enhancing.

To the extent that psychoanalysis justifies its system of thought by science or reason, it promotes a dualistic mode rather than a stance where one roams free in paradox. One side of the dualism is elevated above the other and justified as being superior—by reasoning usually created by the superior side of the duality. When one side is considered the lesser or is distorted, it can diminish the whole and create false perceptions of all its parts. When logic finds itself helpless to grapple with the complexity of the human psyche, in which contradictions and multiple levels exist simultaneously, it comes up with paradox.

In the realm of dreams, the poetic, imagination, and the symbolic, polarities coexist and recombine. In the creation of metaphor and symbols, the least valued or understood of the two sides of a polarity is often brought to light in fuller dimension, transforming the meaning of the whole as well as both polarities. The symbol or metaphor thus conveys the unity of elements or the indispensability of both sides to the whole, in a way that logic regards as paradoxical.

The energy that produces images and symbols is not easily explained. Bachelard (1987) states that "if we limit ourselves, as psychoanalysis often does, to translating symbols into human terms, we neglect an entire field of study—the autonomy of symbolism. . . . Psychoanalysis has been no more able than psychology to find proper means of estimating these forces" (p. 67).

That part of self that is not a product of history, social interaction, biology, or culture but a conduit to another realm—a gift—is not explicable or interpretable by psychoanalytic theory. This self is experienced by artists as inspiration or as dictation of thought, that comes without choice. As Louis Simpson says, "Poetry must be conceived as a force beyond the self and the poet a medium of that force" (1986, p. 10) and "Poetry is essentially mysterious. While he is writing the poet has in mind another self, more intelligent than he. The poet is reaching out to the person that he would be . . . a sense of reaching that can never be satisfied" (1972, p. 199).

In a conception of self consisting of ego, superego, and id, where is there room for this experience of the self? Those who value this experience of communion with another realm, above all else, may sacrifice many other aspects of life—relationships, material comforts, "success"—for the sake of their gift. To make such a mess of one's life for this, may appear as a kind of madness. It involves both a suffering and kind of ecstasy that psychology might too easily see as sickness.

It is the area of creation which Balint (1968) characterized by the number *1* (as opposed to *3* for the oedipal conflict and *2* for the area of the basic fault) when he said, "No outside object is involved, consequently there is no object relationship and no transference. That is why our knowledge of these processes is so scanty and uncertain. Our analytic methods are inapplicable in this area and thus we have to resort to insecure inferences and extrapolations" (p. 24).

Emily Dickinson (1862) anticipated this inadequacy:

> Much Madness is divinist Sense—
> To a discerning eye—
> Much Sense the starkest Madness—

'Tis the Majority
In this, as All, prevail—
Assent—and you are sane—
Demur—you're
    straightway dangerous
And handled with a Chain

Freud had a difficult time establishing a comfortable relationship between art and psychoanalysis. He explored works of art and literature for
ideas to work into theory; the most famous is his oedipal conflict, derived
from Sophocles. He saw poets and dramatists as being on the pulse of truth
long before it was systemized by scientists and social scientists. He also
elevated art, seeing it as beyond the scope of psychoanalysis. In his "Auto-
biographic Study" (1925), he said that psychoanalysis "can do nothing
towards elucidating the nature of the artistic gift, nor can it explain the
means by which the artist works" (p. 65). And some years later (1933), in
relation to the understanding of women, he advises us to "turn to the poets"
(p. 135). Yet he saw the motivating forces of symbolization and fantasy,
the essence of artistic creation, as being either sublimated sexual energy
or unsatisfied wishes: "an unhappy person never fantasizes, only an unsatisfied one" (1907, p. 146). Primary process was to be under the control
of reality-adaptive secondary process. On occasion, Freud turned poets
away from his practice, telling them that psychoanalysis would not be good
for their work.

If psychoanalysis historically has deemed its method inadequate to the
artistic, and in opposition to the spiritual, hasn't it affected our way of listening to and esteeming these areas of a person's life? Has not psychoanalytic theory, in its emphasis on sexual and relational health and development, repressed and blinded itself to this delicate but essential aspect
of existence? Have not these twins in some way been the abused children
of psychoanalysis who are now valiantly trying to make their perceptions
and voices heard and included?

SOUL MURDER

A patient's explosion of anger, or honest confrontation of an analyst, can
be an act of trust that was never possible in childhood. Defining this anger

as "negative" or a sign of "illness" as opposed to an act of courage or transcendence can mean the difference between enhancing a soul or damaging it. Winnicott's (1971) use of paradoxical thinking advanced theory with the idea that the destruction of an object allows a patient to make the object of value and use, to discover it is there while freeing himself from bondage to the object. This process requires the analyst to understand that the anger is an appeal to him as a good object. He must therefore not identify himself as a bad object, by responding defensively or narcissistically, or by retaliating. Winnicott (1969) makes it clear that the patient's "destruction" is innocent—the patient expects that the other will survive. If the expectation is not met the outcome will then be as Ghent (1992) describes:

> He or she [the patient] has been implicitly defined and labeled as destructive by the very fact that the object has been destroyed. The . . . subjective object never becomes real but remains a bundle of projections and externality is not discovered. . . and finally, fear and hatred of the other develop. [p. 149]

All forms of nonretaliation are not alike. A manifestly benign response on the part of an analyst can have varying inner meanings. He may be covering an inner irritation, contempt, or lack of understanding with a "professional" acceptance. He may use an "affirmative stance" (Kohut 1972) to counter internally punitive, or unconsciously self-critical inner objects, or take a stance of love and tolerance (Freud 1916), or may "permit the patient to express the thoughts, feelings and wishes that are opposed by punitive, unconscious, self-criticism" (Kris 1994). But all these stances are somewhat paternalistic and assume a pathology in the patient rather than an exertion of health or courage. The listening that understands the paradoxical nature of the patient's "anger" and esteems it for its courage will welcome this protest and so bring into being an aspect of the patient that has never been present before.

What goes on in the silent listening of therapist to patient and patient to therapist will eventually be revealed and will affect the outcome of the treatment. Listening is never neutral. It is always "filled" with an analyst's thinking, and the quality of his or her understanding, and a patient will intuit this. Perhaps feeling loved comes from one grasping that the other's listening approaches some truth about an inner state. And the absence of this may create hate. Though the external response may be the same, the understanding *in the listening* will effect different resolutions in the patient.

If the patient's involvement in this process fails to bring about a favorable resolution, hope is diminished and he/she is less likely to try again. Perhaps that is why, in the Bible, soul murder is considered "the one unforgivable sin." The sapping of life—the turning of an opportunity for love into hate—is an invisible crime; the effect of it goes on killing throughout a person's life. Shengold (1989) describes soul murder as "the deliberate attempt to eradicate or compromise the separate identity of another person. The victims of soul murder remain in large part possessed by another, their souls in bondage to someone else" (p. 2).

The inescapable dilemma of the abused child (and for most all kinds of abuse) is how to maintain his or her perceptions and still retain a good object. Most often, the child sacrifices his or her own perceptions to maintain the object. The same holds true in many adult love relationships. The demand from the other—"see it my way or I will withdraw my love"—for one dependent on another can be tantamount to saying "see it my way or I will kill you." Living with this, the person so threatened narrows, restricts, and denies his/her experience and perception in order to appease the rage or narcissism of the other. Rather than expansion of self, the narrowing of self, through the destruction of perception or inner freedom—under threat of loss of love—is the essence of soul death. The experience of freedom necessary for expansion toward wholeness is replaced, in order to survive, by a feeling of restriction. Also, as Shengold (1989) writes, "It is exactly the ability to feel that is so vulnerable to ruin and mutilation, especially the ability to feel love" (p. 84).

Is there not a dangerous parallel between the abused child whose perceptions are overridden by the rational, knowing ideas of adults, and a patient diminished and ignored in aspects of him/her self by a theory that potentially overvalues one side of his existence over another? Our patients, who come to us with the vulnerability of children and lovers and the "willingness to repeat" their masochistic submission patterns that are the echoes of their past, are so easily hurt again unless we guard against our potential to recreate what they are trying to escape. In theory, the murdering of soul can become through technique and through unexamined aspects of the analysts' countertransference the murdering of souls in patients.

Narcissistic investment in a theory that doesn't allow for its own negation can keep a patient in bondage to a pernicious past, and bound to an identity which compels him to repetitive attempts to make things come out right. This can lead to hopelessness, a feeling that the present or future can be no different than the past . . . and so a kind of soul death or dying.

The understanding of the need for a paradoxical reaction on the part of a healer or mentor has long been a part of the wisdom of religions and poets. In Buddhism, it is a well-known saying that to reach enlightenment, one must destroy or "kill" his teacher. And Walt Whitman (1855), preceding Freud, had said "He most honors my style who learns under it how to destroy the teacher" (p. 72).

CONCLUDING THOUGHTS

I do not mean to polarize the realms of the poetic and of reason. There are psychoanalyses rich in the poetic process and poems that depend heavily on reason. My concern in this paper has been to highlight a tendency in psychoanalysis, going back to its origins, that can both entrench certain patients in traumatic experiences from their past and ignore or minimize certain fragile aspects of the artistic or spiritual self and so not adequately nourish them.

Is there a basic morality in an analyst's stance that can protect against that tendency? I believe there are three relevant factors. The first is an ongoing awareness of the basic duality of reality. André Green (1986) says duality is the irreducible basis of intelligence, leading to the creation of a third entity, namely symbolic activity (pp. 18–19). Every utterance of a patient or analyst assumes another possibility, which may then transform to a third, so meaning is never assumed or imposed. Analysts can err in thinking either that their "objective" responses, based on theory or learning, have truth, or that their "intuitive" responses from the unconscious are inherently true. Both the objective and subjective can be contaminated by bias or countertransference unless checked by a reflective consciousness wondering what a communication might be or how else it can be seen. The second factor is what many poets have in varying ways described as the essence of the poetic process—a suspension in the beliefs of the self for another's sake. And the third is a commitment to the truth of the unconscious over and above the analyst's commitment to theory, institutions, or his own biases. Violating this commitment is a betrayal of the patient for narcissistic or security concerns of the analyst.

Integrity, commonly thought of as an adherence to a code of approved behavior or morals, really means wholeness. It requires inner flexibility, an openness to experiences in the world and within oneself, an ability to ride cycles of success and failure, illusion and disillusion; and it leaves a sense of the indispensability of one for the other and of a commitment to listening from a stance of "not knowing." With such a stance the analyst is more likely not to impose meaning but instead to discover the unique meaning of each utterance or behavior.

The polarity of creativity and power is a relatively new frontier in psychoanalytic exploration. Nietzsche (1887) saw the opposing and innovative forces of the creative spirit as achieving a new kind of power, one not obedient to reason or existing external moral forces. He in fact saw the "good" man, the one who is obedient to reason and a logical morality, as potentially dangerous, "enabling the present to live at the expense of the future" and perhaps endangering man's potential to "reach the peak of magnificence of which he is capable" (p. 155).

Buber (1958) thought psychoanalysis could be helpful up to a point, but then became an obstacle to the essential I–Thou relationship because of its limitation on true mutuality. He wrote that in the I–Thou relationship, "No system of ideas, no foreknowledge, and no fancy intervene between I and Thou. . . . No aim, no lust and no anticipation intervene between I and Thou. . . . Every means is an obstacle. Only when every means has collapsed does the meeting come about" (pp. 11–12).

Buber understood that to experience one's own wholeness, one must have available the wholeness of the other and that it is only in partnership and dialogue that a person can experience himself as a whole—in a relationship where both reveal and perceive and have forsworn the security armor of preconceptions.

Where the primacy of soul is not acknowledged—in its workings apart from the logic of the world, apart from reason as we have been conditioned to understand reason—crimes against the soul go unnoticed and unpunished, though their consequence to the self and the world can be more monumental than crimes that break the laws of civilization. The aim of the life of the spirit is to put its unique stamp on the world, not to be stamped by it.

I think that developing theory and technique which foster awareness and understanding of the patient's needs and frustrations in relation to the creative and spiritual would address suffering not now understood in relation to this plight and could release joy now contained by failure to acknowledge the centrality of such needs.

A poem has no ax to grind. It presents itself with aesthetic power and lets the reader go, or captivates him. Poems endure for centuries. Reason and theory try to convince and hold you to their point, yet they easily fade and are replaced by other ideas.

Robert Frost says a poem inclines toward the impulse, assumes direction with the first line laid down, runs a course of lucky events, and ends in clarification of life and a momentary stay against confusion (Weinstein 1995). Could this not be a description of an analysis as well?

REFERENCES

Bachelard, G. (1987). *On Poetic Imagination and Reverie.* Dallas: Spring.

Balint, M. (1968). *The Basic Fault.* London: Tavistock.

Bion, W. R. (1963). *Elements of Psychoanalysis.* London: Heinemann.

Buber, M. (1958). *I and Thou.* New York: Macmillan.

Coleridge, S. (1817). Biographia literaria. In *Coleridge, Poems and Prose,* ed. P. Washington, pp. 227–237. New York: Knopf.

Dickinson, E. (1862). Poem no. 435. In *The Complete Poems of Emily Dickinson,* ed. T. H. Johnson, p. 209. Boston: Little, Brown, 1960.

Dupont, J., ed. (1995). *The Clinical Diary of Sándor Ferenczi.* Cambridge, MA: Harvard University Press.

Freud, S. (1907). Creative writers and daydreaming. *Standard Edition* 9:141–156.

———— (1916). Some character types met with in psychoanalytic work. *Standard Edition* 14:309–333.

———— (1925). An autobiographical study. *Standard Edition* 20:7–74.

———— (1933). New introductory lectures on psychoanalysis: femininity. *Standard Edition* 22:112–135.

Ghent, E. (1992). Paradox and process. *Psychoanalytic Dialogues* 2:135–159.

Green, A. (1986). *On Private Madness.* Madison, CT: International Universities Press.

Jung, C. J. (1910). *Memories, Dreams, Reflections,* ed. A. Jaffe. New York: Pantheon, 1963.

Kohut, H. (1972). Thoughts on narcissism and narcissistic rage. *Psychoanalytic Study of the Child* 27:360–400. New Haven, CT: Yale University Press.

Kris, A. O. (1994). Freud's treatment of a narcissistic patient. *International Journal of Psycho-Analysis* 75:649–664

Laforgue, J. (1917). *Oeuvres completes,* vol. III. Paris: Mercure de France.

Nietzsche, F. (1887). *The Birth of Tragedy and the Genealogy of Morals*, trans. F. Gollfing. New York: Doubleday, 1956.

Rank, O. (1930). *Art and the Artist*, trans. C. Alkinson. New York: Norton, 1989.

———(1941). *Beyond Psychotherapy*. Camden, NJ: Haddon.

Rilke, R. M. (1963). *Letters to a Young Poet*. New York: Norton.

Shengold, L. (1989). *Soul Murder*. New Haven, CT:Yale University Press.

Simpson, L. (1972). *North of Jamaica*. New York: Harper & Row.

———(1986). *The Character of the Poet*. Ann Arbor, MI: University of Michigan Press.

Weinstein, A. (1995). Understanding literature and life: drama, poetry and narrative. Superstar Teaching Series lecture. Springfield, VA: The Learning Company.

Whitman, W. (1855). Song of myself. In *Leaves of Grass and Selected Prose*, ed. B. Scully, p. 72. New York: Holt, Rinehart & Winston, 1949.

Winnicott, D. W. (1969). The use of an object. *International Journal of Psycho-Analysis* 5:711–726.

———(1971). *Playing and Reality*. London:Tavistock.

15

Whither Psychoanalysis? Thirteen Theses in Justification and Outline of a Project[1]

Lawrence Jacobson

1

Clinical psychoanalysis in the United States is in a crisis. In areas such as literary and cultural studies, psychoanalysis is more—and more deeply— appreciated and used than ever before, but in the clinical realm it feels and is under threat. It feels attacked, unappreciated, underutilized, and shows definite signs of slipping confidence. The question arises: Is America decathecting its psychoanalysis?

It is in managed care that the object of the fear is generally located these days. But recall that not very long ago the greatest object of anxiety was Prozac. People would cease to examine their lives because a powerful feel-good pill would be chosen instead. I think we need a broad, deep, and self-searching analysis of the state of American psychoanalysis. A psychoanalytic view would consider both the crisis and managed care as symptoms, and look to underlying factors or the context for illumination.

Earl Witenberg has said that most therapy relationships that end prematurely die from boredom. It might seem odd to suggest that clinical

1. This is a slightly revised version of a paper delivered at the Clinic Conference of the William Alanson White Institute, October 17, 1995.

psychoanalysis should heed that aphorism at a time when it is widely agreed that American psychoanalysis is in fertile ferment in theory and technique. But perhaps none of this ferment has disturbed a constraining and ultimately draining stasis about: What is the point of all this psychoanalysis? What is distinctive about it? It is a deeper and more lasting kind of therapy than any other, is mostly what our answers amount to. As long as depth and durability are valued, that's fine, though hardly inspirational. Much of the contemporary reformulating and rethinking goes on as if the question of the point of psychoanalysis is settled and there is nothing interesting to be asked there.

It is time, perhaps, to question the adequacy of efficacy, to state, find, or refind psychoanalysis's potential and distinctiveness. We must begin by looking at the purpose and effects of clinical psychoanalysis in, and in relation to, its social and historical situation. That is, to look at it as not merely a clinical but as a social activity, an activity of the society.

PSYCHOANALYSIS AS A SOCIAL ACTIVITY

2

The imperative to consider social and historical context arises not just because of our current cultural situation. It is implicit in the relational paradigm. Jay Greenberg, for example, in a 1995 article defines the "interactive matrix" as "the beliefs, values, commitments, hopes, needs, fears, wishes, and so on that both analyst and patient bring to any particular moment in the treatment. . . . We cannot even describe an intervention meaningfully without understanding the interactive matrix within which it is made. . . . every event of an analysis becomes what it is and acquires its meaning within [this] context . . . whether the analyst thinks so or not" (pp. 11, 14, 21).

To explain himself Greenberg uses Wittgenstein, whom he summarizes:

> The meaning of a word . . . can be known only when we understand the broad context within which it is used. We cannot know what the word "means" to a person speaking it unless we know its function, unless we know what the speaker is trying to do with it. . . . Like Wittgenstein, I think of this idea in terms of the rules of games. There are games—football comes to mind—that sanction certain actions that in other contexts are considered criminal. Tackling somebody who is trying to get someplace quickly is an act of random violence on the street; in the stadium it

can be a game-saving act of heroism. What the act means—what it *is*, really—depends upon the circumstances within which it occurs. We can say very little about one person tackling another unless we know what game they are playing. [p. 13]

Greenberg's shift from words to acts is apposite, for what he says is so of gestures and affects, not merely words. The "cool" of a black man, for example, is utterly different in meaning from the same words, gestures, and affect in a white man—it is part of a different "game."

Greenberg does not go there, but clearly this conception takes us beyond the analytic dyad, into the cultural field, to understand what is going on in a psychoanalysis. We cannot understand what is going on between any analyst–analysand pair without knowing what game they are playing. Greenberg means what games each of them brings to the moment, but we must also ask, if we are to understand the analytic pair, what game are they playing together, what game is this peculiar activity, psychoanalysis?

3

By looking at psychoanalysis as a social activity, we look at it as one among the social discourses in which the issues of the culture are worked out. Similarly, pedagogy and politics, Freud's other two impossible professions, the law, religion, and the natural sciences, are social activities.

I will use the expression "cultural field" to refer to the environment of psychoanalysis, the realm of human interaction of which the social activity of psychoanalysis is a part. The cultural field is not a way of referring to "the field of interpersonal relations" but to something larger, which comes before interpersonal relations. The cultural field is the field in which whatever is going to count as interpersonal relations is worked out; it is the *ground* on which interpersonal relations is *figure*. The cultural field is the realm from which the input into the social activity is drawn, and the field of its potential effect. In both roles—as input into psychoanalysis, and as where one would look for psychoanalysis's effect—the cultural field includes but extends beyond the individual analysand. The individual analysand is a representative of and carrier for the culture.

There are two directions from which the cultural field interpolates its way into a clinical psychoanalysis: from the outside in, and from the inside outwards. Looking from the outside in, the "cool" of the black man, for example, is a response to multiple social patterns of domination of black men that press for feelings of hurt and abjection as well as economic subjection. The highly educated and articulate white psychoanalyst perforce represents these cultural patterns of domination in his person and his identification with psychoanalysis, a field that has historically emphasized personal rather than social responsibility for individuals' affective lives. The social and cultural formations that contain and enforce aspects of gender identity are similarly impelled into the psychoanalytic situation, as is widely recognized.

Social and cultural factors work also from the deepest inside of the psychoanalytic participants, outward into the psychoanalytic relationship. Social patterns of representation and domination are formative of the earliest relational experiences of the analysand and analyst. The infant crosses a threshold into language, which, with particular symbolic relations, gives form to experience. Language is a field for idiosyncratic symbolic associations reflecting the unique experiences of the analysand, but also it embodies cultural and subcultural webs of association and dissociation which are given, already formed, as far as the individual infant is concerned. Language constitutes a culturally given template to which the infant's experience must conform, and in terms of which problems in living are defined. This process is at work, moreover, even before the infant enters any realm of differentiated existence or shared verbalizable meaning, carried for example through the parents' affective responses and expectations of the infant such as of greater activity for a boy than a girl. To use Bollas's phrases, the cultural field inheres in the earliest "transformational object" experiences, the deepest "unthought knowns" of the analysand.

Nor can we ignore the effects of cultural factors on psychoanalytic theory. I take it that psychoanalytic theory is like a prism through which the analyst sees the patient and through which the patient must work to find the analyst. Psychoanalytic theory is thoroughly imbued with the assumptions, values, and metaphors of the culture at large. Freud's hydraulic metaphors, the very notions of self and health, and such contemporary notions as the multiplicity of self and an emphasis on dissociation over repression, are examples of the playing out of cultural shifts in psychoanalytic theory, and hence in the kind of game psychoanalysis is, which changes with the culture.

That the cultural field works from the inside out and the outside in to the psychoanalytic space undermines the distinction between inside and outside. What is inside turns out to be outside, and vice versa. This interfusion of inside and outside is an essential part of what is occurring in a psychoanalysis and of how psychoanalysis works.

To be sure, it is crucial that this inside–outside interfusion goes on in a very private and confidential space. The boundary of privacy maintains a segmentation between the domains of the personal and the political/cultural; and between the clinical psychoanalytic and the nonclinical psychoanalytic. The interfusion and the segmentation are equally of the essence.

4

Psychoanalysis is also an entity in itself, separable from the analyst and analysand. Psychoanalytic ideas and practice have permeated contemporary culture, which is full of notions and stories, often contradictory and paradoxical, about psychoanalysis. Every patient brings this into the room, consciously and unconsciously. So does every analyst. There is a transference to psychoanalysis itself, determined in part by the cultural location of psychoanalysis, the effect and role of psychoanalysis in the society at large, and, for the analyst, the analyst's experience of and relation to his or her training. In other words, there is always a third entity in the psychoanalytic situation: the analyst, the analysand, and psychoanalysis itself.

An arena in which psychoanalysis implicates itself into the clinical situation particularly intensely occurs in psychoanalytic training. From reading, didactic events, supervision, and personal analysis, a tradition is incorporated and integrated, more or less, and becomes part of the analyst's nature. Even if a psychoanalyst definitively rejects some parts of the tradition, that too is part of this tradition. This incorporation of psychoanalysis then inhabits the psychoanalyst, much of it literally as habits—habits of interpretation or responsiveness, habits of referring what occurs to psychoanalytic traditions. The notion of the observing ego refers to psychoanalysis inhabiting the psychoanalyst: the internalized relationship with psychoanalysis monitors the analyst's relationship with the patient.

The psychoanalytic entity is composed of traditions, experiences, canonical texts. It is this entity, psychoanalysis, that cures (if anything does)—not the analyst, but the third party, psychoanalysis, or, if one prefers, the psychoanalytic process. This must be asserted against the truth—which I don't deny—that the person of the analyst is also determinative of the cure. We must allow ourselves that paradox.

There is a useful analogy in legal practice: two people in conflict by putting it through the social activity and entity of the law. They each employ an attorney, who in turn may further employ a judge, who will ne-

gotiate and ultimately resolve the conflict by reference to their traditions and canonical texts and cases. The persons of the attorneys, the judge,
and so on, will be very much determinative of the course and outcome of
the process. Yet at the same time it will be the law that "cures" the conflict; the individuals are the medium for the process of the law that works
through them. Similarly, the analyst is the medium for the process of psychoanalysis; it is the social activity and entity of psychoanalysis that cures,
that is at work through the individual psychoanalyst.

5

All social activities as a major dimension tell stories about the cultural field.
These stories inevitably transmit knowledge and values beyond what their
practitioners know. For example, economics tells stories about monetary
relations, movements of money, and monetary value and its relations to
human activity; and it implies assumptions about motivation and value. All
social activities have moral, ethical, and political consequences. This is as
true of the natural sciences as of any other social activity. The natural sciences provide one way of talking about things, with no objective superiority over others apart from how compelling their stories are felt to be, and
their use value, which is the value of predicting. The activity of the natural
sciences thus says—in a statement that is not merely found compelling but
is socially dominant—"the good life is one in which things are known and
understood in such a way that maximally predicts what occurs."

Psychoanalysis also tells stories, about development, about what moves
people, about what people are made of, about what makes a life worth living, that sometimes seek to predict futures but mostly make very different
statements from natural scientific ones. The case can be made, and increasingly is made, that psychoanalysis is a moral discourse, less a field making
claims of fact than one making claims about what makes a life worthwhile.

PSYCHOANALYSIS AND SOCIAL REALITIES

6

Now, having made these preliminary remarks about psychoanalysis as
a social activity and entity, I want to look at the social and historical
context—necessarily in very broad brushstrokes and without claim to

the only true account. Looking back to medieval life, say over the last 700 years, western civilization may be seen as containing a project of human emancipation, emancipation from, on the one hand, the overriding domination of Nature—short and brutish lives of scarcity and vulnerability to famine and illness—and on the other hand from animism, from the experience of ourselves as embedded in a diffusely spiritual, magically ordered and managed world. The Renaissance rediscovery of classical learning and the Reformation challenge to religious authority grew into one of the great positions in this emancipatory project, reaching a height in the mid-eighteenth century, of the Enlightenment: the ideal of autonomy and maturity gained through reason, a reason conceived as abstracted, as independent of us. Reason and its handmaiden, science, push back the bounds of the sacred and the uncontrollable. Using reason we achieve a progressive mastery of internal and external nature. Reason provides authority; progress occurs by disenchantment, the ridding of illusion. From the late eighteenth century, another great position emerged, a counter-Enlightenment, Romanticism: this embodies ideals of authenticity and integrity to a creative self, a self that embodies an organic will for self-expression and self-realization. An organic, creative self rather than impersonal reason marks the distinctively human and provides authority.

Freud embodies elements of both Enlightenment and romanticism. He is the reasoning conquistador of the unconscious, for whom, though, the ego is mere rider of the horse who must steer where the horse wants to go. And Freud undermines both positions. The Enlightenment ideal of reason shades into rationalization, and the Romantic ideal of self becomes decentered and segmented: self is constituted by other (identifications) and self is unconscious to self. Reliance on the authority of reason, and reliance on the authority of self, were both destabilized by Freud. Finally, in this history in broad brushstrokes, comes symbolic interactionism and American pragmatism, Sullivan, and relational theories. Our selves are products of reflected appraisals and interpersonal interactions, utterly social constructions. The real, in any other sense, either as reason which is objective and independent of us, or as a self which transcends reflected appraisals, the real other than "that which is consensually validated," recedes.

Another trend has occurred in conjunction with these shifts in our sense of ourselves and in what counts as real and human. The Western emancipatory project has been most successful not in mastery of ourselves but of nature. This mastery of nature has occurred through instrumental reasoning, or technical rationality, which is the kind of reasoning used in order to most economically apply means to achieve a given predetermined end. Maximum efficiency, the best cost-output ratio, is its standard of success. Instrumental or technical rationality has become progressively more dominant over the last two centuries—as Max Weber emphasized early in this century—to the exclusion of any other form of consideration that may be more applicable to serious moral deliberation. (Moral reasoning is quite different from instrumental reasoning; it involves determining ends in the very process of the reasoning, whereas instrumental or technical reasoning is about getting to an end already defined.) On the largest social scale, instrumental or technical rationality has been apparent in the social engineering that has characterized this century—the "-isms" to create the desired society and citizen. Now, the socially constructed person is a necessary corollary to this trend of the progressive takeover of instrumental reasoning. If you want to socially engineer a society and its citizens, you need a notion of the person which is as much as possible socially determinable. If the self as a product of interaction didn't exist, he'd have to be invented.

Technical reasoning pushes out moral reasoning. Instrumental values displace other values. One stage in this process has been, in Christopher Lasch's phrase, the family as "haven in a heartless world." The process of industrialization since the nineteenth century, with the need for efficiency in the capitalist enterprise and in the modern state, meant that first the public realm of work became progressively dominated by instrumental values, while traditional values for some time continued in the havens of the family (embodied especially by women) and religion.

Now these havens—as they inexorably would—are breaking down. It is not that the family or religion stops functioning, but that they too become instrumentalized—valued as a means to something else. The family is guarded now largely because it is seen as essential for the production of well-functioning children, who become not criminals but useful adults—which is to say producers and consumers. This now extends to the mental health field, which in its mainstream becomes increasingly obviously directed at the maximally efficient maintenance of efficient producers and consumers. Selves and psyches are valued as means, not ends. Thus, we arrive at managed care. [2]

---

2. For the purposes of simplicity I have been talking of *the* culture and *the* language, as if they are monolithic. Fortunately, however, they are not, and internal contradictions

As a corollary to this social process, the self that successfully (or efficiently) lives in this society is instrumentalized. The self is not merely seen but sees itself as having value in terms of its efficient adaptation, its production and consumption. The self is not valuable in itself but as means to other ends. This was seen very clearly by Fromm in his description of what he called "the marketing orientation," in which we value ourselves by our value in the market, by how we are valued by others, so that we inevitably must market ourselves, and be as adaptable as possible.

Thus we have among the social symptoms the glorification of what has been called "the saturated self," full of experiences, even full of relationships, but shallow, embedded in the present moment, and politically apathetic. We have pathologies of meaninglessness. And whereas social adaptation was for Freud necessary for treatment, now social adaptation is often the most resistant of impediments to a treatment of any depth.

Unlike in Fromm's time, or as was only beginning as Fromm wrote in the 1940s, we now face the issue of the mental health field as utterly ceasing to contest this process of market orientation and overwhelmingly functioning as a fellow-traveller, fixing the malfunctioning, adopting an ethos of means–end efficiency, where the end is defined and targeted from the beginning, rather than the end as something that emerges within the process. It thus assists in the creation of the instrumentalized, efficient and adaptable, market-oriented self.

7

Relational and interpersonal thinking may be merely a footnote to this trend.[3] The notion of the self as interpersonally created in a relational matrix—and that there is really no other self than that—follows from this larger cultural trend of the modern world and supports it. This should make us distinctly uncomfortable: we may be part and parcel of the very forces that threaten us. Whatever else we may think of the "classical" Freudian

---

and interstices amidst cultures and languages provide degrees of freedom. The simplification seems appropriate, though, for my purpose is to highlight a powerfully totalizing trend—one that tends to subsume other possibilities—within contemporary culture.

3. In this chapter I use "relational" and "interpersonal" as if the terms are synonymous. I am focusing on concerns which I believe are common to both, so that the distinction between them, though important in many contexts, seems unimportant in this one.

drive conception, in placing the individual as intrinsically asocial and in opposition to civilization it gave a potential traction against social forces. There are twin dangers for interpersonal/relational analysis. Firstly, though relational analysis—*because* of this intertwining with the modern world—may be the best analysis for selves living in it (which I think *is* true) it may *instead*, if it does not attend to this dilemma, become a reflection of the culture rather than engaging contestedly with it. I am reminded of Juliet Mitchell's 1974 book *Psychoanalysis and Feminism*. Freud had been lambasted by feminists for his patriarchal values. Mitchell reformulated or reread Freud: Don't read Freud as a reflection of his patriarchal society, she essentially said, but as an analysis of it, of life within it, of how it is internalized and transmitted, and so on. Her reading was seminal in the resurgence of feminism's ongoing interest in psychoanalysis. The contemporary danger for interpersonal/relational analysis is to make the opposite step: in trying to accommodate to contemporary realities, and with social reality—as Marcuse (1955) first emphasized—so deeply built into its very theory, it ceases to be an analysis of the individual in social reality and comes to merely reflect the position of the individual in contemporary social reality.

The second danger: I do not think that relational analysts directly foster instrumental selves (though I have some qualms which I will refer to later) but for relational analysis not to foster instrumental selves there must be a noninstrumentalizing analyst who fosters a noninstrumental analytic relationship. In much interpersonal/relational thinking there is little basis for the analyst empowering the analysand against instrumentalizing social trends other than by the analyst being a good noninstrumentalizing person. In other words, it does not rest on a strong notion of the third entity, psychoanalysis itself, as noninstrumentalizing. This psychoanalysis risks becoming another "haven in a heartless world" or "haven in a heartless mental health industry," which is ultimately not a viable position. There needs to be some active *contesting* of the instrumentalizing social trend, a contesting that is *integral* to the clinical psychoanalytic process.

8

In summary so far, the question of "What is this game, psychoanalysis?" can only be answered by understanding psychoanalysis's position in relation to the culture. Does psychoanalysis relatively seamlessly take its place within these social-cultural trends, as a treatment through which the patient can hope to come to live less problematically within them? I think that is ultimately unviable. Or does psychoanalysis contest the culture, and if so how?

The question is one of the relation between clinical psychoanalysis and social, consensually validated reality. Obviously, psychoanalysis *is* a social reality itself, and goes on within social reality, so how then can it also contest it? If there is an answer to this then it is also the answer to how psychoanalysis can provide itself and its patients with traction, with a subversive power, against social forces. It is this traction, this location—within social reality yet also contesting and subverting it—which may be what really distinguishes, or should really distinguish, psychoanalysis from psychotherapy.

FIVE PROPOSALS

9.1

Psychoanalysis not only tells its stories, as do all social activities, but psychoanalysis is essentially about storytelling. More exactly, psychoanalysis is about what effect a story makes.

Consider psychoanalytic training: didactic events, reading, supervision, personal analysis. All of this has to do with stories. Some of them are scientific stories such as accounts of development. Many are stories about other analysts and the stories they told, ranging from canonical texts and case histories to gossip. (Incidentally, gossip has an enormous and unacknowledged role in analytic training.) And there are stories about ourselves, told by our analysts and supervisors and patients. Most essential, though, is not the content of these stories, but the experience of their use and effect. The essence of psychoanalytic training is coming to know what happens when storytelling goes on, what difference a story can make. Not the content of the story, but what a storyteller does with and through a story.

Thus the constant analytic clinical attention is on "What is the effect of the patient telling me this story?" or ". . . of my telling the patient this story?"—*that* is the quintessential analytic material: the transference and countertransference. When I analyze a patient's expression and suggest a piece of story about the patient (and inevitably about myself) it is always a self-analysis, a referring or comparing of the patient to myself, comparing what I feel about the patient's response to what I have felt of others' responses to me and my response to others, where "others" are not only people but readings and traditions. And the patient is doing the same, which influences the patient's responses to which I am responding. There is a constant cross-referring of stories, within and between us, which is going on mostly unconsciously on both of our parts. There is a constant imparting of knowledge of which neither of us is in gull possession, just as any good story means more than its teller can know. That a story means more than its teller can know makes for the dimension of communication between the unconscious of analyst and analysand, and makes for the aspect of keeping the future open rather than indoctrinating the patient with our expertise. This is what cures, if anything does, in some way more than teaching the patient to live less problematically within consensually validated social constraints.

By this account, then, the analyst is a kind of reader. The analyst is a reader who tells stories, and a reader who is aware that every reading is itself a telling a story about what is read (by referring it to other read stories). I am not in any way reducing the patient here to a text: the patient is also a reader who tells stories.

The meaning of any good story is greater than the teller knows. The meaning is also more than what the words denote. The meaning can only by grasped in the use and effects of the words in the context, including all that we describe as the affect in the situation, the nonverbal aspects, gestures, tones, rhythms, and silences. Thus, a psychoanalytic reading looks beyond the content of a story to what has been called its illocutionary force, and at speech not as mere content but as performative act.

This point I am making can be related to Edgar Levenson's advice that if you want to know what is unconscious when a patient is telling you something, then look to what is being enacted between you and the patient in the telling. If you just consider the content of what the patient is saying you will miss a major part of what is unconscious, which is only apparent in the effect of the telling, in the telling as performative act, with illocutionary force.

9.2

That psychoanalysis is essentially about the effect of stories implies that psychoanalysis must attend to how it reads its own stories. Many doctrinal disputes may be usefully dissolved by attending to *how* psychoanalysts read rather than *what* story is read, or which psychoanalytic story is better than another. This view holds praxis—the effect of a theory—as having primacy over theory itself; it declines to see theory as something ruling over practice from some higher domain. If you want to understand a theory, look not to the theory in itself, but to the effect of the theory. This is a psychoanalytic reading of theory, which is much the same as a psychoanalytic reading of a patient.

Here we cannot avoid the question of how Freud is read. It should give relational and interpersonal analysts reason to pause that, for the humanities, psychoanalysis is very much about Freud, and these are branches of the humanities that are not known for their conservatism. Are they struggling with obdurate old-fashioned theory because they are unaware of modern interpersonal/relational thinking, or are we misreading?

It is often pejoratively stated that some analysts treat Freud like a Bible, but that raises the question of how a Bible should be read. A problem that has been widespread in American psychoanalysis, across all schools (as well as among the scientific critics of psychoanalysis), has been reading Freud as *fundamentalists* read a Bible, as literal claims of fact, rather than as—arguably—a Bible should be read, for its effects. An enormous effort is put into the *content* of Freud's stories in a desperate attempt to try to make him internally consistent when he often was not: Was he object-relational or a drive theorist? What *was* his position on homosexuality, female sexuality, the centrality of the Oedipus complex? Is what he said true, does it fit the facts? I suggest that this fails to be a psychoanalytic reading of Freud; because it fails to distinguish his illocutionary force from his content, it does not seek to understand his theory by its effects, or, more accurately, only superficially so.

Edgar Levenson has said that a psychoanalytic understanding of what the patient is saying is to be gained by attending to what is being enacted in the transference–countertransference, as the saying is happening—in the effect of the saying, as I am putting it. So we might expect a psychoanalytic understanding (reading) of Freud to be gained by attending to what becomes enacted in the relationship with Freud when analysts read Freud. And Freud is a big problem for American clinical psychoanalysis, a disturbance that haunts it. Large segments of American psychoanalysis therefore avoid him, or define themselves against him, or profess belief in him but somehow easily amputate parts (the death instinct is a favorite), or otherwise seek to press a consistency and respectability onto his theory that is not there. I read this as an enactment which indicates that American psychoanalysis is seeking to disown something about Freud and itself: that Freud and psychoanalysis are about destabilizing, decentering, disturbing all categories and complacencies.[4] Psychoanalysis destablizes certainties about stories: it disturbs stories people tell like "this suffering is bad for me and I don't like it"; the coordinates that are used to structure stories, like the coordinates of self and other; and stories about what relating and understanding are. American psychoanalysis has lost this disturbingness, as Freud predicted. Ironically, portions of American popular culture know better: When Freud can be blamed in the early 1980s for the dismissal of stories of child sexual abuse, and then a decade later blamed for encouraging belief in them, then something is being expressed about a slippery villain who defies and undermines our accepted categories—our fantasies of common sense.

9.3

To say that psychoanalysis is about the effect of stories is to say also that whereas psychology and psychiatry are concerned with facts, consensually validated social realities, psychoanalysis is concerned with acts. One may say "X relates to Y this way because of these constitutional or biological factors and these relational factors." That is fair enough as fact. Psychoanalysis begins when these facts are taken as performative acts and explored for their effects. This destabilizes them as facts, and thereby gives the individual emancipatory potential in relation to the facts, the social reality.

For psychoanalysis, in contrast to psychotherapy, when the facts are called on (like "I suffered this trauma") this is given weight, but weight as a performative act rather than as a fact. Now this performative act is not voluntary—the act is not transparent to the actor—and we can never forget that psychoanalysis is engaged with and in suffering. I am certainly not presenting here some notion of "mere" performative act that disregards or devalues the patient's suffering or reality. But in considering

---

4. Freud was not totalistic about this. He also was concerned with control and prediction, but that is not the part disowned by mainstream American psychoanalysis. Rather, it is the part that was valorized—Hartmann's Freud—and then reacted against by more progressive branches of American psychoanalysis as if it was the whole Freud. That, in conjunction with the ameliorative tendency in the more progressive branches of American psychoanalysis, led to the conservative and progressive branches equally marginalizing the disturbing Freud.

emancipatory potential in relation to social reality and facts, psychoanalysis must not forget that reality is the best defense.

The controversies and tangles around the validating of memories provide an example of the difficulties that arise in trying to define and contest a position without being clear about the relation of psychoanalysis to social reality. Whatever "validating" means psychoanalytically, which is a complex question, it does not mean confirming facticity. Whether recovered memories are "objective reality" stories or not is a side issue for psychoanalysis, which some psychoanalysts may seek to answer by joining their psychoanalytic experience with some *other* expertise and interest, but which is not a psychoanalytic question or answer.

A scientist may say, "You psychoanalysts do this, but it is not validated or real," to which the psychoanalytic reply is a question: "What is the effect of your conviction that that kind of validation is the only qualification for something to count as real?" That is not the only possible reply, but I do suggest it is the only *psychoanalytic* one.

There are psychoanalytic propositions, and consensually or scientifically validated facts are often important in a psychoanalysis. The relevant issue is not the proposition per se but its use: what game, what social activity it is part of. Some psychoanalytic developmental or process notions (Oedipus complex, defense, containing, and so on) may be used scientifically (to formulate an experimental hypothesis) and be found useful or not in that social activity of prediction. A psychoanalytic use of a proposition— whatever its status in another game—is quite different. Psychoanalysis uses propositions as positions from which to question. It is essential that these positions themselves are in turn questioned. Statements in a psychoanalysis are the verbally formulatable elements of the analyst's convictions from which to unravel the effects of the analysand's convictions, in turn to be unraveled themselves for their effects.

Thus, an effective psychoanalysis subverts the hold of facticity by the exploration of its effects, effects which are neither vague nor abstract but often real and concrete. Hence, the first proposal on how to contest social reality while being part of it: read psychoanalysis as about the effect of stories.

10

The second proposal is: theorizing psychoanalysis is very important. What I mean by theorizing is perhaps not the usual meaning but this: the disembedding of psychoanalysis at any moment from its necessary embeddedness in the social matrix—just as we seek to disentangle clinically from the inevitable transference–countertransference enactments of a psychoanalytic relationship. Every theoretical light casts shadows, every form of knowledge has its unconscious, and so becomes embedded in enactments of what it cannot think.

To take one series of such moments. In mainstream American psychoanalysis of the 1940s and at least into the 1970s, there was an overreliance on the content of interpretation and on the cognitive content of insight. This led to a movement to disembed from that by theorizing the relationship, the interaction, as the curative factor, in contradistinction from interpreting. There would have been no way at that time to make a place for or to theoretically and clinically elaborate the relationship or interaction except by conceiving it in opposition to the analyst's act of knowing and conveying the knowledge in verbal interpretation. But that very dichotomy, splitting knowing from interpersonal experience of relationship, carried the seeds of its own embeddedness— embeddedness in the cultural splitting of intellect from feeling, embeddedness in the cultural valorization of the saturated rather than the reflective life, and more. To unstick from such inevitable enactments is not to retrogressively take the other side, but to move further with another turn of the screw.

My theorizing in this essay is as historically contingent as any other. Seeking to disembed clinical psychoanalysis from certain predicaments, this writing cannot escape embeddedness nor claim a special higher consciousness of it, an "awarer than thou." The most that can be hoped is that its own embeddedness is not yet relevant. Ricoeur wrote of psychoanalysis as embodying a "hermeneutic of suspicion." Let me paraphrase that as "an interpretive strategy of suspicion about whether anything said or done is merely what it claims to be." So I suggest psychoanalysis needs to have a hermeneutic of suspicion about its own theory: to always suspect its own theory is a rationalization, or a holdover from an old battle, or an unacknowledged compliance with the social milieu.

11

I have already said some things about instrumental or technical reasoning. The term goes back to Aristotle, who sorted human reason into three realms: *techne* (technical reasoning); *theoria* (pure speculation—truth for its own sake); and *praxis*, moral/political reasoning; "practical reasoning" and the "pragmatic" derive from the same root. In technical reasoning, ends are already known, independent of the agent, and socially given: build a house, get to the moon, remove hallucinations, remove suffering. In praxis, the very process involves the working out and determining of ends. Thus my third proposal: psychoanalysis is praxis, not techne.

This is not an imperative of purity—praxis is so difficult to theorize because it involves elements of theoria and techne. But I do imply that psychoanalysis must be suspicious of all instrumentalizing. It is hard to overstate both the importance and difficulty of this, because the social forces toward instrumentalizing are so powerful. Notice how the very term "pragmatism" has been itself assimilated to technical reasoning. In popular usage "pragmatism" no longer refers to a way of thinking about what ends we seek, but more often is used to justify *not* thinking about ends, as a shallow equivalent of "if it works, do it, and don't bother thinking further about where you're going."

So all technique must be suspect because technique—unavoidable as it is—implies ends and so forecloses other possible ends. Psychoanalysis is anti-closure, not anti-suffering, and not pro-health. We must be suspicious of all social categorizing like diagnoses, notions of what health is, and instrumental techniques, such as medication. These constitute material to be analyzed and lived with, but to speak of integrating them into psychoanalysis is misconceived. Regarding medication, for example: we know that sometimes if a patient would just give themselves a good meal or a good night out it would do them a world of good. We might say that to them and wonder why they cannot give it to themselves, but do we then talk of integrating good meals into psychoanalysis?

What is the authority of psychoanalysis, then, if not a technical authority or authority of knowledge? Here I will sound a bit gnomic because I can only indicate an answer. The authority of psychoanalysis is the authority of a question, not that of an answer, and it is measured in its establishing possibilities for the formation of more stories.

12

Fourthly, professionalization is instrumentalization. Professions are formed and tolerated because they serve social ends. Professionalization can be seen as a social mechanism that contains and domesticates what might otherwise be disturbing to the social fabric. This is very much what medicalization did to American psychoanalysis, or equally, what American psychoanalysts did to psychoanalysis. What role is played by calling psychoanalysis a therapy? Does it allay our guilt by claiming it is good for people? Is it like a parameter to stop things getting out of hand: "We'll limit our conception of what is going on here to therapy" being an equivalent of "Say whatever you feel but don't throw anything around"? Psychoanalysis must develop a hermeneutic of suspicion about its social function, and particularly be suspicious of itself as a profession of therapy, because therapy in the contemporary social context has an increasingly instrumentalizing function, a foreclosing of ends.

This also implies that the individual psychoanalyst must be suspicious of psychoanalytic institutions. Bion captured this well in writing on the container and the contained: the purpose of the institution is to contain and yet further the birth of the insight which threatens to burst it apart. The necessary paradox of the psychoanalytic institution is that it must be a social institution, ordering the social activity, yet at the same time fostering a continuing challenge to its own authority to do so. So there is a responsibility of the individual analyst to interpret back to the institution; the individual analyst has an obligation to disturb the psychoanalytic institution, to disturb it in a psychoanalytic way.

13

Finally, psychoanalysis must maintain what I like to call a robust unconscious: an asocial, nonverbal unconscious, a "radical imaginary," to use Castoriadis's term. Such a notion of the unconscious gives traction and subversive power to the individual in the social-symbolic arena: the unconscious as an asocial resource, not domesticated, not a kind of supervisor of a good therapeutic relationship, but as a continuing disturber, a trickster.

For there is a trend in interpersonal/relational thinking to domesticate psychoanalysis, to make it comprehensible, palatable, marketable. The body as well as the unconscious tends to become subordinated to something called relatedness, the highest value. In some accounts it is as if the body and the unconscious serve relatedness, which instrumentalizes them.

Psychoanalysis should instead foster an appreciation of our strangeness, of how foreign we really are—or really can be if we are lucky—to ourselves. I think that some recent clinical writing, particularly about affect or emotion, about dissociation and multiple selves, and new ideas about authenticity, is trying to maintain some ways of talking about how strange we are—now that we no longer permit ourselves to talk of strangenesses like instincts. But the quasi-scientificness of psychoanalytic discourse here presents a paradoxical challenge, for as soon as we begin to talk about our strangeness within the current modes of psychoanalytic discourse, we are trying to render what we are talking about more transparent, familiar, accepted, unstrange. For psychoanalytic journals, like psychoanalytic institutes, serve not only to foster the birth but also to contain the insight that threatens to burst them apart. So this challenge—the challenge to maintain a robust, asocial and nonverbal, subversive unconscious, and a sense of our own strangeness—is not merely a clinical and conceptual challenge, but a challenge to how we express ourselves. It calls for a willingness to *act* strangely and sound strange.

I am reminded here again of Bion, who wrote that "development itself is not an object that can be 'desired.'" I read this as Bion pointing out that development is something one does in relation to social reality, as his uncoupling pleasure and desire from the social realm, and as his claiming that psychoanalysis should not have a normative notion of development. Value the impossibility of psychoanalysis, and read all psychoanalytic writing as an articulation of psychoanalysis's necessary failure to make sense of what is going on, because it is in the patient's coming to know this necessary failure that he may come to appreciate himself.

BIBLIOGRAPHICAL NOTE

I have not used the usual format for citing works in a text for a few reasons. I did not want to break up the reading with lists of names and dates. Most of the important influences on my thinking are pervasive through the paper in a way that could not be represented by citations in specific locations. Moreover, the traditional citation method suggests layers of accumulation and possession of knowledge which are true to neither the purpose nor the experience of writing this paper. In what I imagine is a common experience, I am constantly finding I have been influenced by people whom I not only do not remember, but am sure I've never read.

So this work stands or falls with less than the customary scaffold of scholarship. I do, however, give references below for works referred to in the text, plus a few other pieces I want to highlight for their influence of the pervasive kind, specifically for their stretching relational horizons. These are Forrester and Phillips for their attention to what slips past the field's grasp, Felman (whose ideas especially influenced Section 9) and Forrester for their readings of Lacan and of psychoanalysis as about story-telling, and Kristeva and Phillips for their sense of our essential strangeness to ourselves.

REFERENCES

Bion W. R. (1970). *Attention and Interpretation*. London: Tavistock.
Bollas, C. (1987). *The Shadow of the Object*. New York: Columbia University Press.
Castoriadis, C. (1975). *The Imaginary Institution of Society*. Cambridge, MA: MIT Press, 1987.
Felman, S. (1977). Turning the screw of interpretation. In *Writing and Madness*, trans. M. N. Evans, pp. 141–247. Ithaca, NY: Cornell University Press, 1985.
——— (1987). *Jaques Lacan and the Adventure of Insight*. Cambridge, MA: Harvard University Press.
Forrester, J. (1990). *The Seductions of Psychoanalysis*. Cambridge, England: Cambridge University Press.
Fromm, E. (1947). *Man for Himself*. New York: Holt.
Gergen, K. J. (1991). *The Saturated Self*. New York: Basic Books.
Greenberg, J. (1995). Psychoanalytic technique and the interactive matrix. *Psychoanalytic Quarterly* 64:1–22.
Kristeva, J. (1982). *Powers of Horror*. New York: Columbia University Press.
——— (1991). *Strangers to Ourselves*. New York: Columbia University Press.
Lasch, C. (1977). *Haven in a Heartless World*. New York: Basic Books.
Levenson, E. A. (1988). Show and tell: the recursive order of transference. In *The Purloined Self*, ed. A. H. Feiner, pp. 201–209. New York: Contemporary Psychoanalysis Books, 1991.
——— (1991). Clinical case seminar. William Alanson White Institute, New York, Sept.–Dec.
Marcuse, H. (1955). *Eros and Civilization*. Boston: Beacon.
Mitchell, J. (1974). *Psychoanalysis and Feminism*. London: Allen Lane.
Phillips, A. (1993). *On Kissing, Tickling, and Being Bored*. Cambridge, MA: Harvard University Press.

———— (1994). *On Flirtation.* Cambridge, MA: Harvard University Press.

Ricoeur, P. (1970). *Freud and Philosophy.* New Haven, CT: Yale University Press.

Weber, M. M. (1921). *Economy and Society,* ed. G. Roth and C. Wittich. Berkeley, CA: University of California Press, 1979.

Witenberg, E. G. (1989). Case seminar in psychoanalysis. William Alanson White Institute, New York, Sept.–Nov.

16

Coming Apart at the Seems: The Self in Postmodern Theory and Postmodern Worlds

Carolyn C. Grey

When a colleague heard I was writing a paper on a postmodern theme, she asked me a riddle: "What do you get when you cross a mafioso with a postmodern theorist?" Predictably, I gave up, so she answered, "You get an offer you can't understand."

As the riddle suggests, some of the most influential postmodern writers address their audience from the giddy heights of theoretical abstraction, rarely relating their work to the earthbound, lived experience of real people. Nonetheless, in spite of the bad rap they get from advocates of intelligibility, their work has the potential to rescue contemporary psychoanalysis from suffocating epistemological doubts, and dead-ended, decontextualized, one- and two-person theories of development, psychopathology, and clinical practice.

There are numerous conflicting postmodern voices. But the important contributions of social constructivism, deconstructionism, post-structuralism, and hermeneutics are twofold. First, they locate the human self in specific sociocultural-historical contexts, viewing subjectivity as arising through immersion in social experience, including the values, beliefs, and practices of local communities and families. Second, they examine the theories we build to describe, explain, and heal the self as products of history and culture. In thus situating the human subject, and in providing analytic tools to unearth the social meanings and consequences of psychological theories, and the interests they represent and reproduce, postmodern writers challenge psychoanalysis to broaden its base of observation and seek validation in fields of knowledge outside its own narrow perspectives.

In the following discussion, I offer a tentative bridge between psychoanalysis and postmodern thought. I begin with an illustrative postmodern dilemma, then trace the development of psychoanalysis toward a social constructivist paradigm of identity. There follows a discussion of the concept of "discourse" as a bridge between psyche and culture. Finally, there's a case in which this concept is used psychoanalytically to illuminate a life.

THE SELF AS SOCIAL CONSTRUCT

Let's start with a TV talk show I watched last year.

There was a panel with four transsexuals—all previously male, now female, and all unusually attractive as women.

The climax of the show came when one willowy blond, Janice, announced that she was a lesbian. The audience, previously entranced, now murmured its shock and confusion. One woman jumped to her feet, pelting Janice with a series of incredulous questions. "I don't get it," she said. "Are you telling me you're attracted to women? Not men?"

Janice: "That's right."
Woman-in-audience: "Then why didn't you stay a man? You could have had all the women you wanted."
Janice: "I don't want to be a man. I want to be a woman."
Woman-in-audience: "But you don't want men?"
Janice, patiently: "No, I want to be with another woman."
Woman-in-audience, now desperate: "Then what—what ARE you?"
Janice, with a shrug: "It beats me."

While many of us, like the anonymous interlocutor, probably get queasy with gender bending, Janice's composure under fire raises a very postmodern question: What's the big deal? What makes us so wedded to our conventions and so blown away when they're shattered? What would we, or could we think if Janice, who once seemed to be a man, and now seems to be a woman, decided to dress in men's clothing? Will it advance our understanding, or hers, to call her a transsexual-lesbian-transvestite? "It beats me," says Janice.

Probably bending gender and sexuality makes us crazy because, like the woman in the audience, we, as people and as psychoanalysts, have taken for granted that the male/female divide, and heterosexuality, are not only moral and healthy, they also constitute foundational human nature. But Janice, and the social/technological world that makes her possible, expose the constructed nature of the self, including both gender and sexuality. They tear us away from our culture's conceptual moorings—the value commitments and obligatory traditions—that define major aspects of our selves and our proper relations with others. We are left adrift on an uncharted, foggy sea.

And gender is just the tip of a relentlessly melting iceberg—only one of the most obvious signs of destabilization of identity in Western culture, and probably most of the world touched by it. We have direct contact with increasingly diverse culture groups and are informed by the mass media of the most inspiring and appalling aspects of unfamiliar humanity across the globe. Further, we are more and more likely to suffer either voluntary or involuntary relocations into new cultures, and dislocations from our own families and communities. Thus there are continuous challenges to the traditions, commitments, and certainties that in the past defined most human selves—gendered or otherwise. Particularly in the West, where liberationist revisions of identity abound, gender, social class, race, and ethnicity are no longer infallible coordinates on the map of life's possibilities.

In this postmodern world, the self becomes a problem (or an opportunity) to itself to construct, to construe, and to present to the world. Moreover, the self becomes a problem to the human sciences, including psychoanalysis, because our prior conceptions of selfhood have been exposed as products of our culture.

The current intellectual ferment concerning issues of self, or identity, is particularly important for us as analysts. That is, for psychoanalysis and psychology as scientific disciplines, the central questions have always been: What constitutes a human self? How does that self evolve? and, What is its relation to other selves? Within psychoanalysis there have been two kinds of answers. Broadly speaking, one is essentialistic, biologistic, and individualistic, while the other is proto-constructivist, experiential, and social.

In keeping with essentialism in nineteenth-century philosophy and science, our analytic forbears confidently defined the human self as contained within its physical body, driven by innate biological instincts and their developmental vicissitudes. The sexual instinct was the universal primary human motive, and gender the bedrock of human character. In this scheme, people were "objects" loved or hated for the gratifications or frustrations they occasioned.

As an alternative to orthodox developmental maps, theorists from the interpersonal/cultural and object relations schools reconceptualized rock-bottom human nature as constituted not by sexuality, but by sociality—a psychological interconnectedness with other people as fundamental to psychological life as oxygen is to bodily existence. In this account, biology defines basic survival needs and the boundaries of our capacities and limitations. It also confronts us with predictable existential challenges. But the ways individual selves construe and act upon biological facts of life depend on the social relations that give meaning to experience and shape character.

While object relations and interpersonal theories share these fundamentally social assumptions, they differ radically in the range of social relations considered clinically relevant to individual development. In object relations theory, mother and child, and maybe father, exist in a trans-historical, transcultural space where the child's character is forged and fixed through early fantasies and patterns of dependent relatedness. The early interpersonal school also emphasized the importance of childhood experience with intimate others. But, in keeping with their interest in cross-cultural studies, they believed the cultural community shaped the family itself, thus influencing the child's experience of the world in terms of community values and beliefs (Fromm 1941, Horney 1939, Sullivan 1953, C. Thompson 1950). Further, Sullivan theorized the importance of others outside the family in the growing child's development—peer groups, non-family authorities, chums, lovers, and occupational groups of adult life.

Unfortunately, for the most part, psychoanalysts failed to follow through on the effort to construct a systematic account of the self in social terms. However, social science research has sketched a field of radically different perspectives, making essentialistic, biologistic accounts of human nature increasingly less tenable. For one thing, within the arena of gender, our transsexual guide Janice reminds us that bits and pieces of anatomy, which Freud and others believed constituted the human subject, can now be reassembled or redefined almost at will. Further, Money (1973, 1987) has shown that gender identity and choice of sexual partner match sex of rearing rather than biological sex, when labels and bodies are at odds. And, while all known societies differentiate between men and women, the specific characteristics ascribed and permitted to each sex vary from culture to culture, as does the rigidity of lines between the two sexes.

Even among subcultures of our own society, there are wide differences in what is permissible for male and female identities. Upper-class career women arguably have much more in common with their husbands than with working-class women whose choices are limited by economics and more rigid role constraints.

Gender has assumed a privileged place in contemporary constructivist theory. However, other aspects of identity are equally constructed, both at the level of theory, and at the level of individual subjectivity. For example, take the self as entity. The normative, healthy adult American self is construed as self-contained, self-defined, the origin of its own psyche and author of its destiny (Bruner 1990, Cushman 1991, Geertz 1985). Yet, for many traditional cultures, including Japanese, Islamic, Hindu, and Chinese, the self has no meaning apart from its web of connections and mutual responsibilities with family, tribe, and even Nature (Heelas and Lock 1981, Roland 1990). Westen (1985) reports that "something is clearly in need of explanation when one is confronted with an Australian [aborigine] who is convinced that he is, in every ontological sense, a turtle" (p. 250).

The Zen monk V. S. Hori (1994) illustrates the difference between ethnic Buddhist and American selves in his cautionary tale of a Buddhist retreat he attended in 1992. Chinese-American participants joined in order to derealize the self, to break "habits of selfishness . . . in order to become open, responsible, and compassionate with others." One Chinese woman said that "meditation made her realize how selfish she usually was; she wanted . . . to bow down to her family [and] perform some deep act of repentance" (p. 48). With equal sincerity, American converts valued the "long hours of meditation for help[ing] them get in touch with themselves, giv[ing] them strength . . . to cope with the pressures of society, and assist[ing] them in the process of self-realization" (p. 48).

In sum, cross-cultural and other social science observations have made it clear that the self—whether viewed from the perspective of its gender, or its sexuality, or its entire being, cannot be construed without reference to the full range of influences brought to bear through the web of relations that constitutes a culture.

In recent years, within psychoanalysis, feminist theorists have carried the project of linking the psychoanalytic self to the culturally embedded self (e.g., Benjamin 1988, Chodorow 1989, Flax 1990, Gilligan 1982, Goldner 1991, Grey 1993). They have explored the ways prevalent ideologies and practices produce selves that take for granted their own gendering, assuming male dominance and superior value. And they have noted that both male and female gender categories contain imperatives for identity, including heterosexuality, which are enforced not only by social acceptance or rejection, but more importantly by conscious and unconscious anxiety, shame, and self-rejection engendered in the person who violates them (Grey 1991, 1993). In short, they have explored important ways in which culture shapes subjectivity through gendering.

Other ubiquitous social categories that analysts are only beginning to note clearly influence individual identities as well as the analytic process (Altman 1995, Foster 1993, Grey in press and 1993, C. L. Thompson 1987, 1995). Social class is probably the most powerful because it subsumes other categories. But race, nationality, ethnicity, religion, and age all contribute to defining a range of thinkable, acceptable, personal characteristics, aspirations, values, and actions.

CULTURAL DISCOURSES
AND THE CONSTRUCTION OF IDENTITY

The postmodern concept of discourse can help us to map the complex relations between the psyches of individual people and the cultures that make them intelligible. In this usage, "discourse" refers to a system of meanings and beliefs held in common by members of a culture group. The group's discourses are interpretive frameworks for understanding human experience. But they are not simply conscious cognitive categories and explanations. They may function outside awareness, or in the realm of common sense in which they are conscious but unexamined, taken-for-granted assumptions about reality. Discourses in this sense map solutions to both existential and practical problems-in-living in a particular social and material world. They define what people of various categories—ages, genders, sexualities, races, classes, and tribes—are like, or what they should be like, and how they should interact with and value each other. Discourses thus engender motivation within individual psyches, serving as guides for thinking, feeling, willing, and acting. As Frosh (1989) says, they are "not simply a way of looking at things, [they are] a way of living them" (p. 188). While postmodern theorists like Foucault focus on destructive power and value inequities embedded in discourse, discourses also delineate the boundaries of conscience, exalted ideals, deeply felt pleasures, and positively valued identities. Moreover, they generate and support acceptable structures for our communal lives—for our nuclear or extended families, for our religious, economic, and political institutions, and for our local communities.

This description does not imply a single party line for any aspect of reality addressed by discourse. Rather, there are usually multiple possibilities, alternative interpretations, paths of action, and patterns of relatedness to others. For example, take gender. In contemporary urban American society, there are coexisting discourses from different subcultures that describe, produce, and legitimize a variety of masculine identities. These include the traditional paterfamilias, a faithful, protective, benevolent autocrat whose stiff upper lip and determination guarantee the good life for himself and his loved ones. Then there's the macho man, sexy, aggressive, physically strong, who conquers multitudes of women and defends his honor with violence at the lift of an eyebrow. Then, too, there's the contemporary, educated, liberal, middle-class male, whose culture group's discourse enjoins him to be in touch with his feelings, to share those feelings with significant others, and to share power with his wife, and even his children.

These discourses can produce George Bush, Sylvester Stallone, and an ideal male analyst respectively. But they can't encompass the Ilongot tribesman who can only achieve full male selfhood when he takes "an 'enemy's' head . . . in an appropriate state of anger . . ." (Bruner 1990, p. 41). Nor can they explain the Sambian boy whose masculinity depends on fellating older males for several years (Herdt 1981). And then there's Janice, our transsexual lesbian cross-dresser. He/she operates outside our prevalent gender discourses, which may explain our alarm, and her/his quandary in explaining him/herself. In sum, while there may be some universal, or almost universal aspects to gender and gender relations, we cannot understand a particular individual's gender, and its implications for her/his relations with others, unless we know the ideologies and practices of her/his local, historically situated culture group. This way of conceiving gender abandons the old two-kinds-of-cookie-cutter model for one in which gender is defined as the discourses of a specific culture group that describe and prescribe a variety of ways of being and living male and female. It locates gender in social practices, values, and beliefs that become part of individual psychology, defining not only qualities of male and female persons, but also the relations between them.

The ways of living represented in discourse may be explicit in formal doctrines (like the Ten Commandments or the U.S. Constitution), or in that hodgepodge of colloquial wisdom we call common sense. They may also be represented implicitly as themes, unarticulated assumptions, and fragmentary images in such diverse cultural products as the arts, literature, advertising, and academic disciplines. For example, America's brand of individualism is explicit in the Bill of Rights, and implicit in myths of the old West, Hemingway's novels, Marlboro ads, and the developmental theories of psychology. The discourses of individualism are not simply conscious stereotypes. By shaping individual psychology, both directly and through the mediation of meaningful others, they produce aspects of character in such diverse Americans as Walt Whitman, Susan B. Anthony, Barbara Jordan, Michael Milken, and O. J. Simpson.

Most significantly for us, the discourses of individualism have shaped American psychoanalysis for good or ill. For example, these discourses are represented in the image of what Cushman (1991) calls the "masterful, bounded, feeling self" (p. 206), idealized in Daniel Stern's (1985) theory of infancy. They produce our subversive clinical practice that challenges the group's and family's authority over individual psyches and life narratives. And they determine our failure to conceptualize communal needs and responsibilities as we urge our patients, above all, to get in touch with, forgive, and realize their selves.

In this conceptualization, culture is no longer an abstract entity "out there." Nor is it a layer of superficial conformity that can be stripped away to reveal true selves. Rather, our inner lives are constituted and given meaning within the range of discourses that also constitute our culture groups.

If we incorporate these ideas into psychoanalytic developmental theory, the individual's life story goes something like this. A child is born into a social world. She is primed by her irreducibly social nature to receive multiple, often contradictory meanings conveyed through the emotions, gestures, and later words of intimate others. Starting at birth, the child gradually becomes an increasingly competent interpreter and synthesizer of these meanings—gradually making sense of the world and her place in it. Also, from birth, the child produces meanings—communicating her needs, fears, and interests. Intimate others give back confirmatory or contradictory messages, shaping the child's understanding of herself and her relations with others. The family's contribution to individual identity is twofold. Valuations of the self and its qualities are established through the family's emotional climate and specific patterns of interaction. Second, family members both enact and directly teach positions within the cultural discourses available to them. They induct the child into their version of her right and proper gender, her ethnic identity, and the manners, morals, taboos, and rituals of her social class or caste. In this way, the family is a primary subculture, constituted within a larger subculture, within broader communities.

The family's influence is powerful, not because it is different in kind from nonfamily influence, but because, in our culture of nuclear families, it is relatively intimate and constant. Further, its intimate influence extends in time, usually (in our culture) through adolescence. But inevitably, from very early on, discourses of the outside world become available to the child, and later the adult, as she is exposed to nonfamilial others. Increasingly, opportunities open to redefine herself and her relations for good or ill. Witness transformations of self that obtain in Western adolescence and in adult experiences like parenthood, professional training, and, of course, in psychoanalysis. How child or adult tentatively or certainly puts together this world of available meanings, and her self, depends on the lessons about life that are consciously and unconsciously learned in the family and the outside world. They depend, too, on the child's or adult's ability to negotiate ambiguities and contradictions. This in turn depends on "what the child brings to the world, her or his . . . constitution, the inevitable permutations and distortions that occur in the incorporations of experience," and in "ongoing, unconscious experience" (Flax 1990, p. 122). In sum, the unique individuality that psychoanalysts investigate and hope to rescue is both a fluid construct, and a constructed and fluid reality. It results from the continuous interplay between the person's own capacities, and complex social influences which define possible and permissible selves within specific cultures.

FROM THEORY TO PRACTICE

These propositions have crucial importance for clinical work. They provide a conceptual framework for construing a personal history, formulating analytic issues, suggesting fruitful lines of inquiry, and locating transference–countertransference binds.

The following case involves an increasingly significant problem in American culture and analytic work. Socioeconomic mobility and ethnic dispersion leave many people without secure, culturally legitimated identities. Clashes between discourses of their old and new culture groups may create alienation from the culture of their families and old communities, and insecurity in the culture of new, often more privileged groups. In describing the case, I will illustrate the interplay between broad social influences experienced by the patient and the idiosyncratic familial experiences psychoanalysts traditionally investigate.

The patient, J. Cecil Grantham, was a middle-level advertising executive. He was 39 years old, white, Anglo Saxon, Protestant, heterosexual, and male. Eight years ago, he drove up to my office in a mid-sized BMW, wearing a dark blue suit, rep tie, monogrammed shirt, and tasseled loafers. A Burberry raincoat was draped over his arm, plaid lining discreetly exposed. In an embarrassed, halting voice, he told me about the stormy affair that he feared would break up his seventeen-year marriage.

From the beginning, I formulated Grant's problems in living in terms supplied by psychoanalytic discourse. It was not my intent to proselytize. I was simply calling it like I saw it. Grant was paralyzed in work, love, and friendship. He was constantly anxious about being put down or outdone by co-workers, and terrified that some superior would criticize his work or find him personally ridiculous. At home, he and his wife lived an active social life comprised of parties, games, and sports shared by an upper-class community. In these gatherings, he felt continuous pressure to prove his worthiness through witty conversation, demonstrations of esoteric knowledge, sartorial perfection, and superior performance in elitist sports like fly-fishing and sailing.

On those rare occasions when they spent time alone, he and his wife maintained a well-bred emotional distance breached only by occasional bickering over trivial household arrangements. In their late thirties, after seventeen years of marriage, they had no children, and had never discussed whether they wanted them. No wonder, then, that Grant was starved enough to be swept up in an affair.

In analytic discourse, one might summarize by saying that Grant was a very fearful, dependent man whose insecurity about his own worth curtailed appropriate self-assertion and ambition, impaired his capacity for emotional intimacy, and made him seek comfort in conformity to his social group's way of life.

At the start, I was lulled into an illusory sense of common basic values and therapeutic goals by similarities in our socioeconomic backgrounds—years of education, cultural interests, and economic status. Indeed, Grant did want to feel less anxious, and to be more successful in his career. But much of my formulation, suggested tactfully over time, was met with bewilderment and discomfort. His history reveals the sources of uneasiness in our dialogue.

Grant had been raised in a small town outside Philadelphia. His father, Fred, was a well-liked, modestly successful businessman of limited cultivation and drive. His mother, Emma, on the other hand, had grown up poor, but was actively intelligent and ambitious. For as far back as Grant remembered, his mother's imagination was captured by the privileged lives of the old, rich, and landed families living like British aristocracy on estates outside town. Barred from their charmed circle, she took her boss, Dr. Williams, as a more plausible representative of refined living. She emulated his intellectual interests, created an English garden like his, and began collecting antiques.

Over time, Emma turned to Grant to share her emerging vision of the good life, all the while making it clear that he should not imitate his lowbrow, low-class father. Grant remembers her excitement in planning a wine-tasting party. He remembers, too, how thrilled she was when his ballroom dancing teacher singled him out as a particularly graceful, courtly dance partner.

Grant's informal education in the discourses of more patrician life took place in church and school. Emma took him to the local Episcopal church where their upper-class neighbors seemed to attend more to socialize than to worship. Significantly, every minister Grant remembers drove a Mercedes Benz. Here, the aristocratic community functioned as a closed group defined by inherited wealth, school ties formed in elite colleges, quiet but expensive good taste, and a sense of noblesse oblige toward those less fortunate than themselves. The religious authority of the church seemed to legitimate their lives of leisure and pleasure through an implied code of election.

Grant's formal secular education enhanced the messages of religious experience. His parents sacrificed to send him to private academies with sons of the aristocracy. There, peers and educators alike initiated him into the values of athletic achievement, civic participation, and broad knowledge in literature and the arts. Their moral imperatives were fair play, good manners, and a stiff upper lip. Disclosure of inner feelings was unthought of in these circles. Sent to boarding school at 12, Grant grew distant from his parents, particularly as their continuous conflict became increasingly stressful for him. The privileged and apparently secure lives of his upper-class schoolmates beckoned as a safe haven, an alternative source of comfort and confirmation. His need to belong insured that their discourse would become his own deeply felt convictions about how life should be lived, and how needs could be legitimately satisfied.

In his adult life, one of Grant's major dilemmas arose from the conjunction of class and gender discourses in the arena of work. As an upper-class man, he expected himself to provide the means for his family fully to live the aristocratic life. But Grant's paralysis in the face of important career challenges was supported by social class and religious codes that valued inherited status and wealth, while devaluing scrimping and opportunistic scrambling after money or position. His ideal was to be a dollar-a-year man in a prestigious, worthy, public interest organization. Violating the aristocratic code threatened his social identity and self valuation. But failure aggressively to pursue advancement limited Grant's ability to participate in his reference group's expensive social life.

Grant's problematic legitimacy was painfully evoked in a dream. He had attended a Kentucky Derby party at the elegant home of friends whose wealth and social position came from blue-blood families. "That night," he said, "in the dream, I was in a tenement sort of building in an urban setting. A neighbor asked me to be a bag man for the mob. I thought, 'I'm always looking for money, so I'll do it.' . . . Then I'm scared other neighbors will see I'm hooked up with the mob. . . ."

Grant had learned and was living the discourses of aristocratic life. His tastes, pleasures, values, and behavior were all consonant with their dictates, and he valued himself in their terms. Unfortunately, those same terms defined him as a class-crosser, a violator of boundaries, a hanger-on. So, in spite of his friends' genuine affection, he felt illegitimate, vulnerable to exposure, and alone.

The course of my work with Grant was marked by ideological jolts. For one thing, there was the issue of intimacy. As the bearer of the analytic community's discourse, I inquired about and interpreted Grant's reticence, assuming he naturally would want to share his deepest hopes, fears, and passions with his wife. My dogged pursuit of this issue finally led to their working through some difficult conflicts, and deciding to have children. But the depth of intimacy that I envisioned in marriage and friendship remained foreign. It simply is not done or thought in his community's discourse of relatedness. Sharing activities seemed to provide the affirmation and security provided by self-disclosure in the analytically sensitized educated middle class. Nor is intimate knowledge of the self highly valued, except as a tool for dealing with emotional emergencies. As Grant began to be less anxious and more assertive, his motivation to look inward waned.

Perhaps the most pervasive problem arose from my egalitarian individualism. My commitment to personal fulfillment and freedom of choice is deeply ingrained, as is my revulsion against conformity, authority, and hierarchy—at least in principle. Community commitments seemed threatening to mature autonomy. Of course my personal predilections are rationalized in analytic discourse and the discourses of the middle class in general. Needless to say, I found Grant's need to belong, and the way he expressed it through being like his friends, ideologically irritating. "For God's sake," I wanted to say, "for once, do your own thing."

Finally, my brand of individualism mandates a puritan work ethic, with a pull-yourself-up-by-your-own-bootstraps twist. While I pride myself on making a career, Grant was committed to looking like he didn't need one. This puzzled and annoyed me. Indeed, it was clear that this orientation served a defensive purpose in rationalizing Grant's retreat from challenge. But it was not an idiosyncratic neurosis. Rather, it was a value position of a tradition-based culture group at odds with contemporary American individualism.

In sum, my values and therapeutic goals seemed common sense to me. I was only dimly aware at first that I was using them to disparage Grant's way of life. Because of my underdog sympathies, this is less likely to happen with patients of lower social class or members of obviously devalued groups. In any case, my own conformities—and a conflicted desire for a warm, confirming community—went unexamined.

Over time, I realized that Grant and I live in different discourse communities, and began to appreciate the value that his community had for him. While it remains difficult for me to imagine living as Grant and his wife do with each other, it became clear that they were generally loyal, supportive, and consistently involved in each other's lives. I also realized that Grant shared with his group pleasures and interests that enriched his life.

In the end, I was painfully aware that my ideal analytic outcomes only partly matched Grant's felt needs, or life in his culture. Recognizing the conflict between discourses was critical for establishing an analytic dialogue and empathic connection that allowed Grant to achieve greater comfort in his life through our efforts.

CONCLUSION

Psychoanalysis has claimed the territory of the private, unconscious, and uniquely individual aspects of human experience. No other discipline offers us such effective methods for exploring that territory. However, by clinging to the old, misleading dichotomies between intrapsychic and interpersonal, nature and nurture, self and culture, we have misconstrued the influence of our communal lives in shaping individual psyches and life narratives. Our status as a scientific discipline suffers accordingly.

Our clinical work, too, suffers from our failure to understand the impact of cultural communities on the psyches of the people with whom we work, and on our own culturally shaped participation in the psychoanalytic engagement. And our belief in the necessity of unique, autonomous individuality leads us systematically to neglect or devalue the enrichment and comfort potentially available in community, and in commitment to causes beyond the self.

To take up the postmodern challenge, we need to go beyond the one-, two-, or even three-person psychologies of traditional psychoanalysis, to map the formative influence of cultural communities on emergent selves, as well as the institutions, beliefs, and practices of psychoanalysis. If we apply the postmodern tool of deconstruction to our own theories and practice, we will recognize psychoanalysis itself as a subculture with what Cushman (1993) calls its own "moral discourse." As Bellah and colleagues (1985) put it, we proffer "a normative order of life, with character ideals, images of the good life, and methods of attaining it" (p. 47). From the deconstructive perspective, there should be no foregone conclusion about what constitutes normal psychic development or what the endpoints of our analytic project should be. The endpoints we have taken for granted— like heterosexuality, the gendered psyche, the work ethic, intimacy, authenticity, and autonomy—are our analytic and middle-class culture's way of meeting the challenges of life and human relations. Whether we hold to them or revise them should be decided on the basis of their validity and usefulness in a particular personal-social-historical context. Our analytic discourses can be challenged and enriched through what postmodernists call "interesting conversations" with bearers of alternative visions of human nature and human needs.

REFERENCES

Altman, N. (1995). *The Analyst in the Inner City: Race, Class, and Culture through a Psychoanalytic Lens.* Hillsdale, NJ: Analytic Press.
Bellah, R. N., Madsen, R., Sullivan, W. M., et al. (1985). *Habits of the Heart: Individualism and Commitment in American Life.* New York: Harper & Row.
Benjamin, J. (1988). *Bonds of Love: Psychoanalysis, Feminism, and the Problem of Domination.* New York: Pantheon.
Bruner, J. (1990). *Acts of Meaning.* Cambridge, MA: Harvard University Press.
Chodorow, N. J. (1989). *Feminism and Psychoanalytic Theory.* New Haven, CT: Yale University Press.
Cushman, P. (1991). Ideology obscured: political uses of the self in Daniel Stern's infant. *American Psychologist* 46(3):206–220.
——— (1993). Psychotherapy as moral discourse. *Journal of Theoretical and Philosophical Psychology* 13(2):103–113.
Flax, J. (1990). *Thinking Fragments: Psychoanalysis, Feminism, and Postmodernism in the Contemporary West.* Berkeley, CA: University of California Press.
Foster, R. (1993). The social politics of psychoanalysis. *Psychoanalytic Dialogues* 3(1):69–83.
Fromm, E. (1941). *Escape from Freedom.* New York: Rinehart.
Frosh, S. (1989). *Psychoanalysis and Psychology: Minding the Gap.* New York: New York University Press.
Geertz, C. (1985). From the native's point of view: on the nature of anthropological understanding. In *Local Knowledge,* pp. 55–70. New York: Basic Books.
Gilligan, C. (1982). *In a Different Voice: Psychological Theory and Women's Development.* Cambridge, MA: Harvard University Press.
Goldner, V. (1991). Toward a critical relational theory of gender. *Psychoanalytic Dialogues* 1(3):249–272.
Grey, C. (1991). Relatedness as purpose: a psychoanalytic inquiry into gender imperatives for women. *Contemporary Psychoanalysis* 27(4):661–680.
——— (1993). Culture, character, and the analytic engagement: toward a subversive psychoanalysis. *Contemporary Psychoanalysis* 29(3):487–502.
——— (in press). Conduct unbecoming: female inversion and social disorder. In *She Foreswore Her Womanhood: An Interdisciplinary Look at Freud's Female Homosexual,* ed. R. Lesser and E. E. Schoenberg. New York: Routledge.
Heelas, P., and Lock, A. (1981). *Indigenous Psychologies.* London: Academic Press.
Herdt, G. H. (1981). *Guardians of the Flutes.* New York: McGraw-Hill.

Hori, V. S. (1994). Sweet and sour buddhism. *Tricycle: The Buddhist Review*, Fall, pp. 48–52.

Horney, K. (1939). *New Ways in Psychoanalysis*. New York: Norton, 1996.

Money, J. (1973). Gender, role, gender identity, core gender identity: usage and definition of terms. *Journal of the American Academy of Psychoanalysis* 1:397–402.

———(1987). Propaedeutics of diecious G-IR: theoretical foundations for understanding dimorphic gender-identity/role. In *Masculinity/Femininity*, ed. J. Reinisch, L. Rosenblum, and J. Sanders, pp. 13–28. New York: Oxford University Press.

Roland, A. (1990). The self in cross-civilizational perspective: An Indian–Japanese–American comparison. In *The Relational Self*, ed. R. C. Curtis, pp. 160–180. New York: Guilford.

Stern, D. (1985). *The Interpersonal World of the Infant*. New York: Basic Books.

Sullivan, H. S. (1953). *The Interpersonal Theory of Psychiatry*. New York: Norton.

Thompson, C. (1950). *Psychoanalysis: Evolution and Development*. New York: Grove.

Thompson, C. L. (1987). Racism or neuroticism: an entangled dilemma for the black middle class patient. *Journal of the American Academy of Psychoanalysis* 15(3):395–405.

———(1995). Self-definition by opposition: a consequence of minority status. *Psychoanalytic Psychology* 12(4):533–545.

Westen, D. (1985). *Self and Society: Narcissism, Collectivism and the Development of Morals*. New York: Cambridge University Press.

17

Psychoanalysis and Community: Mutual Need, Volatile Interface

Donald Moss

In reading the English-language psychoanalytic literature of this century's first four or five decades, one is impressed not only with the regular appearance of theoretical and clinical feats of startling imagination and brilliance, but even more with the widespread authorial confidence that the work of writing psychoanalysis—regardless of Freud's somewhat excessive protestations to the contrary—will matter to a wide audience, and that, in general, psychoanalysis can be presumed to occupy a secure location in the wider culture. For at least forty years, no noticeable professional or theoretical anxiety seems to interfere with the theory's presumption of its own substantial cultural weight. In spite of having to continuously refine the terms of its own conceptual ground, there is no hesitation, no appeal to extra-psychoanalytic legitimating authority. Psychoanalysis emerges articulately and steadily; there is a sense of a continuous improvisational giddiness in this emergence; the theory codifies itself on the fly.

Early psychoanalytic theory is written with a sense of strength and mastery. There is little sign of apprehensive iconoclasm. The work emerges as though it were responding to a cultural demand. This sense of mastery is present not only in the self-conscious production of Freud-as-genius, but more impressively, in work written by what Michael Jordan calls the "supporting cast"—work which calmly aims for unfettered observation and relatively pedestrian systematicity. Exemplary here is Otto Fenichel's work, both the *Collected Papers* (1953) and the monumental textbook, *The Psychoanalytic Theory of Neurosis* (1945). Following in, and covered by, Freud's tracks, Fenichel writes a psychoanalysis which easily moves back and forth between clinical arcana and well-known social phenomena: anti-Semitism, boredom, the excesses of warriors. The pertinent field seems without limit—the traditionally clinical, the newly mapped extra-clinical, and the interpenetrations of subjectivity and history. The so-called Freud-Marx problem briefly assumes a position of dominance within the humanities—in the radical effort to understand and interpret the determinants of repression so as to contribute to the possibility of liberation.

Psychoanalytic theory in these decades takes liberties; it seems to go where it likes. Fenichel's texts are, in that sense, representative. They not only find their place, they make their own place, firmly within and critical of the libertarian/enlightenment tradition. That tradition is assumed alive and vital; capable, even eager, to absorb the kind of critique offered by the radical epistemological premises of psychoanalysis. These early psychoanalytic texts forswear any gesture of apology toward the tradition in which, and to which, they have been written; they display a kind of epistemological swagger, and indicate no thirst for extra-psychoanalytic legitimation.

The libertarian/enlightenment hermeneutic—no matter its long-standing habit of careful scrutiny, its intellectual and structural resistances—could accommodate psychoanalysis without rupture or crisis. Psychoanalysis, though self-consciously iconoclastic, could, and did, take on the status of an elaborate extension, a modification of already existing modes of thought and representation, many of which—Marx's certainly included—had themselves emerged as iconoclastic and as such bullied their way into the tradition. Ezra Pound's modernist ethos, "Make it new," provided a thematic rationale for the relatively easy integration of psychoanalysis into what, well into the twentieth century, could still be thought of as the "classical" libertarian/enlightenment tradition. Its integration was akin to the integration of Schoenberg and Berg, say, or Faulkner and Joyce, into their respective classical canons. What was new and progressive could be patched on, nearly seamlessly, to a cultural cluster whose trajectory had long ago developed the means and appetite for integrating the "new and progressive."

No such confidence characterizes contemporary psychoanalytic writing. Today, one reads the output of a wounded discipline, a discipline in search of both salve and prosthesis, reassurance and support, a displaced discipline suddenly preoccupied with its market position, its capacities to compete, its shifting cultural place. Not only is the intellectual élan gone, but more importantly, the tradition which nurtured that élan has been torn asunder. We no longer are participants in a widespread assumption that progressive thought might actually foment progressive change, that thoroughgoing interpretation might induce thoroughgoing social and subjective transformations.

The tradition ruptured, its place jeopardized, psychoanalysis—both in the form of its institutions and of its individual practitioners—has begun casting about for a new tradition, now often called a "community," in which it can again be comfortably housed. To whom will it appeal, on what grounds, making what promises, offering what vision of what possibilities? Freud's (1895) terrible dictum that psychoanalysis can merely help "transform neurotic misery into common human unhappiness" (p. 305) would hardly suffice today. The melancholic dimension of the theory has, for now, to be obscured as it pursues an audience.

The following reflections have been instigated by a sustained consideration of that pursuit.

The bond linking "community" to "psychoanalysis" is an unstable one. Unions are rare and usually transient. Such unions depend upon a continuous expenditure of energy. Without such expenditure, the two terms seem parts of two separate domains—in one, there are the objects and problems provoking the theory and practice of psychoanalysis, in the other the objects and problems provoking the theory and practice of community. The two domains, though separate, exist in uneasy proximity to each other, hovering in what seems a relation of complementarity. They meet edge to edge, border to border, in a relation resembling that of concave to convex, or more pertinently, of negative to positive, and therefore of neurosis to perversion.

As in the relation between neurosis and perversion, in the relation between psychoanalysis and community, each term seems to license the enactment of what the other term interdicts. From the one domain, psychoanalysis seems to both propagandize and provide the means for a first-person singularity which would transgress all limits and therefore radically negate community's essential first-person plurality. And from the other, community, by setting up non-negotiable conditions for membership, in the form of its laws of operation, its rules of order, appears as the medium through which first-person singularity is muted and forced into submission. Psychoanalysis licenses a singularity which community interprets as transgressive. Community enforces an order which psychoanalysis interprets as deforming. Community punishes excessive singularity with one or another form of exile and object loss.

Access to the community's objects depends upon obedience to its laws. Psychoanalytic inquiry addresses the subjective elaborations linking object access and obedience to law. In clinical work, the effective presence of law can be inferred by the irreducible fact of anxiety.

Each of the dangers that anxiety signals, after all—the impending loss of the object, of the object's love, castration, and superego disapproval—are sensed by the anxious first-person subject as inevitable retribution for a transgression of law. Pursue that thought, that image, that wish and the consequence is a more or less attenuated version of exile. You will lose access to objects, to their love, to their sexual promise, to their ethical approbation.

In an indirect sense, then, in the clinical situation the presence of anxiety invariably marks a point at which an acute concern about community—about access to objects—impacts the free associational efforts of the first-person singular voice. I mean community here as a construction of both fact and fantasy, a construction which, though, regardless of its makeup, is real enough to underwrite the searing sense of reality which accompanies all anxiety.

From the point of view of clinical psychoanalysis, both community and anxiety exert an identical presence; they have an inhibitory effect on free association. Anxiety speaks by way of the voice of the community; the community speaks via the voice of anxiety. The apprehension of danger drives the singular voice toward the ostensibly safer pluralities of community. Community legitimates an otherwise inchoate anxiety and provides it with all of its local forms and reasons.

Community and anxiety, then, since they can speak for each other, can also mask each other. Clinical thought is incapable of effacing this mask since, in clinical effect, the two, community and anxiety, are identical. Suddenly it is the other which speaks. As other to the speaker, the two terms share the same voice, whose fundamental message is inhibition. This apparent convergence of voice marks the site of the most recondite of clinical resistance. The voice of such resistance grounds itself in community: it is not I, it says, who stops me from speaking-thinking-wanting-imagining, but rather it is the others, them, their law, who insist that now is the time to stop this speaking-thinking-wanting-imagining.

I do not mean to imply a relation of pure opposition between first-person singular and first-person plural voices. Babies without voice turn into people with voice only by way of their insertion into communities. And in turn, in order to survive, such communities—couples, genders, families, classes, states—must provide sites for these insertions, and the provided sites must offer something more than inhibition. They must offer a regulatory apparatus which not only inhibits, but also can promise, and deliver, sufficient measures of both pleasure and control. One senses one's insertion into a community by way of the effect one feels from this regulatory apparatus, the mix of opportunites and constraints which set the terms on both internal and external life.

These terms are codified in three tiers—as order, as justice, and as reality.

Clinical work calls into question each of these three central terms. The clinical focus, though, is not at all disinterested. The fundamental rule—say everything that occurs to you—can be followed only if the shared voice of anxiety and community is barred from the clinical setup. When that voice nonetheless appears, its appearance is therefore transgressive, and often transferential. The sequence is paradigmatic. The singular voice, anxious, turns itself plural and suddenly finds itself in the company of a familiar other, an other it knows as "we."

In psychoanalysis, Ricoeur's (1986) famous "hermeneutic of suspicion"—by which he links the thought of Freud, Marx, and Nietzsche—suspects such company most of all. This suspicion is without limit. From the point of view of the community, it is this dimension of limitless suspicion which gives psychoanalysis its perverse valence.

Psychoanalysis rides the voice of the singular so as to both discover and transgress the limits set by plurality. At its most raw, on its skin, on our skins, the tension between our allegiances to psychoanalysis and our allegiances to our communities is felt as an ethical tension: a tension between incompatible notions of justice, order, and reality, a tension, as Lacan would have it, classically prefigured in Antigone and Creon, and as Freud would have it, in Oedipus.

The tension is irresoluble. On each side—the singular and the plural—vital, and incompatible, interests are being protected. I want to sketch out some of those vital interests, and to highlight the possible integrity inherent in ambitions to protect them.

I begin with the long-standing wariness psychoanalysis has displayed toward the idea of "community." Precisely because of the regressive and authoritarian uses to which this wariness has been put, the rationale supporting it warrants our ongoing attention. The general tone of that rationale is constant. Its appeal is ethical, an appeal which, at base, will claim that community involvement undoes and perverts the founding impulse of psychoanalysis, an impulse whose integrity depends upon its splendid isolation. The ethic of this appeal is long-standing. It celebrates the integrity of individual desire, of wanting. There is Antigone and Creon and there is also the dialog between Christ and the Grand Inquisitor. Christ returns to Seville and heroically remains silent and alone, again refusing the temptations of magic, mystery, and authority, the temptations whose acceptance alone would grant him access to the world he claims to love, access to community.

The ethic here is a clinical one, though grounded not only in the defense of particular individuals, but more fundamentally in the very idea of the individual. It conceptualizes the individual as undergoing a relentless, often silent, insidious assault. It is an ethic of the unique, the authentic, the genuine, an ethic of melancholy, of loss, of resignation, of "common human unhappiness," an ethic of modernity.

This ethic places community where Adorno (1981) placed jazz. It argues that the appeal of community is a regressive, and finally moralistic, one. It claims that a careful—psychoanalytic—approach to this appeal will invariably reveal an aggrieved and accusing voice, a parental and conservative voice, the voice of order, of restoration. That voice will insist that only when controlled can psychoanalysis redeem the latent promises it assumed at the moment of its origin.

The voice of this psychoanalytic-singular ethic, however, will insist that no matter how contemporary the community referenced in whatever the local version of "community psychoanalysis," the community referenced is a stand-in for traditional order. Psychoanalytic ethics here would insist on a principled antagonism to all such tradition. It could even be yoked to an only slightly paraphrased Marx (1852) and work to unburden the singular voice from all that weighs like a nightmare on the heads of the living.

That such an ethical cluster can, and has, been used as ethical camouflage, does not invalidate its integrity. What has been camouflaged behind this ethic is infamous—a self-interested disengagement, a systematic muteness regarding the erupting urgencies of contemporary life. If one wants to move the psychoanalysis which grounds itself in the ethic of the heroic individual into the community, one must be able to seduce it. The terms of the seduction must offer this ethically grounded psychoanalysis a point of insertion from which both its use as camouflage can be exposed and its integrity protected; neither exposure nor protection, alone, will do.

The integrity of plurality's voice—the voice of class, race, gender, sexual preference, the voice of determinants more than of individuation—is also grounded in an ethic, an ethic which gives priority not to individual identity but rather to the sets of identifications from which such identity derives. This ethic locates danger not in object loss, but in disidentifications. It aims at the defense of that which one has come into, that which has been there before and has therefore set the terms for what one might become. This ethic protects sources and origins. A recent collection of readings in black philosophy catches the spine of this ethic in its title, *I Am Because We Are* (Hord and Lee 1995). It is an ethic of affirmation rather than of melancholy, of finding rather than of loss, of continuity rather than disruption. This ethic sees in the hypertrophied singular and in psychoanalysis an abandonment of the very possibility of decency, sees in the singular voice an excess which betrays historical promise. As Walter Benjamin (1969) put it, it sees in modernity's pursuit of the singular an intoxication with the vision of liberated grandchildren, a vision doomed to futility because it depends upon the forgetting of enslaved ancestors.

To entice this ethical voice of first-person plurality into cooperation with the psychoanalytic project in particular, and with the first-person singular project in general, will also take acts of seduction. In order for such seduction to succeed, the singular must be theorized broadly enough to include something other than the self—the beautiful as something other than the singular, genius as something other than individual, realization as something other than accomplishment. Such theorization is potentially available to psychoanalysis. It will depend upon an as yet unconcluded, meticulous reconsideration of the status of the ego, and of ego psychology, and particularly of the relation between values and clinical observations which underpins its crucial notions of autonomy and management. (Ricoeur, for one, performs such a reconsideration brilliantly in *Freud and Philosophy* [1986] when he reconciles faith with interpretation. It remains to be seen whether his work can be transposed into a radically secular sphere.)

The seductions I am speaking of here are long-term projects. They entail reworkings at the very center of our notions of the relations between the singular and the plural. Shorter-term projects are necessary. For now, it seems to me that the only people capable of mounting such projects are those for whom, whatever threat the community might pose to psychoanalysis, this threat is less severe than the one posed by their consciences when they realize the shoddy psychoanalytic posture which has long been camouflaged by a heroic psychoanalytic ethic. Even a cursory glimpse at contemporary historical development will lead one to side with a century of ruthless psychoanalytic inquiry in concluding that conscience is a terribly shaky ground on which to mount a practice. For the moment, however, it seems to me that, regarding community psychoanalysis, we have little else, and that therefore the risk of proceeding with conscience as a guide is a reasonable one.

I now want to offer conscience at least one supplemental item. Psychoanalytic theory is a theory of work, a theory of what makes work both possible and impossible. Psychoanalytic work, like any work, including community work, aims to first discriminate between wishes and to then render the realization of some, the postponement of others, to see to the propagation of wishes across generations. Even more than a theory of work, though, psychoanalysis is a theory of resistance. In the theory, resistance and work define each other negatively, in the same way that neurosis and perversion do, in the same way that the singular and the plural do. Psychoanalysis, then, can offer itself to the community in terms nearly identical to those with which it offers itself to an individual: as a means by which to theorize, illuminate, and contend with resistance, a means by which to finally get the work done. Psychoanalytic theory does not define what the work is. Its first-person speaker does that. The theory aims only to make that first-person work a possibility. Psychoanalytic thinkers could be similarly employed by any unit whose aim is work. Their job would be to interpret resistance and to do so ruthlessly until either the work was completed, or was reconceptualized, or, as might be likely, they were fired.

REFERENCES

Adorno, T. (1981). Perennial fashion—jazz. In *Prisms*. Cambridge, MA: MIT Press.

Benjamin, W. (1969). Theses on the philosophy of history. In *Illuminations*. New York: Schocken.

Fenichel, O. (1945). *The Psychoanalytic Theory of Neurosis*. New York: Norton.

———— (1953). *The Collected Papers of Otto Fenichel*. New York: Norton.

Freud, S. (1895). Studies in hysteria. *Standard Edition 2.*

Hord, F. L., and Lee, J. S. (1995). *I Am Because We Are: Readings in Black Philosophy.* Amherst, MA: University of Massachusetts Press.

Marx, K. (1852). The eighteenth brumaire of Louis Bonaparte. In *The Marx–Engels Reader*, ed. R. Tucker, p. 437. New York: Norton, 1972.

Ricoeur, P. (1986). *Freud and Philosophy: An Essay in Interpretation.* New Haven, CT: Yale University Press.

18

Dorothy to Toto: I Don't Think We're in Kansas Anymore[1]

Robert M. Prince

My 3½-year-old already has had a year more computer experience than some of my colleagues and many of my teachers. Where twenty years ago I remember graduate students signing up months in advance for a half hour on a terminal, his favorite **toy** is exponentially more powerful than the mainframe they hooked up to. While his brother, who was born just about the same time as the personal computer, but is only older by six years, was able to recite the alphabet by this age, he cannot. He can, however, use the enhanced keyboard, and speak a language that allows him to enter simple DOS commands. Where I often get stuck in an application like a fish out of water, kicking myself for wasting hours of intense concentration on what turns out to be a failure to attend to simple, logical directions, he intuitively navigates through GUIs (that is, graphical user interfaces) with delighted mastery. My older child used to delight in manipulating his toy figures and could be overheard making up stories about them. This child prefers to interact with a computer world, identi-

---

1. Presented at the 7th Biennial Conference of the Psychoanalytic Society, New York University, March 5, 1994.

fying with a figure on the screen, one which, depending on the program, he is able to select or design himself, and which he uses to explore a virtual landscape.

There are consequences to this kind of experiencing that go beyond the obvious. For example, I had noted, prior to his discovery of the computer, that he seemed to be developing a very nice attention span which I might have adultomorphized as a pacing and sense of time that adumbrated a capacity for deep relating to and thorough digesting of experience. As his interaction with the dramatic audio and visual stimuli provided by the computer increased, he seemed to lose this beginning quality of patience, habituate more quickly to his play—on the computer and off—and crave more intense and different sensory input. Another possible effect was suggested one day when we were stuck in heavy bridge traffic. As we went through the toll booth, the traffic cleared and he exclaimed, "Hooray, we're at the next level." These examples suggest to me a possibility of externally determined differences in the organization of play, structuring of reality, and development of ego functioning not only across the generational gap between myself and my children but also over the space of time between a younger and older sibling.

I would like to turn my attention now to another set of changes that has taken place over the course of a generation. Not so long ago, psychoanalysts enjoyed the highest status among mental health practitioners. Although we may have been seen as a bit eccentric, we were also regarded as the best trained, on the cutting edge of psychological and social thought. Today we are advised to omit reference to psychoanalytic training on our applications to provider panels. Despite this having been a period of tremendous intellectual challenge and growth as seen from within the psychoanalytic realm, by outside psychoanalysts we are seen as static and often patronized as latter-day Luddites resisting inevitable progress. Having fallen from grace, we are assailed from all sides. Is there a connection between these observations of my children, which really have to do with questioning the magnitude and depth of the psychic effects of new developments, and of the place of psychoanalysis in modern culture?

Psychoanalysts have taken conflicting positions on the relationship of the surrounding culture to the psyche. Freud was ambiguous. His revision of the seduction hypothesis has been taken to suggest an emphasis on inner reality over an external world. However his explicitly sociological and anthropological writings reflect a position that it is the demands of the culture that initiate psychic conflict. Subsequent psychoanalytic views range from the extreme instinctual determinism of the Kleinians who see the outer world as only serving to confirm pre-existing fantasies to a mid-position that culture provides the materials for defense, to the polar extreme deterministic position of social constructivist school. Similarly, analysts range from seeing theory as developing in the consulting room independent of the surround to those like Wallerstein (1995), who regard psychoanalysis as exquisitely sensitive to the *zeitgeist*. More extremely, Spence (1993) emphasizes the centrality of context and explores psychoanalytic theory and practice as a *projection* of the *zeitgeist*.

If there is considerable diversity among analysts, analytic biographers tend to be more uniform in relating analytic positions to historical and cultural currents. Biographers of the analytic innovators, beginning with Freud, stress their relationship to the prevailing intellectual currents and scientific paradigms. Thus Freud has been understood in terms of the best that nineteenth-century European science had to offer and Sullivan has been interpreted in terms of his relationship to the logical positivist movement and a uniquely American ethos. However, there is a continuum of beliefs about the nature of historical change. The conservative position is expressed in the aphorism "The more it changes, the more it's the same." Nietzsche elaborated this idea into a cyclical vision of history which in turn is elaborated in psychoanalytic theory as the repetition compulsion. A *New Yorker* cartoon portrays it as one young adult saying to another, "I guess Beavis and Butthead are the Ren and Stimpy of our time." At the other pole is a Hegelian view of progress which posits the possibility of a break in the circle and a movement in a line toward an end. Are the developments we are seeing today, dramatic as they may seem, essentially surface phenomena on the circumference of the circle or representative of a historical novum?

One tool that can be used to address this question is Thomas Kuhn's (1970) model of scientific revolution. Arguably the most influential text of this century in philosophy of science, his *The Structure of Scientific Revolutions* offers a sociohistorical interpretation of science. Kuhn conceptualizes the paradigm as a lens through which nature is observed. His construction of the paradigm emphasizes a theory represented by an exemplar case (the "paradigm case") which arouses interest, demands explanation, and which organizes a delimited set of observations which are deemed to be relevant by the consensus of a community of practitioners. Kuhn presents a coherence rather than a correspondence theory, one thus oriented to the pragmatics of science. Further, Kuhn writes, "Paradigms gain their status because they are more successful than their competitors in solving a few problems that the group of practitioners have come to recognize as acute" (p. 23). Freud's discovery of psychoanalysis constituted a revolution, that is, the creation of a new paradigm for understanding human mind and behavior. This paradigm shift in psychology was compatible with other simultaneously occurring shifts in science and culture—for example, the assumption of a natural world defined by rational laws—such that it could attract gifted practitioners and generate inquiry. From an external vantage, the psychoanalytic paradigm can be construed as having replaced older paradigms and then itself having come under challenge from newer ones. From an internal vantage point, a multiple of competing psychoanalytic paradigms have emerged. Ferenczi's empathic method is an early example. Sullivan's interpersonal theory is another. However, many psychoanalysts continue to struggle to reconcile the multitude of psychoanalytic perspectives and have not recognized the kind of fundamental transformation that has occurred in, for example, general psychiatry, where a paradigm based on brain chemistry has prevailed. One might take the point of view that current challenges to psychoanalysis, while more strident, can be understood as yet another expression of essentially familiar repressions and resistances. Alternatively, it can be considered in terms of the "incommensurability" of the psychoanalytic paradigm with the emergence of new paradigms in the surrounding culture.

Reminiscent of Dorothy in *The Wizard of Oz* who awakens to a strange environment far away from her native Kansas, Wallerstein (1975) described psychoanalysis as originating in what might be thought of as Kansas, that is, a stable world in which there existed

> an ordering of things and the assumptions that bound them into a coherent pattern of meaning that people of intelligence and good will could not just agree upon, but . . . could take for granted. . . . There was . . . an implicit *consensus about reality* . . . [the] . . . impinging impact [of which] . . . could be subsumed under the apt phrase . . . the "average expectable environment." [p. 416]

In a previous work (Prince 1985), I have argued that the massive historical event of the Holocaust that occurred at the end of the first half of the century fundamentally altered humankind's assumptions about the nature of the possible and the organization of reality. Here I will argue that the dizzyingly rapid technological, social, and political transformations of the last quarter century, including the ideological changes consequent to the end of the Cold War, are currently accelerating at a pace that makes our current world unrecognizable to the world that developed and nourished psychoanalysis.

Let me at this point illustrate my thesis with examples of radical transformations of modern culture with a suggestion of how they clash with the psychoanalytic paradigm. First is the experience of time and space as a paradigm for interacting with the world. As analysts, we have developed an extended sense of time with patience for the slow pace of change. This contrasts with a world that has been moving faster and faster and is still accelerating. In almost every field we see the compression of time and change. The speed of the microprocessor doubles every eighteen months. The president of a telecommunications company tells me that his systems become obsolete and are replaced every six months. The journal has been found to be too slow a medium for the exchange of scientific information and has been replaced by the instantaneous transmission made possible by bulletin boards along the Internet and E-mail. New technologies change how people live their lives literally overnight. John Malone and Bill Gates (whose company, Microsoft, dates back only to 1975) have independently commented that the profits they each anticipate in the year 2000 will come from products as yet inconceivable that will alter our lives.

Using a similar time frame, the liftstyle of a patient beginning treatment today would be transformed before his analysis was half over. However, new products might force the analyst to modify some key considerations about human adaptation. For example, I recently saw a successful businessman whose ambivalence about staying in his marriage brought him into treatment. This was a man who was in constant motion, often crisscrossing the continent by plane several times in the course of a week. His outstanding feature was a cellular telephone prosthetic. He was on the phone when I greeted him in the waiting room and was barely out the door before he was back on it. His state-of-the-art Motorola sky pager allowed him to be found at any time, anywhere, including my office. This was a man who could neither make a commitment to another person nor be alone. Technology made it possible for him to never be at home but always have the illusion of being in touch and thus obviated the tension that might have motivated him to remain in treatment.

The second aspect of the current surround is the explosion in information technologies, a development that clashes with the prevailing psychoanalytic relation to information, which stresses either its unavailability or the painstaking work of making it available through analytic process.

It is true that some analytic thinkers have attempted to apply information models. However, their lack of significant support contrasts with the preoccupation of the surrounding culture with the abundance of information. IBM is developing a holographic medium, soon to be commercially available, that will store either the *Encyclopaedia Britannica* or thirty hours of video on a disk the size of a penny. Last week's prevailing metaphor (remember the excitement that attended the announcement of "the information superhighway"?) is old news today. And in a world that may not have the time to wait for people to speak their minds, we have developed imaging technologies that allow us to literally look into their brains and watch their thoughts and feelings appear on a screen. It is just barely science fiction to expect a dictionary of the morphology and neurochemistry of mental contents. It will fit on the same shelf as a disk containing the genetic code for human attributes.

The explosion in the availability, retrieval, and communication of information shifts the ground under the psychoanalytic enterprise. Just as individual variations in the oral tradition came under pressure from the advent of the written word, so the potential for standardization of the sublime individuality of psychotherapy becomes possible. Case review by managed care companies is made possible by databases and computerized protocols. Already we are seeing treatment manuals and the introduction of so called standards of practice. The brand new ability to manage huge quantities of information has made confidentiality, once so central to the treatment ethos, an anachronistic concept.

Still a third shift from Freud's time to the present has to do with the radical revision of assumptions about social roles and relationships, including sex and gender, and family roles and configurations, and identification with and belonging to a community. It becomes infinitely more difficult to analyze a person's adaptation in society when the society is in dramatic flux. An example, perhaps even a paradigm case, is the professional woman whose chief complaint is depression resulting from difficulty finding a partner. There was a time, and not so long ago, when it may have been appropriate to use individual dynamics and family relationships as the lens through which her situation could be understood. Today, there has to be a major consideration of the psychology of *not having models* (even those existing for the sole purpose of being rejected) and being, like it or not, an explorer of previously uncharted social territory. And anyone bold enough to aspire to the status of an "expert in human relations" might be given pause by the possibility that the relations one has become expert in may no longer exist and the relations one may want to become expert in do not yet exist.

If psychoanalysis added a new psychic reality to the discourse of experience, a newer domain, virtual reality, must now be included. Certainly the computer-generated perceptual experiences that are now almost and soon will be indistinguishable from actual ones will have to modify the psychoanalytic conception of fantasy and play. Important to understanding new patterns of human organization, social and personal, is that, as people experience alienation or the disintegration of their actual communities, they are creating new ones in cyberspace. The cooperation and generosity that once facilitated living in the real world (but which have given way to the forces of social disintegration) have been rediscovered in virtual communities that have been created on what its population calls "the Net." People log on, friendships are made and, on occasion, people warp back into real space and marry. The virtual community, demonstrating some continuity, even has a red-light district, that is, its pornographic bulleting boards. While writing the original text of this chapter, I cited a magazine with the vertiginous title *Open Computing: The McGraw-Hill Magazine of Unix and Interoperable Solutions*. In it, I had discovered and made note of an editorial which complained of the absence of an Internet psychological help line. Now, only three years later, painfully aware of a plethora of such web sites, I can barely remember the state of mind produced by that complaint.

Consideration must also be given to the values implicit in psychoanalysis, that is, its moral paradigm. Freud was fond of the quotation "What is moral is self-evident" (Wallerstein 1975). There are overwhelming challenges to this position. First the medical and biotechnology revolution has challenged the sanctity of life by calling its very nature into question. Our ability to defy death may in many instances betray life. The possibility of genetic engineering raises serious questions about our conception of free will, determinism, and what it means to be human. Reproductive technologies pose real moral dilemmas. And certainly, when economics and the question of the allocation of limited resources are thrown into the deliberations, morality ceases to be clear—much less "evident." Even our consideration of the aims of therapy is less than straightforward. While psychoanalytic therapy involves the enhancement of functioning, such is now also the case for pharmacotherapy. The only evident morality here is the dilemma. In his *Brave New World* (1946), Aldous Huxley presented the frightening image of a populace satisfied and pacified by a drug called

Soma. The serotonin re-uptake inhibitors have arrived, and they work passing well. Their next generation is on the way and the trouble is they're better. Combined with developments in other therapies, the Freudian aphorism that begins, "Where id was . . ." may be replaced by, "Where cosmetic psychopharmacology was, cosmetic genetics will be."

The consequence of all these changes is a fundamental transformation from the culture that gave rise to psychoanalysis, that is, a shift from what Margaret Mead (1970) terms *prefigurative* to what she calls *postfigurative.* In a prefigurative culture, the older generation serves as a guide to the younger, having the responsibility of imparting knowledge and wisdom. A grandparent looks at the newborn and can anticipate the course of the child's life. In prefigurative culture, knowledge is timeless. Irving Howe (1976) expressed it in *The World of Our Fathers*: "The *Talmud*," he wrote of the Jews of the shtetl, "was their daily newspaper." In contrast, postfigurative culture renounces tradition for change. The authority relation between the younger and older generation is reversed as it is the former that is always closest to the latest understanding about the world, how it works, its new relationships. In prefigurative cultures, children may go through a phase believing they know more than their parents. In postfigurative cultures, they do.

The psychoanalytic paradigm belongs to prefigurative culture. Its educational model depends on the handing down of clinical wisdom. It assumes that history provides continuity and identity. Its cornerstone is the analysis of authority which requires the patient's willingness to believe in the analyst's authority. The paradigm case of classical psychoanalysis was the Oedipus complex, with its emphasis on the child's transgressions. It is perhaps a small sign of their struggle to find a niche in our current culture that analysts are beginning to recast the case into the Laius complex, with emphasis on the father's arrogance and abuse of his authority. Similarly, Ferenczi's clinical contributions with their emphasis on mutuality, and Sullivan's ideas about participation—whether or not their origins are acknowledged—are reverberating in current psychoanalytic discourse.

Freud developed a paradigm for studying human nature that succeeded because it mirrored the aspiration of the physical sciences that strove to bring lawfulness to the natural world. It is perhaps more than a linguistic anomaly that one of the current paradigms flourishing in the sciences has been given the name *chaos theory*. Psychoanalysis, perhaps preoccupied by the excitement of its internal ferment, has failed to be sufficiently attentive to the paradigm shifts taking place in the world around it. As such, it is threatened as never before, and extinction is a possibility. And that would be tragic, because as far as I can see, psychoanalysis is the only current paradigm that promotes the Socratic maxim of the examined life—*know thyself.* And self-reflection, in these tumultuous times, may be humanity's best hope for survival.

REFERENCES

Howe, I. (1976). *The World of Our Fathers.* New York: Harcourt Brace Jovanovich.
Huxley, A. (1946). *Brave New World.* New York: Harper Brothers.
Kuhn, T. (1970). *The Structure of Scientific Revolutions.* Chicago: University of Chicago Press.
Mead, M. (1970). *Culture and Commitment: A Study of the Generation Gap.* Garden City, NY: Doubleday.
Prince, R. (1985). *The Legacy of the Holocaust: Psychohistorical Themes in the Lives of Children of Survivors.* Ann Arbor, MI: University of Michigan Research Press.
Spence, D. (1993). The hermeneutic turn: soft science or loyal opposition? *Psychoanalytic Dialogues* 3:1–10.
Wallerstein, R. (1975). Psychoanalytic perspectives on the problem of reality. In *Psychoanalysis and Psychotherapy,* ed. R. Wallerstein, pp. 415–441. New York: International Universities Press.

19

The Literary Critics Take on Freud: An Assessment of Their Critiques

Robert R. Holt

Once upon a time, long ago and far away, a poor but honest couple lived in a simple hut by the side of a great dark forest, with their baby boy. From a witch's prophecy the beautiful young mother knew in her heart that the child was fated to become a great hero. Soon the little family fell upon hard times, and had to move from the boy's beloved fields and forests to a cold, hostile metropolis. Struggling against contempt, rejection, and poverty, for he was a member of a persecuted minority, the boy studied hard and excelled in school. Already in college, he showed signs of scientific genius. To make a living so that he could marry the girl of his dreams, however, he became a doctor and struggled for years in obscurity.

He had one friend who stood by him in his lonely adversity, and who believed in his latent genius. Alas, this man turned out to be a mad scientist who temporarily filled his head with crazy notions, and for awhile he teetered on the edge of mental illness himself. But by a heroic and unprecedented effort, he looked into the dark chasm of his own unconscious mind and found there the secret of the human soul. Seizing it, he cured himself, broke free from the clutches of his false friend, and offered his great discovery to a suffering world. At first, contempt and ridicule were his bitter lot. Gradually, however, a small band of brave companions formed around him and began spreading his revolutionary healing methods and scientific theories. Despite many hardships he persisted, and when he died he was acclaimed the greatest scientific genius of the age.

At the same time, O best beloved, there emerged in the same country an evil schemer. He too was a Jew, but persecution and ostracism awoke in him the burning ambition to rise from obscurity by hook or by crook, wresting wealth and power from a hostile world. Stealing the ideas of others while pretending to have thought them up himself, he somehow succeeded in hoodwinking a gullible public into believing his preposterous and dirty-minded theories, so that he and his unscrupulous collaborators became rich and famous. How was he able to do it? Did he sell his soul to the Devil? Some say it was because he happened to have a great literary talent; others sadly declare that he was merely the shrewdest, most charismatic con man of his time. But in the end he was unmasked and all genuine scientists recognized him for the charlatan he was.

For a long time, we had to choose between these two mythical Freuds; there simply were no others available. Beguiled by the power of his ideas to throw new light on old problems, the overwhelming majority of American intellectuals chose the more attractive of these fairy stories and performed Tertullian-like feats of believing the incredible. Gradually, however, a breed of scholars emerged who were neither frightened or scandalized by Freud's ideas, nor bound to them by professional loyalty and filial gratitude. Some began studying his texts in light of a sophisticated knowledge of their scientific, literary, political, and cultural contexts. They treated his own accounts of his life and hard times with quizzical skepticism and looked for independent primary sources to check them out. Others critically analyzed his theories with the tools of the philosophy of science, while laboratory colleagues with an intimate familiarity with Freud's hypotheses attempted to test them by modern research methods.

This new breed of critics differed from the perpetrators of the bad-Freud myth (who rarely bothered to read much of what he actually said) in two ways: they knew the canon, often better than most training analysts; and they were also well trained in other critical disciplines. Yet most guardians of the Freudian flame greeted their fresh findings with the old familiar charges of resistance to unpalatable truths, or of suffering from unanalyzed father-transferences, or of being mere envious publicity-seekers. Some psychoanalysts adopted the newly modish dodge of declaring exposés of faults in Freud's scientific method irrelevant, because he had created a hermeneutic doctrine answerable only to another (happily more lenient) methodology and epistemology. Nevertheless, the new subdiscipline of "'Freud studies" grew and produced a number of serious and useful critical reappraisals (e.g., Eagle 1984, Ellenberger 1970, Gelfand and Kerr 1992, Grünbaum 1984, 1994, Sulloway 1979).

Beginning just two decades ago, however, another kind of critique of Freud and psychoanalysis began to appear from a new source: literary critics (including professors of literature and humanities).[1] Of course, humanists and students of literature began very early to take an interest in psychoanalysis, many becoming lay analysts themselves or writing extensively on what was known as "applied psychoanalysis." Largely an *un*critical endeavor, this body of work included several works on Freud's prose (e.g., Mahony 1982, Schönau 1968) and appreciations such as Trilling's *Freud and the Crisis of Our Culture* (1955).

The newer contributions to Freud studies by scholars from the humanities (excluding, for present purposes, philosophers) may be roughly divided into two groups: those that focus on Freud's texts, their rhetoric and logic; and others that deal with historical, cultural, and scientific issues.

THE WORK OF TEXTUAL AND RHETORICAL CRITICS

Timpanaro

The earliest of the former type is the work of an Italian scholar, Timpanaro (1974). Unlike the other authors considered here, he is a textual critic—a practitioner of what he calls the science of critically examining texts, especially the texts of old books that have had a history of repeated reproduction by hand-copying. Noticing that each manuscript volume of a given work varied from others by errors introduced in the process of copying when that was the only available method of "publication," scholars began recognizing recurrent types of errors, then developing a set of methods and rules for correcting them. The result is textual criticism, a discipline now with a considerable body of careful scholarly literature.

---

1. The first I know of, in a book by Stanley Hyman (1962), goes back thirty-five years. He writes, both appreciatively and critically, about Freud's use of imagery and several rhetorical devices; but his book has been largely overlooked in the current literature.

Having turned his highly honed set of most apposite skills to *The Psychopathology of Everyday Life*, Timpanaro (1976) produced a reasoned, logical, and thoroughly convincing little book, which differs in several ways from the others considered here. Though the result is as devastating to psychoanalytic methods as any other, this author never loses his conviction that Freud was "a thinker who for better or worse was unquestionably one of the intellectual giants of our century and who pioneered new horizons *even for science*" (p. 88 n, original italics).[2] He is even willing to admit that in a restricted set of instances Freud makes a convincing case for the motivational determination of slips of the tongue, advancing a persuasive case that instead of having provided a definitive explanation, Freud has made a modest contribution to the expansion of textual criticism. And yet, he adds, Freud errs in failing to consider a patient's slips in relation to the whole personality and neurosis, but treats each slip as an isolated phenomenon.

His analysis of a celebrated slip of the tongue, the second Freud discussed in his book (1901), nicely exemplifies Timpanaro's method. On the basis of associations to the omitted Latin word *aliquis* from a quotation from Virgil's *Aeneid*, Freud concluded that it was caused by a concealed concern that a man's lover might have missed a menstrual period. Timpanaro recognizes it as a typical error, very common in quoting poetry, of *banalization*. That means substituting something ordinary and expected for the unexpected. It happens that the sentence can't be translated directly and simply into German (or English or Italian), just because of the odd presence of the word *aliquis*, which seems not to fit. The easiest way to correct what seems (to someone ignorant of Virgil's subtlety) to be a mistake is to drop this one word in the translation. He quotes German translations of Virgil that do just that. Moreover, dropping *aliquis* does not destroy the Latin line's correct rhythmic stress as one quotes it.

The other error, *ex nostris ossibus* for *nostris ex ossibus*, is also easily explained: it's an unusual order in Latin, which doesn't occur at all in German (or English). Even in Latin, the "erroneous" order was more common. Thus, both "slips" are banalizations, which are quite plausible and retain the desired meaning and rhythm.

This account, Timpanaro (1976) exclaims, "is the simplest and most economical explanation possible" (p. 48). That is too strong, far beyond

---

2. Throughout, italics in all quotations are present in the original unless explicitly noted as added by me.

what he has demonstrated; he might better have added that it anteceded Freud's, and a new theory has the burden of showing that it can displace an existing one with some added virtue such as greater economy or scope.

Timpanaro then protested that "by passing through so wide a range of transitions [as Freud did in pursuing a chain of associations], one can reach a single point of arrival from any point of departure whatever" (p. 48). He demonstrates plausible routes by which Freud could have arrived at his conclusion if *any* one of the words in Virgil's sentence had been forgotten. That might not have been a valid objection, *if* Freud had scrupulously held back from steering the course of associations, which Timpanaro shows he had not done.

Timpanaro apparently does not realize that making a plausible case for *his* explanation does not permit him to conclude that "the connexion established by Freud . . . has not the slightest substance" (p. 53). At most, he can say that Freud's causal linkage is speculative, not convincingly substantiated, and that the burden of proof is on any defender of Freud to show that his explanation is preferable to Timpanaro's.

Freud rejected physiological and linguistic explanations of slips on the grounds that they were too general, and only his is specific. Timpanaro retorts that any scientific explanation must be somewhat general; "a 'magical' one . . . nearly always has a more 'individualizing' quality." He backs up this statement by an interesting quotation:

> For myths there can be no accidental event. . . . Everything has to be strictly determined, but . . . not by general principles underlying events [or] . . . "natural laws," but by individual purposes and forces servile to them. . . . mythical causality is based on intentions and acts of will as contrasted with rules and laws. [cited in Cassirer 1956, p. 99]

It is particularly striking that Cassirer was not referring to Freud's principle of exceptionless psychic determinism in this context. He is not alone in pointing out this major difference between magical and scientific thought: the former does not admit of coincidences or "chance," a concept central to statistical method and a great deal of scientific theory. Ironically, many psychoanalysts cite this very principle as evidence of how strictly scientific Freud was in approaching "the mind."

Timpanaro admits that emotional disturbances may play a role, but wants a balanced approach giving due weight to *all* the determinants of errors. That wasn't Freud's way. He was so convinced that he had *the* important, neglected, basic reason that he tended to derogate all others as "superficial," exaggerating the role of putative unconscious wishes and conflicts.

Near the end of his short book, Timpanaro puts Freud into intellectual-historical context: He "displays the temper of his time—a period in which psychologism reigned supreme throughout European bourgeois culture and literature. . . . this hyper-psychological bias . . . is, I think, the principal cause of the arbitrary interpretations to which Freud subjects the 'slip,' the dream, and everything we do" (p. 179). This learned and balanced outlook distinguishes Timpanaro from most of the other authors considered here. Yet he too has his own rather uncritical allegiance to an ideology, Marxism. Hence, he criticizes Freud for not being a consistent enough materialist, and deplores as "scandalous" his ignorance of Engels and Marx.

Mahony

Not many years later, Patrick Mahony, a Canadian psychoanalyst who is also a professor of English, began publishing a series of small books on Freud's principal case studies. His previous discussions of Freud's work had been rather more laudatory than critical, but now as he focused his skills of textual study he began to be disquieted by much that he observed. The result is three books in which quite severe criticism alternates with praise and the flattery of imitation—passages where Mahony presents his own "deep" interpretations, usually without acknowledging their speculative and unsubstantiated nature.

In the first[3] of these, Mahony (1984) takes up the famous "Wolfman," the Russian aristocrat whose childhood dream of wolves in a tree gave him his nickname. Initially, Mahony presents and discusses Freud's interpretation of the dream as concealing an infantile experience of observing parental intercourse *a tergo* as if Freud's construction had been factual. By the third chapter, however, Mahony is asking, "A remarkable achievement, granted—but does it accord with reality?" (p. 49). He answers by pulling together several kinds of reasons to believe that this primal scene could not have happened as described by Freud, notably Viderman's (1977) point that it would have been physically impossible for the child to have made the supposed observations. Why, Mahony asks,

---

3. Here I concentrate on the first of the three books. For a critique of the latest (Mahony 1996) see my review (Holt 1997).

did it take so long for an analyst to make such a common-sense criticism?—
Because of "the continuing history of Freud's domination and postmor-
tem presence in the psychoanalytic movement" (p. 51). He then criticizes
Freud's interpretation of the primal scene as necessarily traumatic and as
invoked to explain so much that it finally explains nothing.

Later Mahony suggests that "the fact that up to the age of three Freud
shared the same bedroom with his parents and younger siblings conduced
him to date his patient's primal scene in the same age" (p. 103). He does
not add that this fact makes it a plausible hypothesis that Freud's early
exposure to his parents' lovemaking led him to look for evidence of primal scene material in many of his patients, often—as in the cases of the
Wolfman and Dora—on far skimpier evidence.

This book, like the others that followed, contains two kinds of critique,
which might be called clinical and textual. Under the first heading,
Mahony (1984) criticizes many of Freud's interpretations, offering others of his own, but throughout paying little attention to the issue of evidential basis. The implied approach to the reader seems to be, on the one
hand to appeal to a shared stock of psychoanalytic terms and theories, and
on the other to charm and seduce into acceptance of the author's own ideas
by aesthetic rather than by scientific means. He freely criticizes Freud's
diagnostic and therapeutic decisions, drawing for his own on a motley
variety of sources from competing schools, including Kohut, Mahler,
Winnicott, and Lacan. Ready enough to accuse other analysts of putting
forth interpretations that are on their face implausible to the point of ab-
surdity, he proffers others that strike me as equally unacceptable. For
example, "the dream screen . . . visually represents the wish for a blank,
sound sleep at the breast after nursing" (p. 60), though modern sleep researchers and neurophysiologists concur that the notion of a wish to sleep
which is guarded by the dream is baseless.

On the side of textual criticism, Mahony (1984) is equally erratic.
Throughout his three books, he pays a great deal of attention to Freud's
verbal usages, and the alternate German meanings of key technical terms
and their roots, often pointing out instances in which Strachey's English
subtly but perhaps significantly distorts Freud's meanings and promotes
"a falsely idealized Freud" (p. 117). And yet in his own writing, he sur-
prises us with vulgar errors, for example, treating *schema* as a plural
(p. 60), or misusing *enormity* to mean "great size" (p. 127). He is very alert
to misprints in the *Standard Edition* but missed a few in each of his own
books. Sometimes he criticizes Freud's prose as "obfuscating" (p. 89), but

freely peppers his pages with rare and undefined words (e.g., syntagm, retrogradient, tergal), and he can be careless enough to let a passage like the following appear in print: "The particular bizarre conception of an accordingly physically impossible primal scene was the analyst's and patient's mutual acceptance of it" (p. 117). Such stylistic lapses contrast with occasional clever or even striking phrasing, culminating in the uneven quality of the long poem that concludes the Wolfman book.

A specialty of Mahony's is insightfully pointing out "mimetic" writing, in which stylistic, rhetorical, or linguistic aspects of Freud's text mirror the content. He occasionally analyzes ways in which Freud uses rhetoric, commenting that "his persuasive technique is always fascinating even when his propositions are at their weakest" (p. 100). He can be harsh in his judgments of Freud's arguments: they present a "polka dance of bewildering logic" (p. 88), "another logical whirligig" (p. 89), and "the relentless somersaulting in Freud's reasoning" (p. 93). Similarly:

> During the final months [of the Wolf Man's first analysis] Freud was driven to desperate lengths to find proof of the primal scene. . . . Soberly looked at, accumulative evidence suggests that the final course of treatment fulfilled Freud's own wishes and satisfied what had already been organized in his own mind; if some material was not forthcoming, other parts were tailored to fit expectations. [1984, p. 102]

Partly, Mahony thinks, Freud's desperate need was to persuade himself, "though ultimately he was unconvinced by his own arguments" (p. 103). And yet, at the end, he calls Freud "the world's greatest psychological genius" (p. 130).

Fish

Stanley Fish (1989) devotes the final chapter of a collection of his essays to another dissection of the same Wolfman case.[4] He gets off to a bad start,

---

4. Frederick Crews recently commented (1995, p. 13 n): "The most recent and most promising development in Freud studies is the articulation of . . . [an] understanding of Freud as a self-dramatizing rhetorician. Not surprisingly, it is literary critics who are leading the way." He then cites Wilcocks (1994), Welsh (1994), and Farrell (a book not covered here), adding: "One prototype for such efforts . . . can be found in Fish's *Times Literary Supplement* essay of August 29, 1986." It was reprinted as this chapter (albeit "revised [to its detriment]," says Crews).

however, by misquoting ". . . a report by the Wolf-Man of what he thought to himself shortly after he met Freud for the first time: this man is a Jewish swindler, he wants to use me from behind and shit on my head. This paper is dedicated to the proposition that the Wolf-Man got it right" (Fish 1989, p. 525). Fish, however, got it wrong. In a letter to Ferenczi of February 13, 1910, Freud reported that it was the patient who "wanted to use me from behind and shit on my head" (cited in Brabant et al. 1993).

Fish proceeds to make a rather subtle point concerning Freud's rhetoric, quoting passages that display Freud, in the treatment *and* in his presentation, simultaneously claiming to be giving freedom to patient or reader and setting many constraints: "The pattern is always the same: the claim of independence—for the analysis, for the patient's share, for the materials—is made in the context of an account that powerfully subverts it, and then it is made again" (p. 528). Fish does not accuse Freud of deceit, however; he leaves open the possibility that Freud was unaware that in many ways he made it impossible for the patient or for the reader to exercise real freedom.

Fish then proceeds to detail several devices by which Freud disarms criticism and otherwise makes it virtually impossible for the reader to find a fulcrum upon which to leverage any effective skepticism. One such, for example, is to frame his own situation (as therapist or as writer) in such a way that his behavior seems entirely constrained by external forces over which he had no control. With nice ingenuity, the critic shows us nonobvious ways in which Freud reverses roles, neutralizes criticism, and defends himself against charges of using suggestion and manipulation. But in doing so, Fish uses some of the same devices: overstatement ("what he calls the 'course of the analysis' has been *entirely* determined by him" [p. 538]); dogmatic reductionism ("The *real* story of the case is the story of [the reader's] persuasion" [p. 537, italics added]); and interpretation by reversal of apparent meaning (as in his argument that Freud's declaration of powerlessness is a way to gain power over the reader).

Thus, though Fish starts out with attractive skepticism and ironic detachment, by the end he offers his diagnostic inferences about Freud not as hypotheses but as factual conclusions: "In his relationships with the patient, the analysis, the reader, and his critics . . . [Freud] is driven by the obsessions he uncovers, by the continual need to control, to convince, and to reduce . . . [and] to disclaim any traces of influence. . . ." (p. 540). Not content to expose the teasing device by which Freud feeds the reader's curiosity, announcing that he has information but withholding it awhile,

Fish adds that it is a bit of "anal eroticism" (p. 541). A little later, describing Freud's presumed "pleasure of persuasion," he states that it "is intensely erotic, full of the 'sexual excitement' that is said to mark the patient's passing of a stool; it is . . . anal, phallic, and even oral. . . ." (p. 543). Thus, he embraces the libido theory and Freud's way of using it interpretively despite his original stance.

Borch-Jacobsen

Next, chronologically, comes Borch-Jacobsen (1988), Professor of French and Comparative Literature at the University of Washington, Seattle. The book under consideration was his doctoral dissertation in philosophy, written using "the typical Heideggerian-deconstructive method of interpretation, which consists in following the *internal* logic of an argument to the point where it becomes contradictory and self-destructs." His seeming deference to Freud, therefore, "was only a mask for what I intended to be a ruthless philosophical critique of psychoanalysis" (1997, personal communication).

The author tells us that his topic, the Freudian Subject, is "the key term of Western metaphysics" (Borch-Jacobsen 1988, p. 17), which should warn one that it may be a bit elusive. A grammatical term not used as much by Freud as by Lacan, it is not equivalent to the ego. Indeed, as the author is at some pains to demonstrate, it logically precedes the ego. As soon as the baby *does* anything, even look around, it becomes a subject. In his next book, Borch-Jacobsen explains:

> By providing himself with an unconscious made up of "representations," "thoughts," "fantasies," "memory traces," Freud at the same time provided himself with a *subject* of representation, of imagination, of memory—in short, with the material for a new *cogito*, one simply conceived as more basic and more subjectival than the conscious ego. [1993, p. 19]

New, because Descartes conceived thinking as simply conscious, and when one contemplates the originator of unconscious as well as conscious cognition, the issue gets a good deal more complicated.

The 1986 book is a linguistically informed and witty search for the so-conceived subject through a series of key works beginning with the "Interpretation of Dreams" (1900) and ending with "Group Psychology and the Analysis of the Ego" (1921). The author starts with a contradiction in what

Freud wrote, and instead of taking it as a failing, he assumes that there must be a hidden, deeper meaning, an answer that can be dug out. Although it appears to be a devout exegesis, the search ends with discovering a series of further contradictions and arbitrary inventions, and finally a necessary flight into the grandiose fantasy of an explicit myth. Between the lines, then, Borch-Jacobsen does not so much say outright as he leads the reader to conclude that Freud created a basically untenable theory, the most original parts of which do not work, and one which collapses into its self-created pitfalls.

The book's style is at once highly condensed and discursive, studded with multilingual puns and neologisms, so dense and multilayered as to demand the greatest concentration. No evidence is offered for any of the assertions. The book's detailed and often obscure argument at times proceeds by leaps that seem either arbitrary, unintelligible owing to a bad translation (from the original French), or trapped by its own tropes—failing to descend from a metaphoric discourse to saying plainly what one means. In its course, the author frequently comes to different conclusions from Freud's (e.g., narcissism is violence, or when Freud attributes something to homosexuality it really means sociality), without disputing his fundamental concepts or the premises of metapsychology.

He seems, however, to pull off the feat of making sense of the many contradictions and confusions of "On Narcissism" (Freud 1914) by keeping always in mind the basic point that the self or sense of special individual identity is *constructed* from social interaction. To be sure, in so doing he has to reject and reinterpret a great deal of what Freud says.

It is not easy to convey a sense of what is insightful and useful in this book in a few words; but let me try. Taking at face value several passages in which Freud describes the earliest object relation as a devouring, undifferentiated love–hate of the breast, Borch-Jacobsen (1988) notes that the infant thus begins the process of constituting an ego. The preoedipal relationship to the father is not yet one of love, but of identification also; thus, *"identification creates sympathy, generates a positive bond with others"* (p. 197). This position, the author points out, is "absolutely unjustified, since he [Freud] also gives us all the elements we need to think the opposite" (p. 197). He nicely shows that Freud describes the beginning and the alleged end of the Oedipus complex in the same way: the boy gets into it and out again by identifying himself with his father. Such an account works only if we accept Freud's arbitrary, never explained, ad hoc assumption that, though the ego ideal is described as part of the ego, identification with the ideal is quite different from regressive identification, or introjection into the ego. At the end of the Oedipus complex, the father is incorporated into the ego ideal but must *not* be taken into the ego, which would put the two into direct rivalry again.

A similar paradox plagues Freud's mass psychology, which uses identification with the leader as the source of the social bond: he too must be taken into the ego ideal but not the ego. Freud's way out is to invoke his speculative phyletic notions. The quest for origins cannot stop with the individual but must go to "the collective prehistory of humanity" (p. 234). Freud said it plainly in 1921, Borch-Jacobsen points out: before the individual came the group bond—except for the leader! He is narcissistic and free from all such bonds, though Freud never says how and why. In his second book, the author makes explicit the totalitarian nature of Freud's political psychology of leader and mass, quoting from the Why War letter to Einstein a "dreadful passage" on "the innate and ineradicable inequality of men . . . leaders and followers" (Borch-Jacobsen 1993, p. 25 n).

"Here, as a result, is a myth," Borch-Jacobsen (1988) concludes, "the myth of the mythic birth of the subject" and Freud himself was the self-creating hero. Psychoanalysis, then, "was nothing but a great egoistic dream—that of Freud" (p. 239).

Another book[5] (Borch-Jacobsen 1993) is cast in a similar mold, but being a collection of separate articles and addresses, it resists quick summary.

Let us turn, then, to Borch-Jacobsen's latest book (1996). It differs rather strikingly from the previous two. It is, first, shorter, more simply and engagingly written, and thus a great deal more accessible to the average reader. Unlike them, it concentrates on a single work and tells an engrossing story. Equally noticeable is the change that the author's attitude toward Freud has undergone, but that is perhaps less remarkable because of a similar change in the tone of most of the literature of Freud studies: less respectful, more willing to make wisecracks at Freud's expense, and less guarded in charging him with ethically dubious practices, such as deliberate distortion of his case histories and other data to fit his theoretical preconceptions.

Admittedly, much of what Borch-Jacobsen has to say about Anna O. (Bertha Pappenheim) has already been said by various others. He handsomely acknowledges his debt to several notable Freud scholars, whose previously published (or publicly presented) data he collates and welds

---

5. I neglect here his second book, *Lacan: The Absolute Master*.

into an expanded narrative. If some of it is conjectural, he correctly points out the annoying fact that many issues could be simply and factually settled if Freud's biological and professional heirs would give all scholars equal access to known but embargoed sources.

He has done enough research on primary sources to warrant a book of his own, even though he himself is not responsible for any of its juiciest revelations. My principal cavil is that occasionally, and more often as the story nears its end, his initial tone of cautious scholarliness gives way to undocumented assertions and fairly risky interpretive leaps from not terribly solid data. Offhandedly, he remarks: "'Hysteria' is not a real illness, as we know [therefore, citations of relevant literature are presumably unnecessary] . . . Like so many other 'neuroses,' 'mental illnesses,' or 'psychosomatic disorders,' but more blatantly and spectacularly so, hysteria is an illness that exists for the sake of the cure" (p. 83).

How did he come to be so sure of the factuality of these bland assertions? The book gives us no hint.[6]

I find it hard to argue with his principal conclusion, however: there has indeed been a century of mystification about the famous case Freud singled out as the principal starting point of psychoanalysis. To an unknown but— the author argues persuasively—large degree, the patient's illness, with its extraordinary panoply of dramatic symptoms and the (usually temporary) removal of many of them, seems to have resulted from implicit game-playing between Breuer and Anna. Borch-Jacobsen calls attention to the sensational mesmeric performances of a stage hypnotist, Carl Hansen, which attracted the interest of numerous serious scientists as well as the rest of Vienna during the months just before Anna called in her doctor for help with a persistent cough, and makes a rather convincing case that the subsequent flowering of a "hysteria" may have been directly influenced. Though he was a decent and ethical practitioner and in many ways an excellent scientist, Breuer found in his patient someone who acted out all his expectations, however subtly they may have been conveyed to her, and

---

6. In the same letter referred to above, Borch-Jacobsen (1997) asked me, "isn't there a wide consensus about the fact [sic] that hysterical symptoms are not symptoms of a *real* (objective) illness? . . . If you really want a reference, . . . [see] Edward Shorter's work on psychosomatic illnesses, which convincingly shows how psychosomatic symptoms evolve over time to meet medical expectations." He also remarks that "it is true that I don't cite any sources, mainly because I have my own little 'interactional' theory of hysteria that I intend to develop one day."

she in turn found an ideal audience for theatrical performances of her "caprices" and fantasies. She discovered, too, that he was willing to play the roles she assigned to him, and to spend endless hours helping her to enliven her otherwise tedious life.

With telling effect, the book compares the famous account of the case in "Studies on Hysteria" (Breuer and Freud 1895) with Breuer's own extensive case notes (published in Hirschmüller 1989), showing in detail how an obvious failure was turned into what appears to be an at least partial therapeutic success, clearly under Freud's influence. Freud comes off pretty badly in this book, which mercilessly exposes his many distortions and fabulations about Anna's case. In large part, their untruth is manifest when one reads what he and Martha said to one another about the patient, who was her friend.

Welsh

Another professor of literature, at Princeton, has devoted an engaging book entirely to *The Interpretation of Dreams* (1900). Welsh (1994) tells us that he has given a course on this "masterpiece" for several years, which must include several kinds of commentary besides the literary. This book is full of insightful comments on, for example, the social origins of many aspects of Freud's thought, and it contains some sensible analyses of the theory's questionable standing as science. Commenting on the individualism of psychoanalysis, he notes that it has roots in romanticism, but also in medicine: the practitioner "can hardly avoid noticing that afflictions strike some individuals but not others" (p. 133). Hence the need to treat each patient as unique and to take a personal history.

He begins by insightfully noting the ways in which the writing was an act of wish-fulfillment on Freud's part, admitting nevertheless that its wishfulness does not invalidate it. He notes, for example, that each interpretation fulfills a wish by unveiling it. As he gets into its conceptual basis, Welsh becomes a little more acerbic. After discussing the relations among displacement, censorship, repression, and resistance, he comments:

> Less patient readers may feel that Freud defines these terms by means of one another and confuses them freely because they have no empirical base. [p. 85] . . . To do away with the censorship [however, he adds] would be to do away with the dream book in its most enjoyable part. . . . Still, the concept is mired in such difficulties . . . that it scarcely can be rationalized.

... Freud has no other means of knowing what the censorship, in a given instance has censored than a general knowledge of what is socially permissible to communicate.... [p. 88]

Much of this book dwells on Freud's mastery of self-portrayal. As he tells his own dreams and gives bits of autobiography to illuminate them, Freud manages to win the reader's admiration and sympathy, converted into agreement with implausible assumptions and finally complicity in a process of reasoning that has many gaps. "The effect [of one of Freud's pleasantries] is to make acceptable the evidence" he puts forward and

> to assure the reader of his sincerity once the foolery is over. But Freud's way of seeking approval cheerfully admits to telling lies and speaks of insincerity.... If you enjoy the act, you identify not only with the positive assurances but with the scurrilous admissions.... the pleasures of the book, including wish fulfillment in the argument thereof, carry the author and his readers uncritically forward. [pp. 118–119]

The tone, then, is ambivalent. It is clear that Welsh enjoys the artfulness of Freud's performance, and considers the book a major achievement despite its flaws.

> Freud.... may be a giant—he is a giant—but the arguments on which his gianthood rests have increasingly been challenged. [p. 122] ... History ... is not likely to forget his masterpiece. [It has two main, "indisputable" achievements:] It endorsed the principle ... that each individual is constrained by his or her personal history, and it worked out an especially influential account of narrative. [Neither was] entirely new, but in both areas he focused the attention of the 20th century so decisively that they well deserve to be known as Freudian innovations. On the grounds of publicity, obviously, the unconscious also deserves to be called a Freudian innovation.... [p. 131]

Since I agree with those judgments, I found the book on the whole sensible and useful. At times, however, Welsh overreaches. He devotes a good deal of space to discussing the two case vignettes with which the seventh chapter ends, as illustrations of the devices—besides dreams—[in] by means of which unconscious impulses emerge in behavior despite the censorship. Each occupies one paragraph. The first portrays a girl brought by her mother "to a consultation last year," Freud says (1900, p. 618), whose appearance was surprising: one stocking hung down, two blouse buttons were undone. She appeared unembarrassed by exposing her calf as she reported pain in it, or by her main complaint: that her body felt as if something was stuck in it that was moving back and forth and shaking her through and through. Freud then mentions a male colleague who exchanged a meaningful glance with him, and comments that the mother found nothing meaningful "though she must often have found herself in the situation which her child was describing" (p. 618).

In the second, a boy of 14 comes to treatment for various somatic symptoms declared hysterical, and on Freud's suggestion produces a series of visual images: a checkerboard with various positions and moves one must not make; a dagger on the board, replaced by a sickle and a scythe. Freud briefly rehearses the boy's history, giving reasons for the "suppressed rage against his father" which was responsible for the imagery. Freud tells us that the pictures were drawn from myths in which (for example) "Zeus castrated his father" (p. 619) with a sickle, and that the boy's animus against his father stemmed from his being forbidden to masturbate.

About the first vignette, Welsh says:

> The story omits some facts necessary to show "the intimate and reciprocal relations between censorship and consciousness" and admits others . . . that are gratuitous, such as the dress of the patient and the seeming negligence of the mother—features . . . singled out as "surprising" . . . and "extraordinary." . . . The narrative is more nearly . . . a risible anecdote . . . an obscene joke. . . . [p. 91]

Welsh then quotes extensively from Freud's joke book on smut and the like, calling it "brilliant literary analysis" (p. 92). In many details, this story resembles the typical dirty joke as Freud (1905, p. 99 n) himself describes it. Therefore, with no further ado, Welsh declares: "This story has patently been assembled for the pleasure and instruction of readers. . . . For this reader, its penury as a report and similarity to a joke cast its provenance completely in doubt" (p. 93). . . . "The details supplied for preparation and suspense have almost been too well told" (p. 94).

As to the boy, Welsh quotes a passage from the book on parapraxes where Freud takes up his slip in calling Zeus the castrator of Kronos and attributes it to "derivatives of repressed thoughts connected with my dead father" (Freud 1901, p. 219).

> From this casual admission, it would seem that the fourteen-year-old's knowledge of mythology is Freud's knowledge, and the story so thoroughly

subjective in its telling as to erase the distinction between the boy and its narrator.... In autobiographical passages, this order of deception has come to be taken for granted by Freudians, but if this story is autobiographical, it leaves behind a bad taste in such fanciful details as the parents' divorce or the character of the father. [Welsh 1994, p. 103]

—which make it seem highly unlikely that the passage is autobiographical; rather, Freud is as usual supplying his own associations in lieu of those the patient failed to give.

Welsh goes right on with what he considers the clincher:

It so happens that the stories of the girl and the boy have a connection that antedates by at least five years their appearance [here]; a connection that belies any possibility [sic!] that the consultation with the girl occurred "last year" and leads one to suspect that a good many other narratives in the book were made to order. The malleability of such fictions is apparent, for as it happens, an outline of these two was first roughed in by a paragraph in Freud's theoretical contribution[7] to "Studies on Hysteria" that began with a similar offer of two examples.... [p. 103]

The similarity, on which the author pins so much, turns out to be rather slight: in 1895, Freud was in fact talking about censorship in relation to pathogenic recollections, but both examples were produced by the same male patient. One is an image of a woman whose "dress [was] not properly fastened—out of carelessness, it seems" and the other a picture of two boys who were "guilty of some misdeed" (Breuer and Freud 1895, p. 282). Welsh finds the similarities striking enough to declare that "they are clearly fiction as presented" (p. 104). A little later (p. 108), he refers to the two stories from Chapter 7, remarking, "... I trust I have shown—they are spurious."

Again, the pot is complaining of the kettle's dark complexion, for this is the same author who chided Freud for reaching serious conclusions on the basis of slight evidence bent to his own purposes.

In the penultimate paragraph of the dream book, Welsh says, Freud tries to explain

why unconscious wishes need not be judged in an ethical light or serve as evidence of character. In doing so, however, he not only raises the question

---

7. It is actually from Freud's chapter on psychotherapy; the theoretical chapter was written by Breuer.

of the possible insignificance of the dreams he has studied but suddenly exposes the mechanisms of repression and censorship as completely arbitrary. [Welsh 1994, p. 112]

What Welsh apparently means is that by his effort to deal with this "practical" issue of ethics, Freud suddenly finds himself embarrassed by the insufficiency of his simple theory: he must posit unconscious operations that don't sound like the usual brutal or infantile *Ucs.*, but which he will later call unconscious ego and superego. Likewise, he attributes much more power to "the real forces of mental life" (Freud 1900, p. 621) in consciousness than he had given to the *System Cs.*, foreshadowing much of ego psychology. Despite the weaknesses of these later theoretical innovations, the need for them surely doesn't amount to a sudden exposure of complete arbitrariness. A more appropriate reflection would have been that since he could treat the ethical question only so lamely and incompletely, Freud would have done better to have omitted it entirely, here.

Welsh then (on p. 115) characterizes the dream book's ending as a clown's exit "on the run with an exaggerated bow, a wave, and a wink. . . . I am in danger of travestying the end of the dream book," he concedes, but alleges that a second clown may be needed to put a first in his place. At this point, his imitation of his target's faults seems almost completely conscious.

Wilcocks

The last of the authors who criticize Freud primarily from the standpoint of their own professional expertise is Robert Wilcocks, Professor of Modern French Literature at the University of Alberta, Canada. He is not at all shy about speaking as if he were an expert on scientific method or such medical specialties as neurology, however, though he reveals no relevant credentials. From time to time, throughout his book, Wilcocks (1994) betrays how out of his element he is in scientific and clinical matters, but that does not seem to deter him from making dogmatic pronouncements. We will do better to concentrate on what he has to say when on home ground, as a student of rhetoric and discourse.

The subtitle of his book (*The Rhetoric of Deceit*) epitomizes its tendency to assert its conclusions before arguing them, and hints at its angry, snide, contemptuous tone. In a relatively few pages, Wilcocks decides that

Freud's genius was as a writer, not as a scientist; indeed, he considers science merely a "trope" for Freud—a term the latter brandished defensively and pretentiously without any understanding of how to achieve scientific status for psychoanalysis. In an equally dismissive way, Wilcocks assures us that, as a therapy, Freud's invention has "a failure rate so dire that, in the United States at least, they refuse to publish the figures" (p. 34). The real reason so few figures have been published is that they hardly exist, since too few analysts have been willing to participate in gathering the data. It is purely Wilcocks's supposition that the underlying reason is a "dire" rate of failure, but take notice how he presents it as if it were a fact. (Actually, psychoanalysis has approximately the same rate of success and failure as other psychotherapies; see Erwin [1996] and Fisher and Greenberg [1995].)

Wilcocks asserts that Freud's unearned status as Authority is "a triumph . . . in the face of facts that . . . confounded his theories" (p. 5). What he apparently has in mind is "Jeffrey Masson's disclosures," actually interpretations rather than facts, which few Freud scholars take seriously whatever their orientation. "The deceptions of Freud's rhetoric are at least threefold," we learn in the first chapter: "(1) in the plausible presentation of induction gone wild; (2) in the creation (he named it 'construction') of texts (his own and those of his patients) that appear to justify his hunches; and (3) in the elaboration of a kind of argumentation designed to provoke in the reader a narrative suspense and a willing suspension of disbelief" (Wilcocks 1994, p. 7).

Wilcocks provides many examples of each kind, a number of which (to the best of my knowledge, anyway) have not been remarked by any other scholars. He is capable of shrewd, close reading; he showed me many inconsistencies and self-contradictions that I had not noticed before in various of Freud's works.

Yet there are gaps in his knowledge of psychoanalysis, and he is capable of perpetrating some real howlers. Here are a couple: To have considered that "the cupboard is *not* a symbolization of the womb . . . might have led to some alarming revisions of his *metapsychology*" (p. 188); "For him [Freud], as we know, dreams *were* symptoms" (p. 202). "Freud begins . . . with the basic issue of the *psychological* versus . . . the *organic* view of hysteria. In this paper [Freud 1896] he claims to embrace uniquely the first" (p. 132). Freud actually wrote: "What can the other factors be which the 'specific aetiology' of hysteria still needs in order actually to produce the neurosis? . . . No doubt a considerable quantity of factors will have to be taken into account. There will be the subject's inherited and personal constitution. . . ." (Freud 1896, p. 210).

In addition, Wilcocks's grasp of medical history is insufficient for him to realize that Freud, like others of his era, considered that "infantile sexual experiences" (listed next in the passage just quoted) were considered organic, rather than psychological factors: what mattered was the irritation of the sexual organs and the neural stimuli produced, not the traumatic experience of being overwhelmed and violated. It is only fair to add that very few Freud scholars fully grasped this point before it was fully documented by Bonomi (1994).

Freud's very presentation of psychoanalysis as a science uses figurative language, Wilcocks argues: "its function was to conceal, to deceive, and to make *acceptable*—to its users as to its readers—the subject matter of the discourse" (Wilcocks 1994, p. 27). He soon cites an example of deceit, in "A Case of Paranoia Running Counter to the Psychoanalytic Theory of the Disease" (Freud 1915). Though the case begins with the report that Freud was approached by a lawyer who suspected that his client's demand for protection against a man who was harassing her was pathological, when Freud heard the woman's initial story he says that he was in a dilemma. He either had to give up his theory about the role of homosexuality in paranoia or else "side with the lawyer and assume that this was no paranoic combination but an actual experience which had been correctly interpreted" (Freud 1915, p. 266). Keen-eyed Wilcocks noted the odd phrase, "side with the lawyer" and promptly concluded that "Freud is *lying*" (p. 38, original italics). "Confused," "contradicting himself," "beset by a momentary lapse of memory"—a characterization of this general type seems plausible, but hardly that Freud gratuitously put in the phrase as part of a deliberate effort to deceive. *Cui bono?* we must ask; what gain would there have been for Freud? Wilcocks does not suggest any; instead, he veers off into a comparison of Freud with Edgar Allan Poe, a known hoaxer. A careful reader, seeing here a diversionary tactic that prevents the reader from asking difficult questions, might conclude that "We have thus . . . at once a dismantling of Freud's rhetorical effects and an employment of them in that very demonstration." Amusingly, this is a quotation from Wilcocks himself (p. 323), only he is referring to Fish (1989), seemingly unaware that he might be hoist with his own petard!

Wilcocks can do a rather amusing turn of imagining the chapter on the dream of Irma's injection as a stage monologue delivered in the Mark Twain style. But he quickly passes from a showing that it *can* be read that way to an inner assurance that it must be and therefore "is a highly crafted theatrical monologue (the hidden presence of the public is almost palpable), not a dream analysis" (Wilcocks, p. 248). In doing so, he shows how deftly Freud distracts the reader from raising any skeptical questions, or from noticing that his interpretation makes no mention of infantile wishes, and that it is not so much a demonstration of wish-fulfillment as a plea for exoneration.

Wilcocks then argues that "Equally feasible, and in my opinion far more likely, is that what is called the 'Specimen Dream' . . . is a concatenation evolved by Freud from a series of dreams at different times in the troubled summer of 1895" (p. 248). Only a little later, and after the introduction of no further hard evidence, he writes: "He was lying to Fliess in that letter [of June 18, 1900] about [the usually accepted date of] the Dream of Irma's Injection, and the report in *Traumdeutung* was a complete fabrication written some years after the completed dream(s)" (p. 277, n 64). How like Freud, who could introduce a tentative suggestion and then soon after treat it as if it were a demonstrated fact!

One of this author's frequently used analytic concepts is *the middle mode of discourse*. He borrows it (with full acknowledgment) from a colleague, Nicholas Boyle, who shows how Nietzsche confuses the unwary reader by metalepsis, defined in the Shorter Dictionary as "the metonymical substitution of one word for another which is itself figurative." Here is an example: After quoting another critic's echoing of the charge first enunciated by Fliess, that the "thought-reader" reads his own thoughts into his subject, in a metaphor of mistaking a mirror for a window, Wilcocks writes: "The very strong possibility remains that he had not merely mistaken a mirror for a window (the inductive extrapolations that belabored everyone else with his supposed problems), but that he had mistaken a fairground distorting mirror for the less duplicitous, and less dramatic plain glass of the bathroom vanity" (p. 44).

Wilcocks generalizes the idea of the middle mode somewhat to mean a way of writing in which "indeterminate multivalent phrases obfuscate careful thinking" (p. 274). For example, Wilcocks makes much of the ambiguity and semantic slippage in Freud's use of the concept of castration anxiety. To begin with, he charges neologism: before Freud, castration meant only the removal of the testicles, but Freud distorted it to mean cutting off the penis. (He could have spared his great expenditure of indignation if he had realized that there is a large literature in the 1880s and 1890s on castration of women—typically, clitoridectomy—as a supposed cure for hysteria [Bonomi 1994].) Wilcocks complains that the concept is applied to all boys, whether or not anyone has warned them that it will drop off if they don't stop playing with it, because Freud thought the fear a phylogenetic inheritance (via the myth of the primal horde), and to all girls, who can plainly see that they are already victims of it. So it comes to mean an assumedly universal fear of what might happen to an organ assumed to be anyone's most important possession, even if it was never there between her legs—assumption piled on metaphor heaped on assumption. He surely has a point, here and in many others of his charges, however overblown they usually are.

The very title of this book, *Maelzel's Chess Player*, is metaleptic: it is a tale of a deception perpetrated by a nineteenth-century American mountebank, supposedly unmasked by Poe in an essay that itself is actually a hoax. As Wilcocks tells the story, he constantly compares Poe to Freud, but is a great deal more specific and convincing in detailing the poet's deceptions, intellectual thefts, and forgeries than those of psychoanalysts, to whom they are intended to be attributed by association. But it may be that the author feels that, as a literary man himself, he has license to play fast and loose with figurative language in a way that is off limits to a purported scientist. Perhaps so, but he has lost sight of the fact that his indictment would seem stronger and would stick better if delivered with more care to avoid precisely the same intellectual shoddiness of which he accuses Freud.

MORE GENERAL CRITIQUES

Some professors of literature and similar humanistic studies have only incidentally used their professional skills in the analysis of rhetoric and similar aspects of texts, in their critiques of Freud. I will consider only three examples of this smaller genre.

Gilman

Sander Gilman is the Goldwin Smith Professor of Humane Studies at Cornell University and Professor of Psychiatry at Cornell Medical College. He has held fellowships and appointments in English, history, and the humanities, and has been a visiting professor of literary theory and of

Jewish studies. While he is thus not so easily pigeonholed as some other authors, his book *The Case of Sigmund Freud* (1993) has some right to be considered along with others by literary critics.

This mistitled book is not a case history in any usual sense, but a learned essay on race and medicine, with particular attention to late nineteenth-century notions about the bodies, physiology, and illnesses of Jews. It does of course discuss the ways these themes affected Freud and he them, but it contains no extended presentation of Freud's life and career, interpreted in this new light.

Early on (p. 5), Gilman announces: "My thesis is rather simple: given that the biology of race stands at the center of the nineteenth-century 'sciences of man' . . . it is extraordinary to imagine that anyone who thought of himself as a 'scientist' . . . could have avoided confronting this aspect of science."

So the Jewish scientist was in a serious bind, for science showed that he was inferior. Moreover, a special problem for Jewish doctors was that the Jew was considered inherently diseased, specially vulnerable to and afflicted with a variety of illnesses. Different ones coped with this bind in different ways, naturally.

"Freud is not typical in his response," Gilman notes (p. 6), promising "a detailed study of the strategic devices that . . . Sigmund Freud evolved. . . ." An interesting idea, one thinks; this man has an original approach, which might throw some new light on Freud and how he worked. Then one remembers that, in all that Freud said about Jewishness, he never gives a hint that he was aware of and had to cope with this facet of anti-Semitism.[8] He wrote a lot about discrimination and prejudice, and about the marks it left on him to be part of a rejected minority, but nothing about the special issues that Gilman takes up here.

The consequence is that Gilman is in all-too-familiar a bind. Like Freud, attempting to figure out how patients cope with traumatic memories or pathogenic fantasies of which they are quite unaware but which he felt

---

8. Gilman (p. 25) quotes Freud as saying to Romain Rolland "'I, of course, belong to a race which in the Middle Ages was held responsible for all epidemics . . . and which today is blamed for the disintegration of the Austrian Empire and the German defeat.'" That does not, however, justify the implication that he was aware that in his own time some medical writers accused Jews of being carriers of various diseases, or that such notions were widespread enough to constitute a threat against which he had to erect defenses.

convinced they harbored, Gilman must try to figure out how Freud reacted to a predicament he is postulated to have been in though he gave no sign of having been aware of it. The author makes no mention of this parallel, however, and may be a bit too confident of his thesis.

In a series of chapters, he quotes many contemporary sources that expounded ideas about how Jews were physically and psychologically different, and shows how they became part of medical doctrine in the nineteenth century. The data are clearly there: there *was* a body of such anti-Semitic mythology within medicine—including, interestingly, the notion that hysteria was a peculiarly Jewish disease. But we never get answers to such key questions as these: Just how pervasive was this particular set of stereotypes about Jewish pathology at Freud's time and place? To what extent did it affect him and his circle of Jewish-doctor friends, like Breuer and Fliess? How can we understand their failure to mention it, though they discussed other aspects of anti-Semitism freely enough among themselves?

Gilman's approach is to quote a few writers of the time to the effect that "the Jew was different, and this difference presented itself as a disease" (p. 21), but does not show that they were the rule, not exceptional. There clearly was a lot written, however, about Jewish diseases, some of it by Jews. For example, proponents of emancipation saw Jewish diseases as caused by ghetto life and repression. That doesn't provide the critical information to establish Gilman's thesis, however.

Here is an example of one of the methods Freud used, according to Gilman, to cope with his alleged plight. Taking up Fliess's notion of male menstruation, he tells us that a thirteenth-century anatomist, de Cantimpré, introduced the concept that male Jews menstruated. The myth that Jews kill Christian children to get their blood originated in de Cantimpré's story that a Jewish prophet told Jews that they could use Christian blood to get rid of menstruation. "The belief in Jewish male menstruation continued through the seventeenth century. . . . And the view that attributed to the Jews diseases for which the 'sole cure was Christian blood' persisted into the late nineteenth century" (p. 95). So, by postulating the *universality* of male menstruation (and the closely associated idea of bisexuality), Fliess and Freud managed to get rid of the charge that these were disorders peculiar to Jews.

This book is fascinating for its bits of such esoteric lore, but in the end not adequately convincing. Gilman works hard to find evidence—too hard,

I believe, because when texts he cites are tracked down, what is said often becomes evidential only after the exercise of interpretive ingenuity strongly reminiscent of Freud.

Webster

In an introductory Note to the Reader of his book *Why Freud Was Wrong* (1995), Richard Webster describes himself as no polymath but "a literary critic who had strayed into neurology, psychiatry and the history of medicine." If he has had any formal education in psychoanalysis, psychology, scientific methods, or the philosophy of science, he does not divulge it. He seems to be an autodidact in these fields, which paradoxically may have made it easier for him to pass many sweepingly negative judgments concerning them.

Early in this book, Webster accuses Freud of having "left us no theoretical means by which we might unravel his own deepest motives or analyze his development and his evident sense of mission" (p. 29). Yet he uses precisely the theoretical means of psychoanalytic interpretation to put together his own explanation of the man, complete with early traumas, unconscious motives, and defenses.

The book starts with a section headed "The Creation of a Pseudo-Science," a pretty good summary of works by the main critics of Freud's scientific methods. In Part II, "The Church and the Psychoanalytic Gospel," Webster develops the central thesis of the book, that psychoanalysis *is* a religion. Not to be misunderstood, Webster rejects the *analogy* of religion and psychoanalysis, because "psychoanalysis, it would seem, is quintessentially a religion and should be treated as such" (p. 362).

It may be a mistake to consider Freud's probable identification with God basic. The power of the Austrian emperor was much more real and manifest than the mythic omnipotence of God Almighty. But we don't have to choose between these interpretations! I know how furious many critics become over the glib tendency of analysts to resolve disputes about alternative interpretations simply by invoking overdetermination, concluding that everyone is right. It is too easy a way to escape the obligation to seek data to resolve issues. In this case, however, like many others, there are plenty of data on both sides. Here perhaps Freud was right: unconsciously, we often may maintain mutually exclusive fantasies without having to chose between them. But for Webster, there is no problem of choice; he knows the answer.

Webster seems as monomaniacal about religion as Freud was about sex: stretching the concept as far as possible, interpreting everything that *could* be religious as such, constantly using religious imagery, and talking himself into his own pet interpretations just as Freud did his. He freely admits that he is not the first to be struck by Freud's religious imagery and by parallels between the psychoanalytic movement and religious sects; indeed, he quotes many such observations as if they proved his larger thesis, though he fails even to mention the most diligent and successful of his predecessors, Vitz (1988). What he adds is to put it all together: the evidence that Freud identified himself with religious leaders, the Messiah, and God himself; the sect-like structure and organization of the movement, the worshipful attitudes of the followers, Freud's pope-like behavior, etc. He develops an elaborate conception of Freud's messianic personality, points to more than superficial parallels between psychoanalytic treatment and the confessional, and strives to make psychoanalytic theory seem a form of religious dogma.

Up to a point, it is quite plausible, but Webster seems unable to quit when he is ahead. He might have made a pretty persuasive argument if he were less cocksure and dogmatic, not so eager to overstate his case. He could see that trait as marring the writing of Elizabeth Thornton (1983)—on whose works he nevertheless relies extensively—but not as applying to himself.

Despite these defects, the book's first two parts contain an interesting and competent synthesis of much modern Freud scholarship, worth a carefully skeptical reading, even though Webster himself has done no work on primary sources and presents no new findings. As soon as he tries to go off on his own, he loses all claim to our interest.

Part III of Webster's book, portentously titled "Psychoanalysis, Science, and the Future," lays out an ambitious attempt to survey and pass judgment on all of modern science and intellectual life. Here Webster gives us his own diagnosis of civilization's discontents, many of which he lays at the door of science and its "misguided" pursuit of objectivity. Unfortunately, Webster's defective grasp of science and the limitations of his method cause him to fall on his face so embarrassingly that this part of the work is better passed over in silence. He has the notion, for instance, that because religious thinkers of a rationalist persuasion rejected behavioral evidence in favor of dogma, so too all modern rationalist theories (e.g., science with its attempt at objectivity) must therefore begin by rejecting such reality in favor of presuppositions.

One could not ask for a better example of a critic who relies extensively on the same errors of selective attention to fact, reasoning, and writing as he found in his target. Examples could be multiplied at exhausting length; let me give just a few. One form his argument often takes is reductionism, like you-know-whose. The *Project's* (Freud 1895) "elaborately constructed network of neurones and contact-barriers is nothing more than a work of ingenious fiction," he writes (p. 180), even though no less a neuroscientist than Karl Pribram (1965) saw a great deal of merit in it. As Freud sometimes did, Webster makes erroneous factual assertions about matters with which he can have no direct knowledge and without citing any sources: ". . . no form of therapy which allows elements of the human imagination into consciousness only on condition that they are subsequently 'condemned' by the conscious mind [as he claims is true of psychoanalysis], can bring relief from anxiety. . . . ultimately, the effect of analytic therapy can only be to maintain, rather than dissolve, guilt" (p. 352).

And, briefly, he accuses Freud of the following, all of which are present in his own text: hyperbole and overgeneralization, factual errors, loose reasoning, oversimplifying complex matters, genetic reductionism, selective use of evidence (citing what fits his theory and ignoring what doesn't), and asserting the identity of opposites. Not to mention types of muddled, illogical, and irresponsible thinking for which it would be difficult to find parallels in Freud!

Crews

A professor of literature at the University of California in Berkeley, Frederick Crews was for some years a prominent exponent of psychoanalysis applied to literary criticism. About a decade ago, however, he published a collection of essays, *Skeptical Engagements* (1986), from the previous ten years, several of which recounted his growing disenchantment with Freud and his theories. Since then, his brilliantly written, slashing critiques of psychoanalysis in the pages of the *New York Review of Books*, recently collected in a small book (Crews 1996), have put him at the forefront of what are often called the "Freud-bashers."

Crews resembles Webster in that both are good at assembling and integrating the spadework of others into interesting and plausible indictments; and neither contributes, otherwise, more than minor insights.[9] Yet Crews has two great advantages: a dazzlingly witty and readable style of writing, and much better judgment. His distortions are subtler and more difficult to demonstrate, and he has a far more sophisticated way of creating an apparently tight case. He is also a better and more industrious scholar who makes very few outright factual errors. Consequently, he has rapidly become the *bête noir* of orthodox psychoanalysis and the leading spokesman of those who attack Freud.

Trying to answer his charges point by point is like Hercules's fight with the many-headed Hydra. Every time the brawny hero cut off a head, two others with equally biting mouths appeared. Crews is so prolific, his mastery of rhetoric so facile, that by the time anyone could take apart a single page and analyze its distortions and sly insinuations, he could write several others. Not to mention the fact that the result of such exegesis would be longer, less lively, and far less fun to read than the original.

I will again limit myself, therefore, to the analysis of only one part of his recent book, the section that had appeared in the *New York Review of Books*, February 3, 1994, his rejoinders to letters of protest against the original piece. The contents and style of his earlier four essays on psychoanalysis (also predominantly book reviews), collected into the first chapters of *Skeptical Engagements*, display the same virtues and faults, and do not require separate treatment.[10]

Basically, he proceeds (though by no means all of the time) by seductive stages from reasonable arguments to unjustified conclusions. Even when he makes points with which I agree, he manages to put a pejorative spin on basically sound judgments. It's as if, being so good at giving his knife an extra twist, he can't resist an opportunity.[11]

---

9. In his latest (and not yet reprinted) essays in the *New York Review of Books*, however, Crews (1996) does break some relatively new ground. Despite the presence in it of his usual faults of exaggeration and propagandistic rhetorical tricks, he traces some plausible and probable links between theosophy and related occult mysticisms and the work of a number of psychoanalysts, most notably Jung.

10. Anyone who is interested in a much more detailed (approximately 19-pp., single-spaced) critique of both of Crews's books may write to me at Box 1087, Truro, MA 02666.

11. The pages that follow are part of a letter I submitted to the *New York Review of Books*, only the last 45 percent of which was printed. That incidentally may prove one of my points: that biting and witty invective—however irresponsible it may be—is more readable and hence more publishable than careful rebuttal. The end of the omitted part of the letter is noted in the text.

To begin with the second paragraph of his rejoinder (1995): Many of his critics accuse him, he says, of having a "defective personality, the main sign of which is precisely my incapacity to render a 'balanced'—i.e., predominantly appreciative—assessment of Freud and his brainchild" (p. 106). I have no desire to try to analyze his personality at a distance, and sympathize with his implied resentment of analysts who have subjected him to that all-too-familiar treatment. (I would like to point out, however, that Crews himself is quite willing to analyze Freud's personality—indeed, to diagnose him—without having examined the man directly; see below.) It is possible that some of the complaining psychoanalysts would not have considered an assessment balanced unless it ended up appreciative. In his 1986 book, Crews did admit that Freud and psychoanalysis have *some* merits; but the predominant impression since then is of a willful effort to find as much fault as possible. Hence, I would bet that most qualified but impartial observers who are not psychoanalysts would consider Crews's assessment unbalanced indeed.

His first footnote (p. 107) refers the curious to one of the authorities on whom Crews leans, Macmillan's 1991 *Freud Evaluated*, as "strictly evidence-based." It happens that I spent several months studying that work and more recently its revised edition, and can report that it is a thoroughly mixed bag (Holt 1992, 1997). Indeed, Macmillan's book is flawed by excesses of condemnation reminiscent of Crews's—apparently based on indignation at Freud's shortcomings as a scientist. Its greatest strength is the author's painstaking and devastating critique of Freud's theoretical reasoning and his way of reaching conclusions from his data, not in refuting theories on the basis of evidence. Likewise, the trenchant works of Adolf Grünbaum (also referenced in the same footnote) are notable for their philosophical analysis, not for the marshalling of evidence.

Let me next address some of the main points of his recapitulation. First, "Freud's uniquely psychoanalytic ideas have received no appreciable corroboration, and much discouragement, from independent sources" (p. 108). The core of truth is that this can be said about many of Freud's best-known ideas; but the sneaky part of this one is that he does not specify which are, in his judgment, the "uniquely psychoanalytic ideas." Meanwhile, that sounds as if the core has been shown to be rotten; by no means proved. Later, in discussing another response to his essay, he uses the phrase again in a context that helps clarify that, for Crews, what is "uniquely psychoanalytic" about one of Freud's concepts is precisely its least defensible aspects. Thus, he can feel that the force of his polemic is in no way deflected when contemporary workers successfully seek what is valid and operational in what Freud wrote, for by his definition they thereby leave it "bland" and indistinguishable from any other psychological concept.

Second, Crews charges that Freud's "method of reaching causal conclusions . . . could not have reliably yielded those conclusions by any imaginable path of inference." That statement, on its face, is impossible to assert, until all imaginable paths have been tried. It is a characteristically hyperbolic way of retailing Macmillan's valuable analysis of the causal reasoning in Freud's papers of the 1890s, something less than his complete oeuvre.

The fifth point, that Freud's "perceptions and diagnoses invariably served his self-interest, always shifting according to the propagandistic or polemical needs of the moment" (p. 109), transparently displays the same hyperbole. If it can be shown that in several instances Freud slanted his reports of cases to make them "better" illustrations of his theoretical point, that's enough for Crews to jump to a flat, universalistic statement. In that respect, he emulates the very Freud whose methodological sins he scorns so persuasively.

Sixth, Crews claims that Freud's "therapeutic successes . . . appear to have been nonexistent" (p. 109). Sure, he had lots of failures, even in instances where he claimed success; but what about Ilona Weiss ("Elizabeth von R."), Joan Riviere, Hilda Doolittle?

Seventh, Crews repeats the familiar charge that Freud's "rules of interpretation were so open-ended as to permit him to twist any presented feature to a predetermined emphasis" (p. 109). Granted, the rules are loose, much looser than would be desirable, but not *that* permissive. If they were, Freud would never have complained, as he so often did, that he was having difficulty understanding analytic material or that some dreams were uninterpretable.

The pattern is clear: Crews makes valid criticisms of specific points (or, usually, repeats those of others), and then wildly overgeneralizes or exaggerates them. As a result, the Freud he constructs could do nothing right and was a complete charlatan, incompetent in every respect except for a mysterious power to impress the people who knew him best as decent, kind, brilliant, insightful, creative, and devoted to truth. We would have to conclude him to have been the century's most gifted psychopathic personality if Crews had not already settled on another and incompatible diagnosis: borderline psychotic. Interestingly, he attributes this diagnosis to Josef Breuer and Sándor Ferenczi, though both of them died before the term came into psychiatric usage. I would be grateful if he would cite passages from the works of these two colleagues in which they characterized Freud that way.

In addition to hyperbole, Crews the master rhetorician achieves his denigrating effect in part through the clever use of simile, metaphor, and other figures of speech. What cannot be proved can be insinuated figuratively. For example, Freud's movement acted "*like a politburo* bent upon *snuffing out* deviationism*" (p. 110, italics added). Psychoanalysts never kill or even imprison those who deviate from the official line, as the Soviet Politburo often did, but the difference is negligible to Crews.

Another device Crews uses is to define a highly pejorative label in a way that makes it legitimately usable against psychoanalysis, even though the result is misleading. Psychoanalysis was and remains a pseudoscience, he tells us, "in that it relies massively on unexamined dogma" (p. 110), and so on, failing to acknowledge that the reprehensible characteristics he proceeds to list do not apply to a substantial and growing subset of psychoanalysts and others who are trying to build a creditable science on a reworking of Freud's theories. Dogmatists, experimenters, the methodologically upright, and the absurd, all are tarred with the same brush.

Similarly, those who wrote letters protesting against the exaggerations and unfairness of the original review article are dismissed en masse. The methods of even the most liberal (i.e., the most willing to accept Freud's fallibility), he declares, remain "exactly as subjective" (p. 110) as Freud's. I cannot speak about the work of all the writers, but I know that of Drs. Schimek and Luborsky—both psychologists well-trained in objective, quantitative research methods—and it is simply untrue that their methods of "making advances in insight" are as subjective, uncontrolled, and unreplicable as Freud's.

Here is an interesting example of faulty reasoning: "And since transference can be either 'positive' or 'negative,' without our possessing any guidelines for knowing which kind to expect next, no behavioral consequences flow from it, and it is therefore at once irrefutable and operationally devoid of meaning" (p. 119). Non sequitur! The reason we do not know precisely what kind of transference manifestation to expect next has nothing to do with the defects of psychoanalytic theory: it happens to be true of all behavior of human individuals, along with the behavior of particular atoms as well. Though it is apparently news to Crews, indeterminacy on this level *does* coexist with predictability on a more molar level; fortunately, that applies to people as well as things, and to transference as well as such nonpsychoanalytic concepts as, say, strivings for achievement. Researchers such as Lester Luborsky (1977) and Luborsky and Crits-Christoph (1990) have painstakingly set down guidelines for *statistically* predicting transferential behavior, which they have given operational meaning, building on Freud's work without slavishly following it.

Another of Crews's techniques of argumentation is akin to guilt by association. Transference must be "worse than useless as a guide to the rational addressing of patients' initial complaints" because "the concept inevitably remains entangled in the therapeutically questionable practice of fostering a 'transference neurosis'" (p. 121). The entanglement is purely semantic, however; you can't refer to a transference neurosis without mentioning the word transference. But that elementary point in no way means that if you use the concept of transference you must "inevitably" foster regression in all your patients, nor does that in fact happen.

Closely following is a prize sentence which demands to be quoted in full: "By fetishizing *emotional* distortions on both sides, moreover, the whole transference–countertransference rigmarole deflects attention from the *cognitive* dubiety of psychoanalytic formulations in general and of the analyst's services in particular" (p. 121). (Note the familiar propaganda technique of using colorfully pejorative words [fetishizing, rigmarole] where less emotionally freighted terms [emphasizing, doctrine] would have been more precise. That device enables Crews to smear his target in passing with no felt need to justify the implied judgments, while clouding cognitive discourse with gratuitous affect.) It is, of course, trivially true that if you focus on A you cannot simultaneously devote much attention to B or C. But that fact has nothing to do with the conclusion of the next sentence, which triumphantly (if mistakenly) asserts that he has completely trashed transference.

I forego reprinting the rest of my letter, since it appears on pp. 140–144 of Crews (1995). I would like, however, to comment on his rejoinder (pp. 150–153), which illustrates some other features of his polemical style. I had singled out his charge that "to my knowledge, no modern analyst has renounced the cardinal Freudian investigative tool of 'free association,' which is inherently incapable of yielding knowledge about the determinants of dreams and symptoms" (p. 125). My response had been that "the alleged inherent incapability has not been demonstrated." Instead, Crews simply referred the reader to Macmillan's *Freud Evaluated*, Chapter 15 (Holt 1992). I then gave a brief summary of my critique of that argument; perhaps unfortunately, I concentrated on refuting the claim that the validity of free associations had never been tested, let alone demonstrated, hence the method was worthless.

Crews responded that I had "dodged the issue" and had "ignored" his main point: that there is not and cannot be "any trustworthy path of inference from a patient's verbal associations to the causes of a given dream or symptom" (p. 151). Let me now, therefore, address the "three well-established reasons why this is so" (p. 151).

First, free associations aren't free but are fatally contaminated by suggestion. To be sure, Freud was quite wrong in thinking that his method was free from suggestion and that associations could not be influenced. Contamination is *not* an all-or-none matter, however, as Crews assumes,[12] not in the realm of analyzing data any more than in protecting a water supply. Any coliform bacteria at all in drinking water contaminate it, but water is still safe to drink if the proportion is below x parts per million. Immaculate data are rare, and not really necessary, as long as the degree and kind of contamination is carefully monitored. A patient may have picked up, without the analyst's ever having said it directly, that sexual problems are important causes, so if he produces sexual associations to a dream they could easily be the result of such contamination. But if instead the dream reminds him of some nonsexual problem, or recent political event in which the analyst has never shown any interest, the likelihood of harmful contamination is much less. Hence, this point lacks cogency as an argument that free associations inherently are totally useless in the search for causes.

The second point seems to come down to the valid observation that Freud was mistaken in thinking that an associative link directly indicated a causal link. True enough; but that does not mean that just because A is associated with B it cannot be a cause of B. All I maintain is that one of the possible reasons why a patient associates B to A is that they are causally related. Just showing the thematic affinity is *not* enough to prove it, but it is a piece of evidence—part of a logically tenable method of enhancing the probability of a causal linkage. So, free associations may yield some

---

12. Why do I say he thinks so? Because, in his rejoinder, he claims that "critics have decisively shown [that] the whole process of analyst-patient interaction is steeped in indoctrinating effects" (p. 153). He either honestly believes that the demonstration of a few such suggestion effects amounts to a proof that "the whole process" is hopelessly besmirched, or hopes to influence an unwary reader to believe that such a virtually impossible task has been accomplished.

knowledge about the determinants of dreams and symptoms, even though they are by themselves insufficient for *certain* knowledge.

In his third point, Crews rejects the approach I am urging, that of relying not on a single, fallible bit of evidence but looking for the cumulative value of many convergent bits. He is no doubt correct that if every such bit of evidence is merely a blind guess at a cause, and "if the method of drawing causal inferences from free associations is wild in each individual occurrence, it must also be wild in the aggregate" (p. 152). I am arguing that there is value in indicators with very low probabilities of validity if one can accumulate enough of them; he retorts that no psychoanalyst's inference has more than zero validity, hence accumulating them does no good.

In the printed part of my rejoinder, I went to some pains to explain why I believe that some psychoanalytic inferences have some validity, and how it is possible to work with such fallible indicators to obtain independently verifiable conclusions. For the most part, Crews ignores what I had to say; he tries to wave it aside by the rhetorical question, "how much impact could such studies have on what Holt calls the 'earnest ignorance' of analysts in their daily therapeutic work?" (p. 153)—which is not at all the issue under contention.

Setting aside his snide characterization of my quoting points ("methodological commonplaces") from Reichenbach and Popper as mere attempts at "cosmetic 'scientizing'" (p. 153), I want to point out one other way in which he gives a false impression of my position. Since I concede that psychoanalysts often disagree with one another, he concludes that I agree with his judgment that "they are winging it from start to finish"— if one reads carefully what I have to say (p. 152). The clincher is that I admit that working analysts habitually "neglect the crucial difference between forming hypotheses and adequately testing them" (p. 153) and that research on psychoanalysis should be done by people who know better. By the same logic, Crews should believe that the fact that good research in medicine is done by specially trained medical scientists, not everyday practitioners, means that the latter are proceeding entirely by the seat of their pants, and that all of their diagnostic and therapeutic judgments are blind guesses.

So: yes, I agree that workaday practitioners of psychoanalysis are not trained as scientists and, not surprisingly, they don't perform as such. Moreover, they are not likely to pay a lot of attention to what good, methodologically sound psychoanalytic research uncovers—not the present generation of them. None of that means that I agree with any of Crews's exaggerated denunciations or declarations that no progress in psychoanalysis is possible, in principle. Indeed, he simply ignored my brief explanation of how one can in fact work scientifically with free associations and similar types of data, something that is actually going on in a number of research centers.

Since he has no experience of attempting any such research, it is no wonder that he has so many suspicions and doubts. Having devoted most of my career to learning how to do it and, with the aid of my colleagues at NYU's Research Center for Mental Health, carrying out a good deal of such research, I can testify that it is not easy, quick, or inexpensive; it is no longer fashionable or easy to fund; and the undertaking cannot be recommended to a young scientist eager to get ahead in an academic career— the payoff in publishable findings is too slow. Hence, the future of psychoanalysis as a science is hardly rosy; but neither is it merely a dream of self-deluded people.

Finally, I shall briefly note the occurrence of several other kinds of errors in Crews's rejoinder to the first group of letters (1995, pp. 106–135), not yet discussed here, most of which are amusingly characteristic of Freud himself:[13] Citing a theory as if it were a fact (traumatic amnesia is "physiologically based"; p. 124 n16); false statements of fact (p. 118 n10, p. 118 para. 3, p. 125 para. 2); use of a pejorative (and unsupported) interpretation of an act or statement instead of describing it matter-of-factly (p. 113, third sentence [twice], p. 115 para. 1, p. 120 n12, p. 130 para. 1); and extreme, negative exaggerations, usually converting what should be "often" into "always" or the like (p. 111 n 4, p. 117 n 9, p. 118n ["Every Freudian idea. . ."]; p. 122 para. 1, p. 123 para. 1 ["groundless tenet . . ."]).

The cumulative effect of all these flaws, minor though some may seem when taken one at a time, is to convey the impression of a biased and mean-spirited critic who seizes every opportunity to portray his subject in the worst possible light. Professor Crews shows astonishing diligence in digging up negative information and judgments about Freud, while ignoring or failing to understand a growing and fairly substantial literature produced by psychoanalysts and psychologists who know how to do good

---

13. See my *Freud Reappraised* (Guilford 1989), especially Chapter 3.

scientific work, both in the reconstruction of theory and in empirical research.

This combination of rhetorical overkill (he just can't resist an opportunity to score off of Freud) and systematic neglect of what is being done to reform, improve, and validate psychoanalytic ideas offends every informed reader except those who, like him, write as if they have decided to declare war on psychoanalysis and take no prisoners. What a waste of obviously first-rate talents!

CONCLUSION

So, what does it all amount to? I do not claim that the books under review are worthless because they contain mistakes. Most of them are useful additions to the critical literature on Freud and his ideas. Cumulatively, the valid points made do add up to a serious indictment of Freud's texts: The latter cannot be taken at face value! So much has been shown to be exaggerated, distorted, badly reasoned, erroneously argued, and/or tendentiously self-edited that the burden of proof is on anyone who maintains that *ipse dixit* is any basis at all to believe any particular proposition from Freud's pen.

But most of these critics—notably, Wilcocks, Webster, and Crews—are not content with even so portentous a conclusion. They want us to believe that only a charlatan, liar, and/or psychopathic liar would make these mistakes. My point in demonstrating their own commission of the same roster of writer's sins is to urge more balance in their judgments. Since we all play fast and loose with the absolute and complete truth at times, none of us should think that Freud's demonstrated deviations from veracity are enough to brand him a fraud. And when more or less distinguished literary critics use the same rhetorical tricks they discover in Freud's work, often in the same context as their critiques, should they not try to be more empathic, less condemning, or at least less totalistic in their denunciations?

In the end, a critic can't have it both ways: if he is to indict Freud on the grounds of seductive rhetoric, overly allusive or evasively slippery writing, or of unscientifically vague concepts, overgeneralization of findings, and carelessness with facts, he ought to abjure those tactics himself. And, in fact, none of them completely succeeds in doing so. They are all guilty—some far more than others, to be sure—of similar if not the same rhetorical tricks, weasel-wording, devices of insinuating what they cannot prove, and the same hyperbolic overgeneralization. When challenged, they often accuse the opposition of bull-headed refusal to accept unpleasant truths about a cultural icon and the founding father of a profession, rather than backtracking to what they can validly say—which, ironically, is strong enough! In the long run, overstatement of criticism is not as effective as being straight about it; passionate invective (like its cousin, negative political advertising) may move some members of the public, but it eventually discredits itself.

Don't misunderstand me: I surely don't believe that *tu quoque* is a valid riposte. Freud is not exonerated because his accusers have dirty hands, too. Unfortunately, there is no consensus about what is useful and probably valid about psychoanalytic theory and practice. Some of it is more tacit knowledge than formulas that can be written in books; much of it is complex, contingent, dependent on parametric conditions that have not yet been specified. As a consequence, those who (like literary critics) know psychoanalysis only from books, naturally fail to appreciate what is learned best by the experience of being confronted with and having to make some sense of clinical data. They feel, moreover, that anyone guilty of so many errors and so slippery a way with the truth could not have contributed anything of lasting value. That is simply a non sequitur, even though it has a rough empirical usefulness in everyday life. It was a lot easier to believe surprising and counterintuitive assertions when the man who propounded them seemed to be a paragon of integrity and decency. But remember Beethoven—not a nice man at all, but still a genius whose work has to be evaluated on its own merits.

Psychoanalysts would do better to stop trying to defend the indefensible and, instead, examine their body of theories and findings as dispassionately as possible, emphasizing what is demonstrably useful and valid in it.[14] If the result is that little of the valid residue can be formulated in the way Freud did as much as a century ago, small wonder; it's nothing to be ashamed of, but an outcome that is common in the history of science.

---

14. I invite readers who are seriously interested in collaborating on this task to get in touch with me.

REFERENCES

Bonomi, C. (1994). "Sexuality and death" in Freud's discovery of sexual aetiology. *International Forum for Psychoanalysis* 3:63–87.

Borch-Jacobsen, M. (1988). *The Freudian Subject.* Palo Alto, CA: Stanford University Press.

———— (1993). *The Emotional Tie; Psychoanalysis, Mimesis, and Affect.* Palo Alto, CA: Stanford University Press.

———— (1996). *Memories of Anna O.* London: Routledge.

———— (1997). Personal communication, October 25.

Brabant, E., Falzeder, E., and Giapieri-Deutsch, P., eds. (1993). *The Correspondence of Sigmund Freud and Sándor Ferenczi, 1908–1919,* vol. 1. Cambridge, MA: Harvard University Press.

Breuer, J., and Freud, S. (1895). Studies on Hysteria. *Standard Edition* 2:1–305.

Cassirer, E. (1956). *Determinism and Indeterminism in Modern Physics.* New Haven, CT: Yale University Press.

Crews, F. (1986). *Skeptical Engagements.* New York: Oxford University Press.

———— (1995). *The Memory Wars.* Monograph. New York: *New York Review of Books.*

———— (1996). The consolation of theosophy. *New York Review of Books* 43 (14):26–33.

Eagle, M. (1984). *Recent Developments in Psychoanalysis.* New York: McGraw-Hill.

Ellenberger, H. F. (1970). *The Discovery of the Unconscious: The History and Evolution of Dynamic Psychiatry.* New York: Basic Books.

Erwin, E. (1996). *A final accounting; Philosophical and Empirical Issues in Freudian Psychology.* Cambridge, MA: MIT Press.

Fish, S. (1989). Withholding the missing portion: psychoanalysis and rhetoric. In *Doing What Comes Naturally: Change, Rhetoric, and the Practice of Theory in Literary and Legal Studies,* pp. 525–554. Durham, NC: Duke University Press.

Fisher, S., and Greenberg, R. P. (1995). *Freud Scientifically Reappraised: Testing the Theories and Therapy.* New York: Wiley.

Freud, S. (1895). A project for a scientific psychology. *Standard Edition* 1:295–387.

———— (1896). The aetiology of hysteria. *Standard Edition* 3:191–221.

———— (1900). The interpretation of dreams. *Standard Edition* 4/5:1–621.

———— (1901). The psychopathology of everyday life. *Standard Edition* 6:1–279.

———— (1914). On narcissism: an introduction. *Standard Edition* 14:73–102.

———— (1915). A case of paranoia running counter to the psychoanalytic theory of the disease. *Standard Edition* 14:263–272.

———— (1921). Group psychology and the analysis of the ego. *Standard Edition* 18:69–143.

———— (1940). An outline of psycho-analysis. *Standard Edition* 23:144–207.

Gelfand, T., and Kerr, J., eds. (1992). *Freud and the History of Psychoanalysis.* Hillsdale, NJ: Analytic Press.

Gilman, S. (1993). *The Case of Sigmund Freud: Medicine and Identity at the Fin de Siècle.* Baltimore, MD: Johns Hopkins University Press.

Grünbaum, A. (1984). *The Foundations of Psychoanalysis.* Berkeley, CA: University of California Press.

———— (1994). *Validation in the Clinical Theory of Psychoanalysis. Psychological Issues.* Monograph 61. New York: International Universities Press.

Hirschmüller, A. (1989). *The Life and Work of Josef Breuer: Physiology and Psychoanalysis.* New York: New York University Press.

Holt, R. R. (1965). Freud's cognitive style. *American Imago* 22:167–179. Expanded version in *Freud Reappraised*, Chapter 3. New York: Guilford, 1989.

———— (1974). On reading Freud. In *Abstracts of the Standard Edition of the Complete Psychological Works of Sigmund Freud*, ed. C. L. Rothgeb, pp. 3–79. New York: Jason Aronson.

———— (1989). *Freud Reappraised: A Fresh Look at Psychoanalytic Theory.* New York: Guilford.

———— (1992). Review of *Freud Evaluated; The Completed Arc*, by Malcolm Macmillan. *Isis* 83:698. (Also, review of the revised, paperback edition, MIT Press, 1997, *Psychoanalytic Books*, in press.)

———— (1997a). Review of *Freud's Dora*, by P. Mahony. *Psychoanalytic Books* 8:159–163.

———— (1997b). Review of *Freud Evaluated* (2nd, paperback ed.), by M. Macmillan. *Psychoanalytic Books* 8:397–410.

Hyman, S. E. (1962). *The Tangled Bank.* New York: Athenaeum.

Luborsky, L. (1977). Measuring a pervasive psychic structure in psychotherapy: the core conflictual relationship theme. In *Communicative Structures and Psychic Structures*, ed. N. Freedman and S. Grand. New York: Plenum.

Luborsky, L., and Crits-Christoph, P. (1910). The assessment of transference by the CCRT method. In *Psychoanalytic Process Strategies*, ed. H. Dahl, H. Kächele, and H. Thomä, pp. 99–128. Berlin/New York: Springer-Verlag.

Mahony, P. (1982). *Freud as a Writer.* New Haven, CT: Yale University Press, rev. ed. 1987.

———— (1984). *Cries of the Wolf Man.* Madison, CT: International Universities Press.

———— (1986). *Freud and the Rat Man.* New Haven, CT: Yale University Press.

———— (1996). *Freud's Dora.* New Haven, CT: Yale University Press.

Pribram, K. (1965). Freud's Project: an open, biologically based model for psychoanalysis. In *Psychoanalysis and Current Biological Thought*, ed. N. S. Greenfield and W. C. Lewis, pp. 81–92. Madison and Milwaukee: University of Wisconsin Press.

Schönau, W. (1968). *Sigmund Freuds Prosa. Literarische Elemente seines Stils.* Stuttgart: J. B. Metzlersche Verlagsbuchhandlung.

Sulloway, F. (1979). *Freud, Biologist of the Mind: Beyond the Psychoanalytic Legend,* rev. ed. New York: Basic Books.

Thornton, E. M. (1983). *Freud and Cocaine. The Freudian Fallacy.* London: Blond & Briggs.

Timpanaro, S. (1976). *The Freudian Slip: Psychoanalysis and Textual Criticism,* trans. K. Soper. London: New Left Books.

Trilling, L. (1955). *Freud and the Crisis of Our Culture.* Boston: Beacon.

Viderman, S. (1977). *Le céleste et le sublunaire.* Paris: Presses Universitaires de France.

Vitz, P. C. (1988). *Sigmund Freud's Christian Unconscious.* New York: Guilford.

Webster, R. (1995) *Why Freud Was Wrong.* New York: Basic Books.

Welsh, A. (1994). *Freud's Wishful Dream Book.* Princeton, NJ: Princeton University Press.

Wilcocks, R. (1994). *Maelzel's Chess Player: Freud and the Rhetoric of Deceit.* Lanham, MD: Rowman & Littlefield.

20

Psychoanalysis and Film: The Question of the Interpreter

Nickolas Pappas[1]

The psychoanalytic treatment of art happens naturally. If you have a theory of what human minds do, why not—*how* can you not—apply it to those productions of human minds called works of art? No one denies the need for puzzling art out, any more than the need for identifying the working parts in narrative literature, drama, or film. And here's analysis waiting with a boxful of diagnostic tools.

And yet, when psychoanalysis informs the puzzling-out, the commonest response has come to be neither gratitude nor curiosity, but fullness and fatigue. We are speaking of a satiety so acceptable as to require no defense: non-experts who would grant physicists the right to a cartoon vocabulary (quarks, strong and weak forces) feel entitled to ignore oedipal terror in the Marx Brothers, or castration anxiety behind movie close-ups of a woman's body.

Before asking why the psychoanalytic readings of narrative arts should have dissatisfied their audience, it is worth asking what their wrong turn

1. I am grateful to Stanley Cavell, Hope Igleheart, and David Weissman for conversations that inspired and helped me articulate many of the ideas in this piece. I trust that they will recognize their contributions.

looks like. Take the question as broadly as possible, because if the death of psychoanalytic art interpretation is an event, it has happened among a wide public depressed by coarse-grained problems. And start with two commonplaces—flat-footed, maybe, but still with legs enough to get around:

1. There is something ad hoc about every psychoanalytic interpretation of art. Its outcome is never obvious in advance; not even its general form.

This feature of psychoanalytic readings generally—in therapy, cultural interpretation, and elsewhere—motivates one line of argument by philosophers of science. For the charge that psychoanalysis is unverifiable (Farrell 1981, Grünbaum 1984) means in part that no single cord stretches from a given phenomenon to its diagnosis. If analytic interpretation followed invariant methods, it would specify what reading a work must have, and one way or other these could be checked.

Even friendly observers notice the fact. "The 'Uncanny,'" to take only one example, feels perverse in its reading of "The Sand-Man": Freud might have said something about Nathaniel's illness, or the story's anxieties about women, but he fixed on the blindness/castration symbolism until these other psychodynamics disappeared (Freud 1919). Of course another interpreter could come along and add those considerations—but that's the problem, that the mode of exegesis is not already set. Or take Freud's "On Dreams" (1901). If it had offered a key for explicating all oneiric events, it could at least have found a place among occultist and self-help books. But even when Freud emphasizes the universality of certain dream symbols, he warns that no catalogue of them will substitute for dream analysis. The subject will still have to determine which things in a dream are operating as symbols (Freud 1901, Chapter 9). Add in the quirks that shape any given dream-work, and you rule out the translation manual for dreams, and with it the safe answer to Point 1.

Then the second commonplace, most easily imagined between the teeth of a soured student:

2. Psychoanalytic interpretations leach the pleasure out of a work of art. Their authors seem to have missed the delight art can bring, and thus steer their readers away from it as well.

Too obvious to mention? Too jejune? Freud takes the trouble to deny it, and without the scorn he has plentiful resources for expressing (Freud

1935). Nor has the question died, when a contemporary analyst who writes about film raises it again: "My final argument with many contemporary theorists of whatever stripe is that, in the anhedonic rigor of their enterprise . . . they seem to view pleasure at the movies as a seduction away from clarity about the apparatus' more doubtful operations" (Greenberg 1993, p. 14).

Within aesthetics proper, voices from different quarters are calling for a reintroduction of pleasure to art theory (Novitz 1996). We have permission to ask what the interpreter wants from a movie when the promise of happiness moves closer to being an essential feature of art works; and then we can ask why psychoanalytic readings seem to subvert that promise.

The two objections seem unrelated to each other, even on the verge of contradictory. If anything, you'd expect a freewheeling approach to have more fun in it than one plodding by the book. And maybe the incompatibility of the two objections only exposes both as lazy folk-wisdoms whose disagreement matters no more than the clash between "Absence makes the heart grow fonder" and "Out of sight, out of mind."

Only that the same two objections face the *Republic*'s analysis of tragedy, and it doesn't take much imagination to see the kinships between Plato's (1903b) anti-tragic screed in Book 10 and psychoanalytic readings of film. In both, the psychological theory has preceded the aesthetic discussion; the psychology lends itself to revelatory analyses by virtue of positing that people don't always know what they think or desire; the psychology is supposed to show how art forms work.

For Plato, the psychological theory lets us approach the work of art as if it were a symptom, the person applying it a kind of doctor. But who's the patient? Along with the deep questions of whether Plato's psychological categories capture the elusive effects of mimesis (Nehamas 1982), there is the blunter question of whether he applies them in the right place. Call his theory true and complete; agree with Plato that representational literature equals disease and debilitation (399e, 595b, 608a). Only ask him: If talking about tragedy amounts to talking about something that goes wrong with people's souls, which souls are at risk?

An obvious answer is the souls of the audience. So first Plato has Socrates talk about the spectators of tragedy: all sorts of things can't be depicted, because they produce the wrong psychological effect. Even the finest people, "with very few exceptions," seem vulnerable to degradation by drama (605c, cf. 606a–c). The soul of each finds its inner regime toppled by this invasion of irrationality (605b–c).

If you find it hard to get intrigued by such arguments, that may only show that you're assimilating them to arguments made in late twentieth-century America. Turn down the volume on *Republic* Book 10, leave out the call for total censorship, and you get today's long faces over sex or violence. But the two worries admit of different medical metaphors, which will mean that Plato snares himself in tangles that the modern argument does not. Today's objections to sex or violence tend to permit certain depictions in the art, in their place, but find them harmful in excess or when wrongly presented. We count how many televised murders the average 18–year-old witnesses, how many breasts it takes to ratchet a film up to PG-13. Or we condone words and scenes in an artistically redeeming context (Woolsey 1933). Much like our two guides to eating eggs: not too many, and don't eat them raw.

Plato's conception of the harm in tragedy permits no such amelioration. He could hardly make an exception for tragedies seen infrequently, when Athenians enjoyed at most six days of tragedy a year, and only the most privileged got their hands on the written texts. Nor will artistic merit move the man who wants to flush Homer and Sophocles from his culture. Tragedy damages its audience the way a poison or drug does. It wrecks even the best-built psychic constitutions, because it can work its effects regardless of how judiciously its audience consumes it.

But then Plato has to account for the origins of the toxin, which is to say that he has to find some preexisting soul-corruption that debases the audience. He looks at the author, whose soul gets attracted to certain spectacles rather than to others (605a). The cunning of the tragic playwright does not permit reasonable discussion on the stage, or displays of virtue (605b). So we have traced the audience's pathology to the poet's: he too is governed by the base part of his soul (603a,b).

This is not an unusual move in Plato. Only we still have to explain why this pathology comes to get transmitted in tragedy and not elsewhere. The tragic poet is presumably not prevented from walking down the street; he doesn't unbalance fellow citizens just by existing. There must be something happening in the drama itself. To explain what that is, Socrates shifts again to talk about character. Since representational literature essentially represents human beings (393b–c, 395c–396d, 605a), and since those characters attract attention in proportion to their own imbalance—like their tumultuous response to unhappiness (605a, c–d)—poets obligingly trot out whole crowds of sick people.

We know what Plato means. But now three species of souls contain the corruption he finds in tragedy. Suppose these are not all bad souls: suppose you have a depraved playwright who's trying to put on a good tragedy for a high-minded audience. Will some imbalance still creep in? Or suppose you have an audience in a bad state: Won't they respond to even a moral tragedy by looking at it perversely? The wrong audience can be made worse by even the most moralistic writings. So which of the three elements suffices to make tragedy corrupt? The very ambition in Plato's analysis has robbed it of the direct explanatory power it promised.

Now, one reason for this indecisiveness is the absence of a political account. Plato would prefer to cast his anti-aesthetic in dynamic political terms, as he does in the *Laws* (1903a). The *Republic* scores a point by omitting politics, for when the poet's work is described in the vocabulary of the private, it at least can be ostracized from the realm of knowledge: nothing said truly where nothing's said. But then Plato cannot bring his tools of analysis to bear on the exchange. Applied atomistically, the psychological theory throws itself into an integrated phenomenon without knowing where it applies.

There is another thing, too. Plato refuses to dignify the audience's enjoyment (see 604d, 607d) with a theoretical explanation. Pleasure becomes instead an extraneous element that the serious outside interpreter can put off. Maybe for this reason, Book 10 contains an unusual display of Plato's refusal to be pleased. Socrates, as his author's mouthpiece, admits that he has long loved Homer's poetry, but sets that love aside in his investigations (595b). He compares banishing poetry to denying oneself an unhealthy romance (607e). Plato is going out of his way, as a theorist about drama, to deny himself the pleasure it gives.

Here are the two accusations against psychoanalytic readings of (for example, but as my main example) film: the resolutely unpleased interpreter, and the irresolution over where to apply the psychological theory. Finding the two together in *Republic* 10 makes them look less accidentally linked than before. Maybe something more: if Plato offers us any hints about *why* the two get connected, we have a hypothesis to try out on psychoanalytic interpretations. Say that denying yourself the pleasures usually attendant on a dramatic work means denying yourself a place in its audience. But if you recuse yourself from the customary spectatorial relationship to dramatic works, which is to say from the psychological phenomena in and around them, no place seems obviously where the psychological action is.

I was in a different kind of audience a few years ago, when artists gathered to hear psychoanalysts explain works of visual art. At least that's why they seemed to have come. Staged twice as a *Neurotic Art Show* (Four Walls, Brooklyn [1991], Artists Space, Manhattan [1992]), the event was an art opening with a panel. Both times artists brought pieces to hang in the art space, then returned to talk to three analysts and a psychoanalytic art historian. Both sessions hurried toward the same impasse. After hearing general statements by the panelists, usually suspicious of a category like "neurotic art," the participating artists began asking how analysts might find neurosis expressed in a given work. When the panelists resisted that way of joining art with analysis, some audience members specified that someone take a piece and explain its neurotic sources. The panelists more clearly refused; the artists more clearly enunciated their right to an answer.

In one of the sessions a panelist, Donald Moss, spoke to this repeatedly frustrated wish:

> One is in the position of wanting something from figures about whom attributions can be made, like the ones you just made, but the figures are gone. And one wants something from absent figures, and is convinced that one deserves it, etc. It seems to me that's a kind of a formal set-up whose every solution will be neurotic. [Moss et al. 1991, pp. 27–28]

I understood Moss to return the stymied artists' demands to the context of the analyst–patient relationship, where the demands reveal themselves as wishes for the analyst's love. Turning the question back, as he would have to do during analysis, therefore implies that the demand for an answer belongs in another context, which is to say its home context. But *that* implies that analytical explanations lack a home away from home: they get their use and meaning in a therapeutic setting that confrontations with art and artists can't mimic.

Whether or not Moss meant to import this theoretical analysis into a panel talk, to me his comment suggested a syllogism against analytic interpretation:

> Psychoanalysis is possible only in a structure that mirrors that of the clinical relationship.

No such structure fits the relationship between art works and their *readers*.
∴ No application of psychoanalysis to art works is possible.

The syllogism hints at insight into the open methods of art interpretation. Leave the first premise as vague for now as the crucial concept in it, "the structure of the clinical relationship"; whatever that structure ends up looking like, if it cannot expand to fit aesthetic contexts, then even unanimity in clinical practice would not legislate unanimity in interpretation. Every stab at interpretation will begin by reinventing itself to resemble what goes on between analyst and analysand. We get a problem like Plato's. A psychological theory designed to operate atomistically lacks a structure for applying socially, and so can't fix on a structure for treating art.

The history of attempts to bring psychoanalysis to narrative arts, and to film especially, repeatedly proves that it has inherited Plato's difficulty in specifying the subject. There is life left in "pathography," often Freud's method, according to which one reads a work as the symptom of the artist's impulses (Freud 1907, 1910, Hayman 1981, Jones 1948). But other possibilities exist. Moving the artist away from center stage, the interpreter might analyze the work, where such analyses can look beyond a single artist to genres and techniques (Gombrich 1966, Rank 1932), or ignore artists altogether in favor of characters and narrative structures (Lacan 1973). In a third approach, the interpreter analyzes the audience. Literary studies offer the recent theory known as reader-response, which attempts to unveil the significations in literary works by tracing their readers' identifications and gratifications (Holland 1975, Reed 1982). But spectator analysis has really bloomed in film theory, where a combination of Freudian, Lacanian, and Althusserian doctrines join to show what cinematic storytelling does to its viewer (Baudry 1974–75, 1976, Metz 1982, Mulvey 1975, 1981).

The first striking feature of these approaches is that they lend themselves to placement within the structure of clinical therapy. Somewhere in the interpretive process lies a subject exhibiting the drives and conflicts of the analysand; somewhere else stands an analyst, the interpreter, equipped with specialized knowledge, and so situated as to identify the analysand's blind spots. The second feature emerges in the act of describing the first: the structure being extended to the interpretive context evokes traditional Freudian analysis. Freud and Lacan work as almost completely unrivalled references for the content, methodology, and outcomes of psychoanalytic interpretation.

Partly for this latter reason, the models for applying psychoanalysis face obstacles from within the doctrine itself, and consequently have endured a familiar litany of objections. Say the artist stands in for the analysand: here the analytic paradigm presupposes romantic malaise in the artist. Moreover, interpretation flouts analytical practice by confining itself to a tiny set of data, all extensively reworked: no associations here, no reports of everything that comes to mind. In the case of collaborative arts like film, no single figure emerges as the artist under examination, and every choice of one (e.g., the director) can look arbitrary.

While not all of these problems arise when the art work, or some element in it, lies on the couch, new ones take their place, above all the problem that such "analysis" amounts to an overstretched metaphor. Camera angles have no disavowed wishes.

Films don't dream. Even characters, the closest things to human beings in a movie, fall short of the humanity needed for analysis. And when they don't find the analogy theoretically suspect, critics complain that such applications of analysis tend to produce "reductive" readings, stampeding through the surface of the work to hit its latent content (Lapsley and Westlake 1988, p. 67).

I would add one thing to this list of arguments. The analyst, as traditionally defined, must not be delighted. Freud's insistence on fees for treatment makes the point as well as anything. He equates frankness about money with the frankness about sex that analysis calls for (Freud 1913), and the link between those two taboos reminds us that money will be the analyst's source of pleasure. Then money replaces the pleasure an analyst might otherwise get from this confessional intimacy. Analysts get paid because they don't enjoy what they do, and to prove that they don't (Žižek 1991, p. 61). Bringing such an analyst from the office to the movie theater means conjuring up an interpreter who refuses art's pleasures. The problem is not that an unfeeling interpreter *might* look at art joylessly, but that a traditional analyst *must*. The money only makes art's analyst stranger, a viewer who paid for the pleasure of seeing a film, then pretending to be its analyst: paying to get paid for the trouble.

Interpretations focused on the audience introduce another cluster of issues, especially in the case of film theory, whose range and richness of sources make it hard to flatten into any simple analytic analogy. That Lacanian orientation within film studies known as apparatus theory has returned from its dive into spectators' souls with treasures for thoughtful students of film. Fewer theoretical hurdles stand in the way of this turn to the audience. Spectators, unlike art works, are real humans; unlike artists, they are present to inquiry. Especially in the case of sensory barrages like the movies, we can expect spectators to relinquish their control over the experience.

The structure of the last two decades' film theory builds on the act of watching movies with Lacanian doctrines. Thus the gaze (because film is about voyeuristic looking) and the mirror stage that ties looking to personal identity (Kaplan 1990, p. 10). Cinematic images simulate fantasy, the unfulfillable longing for a lost state of completeness; so the child's passage into language and the symbolic realm forms another element of the theory. With these concepts especially, Laura Mulvey, Jean-Louis Baudry, and Christian Metz work to show how watching a film brings enjoyment by reinforcing the watchers' (false) interpretations of themselves. The swirl of disembodied images coalesces into a story of persons, as if under the direction of a fantasizing consciousness, and so brings the reassurance that you are a single someone: this is what it means to say that viewing constitutes the ego.

Apparatus theory manages to preserve the differences among films even while denying the old critical focus on them. Movies vary in their effectiveness at maintaining the illusion of a unified watching mind (Baudry 1974–75, p. 43, Metz 1974). They vary in their legislation of patriarchal viewing, so Mulvey's use of this analytic approach (Mulvey 1975) also admits different readings of different films (cf. Lapsley and Westlake 1988, p. 78, Mulvey 1981).

But these discriminations among acts of looking do not translate into discriminations among the lookers. The spectator being formed (as children are) becomes no one special. "What we are faced with is another theory of Man, another essentializing gesture" (Doane 1990, p. 55, cf. Rodowick 1982). Set aside one obvious disanalogy with therapeutic practice, that the spectator so equated with every other spectator comes in for an analysis shorn of the idiosyncratic interrogations that actual analyses interrogate, and therefore can't function as a subject. I want to harp on my question: Where do we put the interpreters? Into the audience or out of it? If in the former place, how did they escape the film's effects, when some theorists claim that spectators are blinded to the ideological effects of the film spectacle (Baudry 1974–75, Dayan 1974)? So remove the interpreters from the audience at large. But on the apparatus account, viewing pleasure tends to be the means by which a movie works its problematic effects; so the theory exposing those effects will have to come from an atypical viewer. These interpreters are, by definition, viewers who stand outside the movies' transmission of pleasure (Metz 1982, p. 15). Psychoanalysis again operates outside the social art process it had tried to explain.

Here is my analogy between Plato and psychoanalysis. Where the *Republic* looked away from larger politics in its attack on tragedy, to locate its corruption within each soul's constitution, the psychoanalytic interpretation of film—by virtue of beginning with a traditional clinical model—enters its subject with an atomistic structure rather than a social one. The fate of pleasure becomes a special case of this general condition, as well as a problem in its own right, as the analyst must occupy the same unpleased role that Plato forced himself into. And the same general condition leaves us with no obvious framework for turning analysis into art interpretation, so we face the proliferation of approaches. Psychoanalytic theory is open to more than one site of application to film, much as Plato's division of the soul fit more than one element in tragedy.

The links among these pieces suggests a strategy for thinking about applying psychoanalysis. If we can unearth a way to expand the therapeutic model to accommodate interpreters' pleasure, that expanded story may find itself directing interpretations more surely.

Now, I have been saying that unpleasure enters the story when the analytic interpreter acts out Socrates' suppression of his love for Homer. Interpreters remove themselves from the art's delight under the pressure of the clinical model of a cathected analysand and a wary, emotionally unencumbered analyst. I stand by this picture of what happens during psychoanalytic interpretation, as much as I stand by my suggestions of the picture's effects on interpretive method. It is not an account of how psychoanalytic interpretation goes essentially, because the clinical model powering the interpretive one is far from the only available conception of analysis, even the dominant one. Surely a therapeutic practice that presupposes the analyst's engagement can offer more productive patterns for film's interpreters to follow.

What matters first is to get clear on the cost of available solutions. If the radically indeterminate state of psychoanalytic interpretation strikes you as a thicket to be escaped, and yet that interpretation has to model itself after the activity of analysis, you must either change the picture of analysis that provides the model, or discover a structure that fits the old clinical picture without succumbing to the same problems. One possibility then is to make interpretation resemble what has actually happened in the practice of analysis, say in America, say in the last two or three decades. As a philosopher rather than a psychoanalyst, I can only mark this way with a signpost and then not follow the sign, since I know too little about currents in contemporary analytic practice that could offer guides to the interpretation of film. What I *have* seen of those currents, in the pictures of analysis that Ogden and Blechner describe, does suggest that the analyst's encounter with a patient's dreams and memories can unfold in an intersubjective interplay that would carry over nicely to the scene of interpretation (Blechner 1995, Ogden 1996).

But as a reader of psychoanalytic treatments of film, I don't expect that change to happen soon. Maybe that shouldn't matter. Maybe the interpretive allegiance to Freud and Lacan reflects a better fit between their conception of analysis and features of narrative art (instinct, its frustration and mutation); maybe—having only sociological causes—it doesn't. In any event, if the nonclinical community holds to a vision of psychoanalysis different from the one in practice, it might turn out to be more strategic in the short run to describe a common ground between the two: I mean, to mimic the practice's growing implication of analysts with traditional grounds for a model of interpretation that implicates its practitioner.

Traditional analysis does have names for how such a process might work: transference, counter–transference, self-analysis. Any one of these could be applied to the psychoanalytic interpreter so as to keep interpretations patently psychoanalytic, and still account for their makers' involvement with art. If we say counter-transference, we go back to a picture of interpretation in which the artist or work is the subject (Reed 1983, p. 191, Spitz 1985, pp. 92, 160). While this approach remains saddled with unwanted implications, like that of treating the art work as a symptom, there is greater justification for bringing the reader's reactions into the interpretation, that is, more justification for the interpreter's self-scrutiny.

Calling the interpreter's absorption transferential, by comparison, keeps the focus on the audience. As Stanley Cavell has suggested, the interpreter is now the analysand, with the art work or its maker functioning as analyst (Cavell 1988). I come to a film in search of a new pleasure that harks back to older ones, and on the basis of my expectations form a first interpretation. But in a turn comparable to the analyst's withdrawal, the narrative resists the initial interpretation. And then, by thwarting transference, interpretive frustration can transform an interpreter's excitement into self-examination.

This reversal preserves the other benefits of a turn to the audience, and makes better sense of the compulsion to interpret, aligning the critic's pleasure over a work with a patient's excitement about the analyst. In a word, the model locates interpreters where they have always been, among appreciative audiences for art. And *seeing the work as the analyst* may open the way to a more productive conversation between psychoanalysis and art, in which confrontation with literary, cinematic, and visual works functions as ongoing analysis.

The self-analysis I have in mind spins out of a passage in "Aggressivity in Psychoanalysis," an early paper of Lacan's:

> Because he lived at a similar time, without having to suffer from a behaviorist resistance in the sense that we ourselves do, St. Augustine foreshadowed psychoanalysis when he expressed such behavior in the following exemplary image: "I have seen with my own eyes and known very well an infant in the grip of jealousy: he could not yet speak, and already he observed his foster-brother [at the mother's breast], pale and with an envenomed stare." [Lacan 1977, p. 20]

Augustine (1991) makes the world safe for inner states—that is, for seeing them in other people. He attributes jealousy to a boy who conceptually can't yet attribute it to himself. No puzzle here for Augustine: sins (like neuroses) arise before they can be named, which is what makes confession such hard work.

But the *Confessions* passage also brings along a moment of reflexivity. Augustine's own lustful jealousy delivers itself up for confession once his observation of someone else's hammers home the point that the sin can be present though unknown. The boy's jealousy becomes visible after Augustine has looked for his own, and before he can describe its mechanism. Analysis turns into self-analysis, to the extent that judging means confessing.

In Lacan's terms, this means that watching someone else's ego-formation might nostalgically reenact our own. I argue in a longer version of this essay that such analytical observations derive their pleasurability from being self-analytical, and that self-analysis, so elaborated, helps explain the mix of enjoyment and pathos in art interpretation. Here I only claim that this structure for self-analysis suggests a way of seeing dramatic characters. What makes those characters images of human beings, and prevents them from being real people, is their exaggerated definiteness. They have certain tendencies rather than others, overlap their acquaintances in some respects and not others—but all of this so *firmly*. And this nature they have renders them occasions for self-analytical observation. Identifying a movie's people as personalities means locating them in a realm of formed individuals; but the starkness of their forms replays the young child's elemental ego ideal. So identifying these human images as primal narcissists brings us the adult's joy and pathos over observing and not quite reliving. The flavor of that pathos stems from the gulf between our complexity and the characters' consistency: analysis finds itself enmeshed in self-analysis.

Take these as three existing strategies that can enlarge our options for meeting up with art. Not conclusions, only hints that the idol of the masterful analyst does not have to continue fascinating the interpreter.

I am saying that the pose of indifference baffles traditional analysis when it follows a traditional script in the pursuit of interpretation. And the knowingness of studied indifference also makes the wrong strategy for facing a death like psychoanalysis's.

"Death" gets its appeal from providing a digestible metaphor for those changes after which practices, movements, institutions, and civilizations are no longer possible. But metaphorical death tends to play up one association to its literal meaning and suppress another. Dead cultural practices fall into two different groups, in neither case quite corresponding to dead people: there are the ones that survive their deaths, and the ones that never lived.

In the first case "death" overlooks a practice's survival of itself as its own ghost. Opera, epic, and the western may be gone, but more than their memory lingers. People still write epic poems. Only the writing act dangles outside the institutions and assumptions that had once defined it. So epic can no longer be written automatically—which is to say that it must be written knowingly. Today's silhouettes haunt their form, walking through their history without its noticing them. Here the metaphor reports truthfully that this body once lived, but fudges the matter of the form's disappearance.

The other transformation nicknamed "death" is a genuine case of present nonexistence. It falls short of literal death at the other end, in that the thing never lived. Philosophy's death, like God's, diverges in this respect from the fate of the novel and the silhouette. The bedside watch over philosophy is a watch over the past, because *its* obituary writers claim that philosophy has never been (what it thought it was).

Freud's baby likewise understands itself in a way that makes its death retroactive. Rather than expire within history, it dies today, if it does, because it never lived. Its end in the present discredits its past, which is why its enemies try to kill the present institution by means of assault on that past. Hence the criticism popularized by Jeffrey Masson, who went back to Freud's repudiation of the seduction hypothesis in the knowledge that only this strategy could hit analysis where it lived (Masson 1984)—much as philosophy's executioners assail systematic metaphysics by uncovering originary missteps in Plato. But then the practitioners of psychoanalysis lack the remedy, or anyway the gambit, of carrying on knowingly, ironically. The death of epic poetry turns into a subject for subsequent epic poems; psychoanalysis can only be mourned from the outside.

If the analytic interpretation of art inherits this constraint on its form of death, it inherits along with that the need to understand itself and the psychoanalysis that begot it. My hunt for more reflexive treatments of art is one way of looking for self-knowledge among the uses of psychoanalysis. I take this to be Cavell's concern when he wonders why psychoanalysis has so resisted learning from literature (Cavell 1987). Solving the Platonic problem of where to join psychologies to stories will have to include keeping interpretations of art actively psychoanalytic, if those interpretations may not mournfully survive themselves: if they go on not indifferently and knowingly, but with the earnest full heart of detachment.

REFERENCES

Baudry, J.-L. (1974–75). Ideological effects of the basic cinematographic apparatus, trans. A. Williams. *Film Quarterly* 27:39–47.

———(1976). The apparatus, trans. J. Andrews and B. Augst. *Camera Obscura* 1:104–126.

Blechner, M. (1995). The patient's dreams and the countertransference. *Psychoanalytic Dialogues* 5:1–26.

Cavell, S. (1987). Freud and philosophy: a fragment. *Critical Inquiry* 13:386–393.

———(1988). Psychoanalysis and cinema: the melodrama of the unknown woman. In *The Trial(s) of Psychoanalysis*, ed. F. Meltzer, pp. 227–258. Chicago: University of Chicago Press.

Dayan, D. (1974). The tutor code of classical cinema. *Film Quarterly* 28:22–31.

Doane, M. A. (1990). Remembering women: psychical and historical constructions in film theory. In *Psychoanalysis and Cinema*, ed. E. A. Kaplan, pp. 46–63. New York: Routledge.

Farrell, B. A. (1981). *The Standing of Psychoanalysis.* New York: Oxford University Press.

Freud, S. (1901). On dreams. *Standard Edition* 5:629–713.

———— (1908). Creative writers and daydreaming. *Standard Edition* 9:141–159.

———— (1910). Leonardo da Vinci and a memory of his childhood. *Standard Edition* 11:59–137.

———— (1913). On beginning the treatment. *Standard Edition* 12:121–144.

———— (1919). The "uncanny." *Standard Edition* 17:217–252.

———— (1925). Autobiographical study. *Standard Edition* 20:7–70.

Gombrich, E. H. (1966). Freud's aesthetics. *Encounter* 26:30–39.

Greenberg, H. R. (1993). *Screen Memories: Hollywood Cinema on the Psychoanalytic Couch.* New York: Columbia University Press.

Grünbaum, A. (1984). *The Foundations of Psychoanalysis: A Philosophical Critique.* Berkeley, CA: University of California Press.

Hayman, R. (1981). Kafka and the mice. *Partisan Review* 48:355–365.

Holland, N. N. (1975). *5 Readers Reading.* New Haven, CT: Yale University Press.

Jones, E. (1948). The death of Hamlet's father. *International Journal of Psycho-Analysis* 29:174–176.

Kaplan, E. A. (1990). From Plato's cave to Freud's screen. In *Psychoanalysis and Cinema,* ed. E. A. Kaplan, pp. 1–23. New York: Routledge.

Lacan, J. (1973). Poe's purloined letter. *Yale French Studies* 48:39–72.

———— (1977). Aggressivity in psychoanalysis, trans. A. Sheridan, pp. 8–29. In *Écrits: A Selection.* New York: Norton.

Lapsley, R., and Westlake, M. (1988). *Film Theory: An Introduction.* New York: St. Martin's.

Masson, J. (1984). *The Assault on Truth: Freud's Suppression of the Seduction Theory.* New York: Farrar, Straus & Giroux.

Metz, C. (1974). *Film Language: A Semiotics of the Cinema,* trans. M. Taylor. New York: Oxford University Press.

———— (1982). *The Imaginary Signifier: Psychoanalysis and the Cinema,* trans. C. Britton, A. Williams, B. Brewster, and A. Guzetti. Bloomington, IN: Indiana University Press.

Moss, D., Spitz, E. H., Lichtenstein, D., and Mieli, P. (1991). *The Neurotic Art Show.* Transcript of panel discussion at Four Walls, May 19.

Mulvey, L. (1975). Visual pleasure and narrative cinema. *Screen* 16:6–18.

———— (1981). Afterthoughts on "Visual pleasure and narrative cinema" inspired by *Duel in the Sun. Framework* 15–17:12–15.

Nehamas, A. (1982). Plato on imitation and poetry in *Republic* 10, pp. 79–124. In *Plato on Beauty, Wisdom and the Arts,* ed. J. Moravscik and P. Temko. Totowa, NJ: Rowman and Allenheld.

Novitz, D. (1996). Disputes about art. *The Journal of Aesthetics and Art Criticism* 54:153–63.

Ogden, T. H. (1996). Reconsidering three aspects of psychoanalytic technique. *International Journal of Psycho-Analysis* 77:883–899.

Plato (1903a). *Laws.* In *Platonis Opera,* ed. John Burnet, 5:624–969. Oxford: Oxford University Press.

——— (1903b). *Republic.* In *Platonis Opera,* ed. John Burnet, 5:327–621. Oxford: Oxford University Press.

Rank, O. (1932). *Art and Artist.* New York: Knopf.

Reed, G. S. (1982). Towards a methodology for applying psychoanalysis to literature. *Psychoanalytic Quarterly* 51:19–42.

——— (1983). *Candide:* radical simplicity and the impact of evil. In *Literature and Psychoanalysis,* ed. E. Kurzweil and W. Phillips, pp. 189–200. New York: Columbia University Press.

Rodowick, D. N. (1982). The difficulty of difference. *Wide Angle* 5:4–15.

St. Augustine (1991). *The Confessions,* trans. H. Chadwick. Oxford: Oxford University Press.

Spitz, E. H. (1985). *Art and Psyche: A Study in Psychoanalysis and Aesthetics.* New Haven, CT: Yale University Press.

Woolsey, J. M. (1933). Decision in *U.S. v. One Book called "Ulysses," Random House, Inc.* U.S. District Court, New York.

Žižek, S. (1991). *Looking Awry: An Introduction to Jacques Lacan through Popular Culture.* Cambridge, MA: MIT Press.

21

Frankenstein Meets the Wolf Man: A Meditation on Psychoanalysis and Empirical Research

Anne Erreich

INTRODUCTION

In the old horror movie in which the two monsters, Frankenstein and the Wolf Man (*not* Freud's Wolfman!) meet up, we know they're going to duke it out, with the best monster winning, because the earth isn't big enough for both of them. Does the same scenario obtain for two bogeymen of psychological inquiry, psychoanalysis and empirical research? Some psychoanalysts seem to believe that this is indeed the case, arguing that the methodology and data of psychoanalysis, and that of empirical research, are incompatible and orthogonal (e.g., Wolff 1996). The following essay will explore this premise. It will be argued that findings based on empirical research can and do provide data that are highly relevant to the psychoanalytic enterprise.

One might divide the psychoanalytic pie into three separate, though interdependent, pieces: a model of the mind, a model of development, and a model of therapeutics, or technique. This essay will argue that empirical research from developmental and cognitive psychology makes significant contributions to psychoanalytic models of the mind and development.

Research in psychoanalytic process and outcome will be left aside for purposes of this exploration. Although this kind of empirical research contributes to a model of technique, a different set of arguments regarding the value of empirical research needs to be applied to this domain. That is, although one can imagine that there are universal aspects of mental functioning and human development pertinent to psychoanalytic theory which may best be apprehended via empirical research in extra-analytic domains, for example, cognitive psychology, it is less clear that we will discover equally profound universals regarding therapeutic technique by studying any domain *other* than the psychoanalytic process itself. Hence, this essay will be restricted to the contribution of empirical findings as they pertain to models of mind and development in psychoanalytic theory.

EMPIRICAL ≠ EMPIRICIST

It is not unusual to find analysts arguing against the relevance of empirical data by inveighing against empiricist doctrines as incompatible with a psychoanalytic perspective (Opatow 1989). However, though empiricist doctrines require empirical methods of research, the reverse is not the case. Clarification of the relationship between these two terms requires a brief detour into the philosophical underpinnings of academic psychology.

Empiricism is a philosophical doctrine that proposes that sensory experience is the only source of knowledge, that all cognitive contents are derived directly from sensory experience, and that development can be accounted for by the child's accumulation and transformation of sensory data. Hence, the British empiricist John Locke argued that the mind was a "tabula rasa" at birth, with no preformed structures or content, entirely plastic to the impressions of sensory data. Mental development consisted of copying and organizing experience via certain physical laws, the emphasis being on the proper input of information to the brain.

In the United States, empiricism gained acceptance through the work of psychologists like John Watson (1924), who proposed a behaviorist model of human development. In what might be viewed by psychoanalysts as a curious regression from truth, behaviorism seems to have been a reaction against the prevalence of Gestalt psychology in academic circles, particularly the Gestalt psychologists' interest in introspection and mental phenomena. Watson and his colleagues called a halt to investigations into the "black box" of mind; in fact, they went so far as to deny the relevance of mind in favor of that which was observable and measurable: overt behavior. The infant was presumed to be born with innate reactions to specific stimuli, and with a set of combinatorial processes for analyzing data and forming inductive generalizations or associative connections. Development consisted of the association of other stimuli with the innate ones to elicit ever more varied and complex responses. From these ideas, there developed the familiar concepts of contingent reinforcement, classical and operant conditioning, and finally the attempt by learning theorists such as Skinner to develop all-purpose learning theories that would apply across tasks, developmental levels, and even species (Skinner 1953).

From the first, there was rumbling and grumbling about the impossibility of accounting for human or even animal behavior without making reference to mental events, including motivation and the inherent nature of each species (Jacobovits and Miron 1967). However, the final death knell for behaviorist psychology—and for the empiricist tradition in which it was grounded—was sounded in 1959 by the linguist, Noam Chomsky. In a brilliantly argued review (Chomsky 1959) of *Verbal Behavior*, Skinner's (1957) attempt to account for language, Chomsky demonstrated that language acquisition and use could not be adequately accounted for by behaviorist principles. Taking a rationalist stance, he argued that the sensory data of language, that is, the speech stream, provided necessary but insufficient data for language acquisition, and that any adequate account of child language acquisition would have to include the child's innate system of language processing capacities. Chomsky further proposed that the study of language was part of the larger investigation into the operation of all higher mental functions. Thus was the so-called "cognitive revolution" ushered in by Chomsky's work, and with it, academic psychology returned to an earlier interest in mind, an interest that included mental structures and functions as well as data from introspective reports regarding phenomena as diverse as perceptual imagery and linguistic intuitions.

To return to the point of this detour, the academic research spawned by the cognitive revolution was certainly "empirical" research, but it was by no means "empiricist" or even "behaviorist" in philosophy. On the contrary, for his contributions, Chomsky has often been branded a nativist. The adjectival form of "empiricist" merely refers to results based on experiment or observation; no particular philosophical doctrine is implied. Yet too often those who argue against the relevance of empirical research for psychoanalysis assume that "empirical" = "empiricist." For example, in an article about psychoanalytic education at the undergraduate level,

Hulsey and Cohen (1997) observe that "psychoanalytic ideas seem ever more distant from the wellspring of scientific truth as academic psychology rushes to embrace empiricism and its behavioral and cognitive offspring. Those trained to teach psychology are steeped in the empirical tradition" (p. 16). The second sentence is certainly true, but the first does not compute, because empiricist doctrine could not have "cognitive offspring." The mistaken shift from "empiricism" to "empirical" is clear here. In another example, Opatow (1989) entitles a subheading of his paper "The Challenge of Empiricism: Infant Research" (p. 649), and protests somewhat later, regarding early infant experience, that "a human being is not just a generator of interiorless processes" (p. 658). In fact, many infant researchers are either psychoanalysts or come out of a cognitive tradition which takes the elucidation of mind, including the innate contribution of the infant, as its legitimate mandate. These empirical researchers do not take the infant to be "interiorless," and they are decidedly not empiricists.

INFERENCES REGARDING SUBJECTIVE STATES ALWAYS DEPEND ON MANIFEST BEHAVIOR

We are all, psychoanalysts and empirical researchers alike, faced with the enduring epistemological problem of how we can know the subjective mental states of others when all we have access to is their manifest behavior, that is, language or silence, action or inaction. The question is whether psychoanalytic data are in some way privileged in their capacity to reveal the subjective mental states of others. Psychoanalysts have insisted that psychoanalytic data *are* privileged because they provide direct access to fantasy life and affect. It is true that the conditions of psychoanalytic treatment can promote the kind of controlled regression that allows for the emergence of warded-off affects and fantasies, and that this data may be different from the kinds of data that emerge from some research designs. However, two caveats apply here.

First, psychoanalysts cannot claim to have direct access to patients' subjective states because they do not assume that a patient's manifest presentation (including the content of their language and their manifest affect) represents subjective experience which is somehow self-evident. In fact, most of our technical training is geared to providing us with various principles of decoding and inference-making to be applied to manifest data; we speak of "derivatives" of unconscious fantasies because we do not have direct access to them. Furthermore, it is clear from our collegial disputes that we are often at odds about how to interpret subjective experience from psychoanalytic data. Subjective states of intention and desire are patently not self-evident to patients either, who often "resist" by disavowing or distorting them. Therefore, it is not the case that intentionality and desire are self-evident in psychoanalytic data; rather, they need to be inferred from observable data via principles of clinical inference.

In trying to access mental states from the data of observation or experimentation, empirical researchers also subject their data to inference-making. In both empirical research and in clinical psychoanalysis, what counts as data, and what constitutes rules of inference-making, is theory driven. Freud recognized what is commonly acknowledged in philosophy of science, that no observation is theory-free, and that in fact the theory determines the data: "Even at the stage of description it is not possible to avoid applying certain abstract ideas to the material in hand, ideas derived from somewhere or other but certainly not from the new observations alone" (1915).

To generate principles of inference-making, both psychoanalysis and empirical research make use of hypothetical constructs, concepts for which no direct evidence exists, but which are crucial for inference-making in those domains. For example, the notion of mental representation in cognitive psychology and the notion of aggressive drive in psychoanalysis are both hypothetical constructs, crucial to their respective theories. (Note that there may be direct evidence of aggressive behavior, but the notion of an aggressive drive is a hypothetical construct.) Neither mental representation nor aggressive drive can be directly confirmed or disconfirmed, though either might be replaced by proposing another hypothetical construct that provides a better account of the relevant data. Therefore, in their attempts to access mental states, both psychoanalysts and empirical researchers rely on a comparable methodology; they use procedures of inference-making directed at observable data, which are designated as such by previously agreed-upon theoretical assumptions based on hypothetical constructs.

A second caveat: as noted earlier, it is not the case that interest in subjective experience has been limited to psychoanalytic practioners. Although such experience is difficult to study, cognitive psychologists have compiled a huge literature on the development of mental structures and processes in perception, memory, language, and reasoning (Flavell et al. 1993). It is true that most research in cognitive and developmental psychology has not been interested in the motivational aspects of subjective experience; academic psychology has tended to study the normative rather than the ipsative, and motivational variables are too personal and idiosyncratic for normative research (but see Lichtenberg and Shonbar [1992] for an account of motivational systems in academic psychology as well as psychoanalysis). Nevertheless, there now exists an entire body of research which demonstrates that it is possible to investigate motivational/conflictual variables empirically in adults (Shevrin et al. 1992, 1996), and to study intentionality and desire in infants (Gergely et al. 1995).

One example of empirical research that addresses issues of motivation and defense is illustrated by accounts of the behavior of avoidantly attached children, as they are classified by the attachment paradigm. These 1-year-old children appear rather detached from their mothers when they are present, do not protest when they are left with the experimenter, and show little reaction upon reunion with their mother (Ainsworth et al. 1978). Kagan (1984) accounts for the behavior of avoidantly attached children by arguing that they are simply precociously independent due to constitutional/temperamental reasons. However, most attachment researchers would provide a motivational/defense account, that is, that these children, given their independently confirmed history of maternal rebuff as documented during home observations, are demonstrating defensive behavior in response to their expectation of maternal unavailability or rejection (Ainsworth et al. 1978). This account is strongly supported by another empirical study that demonstrates that when these children are equipped with heart monitors, there is a significant increase in their heart rates when mother leaves the room or returns (Sroufe and Waters 1977). This line of research provides empirical evidence for defensive behavior in 12-month-old children.

It is thus possible to design empirical research that investigates subjective states, including motivational/defensive variables (Cooper 1992); as in clinical psychoanalysis, inferences regarding these states are based on observational data. To argue the irrelevance of this strategy is to call into question the entire enterprise of child psychoanalysis, especially with young children, who do not reliably recount their dreams and fantasies, even at a manifest level.

It seems an unfortunate accident of history that when psychoanalysis came to these shores, it landed in the midst of an academic psychology mired in the empiricist/behaviorist tradition. Attempts on the part of those psychologists to engage psychoanalysis were, not surprisingly, unproductive (Hornstein 1992) and resulted in a permanent split between academic psychology and psychoanalysis. As noted earlier, the cognitive revolution ushered in by Chomsky in the 1960s created a much more hospitable environment for psychoanalytic interests because it resurrected the earlier Gestalt interest in "mind" and mental functioning. Since then, a small but growing number of empirical researchers has begun to bridge the gap by investigating various aspects of unconscious mental functioning, including defensive operations such as repression (Erdelyi 1985, 1996, Shevrin et al. 1992, 1996, Singer 1990). One can only fantasize ruefully about the progress that might have been made had historical events been otherwise.

THE IMPORTANCE OF EXTRA-ANALYTIC DATA FOR A PSYCHOANALYTIC MODEL OF DEVELOPMENT

Psychoanalysis is a discipline that relies on an accurate understanding of the nature of normative development, which provides a yardstick against which to measure pathological development. Psychoanalysts have always understood this and have tried to map normative development proceeding from psychopathology; empirical studies of infancy operate in the reverse direction (Lichtenberg 1983). Freud himself (1905) suggested an extra-analytic procedure to test for the convergence between infant observation and findings in clinical psychoanalysis. (For arguments to the contrary, see the rather surprising essay by Wolff [1996]; though I believe my comments to be relevant to his critique of infant research, I can add little more to the excellent and comprehensive rebuttals by others in the same volume.) It simply will not do to continue to cite the "gedanken" experiments of earlier generations of analysts and philosophers to answer questions regarding either mental functioning or infant abilities when these issues can be investigated empirically, any more than one would look to philosophy to solve questions which can be addressed by experimental physics. For example, the study of the infant's descriminative abilities via the habituation paradigm (e.g., Lewcowicz and Turkewitz 1980) have clearly demonstrated cognitive capacities in the infant that are not compatible with Freud's view that the infant only turns to reality out of frustration, nor with Locke's view of the infant's mind as a tabula rasa, entirely passive and plastic to the impressions of sensory data. We now know that the infant is an active reality constructor from birth, human/nonhuman, as well as internal/external.

It is perhaps worthwhile to cite one well-known example of the kind of mischief that results when psychoanalysts are not adequately informed regarding empirical research on normative development. Bettelheim, writing in 1967 about the etiology of infantile autism, argued against Kanner's (1943) proposal that autism was an inborn disturbance of affective contact; instead, Bettelheim argued that "what Kanner viewed as an inborn disturbance of affective contact may very well be what happens when the inborn ability to relate does not meet the appropriate releasers at the appropriate time . . . because it [autism] may be a very early reaction to their mothers that was triggered during the first days and weeks of life" (pp. 396, 399). By the time of Bettelheim's speculations, there was a growing body of research in developmental psycholinguistics which strongly indicated that language development was a universal, biologically based, critical-period phenomenon, with syntactic and phonological development being very robust, and rather impervious to environmental impact. Not coincidentally, a frequent observation regarding autistic children was their aberrant language development, including significant delays in just these robust, neurologically dependent functions. If psychoanalysts had been able to put these two facts together, they might have been much more hesitant to jump on the "refrigerator mother" bandwagon which located the etiology of autism in the nature of the mother–infant dyad. (See Tager-Flusberg [1988], for a developmental psycholinguistics account of the nature of autistic disturbance.)

Empirical research can also be called upon to confirm, disconfirm, or modify theoretical postulates that were proposed by Freud and others on the basis of retrospective clinical data. The utility of such research is nicely exemplified by a study (Parens et al. 1976) which uses observational data to verify Freud's (1925) developmental assertion that girls enter the Oedipus complex via the castration complex. Parens and colleagues observed that girls' wishes to have a baby emerge via different pathways rather than a unitary one; for some girls it appeared that the wish to have a baby preceded the emergence of the castration complex, and this wish did not appear substitutive or defensive in nature. Although further study with a larger subject pool is necessary, their findings do not support the uniformity of Freud's postulate. The observational methodology employed by Parens and colleagues is not unlike that used by child analysts; that is, they make inferences regarding unconscious fantasy via behavioral data, a methodology that is surely more reliable than retrospective speculations from adult clinical data.

THE IMPORTANCE OF EXTRA-ANALYTIC DATA
FOR A PSYCHOANALYTIC MODEL OF THE MIND

While psychoanalysis has investigated mental contents and functions that have been excluded from awareness for motivated reasons, cognitive psychology has been exploring a much wider arena of out-of-awareness mental activity, of which the psychoanalytic unconscious is a subset. It turns out that there is a great deal of nonconscious mental activity that is neither readily accessible to consciousness nor defensively excluded (Emde 1993, Shevrin 1992). In all perceptual domains, children are in the business of acquiring and storing information for the purpose of generating hypotheses regarding the external world, including people, which allow them to negotiate their environment. One obvious example is the very young child's ability to formulate hypotheses regarding the syntactic rules of its native language from a continuous stream of linguistic input, so as to derive only the correct syntactic rules of that native language, none of which the child or we are able to enumerate unless we do graduate work in linguistics. (Even simple overgeneralization errors like "childrens" and "runned" are evidence of the syntactic acquisition process chugging away out of awareness; children frequently make these rule-governed errors but are unable to articulate the rule(s) that underlie them.)

Findings which indicate that very young children are reliably able to derive complex rules and procedures in a variety of cognitive domains, that these rules are stored in the form of mental representations, and that, though stored out of awareness, these rules determine functioning in their respective domains, provide significant support for a psychoanalytic model of the mind which presupposes the following: that very young children can derive complex rules or expectations regarding (dyadic and triadic) social interaction, including a host of demands and prohibitions; that these expectations/demands/prohibitions can be represented mentally in the form of fantasies (mental representations); that such fantasies can be held out of awareness either because they must be repressed (the kind of motivation related to specific trauma that Freud discovered), or because the fantasies represent expectations that are so much a part of the child's everyday experience that they simply become the lens through which the world is apprehended (as in the establishment of particular attachment patterns due to more subtle cumulative trauma); and finally, that in either case, fantasies held out of awareness continue to influence manifest behavior, affects, ideas, and character traits.

The awareness that defensively excluded (repressed) mental contents are part of a larger system of nonconscious mental activity that provides the underpinnings for all higher mental functioning also provides support for another important psychoanalytic postulate regarding mental activity: that so-called neutral mental functioning occurs only in theory, and that motivational factors impinge on all cognitive functioning, promoting special interests and abilities in an individual, as well as idiosyncratic lapses and deficits. The existence of out-of-awareness mental processing as well as the motivated ability to exclude certain information, are well-documented features of the human mind, as demonstrated by the empirical research of clinicians as well as cognitive psychologists (Erdelyi 1985, 1996, Shevrin et al. 1992, 1996). Of course, the devil is in the details when it comes to accounting for such events. Nevertheless, there exists sound extra-analytic empirical evidence that we clinical psychoanalysts are on solid ground when we make clinical inferences which rely on the attribution of complex, yet out-of-awareness mental processing to young children as well as adults.

CONCLUSION

In our work as clinical psychoanalysts, we engage a singular individual; with their help, and their resistance, we attempt to explore the unique course of their development, and the detailed idiosyncracies of their meaning-making mind. Empirical research has little to contribute directly to that unique and idiosyncratic quest. But it can provide us with very important normative data relevant to development and mental functioning that place parameters on the usual and the possible (e.g., the Parens et al. [1976] example) while ruling out some accounts as highly unlikely (the Bettelheim [1967] example). (Freud [1900] understood this larger role for extra-analytic findings, and made just this point with regard to Potzl's [1917] pioneering experimental work on dreams.) As Seligman (1996) notes, although many traditional psychoanalytic assumptions regarding the infant are falsified by empirical research, the validity of the theories that these assumptions were thought to support does not depend on these assumptions alone. For example, the fact that infants do not appear to be totally immersed in primary process thinking, as Freud proposed, does not detract from his stunning discovery of the unconscious mind's capacity for irrational thought. With respect to drives, again contrary to Freud, infants generally seek to optimize tension rather than to reduce it. But this does not invalidate the relief from *unpleasant* states of tension as an important motivational principle up and down the developmental continuum, and it highlights the interesting question of how to account for those individuals who do seem to seek unpleasant states of tension, such as masochistic behavior.

A fruitful synthesis of empirical and clinical findings should help us to separate the wheat from the chaff of psychoanalytic theory, and, equally importantly, to integrate psychoanalysis into the larger world of scholarship which addresses mental functioning and human development (Erreich 1994). We have much to offer that larger world, especially in terms of the subtleties and idiosyncracies of mental functioning, and the influence of desire/motivation on mental functioning and human development (Wakefield 1992). For example, clinical psychoanalysis offers exemplars of glitches in development (e.g., irrational ideas) and in adult functioning (e.g., parapraxes); any adequate model of the mind and mental development must be able to account for such glitches, just as any adequate model of language development and processing must be able to account for linguistic errors in children and adults. Theories of human development and functioning must be able to account for how things go wrong as well as for what is normative. Thus, we have a great deal to offer to related disciplines that investigate the normative, as well as a great deal to learn from them.

As psychoanalysts, our best hope lies in that not-so-comfortable tension between the ipsative and the normative: the ipsative, as best represented by the singularity and uniqueness that emerges from the psychoanalytic case study method, and the normative, which sacrifices the preciousness of such data for the sake of a more rigorous empirical examination of hypotheses. The best of what psychoanalysis aspires to be resides in the tension between these two kinds of scientific inquiry.

REFERENCES

Ainsworth, M., Blehar, M. C., Waters, E., and Wall, S. (1978). *Patterns of Attachment: A Psychological Study of the Strange Situation.* Hillsdale, NJ: Erlbaum.

Bettelheim, B. (1967). *The Empty Fortress.* New York: Free Press.

Chomsky, N. (1959). Review of Skinner's *Verbal Behavior. Language* 35:26–58.

Cooper, S. H. (1992). The empirical study of defensive processes: a review. In

Interface of Psychoanalysis and Psychology, eds. J. W. Barron, M. N. Eagle, and D. L. Wolitzky, pp. 327–346. Washington, DC: American Psychological Association.

Emde, R. (1993). Epilogue: A beginning—research approaches and expanding horizons for psychoanalysis. *Journal of the American Psychoanalytic Association* 41:411–424.

Erdelyi, M. H. (1985). *Psychoanalysis: Freud's Cognitive Psychology.* New York: Freeman.

———— (1996). *The Recovery of Unconscious Memories.* Chicago: University of Chicago Press.

Erreich, A. (1994). Primary and secondary process mentation: their role in mental organization. *Psychoanalysis and Contemporary Thought* 17:387–406.

Flavell, J. H., Miller, P. H., and Miller, S. A. (1993). *Cognitive Development*, 3rd ed. Englewood Cliffs, NJ: Prentice-Hall.

Freud, S. (1900). The interpretation of dreams. *Standard Edition* 4, 5:1–625.

———— (1905). Three essays on the theory of sexuality. *Standard Edition* 7:125–243.

———— (1915). Instincts and their vicissitudes. *Standard Edition* 14:117–140.

———— (1925). Some psychical consequences of the anatomical distinction between the sexes. *Standard Edition* 19:243–260.

Gergely, G., Nadasdy, Z., Csibra, G., and Biro, S. (1995). Taking the intentional stance at twelve months of age. *Cognition* 56:165–193.

Hornstein, G. (1992). The return of the repressed: psychology's problematic relations with psychoanalysis, 1909–1960. *American Psychologist* 47:254–263.

Hulsey, T., and Cohen, R. (1997). Return of the repressed: analysis and undergraduate education. *The American Psychoanalyst* 31(2):16.

Jakobovits, L. A., and Miron, M. S., eds. (1967). *Readings in the Psychology of Language.* Englewood Cliffs, NJ: Prentice-Hall.

Kagan, J. (1984). *The Nature of the Child.* New York: Basic Books.

Kanner, L. (1943). Autistic disturbances of affective contact. *Nervous Child* 2:217–250.

Lewcowicz, D. J., and Turkewitz, G. (1980). Cross-modal equivalence in early infancy: audiovisual intensity matching. *Developmental Psychology* 16:597–607.

Lichtenberg, J. D. (1983). *Psychoanalysis and Infant Research.* Hillsdale, NJ: Lawrence Erlbaum.

Lichtenberg, J. D., and Shonbar, R. A. (1992). Motivation in psychology and psychoanalysis. In *Interface of Psychoanalysis and Psychology*, eds. J. W. Barron, M. N. Eagle, and D. Wolitzky, pp.11–36. Washington, DC: American Psychological Association.

Opatow, B. (1989). Drive theory and the metapsychology of experience. *International Journal of Psycho-Analysis* 70:645–660.

Parens, H., Pollock, L., Stern, J., and Kramer, S. (1976). On the girl's entry into the Oedipus complex. *Journal of the American Psychoanalytic Association* 24:79–107.

Potzl, O. (1917). The relationship between experimentally induced dream images and indirect vision. In *Psychological Issues*, trans. and ed. J. Wolff, D. Rapaport, and S. H. Annin, 2(Monograph 7):41–120.

Seligman, S. (1996). Commentary on Wolff. *Journal of the American Psychoanalytic Association* 44:430–446.

Shevrin, H. (1992). The Freudian unconscious and the cognitive unconscious: identical or fraternal twins? In *Interface of Psychoanalysis and Psychology*, eds. J. W. Barron, M. N. Eagle, and D. L. Wolitzky, pp. 313–326. Washington, DC: American Psychological Association.

Shevrin, H., Bond, J. A., Brakel, L. A. W., et al. (1996). *Conscious and Unconscious Processes: Psychodynamic, Cognitive and Neurophysiological Convergences.* New York: Guilford.

Shevrin, H., Williams, W. J., Marshall, R. E., et al. (1992). Event-related potential indicators of the dynamic unconscious. *Consciousness and Cognition* 1:340–366.

Singer, J. L. (1990). *Repression and Dissociation.* Chicago: University of Chicago Press.

Skinner, B. F. (1953). *Science and Human Behavior.* New York: Macmillan.

——— (1957). *Verbal Behavior.* New York: Appleton Century Crofts.

Sroufe, A., and Waters, E. (1977). Heart-rate as a convergent measure in clinical and developmental research. *Merrill-Palmer Quarterly* 23:3–27.

Tager-Flusberg, H. (1988). On the nature of a language acquisition disorder: the example of autism. In *The Development of Language and Language Researchers: Essays in Honor of Roger Brown*, ed. F. S. Kissel, pp. 249–267. Hillsdale, NJ: Lawrence Erlbaum.

Wakefield, J. C. (1992). Freud and cognitive psychology: the conceptual interface. In *Interface of Psychoanalysis and Psychology*, eds. J. W. Barron, M. N. Eagle, and D. L. Wolitzky, pp.77–98. Washington, DC: American Psychological Association.

Watson, J. B. (1924). *Behaviorism.* Chicago: University of Chicago Press.

Wolff, P. (1996). The irrelevance of infant observations for psychoanalysis. *Journal of the American Psychoanalytic Association* 44:369–392.

22

The Illusion of a Non-Future: Reflections on Psychoanalysis and Its Critics

Jeffrey B. Rubin

Looking back, at the age of 69, on the potential value of his "life's labours"—the psychoanalytic edifice he had created and developed—Freud (1925) remarked: "Something will come of them in the future, though I cannot myself tell whether it will be much or little. I can, however, express a hope that I have opened up a pathway for an important advance in our knowledge" (p. 70).

The letter Freud received eleven years later from Thomas Mann, Virginia Woolf, Romain Rolland, H. G. Wells, Stefan Zweig, and 192 other writers and artists on the occasion of his 80th birthday offered an unequivocally affirmative response to the hope he had expressed. They hailed him as "the pioneer of a new and deeper knowledge of man," a "courageous seer and healer . . . a guide to hitherto undreamed-of regions of the human soul." Freud, they declared, "penetrated truths which seemed dangerous because they revealed what had been anxiously hidden, and illumined dark places. Far and wide he disclosed new problems and changed the old standards . . . his gains for knowledge cannot permanently be denied or obscured." Even then, in 1936, these writers and artists were able to observe that "the conceptions he built, the words he chose for them, have already entered the living language and are taken for granted. In all spheres of humane science, in the study of literature and art, in the evolution of religion and prehistory, mythology, folklore and pedagogics, and last but not least in poetry itself his achievement has left a deep mark" (Jones 1957, pp. 205–206).

Yet Freud's star—and that of psychoanalysis—seems to be waning in the late twentieth century even as interest within the humanities, arts, and social sciences is increasing. The preoccupation with Freud is suggested by the research of Megill, which indicates that Freud is "the most heavily cited author in social science and arts and humanities indices" (cited in Gelfand 1992, xii, n1).

Since meaning, as Bakhtin (1986) knew, is the product of an interaction or dialogue between reader and text rather than a monological essence waiting-to-be-found in a neutral, fixed manuscript, there is no singular, settled, or definitive Freud or psychoanalysis. "Freud" and "psychoanalysis" are heterogeneous and evolving, a multitude of beliefs, perspectives, and theories, co-treated and transformed by readers from different psychological, historical, sociocultural, and gendered perspectives. For many people, Freud and the eighteenth-century Enlightenment project he exemplified—achieving human emancipation and freedom through the exercise of reason—is now seen as bankrupt. Freud is thus no longer treated as the lodestar he once was in the quest to illuminate the mysteries and complexities of the self.

Indeed, the very nature of the self is hotly contested in contemporary thought. Views of the self obviously have enormous implications for the ways we define, and treat, such issues as the nature of: human nature, psychological health, morality, and relationships. Two traditions dominate current discourse on subjectivity: the traditional Western humanist conception of the self—Descartes' "master and proprietor of nature"—a sovereign, autonomous, unified subject who engages in rational reflection, exercises choice, and experiences freedom; and the poststructuralist, antihumanist view of a subject that is decentered and enslaved, divided within itself, with no organizing center or core, a slave of language and history. The heterogeneous antihumanist tradition is not an entity with "'a common denominator, essential core, or generative first principal'" (Bernstein 1992, p. 8). It is a protean mood with some common features. Antihumanist discourses challenge certain inherited viewpoints about knowledge, self, and world; claiming, for example, that inquiry does not disclose a singular, monolithic truth, the self is not a singular essence, and the image of the world is shaped by those apprehending it.

Humanism is an "embattled notion" in contemporary discourse (Dallmayr 1984). It has come under increasing attack in recent years by critics representing a multitude of perspectives who claim, among other things, that the Enlightenment project has culminated, in the twentieth century, in totalitarianism and nihilism.

In recent years, the viability and even the very existence of the Cartesian humanist conception of the self, arguably our secular god, has been challenged by French philosophers (Jacques Derrida) and psychoanalysts (Jacques Lacan), artists (Francis Bacon) and literary theorists (Paul De Man) among others, who herald the dissolution and "death of the subject" and assert that humans are puppets of, and entrapped by, language and history.

Antihumanist perspectives on subjectivity have been challenged in recent years by critics who point out that the view of the self as a linguistic illusion interferes with the notion of human agency and thus inhibits political engagement. For if there is no subject, then there is no one who is alienated or oppressed, no evil to challenge, and no one to contest it.[1]

Both humanist and antihumanist perspectives on subjectivity, in my view, have something valuable to offer to a contemporary understanding of human beings. Introspection, reason, agency, choice, and freedom, as humanists recognize, exist and are crucial to human being-in-the-world. Human self-blindness and servitude (to language), as antihumanists realize, are also central facets of human life. But in taking a particular facet

---

1. There is a tension in poststructuralist writings between an exemplary challenging of authority, a subverting of inequitable hierarchies, and a championing of the subordinated and exiled, and a theorizing that sometimes avoids epistemological accountability (Ellis 1989) and has had and continues to have quietistic implications (cf. Bernstein 1992). Poststructuralist claims about the essential "undecidability" of meaning and the play of "difference(s)" within a text or theory can serve escapist purposes as well as ethical ends. Such notions can be used to sanction noncommitment and cynical disengagement from life or challenge relations of domination (cf. Flax 1993, p. xi).

In raising questions about poststructuralism, I need to emphasize that its strategies of uncovering tensions and gaps in theories and texts have also been of immense help to me in detecting unconsciousness in psychoanalysis and striving toward greater self-reflexivity. My critique of psychoanalysis might have been hampered without the strategies of reading and thinking often available in poststructuralist writings.

of subjectivity such as reason or the disunity of the self as constituting the totality of it, other central aspects of selfhood are eclipsed, and certain crucial dimensions of self-experience will be neglected. The humanist evasion of self-unconsciousness and the antihumanist neglect of freedom and responsibility, foster an incomplete and impoverished perspective on subjectivity.

Neither humanist nor antihumanist discourse provides a sufficient perspective for understanding subjectivity. Both the rationalistic, egoistic individualism of humanism and the unfree, decentered self of poststructuralism make it difficult to develop adequate accounts of the complexity of subjects. People, after all, are shaped by multiple internal and external factors, including the physical and the cultural, as they attempt to navigate the complex and ever-changing waters of the late twentieth-century world.

Furthermore, by positing false and disabling dichotomies—sovereign self or illusory self, human agency or human imprisonment, freedom or determinism—the humanist–antihumanist debate creates an intellectual logjam in contemporary discourse which impedes an understanding of self-experience. It is difficult if not impossible to apprehend the complexity that is the self when human experience is artificially divided into false dualities. To clearly address the psychological complexity and fluidity of our world, it is necessary to recognize that experiences of self-assertion and communion, the exercise of will and the experience of enslavement, coexist and interweave within a single person.

Freud's work in particular, and contemporary psychoanalysis in general, offers a way of thinking about human subjectivity that avoids both naive, humanist Cartesian conceptions of an autonomous, rationalistic self, and nihilistic, antihumanist notions of a fragmented self lacking the capacity for agency or freedom. Unlike many contemporary writers—Habermas (1968) is a notable exception—I do not villainize the Enlightenment quest for emancipation even as I realize its imperfections and difficulties. From my perspective we must avoid both unproblematized faith in reason *and* nihilistic skepticism about its possibility.

By acknowledging psychic determinism without disavowing the possibility of human freedom, and delineating the shaping power of unconsciousness without devaluing the power of reason, what I would term Freud's *posthumanist* subjectivity challenges the reductive terms that frame the issues in the humanist–antihumanist debate and thereby has something important to contribute to this stalled conversation. There are *im-*

plications in Freud's work and *uses* to which it can be put in late twentieth-century thought that he did not intend and of which he could not have been aware. These implications were foreign to the historical and episte-mological context that served as the horizon of Freud's life and thought. What I am calling Freud's *posthumanist* conception of selfhood is one of various examples. Other examples are discussed elsewhere (e.g., Rubin 1998).

For we are neither totally free nor completely determined; neither unitary nor dispersed, neither powerless nor masterful. We are *both.* Freud —and psychoanalysis—offers resources for escaping the intellectual cul-de-sac that social science and humanist discourses on subjectivity have generated. Psychoanalysis may also have something crucial to contribute to our troubled times—in particular, more workable conceptions of self and other, determinism and freedom—which are essential for survival in the late twentieth-century world.

This may seem like a strange claim, given psychoanalysis' problematic standing in the contemporary world, where it confronts gnawing questions about its theoretical and clinical validity and is generally dismissed as a relic of a bygone age. In the heady, crowded, fragmented, competitive and politically charged critical scene of poststructuralism, postmodernism, post-Marxism, and various feminisms, psychoanalysis, a set of discourses and practices that have potentially heuristic implications for illuminating and transforming human self-understanding and conduct, has been resoundingly devalued, rejected, and marginalized.

In recent years there has been what Roazen (1990) terms a "destabilization of Freud's reputation" (p. xvii) among philosophers, scientists, feminists, literary critics, and even some psychoanalysts. They have accused Freud of utilizing an epistemologically unsound methodology (Grünbaum), being a cryptobiologist (Sulloway), subscribing to and perpetuating a deleterious patriarchal vision (Friedan, Millett, and Greer), conducting himself in a morally problematic manner (Crews) and retreating from psychic truths he did not have the courage to uphold (Masson).[2]

Some questions about psychoanalysis arise because of social conditions in the United States—and perhaps elsewhere—which foster a fear of and

---

2. It would take me too far afield at this point to discuss each of these critiques. Elsewhere (Rubin 1998) I have discussed this topic in more detail. The feminist criticism of Freud's reductionistic and patriocentric account of women is the only one of these anti-Freudian critiques that I find compelling and edifying.

a resistance to a psychoanalytic approach to life. Psychoanalysis can be a threat to a commercialized society in which a quick-fix mentality reigns and a greater premium is placed on conspicuous consumption than self-examination. Pressure from drug companies that are deeply invested in promoting the consumption of drugs rather than the achievement of psychological insight; and managed care organizations (the modern day robber barons), which value their own profits more than the psychological welfare of their clients and promote "anti-introspective treatment methods" (Gedo 1984, p. 170) that promise shortcuts to the complex and laborious work of self-understanding; and a declining standard of living in the United States, which has placed economic constraints on the pool of potential analysands—all have contributed to a devaluation of psychoanalysis. And in a world like ours, in which individuals constantly confront a sense of impotence on many fronts, it can also be profoundly unsettling to face one of the central messages of psychoanalysis, namely that we are not even masters of our own minds (Freud 1917).

Perhaps some questions about the validity of psychoanalysis arise because it threatens to reveal unconscious motives (on the part of critics) that may be based, for example, on self-serving wishes or fears. But other doubts about the usefulness of psychoanalysis are based on genuine problems and limitations within the field. The fact that certain critiques of psychoanalysis may have selfish and reductive motives should not blind us to the very real difficulties with psychoanalysis.

That psychoanalysis is in need of revision is evident to anyone who considers the conflicts within the field about what psychoanalysis is and what it should be. Residues of phallocentrism, sexism,[3] positivism, and scientism remain. The legacy of scientism lives on in psychoanalysis in various guises, including the unproductive debates about whether psychoanalysis is a science. From my perspective, psychoanalysis is not a science. Its purpose, objects of study, and methods are radically different than the traditional conception of science that underwrote Freud's psychoanalysis. To cite three examples: (1) the fact that in psychoanalysis the investigator has an indissoluble influence on what is being investigated

---

3. Despite the variety of attempts from Horney to contemporary psychoanalysts and feminists to revise Freud's problematic account of woman-as-deficient-man, psychoanalysis is still riddled with androcentric biases which inhibit understanding the experience of women, particularly their enriching complexity. I explore one instance of this in greater detail in "Kohut's Bipolar Self Revisited" (cf. Rubin 1998).

clashes with traditional scientific notions of the neutrality and objectivity of the investigator; (2) the possibility of replication in psychoanalysis is deeply compromised by the uniqueness—perhaps the unrepeatability— of the analytic relationship; and (3) psychoanalytic notions do not readily lend themselves to empirical validation as it is normally conceived (Stolorow and Atwood 1986, p. 303). The possibility of validating psychoanalytic hypotheses is profoundly complicated by the reality of unconscious mentation, motivation, and resistance, which renders data highly complex; neither the patient's agreement with or challenge to an analyst's interpretation, for example, is necessarily a sign of validation. Certain crucial facets of psychoanalysis may best be examined, in my view, in the consulting room, not the laboratory. It would be deeply unfortunate if the revolutionary insights about human nature emerging in the unique relationship in the consulting room were thought to be invalid if they had not been nor could not be tested in a laboratory.

Psychoanalysis, in my view, is essentially an anomalous discipline—a depth psychology of human subjectivity—in which the investigator is a participant–observer and the analytic process and the phenomena generated by it are unique, and thus not often amenable to traditional scientific replication or validation. It is not clear to me, for example, how the heart and soul of psychoanalysis—the complex and unique psychoanalytic relationship—might be replicated.

In claiming that psychoanalysis is not a science I am not questioning the importance of "consensually validated observation and reason" (Gedo 1984, p. 159) and I do not mean to devalue or ignore the potential value of empirical research in psychoanalysis. Psychoanalytic propositions need to be consensually validated by analysts and investigators in allied fields. Research in the sense of disciplined and systematic examination and evaluation of findings can be instructive. The work of Weiss and Sampson (1986), as well as others, for example, on the psychoanalytic process or developmental propositions regarding infant–mother attachment and the impact of early environment on normalcy and pathology, has clarified the analytic process by systematically testing the implications of psychoanalytic theory. But science is not the royal road to either The Real or the validation of psychoanalytic propositions.

Not only is psychoanalysis not a science, it should not trouble itself about not being one. Science is not the only way to investigate or illuminate human experience. Given the fact that science cannot answer questions about purposes or meaning, placing all our bets on science when studying human lives may have certain fundamental limitations. Because of this and other issues I would go so far as to assert that the belief in the scientificity of psychoanalysis or the attempt to make analysis scientific "is a symptom of some of its problems" (Flax 1993, p. x), especially the way it is underwritten by the Enlightenment metanarrative of the possibility of objective truth. One of the results of subscribing to such a vision is that it enables analysts to ignore the subjective, power-laden, and political nature of their knowledge and practices. Psychoanalysis would not suffer if the question of its supposed scientificity was no longer posed except in terms of studying the history or sociology of psychoanalysis.

Scientism is not psychoanalysis' only problem. Psychoanalysis also suffers from "unworldliness" (Said 1983), by which I mean a relative neglect of the larger social and historical world in which it is embedded.

There are narcissistic and dogmatic investments in received theory (Greenson 1969); resistances to creative theorizing in the field (Langs 1978); rigidity and defensiveness about its boundaries; and a lack of openness about and intolerance toward those with different points of view. The Byzantine politics and ideological warfare within and among different schools is yet another complication, as are the marginalization of dissidents; the resistance within certain segments of the field to corrective feedback about limitations in psychoanalytic theories and practices; and, most important, insufficient theoretical and methodological self-reflectiveness.

Freud may have discerned a fundamental difficulty in psychoanalysis in the second case in *Studies on Hysteria*. Responding to Freud's question about why she did not tell him that she loved her employer when she knew that she did, Miss Lucy R. replies, "'I didn't know—or rather I didn't want to know. I wanted to drive it out of my head and not think of it again'" (Breuer and Freud 1895, p. 117). In a footnote to Lucy's remarks Freud says:

> I have never managed to give a better description than this of the strange state of mind in which one knows and does not know a thing at the same time. It is clearly impossible to understand it unless one has been in such a state oneself. I myself have had a very remarkable experience of this sort, which is still clearly before me. If I try to recollect what went on in my mind at the time I can get hold of very little. What happened was that I saw something which did not fit in at all with my expectation; yet I did not allow what I saw to disturb my fixed plan in the least, though the percep-

tion should have put a stop to it. I was unconscious of any contradiction in this; nor was I aware of my feelings of repulsion, which must nevertheless undoubtedly have been responsible for the perception producing no psychical effect. I was afflicted by that blindness of the seeing eye which is so astonishing in the attitude of mothers to their daughters, husbands to their wives and rulers to their favourites. [p. 117 n]

A "blindness of the seeing eye"[4] has afflicted Freud and many subsequent psychoanalysts—including myself—as well as mothers, husbands, and rulers. Freud's myriad contributions have been deeply compromised by an epistemological ambivalence at the heart of his life and work. A closer examination of Freud's own life in particular, and psychoanalysis in general, reveals that a conflict between a wish-to-know and a wish-*not*-to-know, or seeing and not seeing psychic truth, is a central facet of Freud's life with his family, and the subsequent history of psychoanalysis. Many aspects of psychoanalysis, including, but not limited to, Freud's self-analysis, his theory of pathogenesis, dream practice, aspects of the institutional history and politics of psychoanalysis, the analytic relationship, and even post-classical conceptions of subjectivity, can be understood as expressions of this epistemological ambivalence. An interest in both decoding *and* concealing the truth frames and haunts both Freud's life and psychoanalysis.

For example, the psychoanalytic situation and method often destabilizes rigid conceptions of self and opens up unforeseen possibilities in living. Yet the freedom of many patients can be subverted by the tendency within psychoanalytic theories of selfhood—including post-Freudian revisionist ones such as Winnicott's True Self and Kohut's bipolar self—to fit analysands into a procrustean conceptual bed of established psychoanalytic concepts and procedures, fostering compliance and self-imprisonment.

As I ponder recent scholarship on Freud, both the virulent attacks (e.g., Crews 1993) and the loyalist, hagiographic defenses, I am struck by this irony: both critics and apologists have compromised our capacity to take the full measure of Freud's complex legacy. The genuine difficulties in psychoanalytic theory and practice are sometimes neglected by loyalists who may deny the need for revision, which renders them insufficiently

---

4. I am grateful to Samuel Weber's (1987) essay on "The Blindness of the Seeing Eye" for drawing my attention to this evocative passage in Freud, although he approaches the topic from a somewhat different perspective than I do.

alert to problems within the field. So they may fail to draw fully on the liberatory possibilities of the psychoanalytic enterprise, and psychoanalysis is thus impoverished.

The resources and potential of psychoanalysis are also eclipsed by critics of Freud (and sometimes even revisionists) who often neglect both post-Freudian theoretical revisions of psychoanalysis and clinical facets of the classical and post-classical psychoanalytic enterprise. There are at least two problems with such critics: (1) they treat the selected aspects of the psychoanalytic corpus that they are interested in—typically classical theory and nonclinical or nonmethodological topics—as if they are representative of the whole; and (2) by neglecting the contributions of post-classical analysts, they deny that psychoanalysis has a history and thereby critique a body of classical analytic thought that many contemporary analysts have significantly amended and moved beyond theoretically, epistemologically, and methodologically. This impedes comprehension of the complexity and fertility of the psychoanalytic enterprise. The theoretical landscape of psychoanalysis looks much fuller when the contributions of post-Freudian perspectives are also considered.

In placing such things as the unscientific status of psychoanalytic discourse or Freud's patriarchal view of women in the foreground, such critics also underplay other radical and important aspects of Freud's "multiple legacies" (Schafer 1992, p. 152). Such studies rarely, if ever, point to the transformative context (the self-reflexive dialogue of analyst and analysand) and liberatory methodology (free association and the analysis of transference, countertransference, and defensive processes) for investigating unconscious aspects of human life, that Freud offers.[5]

Both deifying and denigrating Freud or psychoanalysis—engaging in "Freud piety" (Fromm 1959) or "Freud-bashing" (Gelfand 1992, pp. xi–xii)—precludes the balanced perspective that is essential for reanimating psychoanalysis. It compromises our capacity to use the fertile resources of psychoanalysis and the discoveries of allied disciplines to recuperate what is useful and reformulate what is problematic.

I have a deep love and respect for psychoanalysis. It has changed my life and the lives of many people I have had the privilege of working with. It is an extraordinary tool for increasing self-awareness, healing developmental arrests, resolving conflicts, heightening interpersonal sensitiv-

---

5. The possibilities opened up by Freud's multiple legacies have not been fully actualized in theory or in practice.

ity and compassion, and expanding the range of human freedom. But, as an analysand and later as an analyst and supervisor of other therapists, I have experienced how psychoanalysis can sometimes promote enslavement as well as liberation. For example, even as it fosters an antiauthoritarian stance toward life by questioning both established meanings and the authority humans often irrationally invest in others, it often resembles an authoritarian culture, breeding conformity and submissiveness and sapping creative thought and practice.

But to be apprehended in its complexity, one must steer a balanced course between the Scylla of premature dismissal characteristic of anti-Freudian diatribes and the Charybdis of blind adulation often demonstrated by overzealous Freudians. Such a viewpoint recognizes that psychoanalysis has a vital function for individuals and the world, and also acknowledges that certain psychoanalytic categories and perspectives have to be questioned and in some cases jettisoned or refined.

Mitchell (1993) distinguishes between an "evolutionary" and a "revolutionary" perspective on psychoanalysis. The former, exemplified in the work of Rothstein (1983), stresses the value of tradition and the links with the psychoanalytic past. Two assumptions underwrite this perspective: (1) "the best that has been thought and said" about analysis was thought and said in the *past*; (2) the psychoanalytic past should not be discarded and problematic features can be salvaged.

Evolutionary perspectives tend to neglect both discontinuities between the psychoanalytic present and its past, and unworkable facets of the past—that is, aspects of psychoanalysis that are problematic and need to be replaced. The "revolutionary" view of psychoanalysis—exemplified by Mitchell (1993)—emphasizes the way contemporary psychoanalysis is discontinuous with its past, and the way current theories and practices offer a "novel and discontinuous perspective" (p. 85).

"Tradition" has two clashing connotations. On the one hand, it derives from the Latin *tradere*, meaning to hand over or deliver. From this perspective, tradition is the transmission or handing over of knowledge from the past—the past which connects us to the present. *Tradere* also means to become a "traitor," to betray. So, tradition both contributes to the continuity which is essential to progress in the present *and* interferes with change (Spurling 1993).

Evolutionary perspectives overemphasize continuities with traditional viewpoints. Such a position may grant antiquated concepts a landmark status, making them immune to critical scrutiny and eclipsing the way certain analytic theories and practices in the present represent radical points of departure from its past.

Believing with Mannheim (1936) that no thinker operates in a vacuum and truly thinks by herself, but rather, at best only thinks further than her predecessors, revolutionary claims about radical points of departure seem only partially true. The excessive focus in revolutionary viewpoints on *dis*continuities, may have its own difficulties, such as concealing what is valuable from the past. As the case of Sándor Ferenczi illustrates, this can lead to not fully mining or integrating what already exists, and then attempting to reinvent the psychoanalytic wheel. Despite the recent upsurge of interest in the seminal contributions of Ferenczi (e.g., Aron and Harris 1993), the importance of his suggestive work in the late 1920s and the early 1930s on the intersubjective nature of development and treatment, the analyst's impact on the patient's transference, and the constructive use of countertransference in treatment seems to have been incompletely assimilated in recent analytic writings (Rubin 1998).

Evolutionary and revolutionary viewpoints need not be polarized and incompatible. Psychoanalysis can neither afford to neglect, nor be bound by, tradition. Pursuing new discoveries and innovations while preserving and drawing sustenance from what is useful from the past—and jettisoning what is problematic—is crucial to the development of psychoanalysis. Both fundamental revisions as well as traditional psychoanalytic insights, are, in my view, necessary for psychoanalysis to reach its radical potential. In terms of the former, there is no compelling evidence that the vast majority of analysts find Freud's concept of the death instinct clinically useful in understanding self-destructive behavior. In terms of the latter, Freud's recommendations for cultivating the special state of speaking and listening he termed "free association" and "evenly-hovering attention" offer unique—although not complete—vantage points in exploring human subjectivity. Psychoanalysis is best served when we absorb what is useful from the psychoanalytic present and past, reject what is useless, and add what is specifically our own (cf. Lee 1975).

Psychoanalysis, as I claimed earlier, does offer a way out of the humanist-antihumanist logjam. The problem is that it is deeply compromised by certain outmoded features, including Freud's subjective blind spots—the blindness of his seeing eye—and his nineteenth-century scientism, that is, his overvaluation of science as the foundation on which psychoanalysis rests. The subsequent theories and practices of psychoanalysis have been shaped, and at times delimited, by these and other fault lines in the psychoanalytic edifice. If psychoanalysis is to reach its radical potential and be of real benefit in our world, it will have to develop a capacity for a more thoroughgoing self-reflexivity that was not available to Freud and his contemporaries but is to us.

Reflexivity, from the Latin root *re-flectere*, means "to bend back." Self-reflection, like self-analysis, is beset by a common difficulty: the examination of one's self or perspective inevitably occurs within the limiting and limited horizon of that very perspective. Since one's subjectivity cannot be transcended, reflecting on the partiality of one's own perspective cannot help one eliminate it. But understanding the impact of one's partial perspective on one's thought can sometimes aid in revealing alternative conceptions of self and world.

It seems true that, as the poet e. e. cummings put it, all of us have only halfsight, and there is no single vision that can create the entirety. Psychoanalysis and psychoanalysts are then not alone in the *blindness of the seeing I*: it is to be a key aspect of the human condition. All humans thus confront the dilemma Kierkegaard (1843) pinpointed when he said that "Life must be understood backward . . . [but] it must be lived forward" (p. 111).

Because blindness constitutes our very historical being, the crucial challenge for psychoanalysis and psychoanalysts is not how to eliminate self-blindness—which is impossible—but how to cultivate greater self-reflexivity. We have to pursue knowledge of the human condition while retaining an awareness of both its complexity and its inevitable incompleteness (Mitchell, personal communication).

Reflexivity can take various forms, including "counter-histories" of psychoanalysis that offer alternatives to conventional narratives about the psychoanalytic past, or critical accounts of received theories or practices. Russell Jacoby's (1983) *The Repression of Psychoanalysis: Otto Fenichel and the Political Freudians* is an example of the former. Drawing on extensive letters between Otto Fenichel, Annie Reich, Edith Jacobson, and other politically concerned second-generation analysts, a buried, radical legacy within psychoanalysis emerges. These "political Freudians" extensively reflected on the relationship of psychoanalysis and Marxism, and questioned and challenged received sexual and social codes. Since they hid their radical political leanings when they fled Nazism and fascism and relocated to the more conservative, scientific shores of the United States, they never passed the torch to any students, and their legacy was buried with them. Mitchell's (1993) critique of Winnicott's True Self exemplifies the critique of received theories. Questioning accepted versions of analytic events and reintegrating marginalized figures or detecting the internal contradictions and evasions in apparently coherent analytic theories and practices will contribute to the development of a methodology through which psychoanalysis might become more essentially and continually self-reflective and thereby more relevant to our age.

Psychoanalytic texts are generally devoid of self-reflexivity.[6] It is easier to advocate reflexivity than to practice it. And it is hardest to practice it on one's own work. This creates an interesting tension in the texts of those who—like myself—suggest that no theories, including psychoanalytic ones, are final; that all are partial, essentially contestable, and potentially in need of revision. When theoretical claims in such texts are treated without skepticism, which is what usually happens in the generally unreflexive discourse of most psychoanalysts, then these claims are granted an unchallenged authority that invalidates the author's claims about the partiality of all viewpoints. It is as if one is saying: all perspectives are partial—except my own.

Because this tension can neither be transcended nor avoided, we analysts need to problematize our own perspectives. We need, for example, to reflect more actively on our own theoretical omissions, attempt to notice where our own desires and confusion are smoothed over in our formulations, and where unsolved problems inhabit our discourses. We also need to present alternative interpretations to our own favored constructions, and envision perspectives that may not yet exist, but perhaps need to be imagined.

Employing such a nontraditional, self-consciously experimental format may generate some trepidation because it questions conventional analytic modes of explication underwritten by scientific assumptions of realism, truth, and rationality, which may be central to the self-image of the reader as well as the discipline of analysis as a whole. But attempting to embody the perspective that we theoretically advocate will give the readers of

---

6. The work of Ferenczi (1928), among others, which exhibits an exemplary sense of its own partiality and a conditional belief in its own validity, is an exception illustrating the rule.

psychoanalytic texts an intensified *experience* of reflexivity, as well as a sense of some of the ways it might be fostered.

Because immaculate perception and objective theorizing is impossible, our work will inevitably exemplify the dual status that Linda Hutcheon (1989) terms "complicity" (with the facets of psychoanalysis that we are questioning) and "critique" (of the above), blindness and insight. The willingness to recognize the contingent nature of even our most cherished formulations and continually explore and play with alternatives seems essential to promoting the vitality of psychoanalysis.

I hope it is clear from the story I have told that I view claims about psychoanalysis's death as premature, greatly exaggerated, and unedifying. Does psychoanalysis, however, have a future? Psychoanalysis offers tools to reveal both the way we are shaped and determined by our past and our capacity to be free. To the extent that it forecloses possibilities by thinking that it is The Discipline that Knows, deifies its own theories and practices, and does not draw on Freud's legacy of continual questioning, self-transformation, and evolution, psychoanalysis's future may be limited. To the extent, however, that psychoanalysis acknowledges at once its own capacity to put itself at risk, develop further and ongoing historical, theoretical, and clinical self-reflectiveness, and work through its own self-blindness, we might justifiably conclude that its future(s) are open and worthy of our continued attention.

Psychoanalytic inquiry, according to Freud (1914), is "accustomed to divine secret and concealed things from despised or unnoticed features, from the rubbish-heap, as it were, of our observations" (p. 222). Exploring symptomatic tensions, gaps, or inconsistencies within psychoanalytic theories, institutions, and practices, and cultivating greater theoretical and clinical self-awareness will not lead to the eradication of psychoanalytic unconsciousness or give us access to the unadorned Truth, which does not exist anyway, but it may uncover and mitigate psychoanalytic self-blindnesses and foster greater self-awareness. Blindness will always be part of both the analytic enterprise and of life itself. But by developing a more self-reflexive method, we may extend the unique "pathways" Freud opened up for us and enrich and reanimate the complex, vastly evocative psychoanalytic project.[7]

---

7. This is adapted from a larger work (Rubin 1998). The feedback of George Atwood and Stephen Mitchell greatly enriched an earlier version of this essay. I am grateful to both of them.

REFERENCES

Aron, L., and Harris, A., eds. (1993). *The Legacy of Sándor Ferenczi.* Hillsdale, NJ: Analytic Press.

Bakhtin, M. (1986). *Speech Genres and Other Late Essays.* Austin, TX: University of Texas Press.

Bernstein, R. (1992). Serious Play: The Ethical-Political Horizon of Derrida. In *The New Constellation: The Ethical-Political Horizons of Modernity/Postmodernity,* pp. 172–198. Cambridge, MA: MIT Press.

Breuer, J., and Freud, S. (1895). Studies on hysteria. *Standard Edition* 2:ix–335. London: Hogarth, 1955.

Crews, F. (1993). The unknown Freud. *New York Review of Books,* November 18.

cummings, e.e. (1972). *Complete Poems.* New York: Harcourt Brace Jovanovich.

Dallmayr, F. (1984). Is critical theory a humanism? In *Polis and Practice: Exercises in Contemporary Political Theory,* pp. 133–165. Cambridge, MA: MIT Press.

Ellis, J. (1989). *Against Deconstruction.* Princeton, NJ: Princeton University Press.

Felman, S. (1977). To open the question. In *Literature and Psychoanalysis: The Question of Reading: Otherwise,* ed. S. Felman, pp. 5–10. Baltimore, MD: Johns Hopkins University Press.

Ferenczi, S. (1928). The Elasticity of Psycho-Analytic Technique. In *Final Contributions to the Problems and Methods of Psycho-Analysis,* pp. 87–101. New York: Brunner/Mazel.

Flax, J. (1993). *Disputed Subjects: Essays on Psychoanalysis, Politics and Philosophy.* New York: Routledge.

Freud, S. (1914). The *Moses* of Michelangelo. *Standard Edition* 13:211–238.

———— (1917). A difficulty in the path of psycho-analysis. *Standard Edition* 17:135–144.

———— (1925). An autobiographical study. *Standard Edition* 20:3–74.

Fromm, E. (1959). *Sigmund Freud's Mission.* New York: Harper Colophon.

Gedo, J. (1984). *Psychoanalysis and Its Discontents.* New York: Guilford.

Gelfand, T. (1992). Preface. In *Freud and the History of Psychoanalysis,* ed. T. Gelfand and J. Kerr, pp. vii–xii.. Hillsdale, NJ: Analytic Press.

Greenson, R. (1969). The origin and fate of new ideas in psychoanalysis. In *Explorations in Psychoanalysis,* pp. 333–357. New York: International Universities Press, 1978.

Habermas, J. (1968). The Scientific Self-Misunderstanding of Metapsychology. In *Knowledge and Human Interests,* pp. 246–273. Boston, MA: Beacon.

Hutcheon, L. (1989). *The Politics of Postmodernism.* New York: Routledge.

Jacoby, R. (1983) *The Repression of Psychoanalysis: Otto Fenichel and the Political Freudians.* New York: Basic Books.

Jones, E. (1957). *The Life and Work of Sigmund Freud*, vol. 3. New York: Basic Books.

Kierkegaard, S. (1843). Entry 136. In *The Diary of Soren Kierkegaard*, ed. P. Rohde. New York: Citadel Press, 1960.

Langs, R. (1978). Reactions to creativity in psychoanalysis. In *Technique in Transition*, pp. 473–499. New York: Jason Aronson.

Lee, B. (1975). *The Tao of Jeet Kune Do*. Burbank, CA: Ohara Publications.

Mannheim, K. (1936). *Ideology and Utopia*. New York: Harcourt, Brace and World.

Mitchell, S. (1993). *Hope and Dread in Psychoanalysis*. New York: Basic Books.

Roazen, P. (1990). *The Freudian Left*. Ithaca, NY: Cornell University Press.

Rothstein, A. (1983). *The Structural Hypothesis: An Evolutionary Perspective*. New York: International Universities Press.

Rubin, J. B. (1998). *A Psychoanalysis for Our Time: Exploring the Blindness of the Seeing I*. New York: New York University Press.

Said, E. (1983). *The World, the Text and the Critic*. Cambridge, MA: Harvard University Press.

Schafer, R. (1992). *Retelling a Life: Narration and Dialogue in Psychoanalysis*. New York: Basic Books.

Spurling, L. (1993). Introduction. In *From the Words of My Mouth: Tradition in Psychotherapy*, ed. L. Spurling, pp. 1–17. New York: Routledge.

Stolorow, R., and Atwood, G. (1986). Reply to R. White, M. Basch, and M. Nissim-Sabat. *Psychoanalytic Review* 73(3):301–308.

Weber, S. (1987). The blindness of the seeing eye: psychoanalysis, hermeneutics, enstellung. In *Institution and Interpretation*, pp. 73–84. Minneapolis, MN: University of Minnesota Press.

Weiss, J., and Sampson, H. (1986). *The Psychoanalytic Process*. New York: Guilford.

23

The Shrink Is In[*]

Jonathan Lear

In an extraordinary decision, the Library of Congress this week bowed to pressure from angry anti-Freudians and postponed for as long as a year a major exhibition called *Sigmund Freud: Conflict and Culture*. According to a front-page story in the *Washington Post*, some library officials blamed the delay on budget problems; but others contended that the real reason was heated criticism of a show that might take a neutral or even favorable view of the father of psychoanalysis. Some fifty psychologists and others, including Gloria Steinem and Oliver Sacks, signed a petition denouncing the proposed exhibit; as Steinem complained to the *Post*, it seemed to "have the attitude of 'He was a genius, *but* . . .' instead of 'He's a very troubled man, and . . .'" Though the library assured them that the exhibit "is not about whether Freudians or Freud critics, of whatever camp, are right or wrong," the critics refused an offer to contribute to the catalogue or advise on the show.

---

*This chapter is reprinted from the *New Republic*, December 25, 1995, pp. 18–26, copyright © 1995 by the *New Republic* and used by permission.

Though this was perhaps the most blatant recent episode in the campaign against Freud, it is far from the only one. From *Time* to the *New York Times*, Freud-bashing has gone from an argument to a movement. In just the past few weeks Basic Books has brought out a long-winded tirade with what it no doubt hopes will be the sensational title *Why Freud Was Wrong*; and the *New York Review of Books* has collected some of its already-published broadsides against Freud into a new book.

In many cases, even the images accompanying these indictments seem to convey an extra dimension of hostility. "Is Freud dead?" *Time* magazine asked on its cover, Thanksgiving week, 1993. Whether or not this was really a question, it was certainly a repetition; for in the spring of 1966, *Time* had asked, "Is God Dead?" From a psychoanalytic point of view, repetitions are as interesting for their differences as for their similarities. With God, *Time* avoided any graven images and simply printed the question in red type against a black background, perhaps out of respect for the recently deceased. For Freud, by contrast, the magazine offered what was ostensibly a photograph of his face, but with his head blown open. One can tell it is *blown* open because what is left of the skull is shaped like a jigsaw puzzle, with several of the missing pieces flying off into space. The viewer can peer inside Freud's head and see: *there is nothing there.*

How can we explain the vehemence of these attacks on a long-dead thinker? There are, I think, three currents running through the culture that contribute to the fashion for Freud-bashing. First, the truly remarkable advances in the development of mind-altering drugs, most notably Prozac, alongside an ever-increasing understanding of the structure of the brain, have fueled speculation that one day soon all forms of talking therapy will be obsolete. Second, consumers increasingly rely on insurance companies and health maintenance organizations that prefer cheap pharmacology to expensive psychotherapy.

Finally, there is the inevitable backlash against the inflated claims that the psychoanalytic profession made for itself in the 1950s and '60s, and against its hagiography of Freud. Many reputable scholars now believe (and I agree) that Freud botched some of his most important cases. Certainly a number of his hypotheses are false; his analytic technique can seem flat-footed and intrusive; and in his speculations he was a bit of a cowboy.

It is also true that the American Psychoanalytic Association is a victim of self-inflicted wounds. In the original effort to establish psychoanalysis as a profession in this country, culminating in the 1920s, American analysts insisted that psychoanalytic training be restricted to medical doctors. The major opponent of such a restriction was Freud himself, who argued that this was "virtually equivalent to an attempt at repression." There was nothing about medical training, Freud thought, which peculiarly equipped one to become an analyst; and he suspected the Americans were motivated by the exclusionary interests of a guild. Freud lost: it was the one matter on which the American analysts openly defied the master. In the short run, this allowed the psychoanalytic profession to take advantage of the powerful positive transference that the American public extended to doctors through most of this century. Every profession in its heyday—and psychoanalysis was no exception—tends to be seduced by its own wishful self-image and to make claims for itself that it cannot ultimately sustain. In the longer run, though, psychoanalysis set itself up for revisionist criticism.

Yet, for all that, it also seems to me clear that, at his best, Freud is a deep explorer of the human condition, working in a tradition which goes back to Sophocles and which extends through Plato, Saint Augustine, and Shakespeare to Proust and Nietzsche. What holds this tradition together is its insistence that there are significant meanings for human well-being which are obscured from immediate awareness. Sophoclean tragedy locates another realm of meaning in a divine world that humans can at most glimpse through oracles. In misunderstanding these strange meanings, humans usher in catastrophe.

Freud's achievement, from this perspective, is to locate these meanings fully inside the human world. Humans *make* meaning, for themselves and for others, of which they have no direct or immediate awareness. People make more meaning than they know what to do with. This is what Freud meant by the unconscious. And whatever valid criticisms can be aimed at him or at the psychoanalytic profession, it is nevertheless true that psychoanalysis is the most sustained and successful attempt to make these obscure meanings intelligible. Since I believe that this other source of meaning is of great importance for human development, I think that psychoanalytic therapy is invaluable for those who can make use of it; but, crazy as this may seem, I also believe that psychoanalysis is crucial for a truly democratic culture to thrive.

Take a closer look at the culture of criticism that has come to envelop psychoanalysis. You do not need to be an analyst to notice that more is going on here than a search for truth. Consider, for example, the emotionally charged debate over alleged memories of child abuse. No matter what side an author is on, Freud is blamed for being on the other. Jeffrey

Masson, the renegade Freud scholar who believes that child abuse is more widespread than commonly acknowledged, made a name for himself by accusing Freud of suppressing the evidence in order to gain respectability. On the lecture circuit and in books like *The Assault on Truth* and *Against Therapy*, Masson has emerged as the most charismatic of the Freud-bashers, a self-styled defender of women and children against Freud's betrayals of them. Yet his critique of Freud is dependent on a willful misreading.

It is certainly true that at the beginning of his career, Freud hypothesized that hysteria and obsessional neurosis in adulthood were caused by memories of actual seductions in childhood. Because these memories were so upsetting, they were repressed, or kept out of conscious memory, but they still operated in the mind to cause psychological disease. By the fall of 1897, Freud had abandoned this view, which came to be known as the seduction theory. His explanation was that he had become increasingly skeptical that all the reports of childhood seduction—"not excluding my own"—could be straightforward memories. Masson, however, argues that this was merely Freud's attempt to fall into line with the prejudices of his German colleagues and thus to advance his career.

I find it impossible to read through Freud's writings without coming to the conclusion that it is Masson who is suppressing the evidence in order to advance his career. In fact, Freud never abandoned the idea that abuse of children caused them serious psychological harm, and throughout his career he maintained that it occurred more often than generally acknowledged. In 1917, for instance, twenty years after the abandonment of the seduction theory, Freud writes, "Phantasies of being seduced are of particular interest, because so often they are not [merely] phantasies but real memories." Even at the very end of his career, in 1938, Freud writes that while "the sexual abuse of children by adults" or "their seduction by other children (brothers or sisters) slightly their seniors" "do not apply to all children, . . . they are common enough." It is, therefore, misleading to say that Freud ever abandoned belief in the sexual abuse of children. What he abandoned was blind faith in the idea that alleged memories of abuse are always and everywhere what they purport to be.

Besides, to focus on child abuse is to miss the point. What is really at stake in the abandonment of the seduction theory is not the prevalence of abuse, but the nature of the mind's own activity. In assuming, as he first did, that all purported memories of child abuse were true, Freud was treating the mind as though it were merely a recipient of experience, recording reality in the same passive way a camera does light. Though the mind might be active in keeping certain memories out of conscious awareness, it was otherwise passive. In realizing that one could not take all memory-claims at face value, Freud effectively discovered that the *mind* is active and imaginative in the organization of its own experience. This is one of the crucial moments in the founding of psychoanalysis.

Of course, there is a tremendous difference—both clinical and moral—between actual and merely imagined child abuse. But from the point of view of the significance of Freud's discovery the whole issue of abuse or its absence, of seduction or its absence, is irrelevant. Once we realize that the human mind is *everywhere* active and imaginative, then we need to understand the routes of this activity if we are to grasp how the mind works. This is true whether the mind is trying to come to grips with painful reality, reacting to trauma, coping with the everyday, or "just making things up."

Freud called this imaginative activity fantasy, and he argued both that it functions unconsciously and that it plays a powerful role in the organization of a person's experience. This, surely, contains the seeds of a profound insight into the human condition; it is the central insight of psychoanalysis, yet, in the heated debate over child abuse, it is largely ignored. In fact, the discovery of unconscious fantasy does not itself tilt one way or the other in this debate. Freud himself became skeptical about whether all the purported memories of childhood seduction were actual memories—but that is because he took himself to have been overly credulous. One can equally well argue in the opposite direction: precisely because fantasy is a pervasive aspect of mental life, one needs a much more nuanced view of what constitutes real-life seduction. Because fantasy is active in parents as well as children, parents do not need to be crudely molesting their children to be seducing them. Ironically, *Freud*'s so-called "abandonment of the seduction theory" can be used to widen the scope of what might be considered real seductions.

The irony is that while those who believe in the prevalence of childhood seductions attack Freud for abandoning the cause, those who believe that repressed memories of child abuse are overblown blame him for fomenting this excess. Its real origins, though, are in "recovered-memory therapy," an often quackish practice in which so-called therapists actively encourage their clients to "remember" incidents of abuse from childhood. After some initial puzzlement as to what was being asked of them, clients have been only too willing to oblige: inventing the wildest stories of satanic rituals, cannibalism, and other misdemeanors of suburban life.

The consequences of believing these stories have in some cases been devastating. "As I write," Frederick Crews observes in the *New York Review of Books*, "a number of parents and child-care providers are serving long prison terms, and others are awaiting trial, on the basis of therapeutically induced 'memories' of child sexual abuse that never in fact occurred." But instead of giving Freud credit for being the first person to warn us against taking purportedly repressed memories of abuse at face value, Crews continues:

> Although the therapists in question are hardly Park Avenue psychoanalysts, the tradition of Freudian theory and practice unmistakably lies behind their tragic deception of both patients and jurors.

Crews, who is a professor of English at Berkeley and the éminence grise of Freud-bashers, acknowledges that his claim will "strike most readers as a slur." "Didn't psychoanalysis arise," he asks rhetorically, "precisely from a *denial* that certain alleged molestations were veridical?" Yes, it did. "It may seem calumnious," he writes later, "to associate the skeptical, thoroughly secular founder of psychoanalysis with the practices of Bible-thumping incest counselors who typically get their patient-victims to produce images of revolting satanic rituals." Yes, it does. But Crews is undeterred. He feels entitled to make this accusation, first, because Freud spent the earliest years of his career searching for repressed memories and, second, because Freud *did* suggest certain conclusions to his patients. That is, on occasion he took advantage of the charismatic position which people regularly assign to their doctors, teachers, and political leaders and told patients how to think about themselves or what to do—sometimes to their profound detriment. Like most successful slurs, there is truth in each claim.

What is missing is the massive evidence on the other side. No one in the history of psychiatry has more openly questioned the veracity of purported childhood memories than Freud did. No one did more to devise a form of treatment which avoids suggestion. Looking back, I regularly find Freud's clinical interventions too didactic and suggestive. But the very possibility of "looking back" is due to Freud. It was Freud who first set the avoidance of suggestion as a therapeutic ideal—and it is Freud who devised the first therapeutic technique aimed at achieving it. Psychoanalysis distinguishes itself from other forms of talking cure by its rigorous attempt to work out a procedure which genuinely avoids suggestion.

This is of immense importance, for psychoanalysis thus becomes the first therapy which sets *freedom* rather than some specific image of human *happiness* as its goal. Other kinds of therapy posit particular outcomes—increased self-esteem, overcoming depression—and, implicitly or explicitly, give advice about how to get there. Psychoanalysis is the one form of therapy which leaves it to analysands to determine for themselves what their specific goals will be. Indeed, it leaves it to them to determine whether they will have specific goals. Of course, as soon as freedom becomes an ideal, enormous practical problems arise as to how one avoids compromising an analysand's freedom by unwittingly suggesting certain goals or outlooks. But if we can now criticize Freud's actual practice, it is largely due to technical advances which Freud himself inspired.

One might wonder: Why isn't Freud the hero of both these narratives, rather than the villain? Why doesn't Masson portray Freud as the pioneer who linked memories of child abuse with later psychological harm; why doesn't Crews lionize Freud as the first person to call the veracity of such memories into question? There are rational answers to these questions—in one case that he reversed his position, in the other that even though he reversed himself, he is responsible for a tradition—but neither of them are very satisfying. Rather, an emotional tide has turned, and reasons are used to cover over irrational currents. Part of this may be a healthy reversal, a reaction against previous idealizations. But it is also true that Freud is being made a scapegoat, and in the scapegoating process, nuance is abandoned.

To see nuance disappear, one has only to look at the supposed debate over the scientific standing of psychoanalysis. In a series of books and articles, Professor Adolf Grünbaum of the University of Pittsburgh has argued that psychoanalysis cannot *prove* the cause-and-effect connections it claims between unconscious motivation and its visible manifestations in ordinary life and in a clinical setting. Grünbaum argues correctly that Freud made genuine causal claims for psychoanalysis; notably, that it cures neurosis. But Grünbaum goes on to argue, much less plausibly, that in a clinical setting psychoanalysis cannot substantiate its claims. It is remarkable how many mainstream publications—*Time*, the *New York Times, The Economist* to name a few—have fallen all over themselves to give respectful mention to such abstruse work as Grünbaum's. Mere mention of the work lends a cloak of scientific legitimacy to the attack on Freud, while the excellent critiques of Grünbaum's work are ignored.

There is no doubt that the causal claims of psychoanalysis cannot be established in the same way as a causal claim in a hard-core empirical science like experimental physics. But neither can any causal claim of any

360 ■ The Death of Psychoanalysis

form of psychology which interprets people's actions on the basis of their motives—including the ordinary psychology of everyday life. We watch a friend get up from her chair and head to the refrigerator: we assume she is hungry and is getting something to eat. We can, if we like, try to confirm this interpretation, but in nothing like the way we confirm something in physics. Of course, we can "test" our hypothesis by asking her what she is doing, and she may correct us, telling us that she is thirsty and getting something to drink. But it's possible that she's not telling us the truth. Indeed, it's possible, though unlikely, that she believes that the refrigerator is capable of sending messages to outer space, which will save the world from catastrophe. We cannot *prove* that our ordinary interpretation is correct. At best, we can gather more interpretive evidence of the same type to support or revise our hypothesis.

What are we to do, abandon our ordinary practice of interpreting people? If we want to know what caused the outbreak of the Peloponnesian War, why there is a crisis in the Balkans, what were the origins of the Renaissance, how slavery became institutionalized, we turn to history, economics, and other social sciences for answers. No historical account is immune to skeptical challenge; no historical-causal claims can be verified in the same way as a causal claim in physics. But no one suggests giving up on history or the other interpretive sciences.

Meaning is like that. Humans are inherently makers and interpreters of meaning. It is meaning—ideas, desires, beliefs—which causes humans to do the interesting things they do. Yet as soon as one enters the realm of meaningful explanation one has to employ different methods of validating causal claims than one finds in experimental physics. And it is simply a mistake to think that therefore the methods of validation in ordinary psychology or in psychoanalysis must be less precise or fall short of the methods in experimental physics. To see this for yourself, take the following multiple-choice test:

> Question: Which is more precise, Henry James, in his ability to describe how a person's action flows from his or her motivations; or a particle accelerator, in its ability to depict the causal interactions of subatomic particles?
>
> Answers: (a) Henry James
> (b) the accelerator
> (c) none of the above

You do not have to flip to the end of the article or turn the page upside-down to learn that the answer is (c). Actually, a better answer is to reject the question as ridiculous. There is no single scale on which one can place both Henry James and a particle accelerator to determine which is more precise. Within the realm of human motivation and its effects, *Portrait of a Lady* is more precise than a Peanuts cartoon; within the realm of measuring atomic movements, some instruments are more precise than others.

If psychoanalysis *were* to imitate the methods of physical science, it would be useless for interpreting people. Psychoanalysis is an extension of our ordinary psychological ways of interpreting people in terms of their beliefs, desires, hopes, and fears. The extension is important because psychoanalysis attributes to people other forms of motivation—in particular wish and fantasy—which attempt to account for outbreaks of irrationality and other puzzling human behavior. In fact, it is a sign of psychoanalysis's *success* as an interpretive science that its causal claims cannot be validated in the same way as those of the physical sciences.

How, then, might we set appropriate standards of confirmation for causal claims in psychoanalysis? This genuine and important question tends to be brushed aside by the cliché of the analyst telling a patient who disagrees with an interpretation that she is just resisting. The apotheosis of this cliché can be found in Sir Karl Popper's *The Open Society and its Enemies,* in which Popper argues that psychoanalysis is a pseudo-science because its discoveries cannot be falsified: what counts as evidence is too large and elusive for the total claim of the discipline to be either checked or challenged. Of course, in this broad sense nothing could "falsify" history or economics of our ordinary psychological interpretation of persons, but no one would think of calling these forms of explanation pseudo. And there *is* something that would count as a global refutation of psychoanalysis: if people always and everywhere acted in rational and transparently explicable ways, one could easily dismiss psychoanalysis as unnecessary rubbish. It is because people often behave in bizarre ways, ways which cause pain to themselves and to others, ways which puzzle even the actors themselves, that psychoanalysis commands our attention.

Unfortunately, there is some truth to the cliché of the analyst unfairly pulling rank on the analysand. Would that there were no such thing as a defensive analyst! Yet I believe that when psychoanalysis is done properly there is no form of clinical intervention—in psychology, psychiatry, or general medicine—that pays greater respect to the individual client or patient. The proper attitude for an analyst is one of profound humility in the face of the infinite complexity of another human being. Because humans are self-interpreting animals, one must always be ready to defer to their explanations of what they mean. And yet, suppose just for the sake of argument that it is true that humans actively keep certain unpleasant meanings away from conscious awareness. Then one might expect that any process which brings those meanings closer to consciousness will be accompanied by a certain resistance. It then becomes an important technical and theoretical problem how to elicit those meanings without falling into the cliché, without provoking a massive outbreak of resistance, and all the while working closely with and maintaining deep respect for the analysand. We need to know in specific detail when and how it is appropriate to cite resistance in a clinical setting, and when it is not. Some of the best recent work in psychoanalytic theory addresses just this issue.

Consider this elementary example: an analysand may come precisely five minutes late every day for his session. For a while, there may be no point in inviting him to speculate about why. Any such question, no matter how gently or tentatively put, might only provoke a storm of protest: "you don't know how busy I am, how many sacrifices I make to get here," and so on. Even if the habitual lateness and the protests *are* examples of what analysts call resistance, there is one excellent reason not to say anything about it yet: the analysis is for the analysand. Any interpretation that he cannot make use of in his journey of self-understanding is inappropriate, even if the interpretation is accurate. *If* coming late is a resistance, and if the analyst is sufficiently patient, there will come a time when he will relax enough to become puzzled by his own behavior. He might say, "it's funny, I always seem to come exactly five minutes late," or "I've thought about asking you to start our sessions five minutes late, but I realized I'd only come five minutes later than that." At this point it would be a mistake not to pursue the issue, for a wealth of material may spontaneously emerge: for example, that he wanted to feel that he was in control, and he wanted the analyst to acknowledge him as a serious professional in his own right, and so on. Once these desires are recognized, they can be explored—and sometimes that exploration can make a big difference in how the analysand sees himself and how he goes on to live the rest of his life. Should all of this be avoided because of some flat-footed assumption that the analyst is always pulling rank when she talks about resistance? The problem with the cliché is that it ignores all specifics. It uses the very possibility of invoking resistance to impugn psychoanalysis generally.

What is at stake in all of these attacks? If this were merely the attack on one historical figure, Freud, or on one professional group, psychoanalysts, the hubbub would have died down long ago. After all, psychoanalysis nowadays plays a minor role in the mental health professions; Freud is less and less often taught or studied. There is, of course, a certain pleasure to be had in pretending one is bravely attacking a powerful authority when one is in fact participating in a gang-up. But even these charms fade after a while. The real object of attack—for which Freud is only a stalking horse—is the very idea of humans having unconscious motivation. A battle may be fought over Freud, but the war is over our culture's image of the human soul. Are we to see humans as having depth—as complex psychological organisms who generate layers of meaning which lie beneath the surface of their own understanding? Or are we to take ourselves as transparent to ourselves?

Certainly, the predominant trend in the culture is to treat human existence as straightforward. In the plethora of self-help books, of alternative therapies, diets and exercise programs, it is assumed that we already know what human happiness is. These programs promise us a shortcut for getting there. And yet we can all imagine someone whose muscle tone is great, who is successful at his job, who "feels good about himself," yet remains a shell of a human being. Breathless articles in the science section of the *New York Times* suggest that the main obstacle to human flourishing is technological. And even this obstacle—in the recent discovery of a gene, or the location of a neuron in the brain, or in the synthesis of a new psychopharmacological agent—may soon be put out of the way. Candide is the ideal reader of the "Science Times." Of course, the *Times* did not invent this image of the best of all possible worlds: it is merely the bellwether for a culture that wishes to ignore the complexity, depth, and darkness of human life.

It is difficult to make this point without sounding like a Luddite; so let me say explicitly that psychopharmacology and neuropsychiatry have made, and will continue to make, valuable contributions in reducing human suffering. But it is a fantasy to suppose that a chemical or neurological intervention can solve the problems posed in and by human life. That is why it is a mistake to think of psychoanalysis and Prozac as two different means to the same end. The point of psychoanalysis is to help us develop a clearer, yet more flexible and creative, sense of what our ends might be. "How shall we live?" is, for Socrates, the fundamental question of human existence—and the attempt to answer that question is, for him, what makes human life worthwhile. And it is Plato and Shakespeare, Proust, Nietzsche and, most recently, Freud who complicated the issue by insisting that there are deep currents of meaning, often crosscurrents, running through the human soul which can at best be glimpsed through a glass darkly. This, if anything, is the Western tradition: not a specific set of values, but a belief that the human soul is too deep for there to be any easy answer to the question of how to live.

If one can dismiss Freud as a charlatan, one cannot only enjoy the sacrifice of a scapegoat, one can also evade troubling questions about the enigmatic nature of human motivation. Never mind that we are daily surrounded by events—from the assassination of Yitzhak Rabin to the war in Bosnia; from the murder of Nicole Simpson to the public fascination with it; from the government's burning of the Branch Davidian compound to the retaliation bombing in Oklahoma City—that cannot be understood in the terms that are standardly used to explain them. Philosophy, Aristotle said, begins in wonder. Psychoanalysis begins in wonder that the unintelligibility of the events that surround one do not cause more wonder.

There are two very different images of what humans must be like if democracy is to be a viable form of government. The prevalent one today treats humans as preference-expressing political atoms, and pays little attention to subatomic structure. Professional pollsters, political scientists, and pundits portray society as an agglomeration of these atoms. The only irrationality they recognize is the failure of these preference-expressing monads to conform to the rules of rational choice theory. If one thinks that this is the only image of humanity that will sustain democracy, one will tend to view psychoanalysis as suspiciously antidemocratic.

Is there another, more satisfying, image of what humans are like which nevertheless makes it plausible that they should organize themselves and live in democratic societies? If we go back to the greatest participatory democracy the world has known—the polis of fifth-century Athens—we see that the flourishing of that democracy coincides precisely with the flowering of one of the world's great literatures: Greek tragedy. This coincidence is not mere coincidence. The tragic theater gave citizens the opportunity to retreat momentarily from the responsibility of making rational decisions for themselves and their society. At the same time, tragedy confronted them emotionally with the fact that they had to make their decisions in a world that was not entirely rational, in which rationality was sometimes violently disrupted, in which rationality itself could be used for irrational ends.

What, after all, is Oedipus's complex? That he killed his father and married his mother misses the point. Patricide and maternal incest are *consequences* of Oedipus's failure, not its source. Oedipus's fundamental mistake lies in his assumption that meaning is transparent to human reason. In horrified response to the Delphic oracle, Oedipus flees the people he (mistakenly) takes to be his parents. En route, he kills his actual father and propels himself into the arms of his mother. It is the classic scene of fulfilling one's fate in the very act of trying to escape it. But this scenario is only possible because Oedipus assumes he understands his situation, that the meaning of the oracle is immediately available to his conscious understanding. That is why he thinks he can respond to the oracle with a straightforward application of practical reason. Oedipus's mistake, in essence, is to ignore unconscious meaning.

For Sophocles, this was a sacrilegious crime, for he took this obscure meaning to flow from a divine source. But it is clear that, in Sophocles's vision, Oedipus attacks the very idea of unconscious meaning. In his angry confrontation with the prophet Tiresias, Oedipus boasts that it was his conscious reasoning, not any power of interpreting obscure meaning, which saved the city from the horrible Sphinx.

> Why, come, tell me, how can you be a true prophet? Why when the versifying hound was here did you not speak some word that could release the citizens? Indeed, her riddle was not one for the first comer to explain! It required prophetic skill, and you were exposed as having no knowledge from the birds or from the gods. No, it was I that came, Oedipus who knew nothing, and put a stop to her; I hit the mark by native wit, not by what I learned from birds.

What was Sophocles's message to the Athenian citizens who flocked to the theater? *You ignore the realm of unconscious meaning at your peril. Do so, and Oedipus's fate will be yours.* From this perspective, democratic citizens need to maintain a certain humility in the face of meanings which remain opaque to human reason. We need to be wary that what we take to be an exercise of reason will both hide and express an irrationality of which we remain unaware.

In all the recent attacks on Freud, can't one hear echoes of Oedipus's attack on Tiresias? Isn't the attack on Freud itself a repetition and reenactment of Oedipus's complex, less an attack on the father than an attack on the very idea of repressed, unconscious meaning? One indication that this is so—a symptom, if you will—is that none of the attacks on Freud addresses the problems of human existence to which psychoanalysis is a response. From a psychoanalytic perspective, human irrationality is not merely a failure to make a coherent set of choices. Sometimes it is an un-intelligible intrusion that overwhelms reason and blows it apart. Sometimes it is method in madness. But how could there be *method* in *madness?* Even if Freud did botch this case or ambitiously pursue that end, we still need to account for the pervasive manifestations of human irrationality. This is the issue, and it is one which the attacks on Freud ignore.

The real question is whether, and how, responsible autonomy is possible. In the development of the human self-image from Sophocles to Freud, there has been a shift in the locus of hidden meaning from a divine to the all-too-human realm. At first, it might look as though the recognition of a dark strain running through the human soul might threaten the viability of democratic culture. Certainly, the twentieth-century critiques of Enlightenment optimism, with the corresponding emphasis on human irrationality, also question or even pour scorn on the democratic ideal. It is in this context that Freud comes across as a much more ambiguous figure than he is normally taken to be. In one way, he is the advocate of the unconscious; in another, he is himself filled with Enlightenment optimism that the problems posed by the unconscious can be solved; in yet another, he is wary of the dark side of the human soul and pessimistic about doing much to alleviate psychological pain. He is Tiresias and Oedipus and Sophocles rolled into one.

If, for the moment, we concentrate on the optimism, we see a vision emerge of how one might both take human irrationality seriously and participate in a democratic ideal. If the source of irrationality lies within, rather than outside, the human realm, the possibility opens up of a responsible engagement with it. Psychoanalysis is, in its essence, the attempt to work out just such an engagement. It is a technique that allows dark meanings and irrational motivations to rise to the surface of conscious awareness. They can then be taken into account; they can be influenced by other considerations; and they become less liable to disrupt human life in violent and incomprehensible ways. Critics of psychoanalysis complain that it is a luxury of the few. But, from the current perspective, no thinker has made creativity and imagination more democratically available than Freud. This is one of the truly important consequences of locating the unconscious inside the psyche. Creativity is no longer the exclusive preserve of the divinely inspired, or the few great poets. From a psychoanalytic point of view, everyone is poetic; everyone dreams in metaphor and generates symbolic meaning in the process of living. Even in their prose, people have unwittingly been speaking poetry all along.

And the question now is: To what poetic use are we going to put Freud? Freud *is* dead. He died in 1939, after an extraordinarily productive and creative life. Beneath the continued attacks upon him, ironically, lies an unwillingness to let him go. It is Freud who taught that only after we accept the actual death of an important person in our lives can we begin to mourn. Only then can he or she take on full symbolic life for us. Obsessing about Freud *the man* is a way of keeping Freud *the meaning* at bay. Freud's meaning, I think, lies in the recognition that humans make more meaning than they grasp, that this meaning can be painful and disruptive, but that humans need not be passive in the face of it. Freud began a process of dealing with unconscious meaning, and it is important not to get stuck on him, like some rigid symptom, either to idolize or to denigrate him. The many attacks on him, even upon psychoanalysis, refuse to recognize that Freud gave birth to a psychoanalytic movement which in myriad ways has moved beyond him. If Freud is alive anywhere, it is in a tradition which in its development of more sensitive techniques, and more sophisticated ways of thinking about unconscious motivation, has rendered some of the particular things Freud thought or did irrelevant. Just as democracy requires the recognition that the king is dead, both as an individual and as an institution, so the democratic recognition that each person is the maker of unconscious, symbolic meaning requires the acceptance of Freud's death. What matters, as Freud himself well understood, is what we are able to do with the meanings we make.

Index